40.00
80E

D0078286

BEST METHODS
FOR THE
ANALYSIS OF CHANGE

RECENT ADVANCES, UNANSWERED
QUESTIONS, FUTURE DIRECTIONS

BEST METHODS
FOR THE ANALYSIS OF CHANGE

RECENT ADVANCES, UNANSWERED QUESTIONS,
FUTURE DIRECTIONS

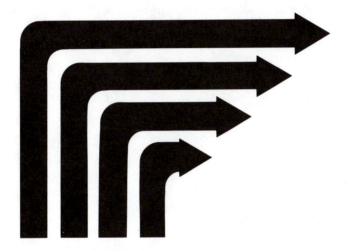

E D I T E D

BY

LINDA M. COLLINS

AND

J O H N L . H O R N

American Psychological Association
Washington, DC

BF
637
.C4
B48
1991

Copyright © 1991 by the American Psychological Association. All rights reserved. Except as permitted under the United States Copyright Act of 1976, no part of this publication may be reproduced or distributed in any form or by any means, or stored in a data base or retrieval system, without the prior written permission of the publisher.

Published by
American Psychological Association
1200 Seventeenth Street, NW
Washington, DC 20036

Copies may be ordered from
APA Order Department
P.O. Box 2710
Hyattsville, MD 20784

Designed by Paul M. Levy
Cover artwork by Beth Schlenoff
Typeset by Harper Graphics, Waldorf, MD
Printed by Edwards Brothers, Inc., Ann Arbor, MI
Technical editing and production coordinated by Linda J. Beverly

Library of Congress Cataloging-in-Publication Data
Best methods for the analysis of change : recent advances, unanswered questions, future
  directions / edited by Linda M. Collins and John L. Horn.
       p.   cm.
    Includes bibliographical references and index.
    ISBN 1-55798-113-2 : $40.00
    1. Change (Psychology)   2. Psychometrics.   I. Collins, Linda M.
  II. Horn, John L.
  BF637.C4B48 1991
  155.2'4—dc20
                                                                91-20462
                                                                CIP

Printed in the United States of America
First edition

CONTENTS

CONTRIBUTORS

Laura A. Baker, *University of Southern California*
Vern L. Bengtson, *University of Southern California*
R. Darrell Bock, *University of Chicago*
M. W. Browne, *Ohio State University*
Norman Cliff, *University of Southern California*
Patricia Cohen, *Columbia University and New York State Psychiatric Institute*
Linda M. Collins, *University of Southern California*
Robert Cudeck, *University of Minnesota*
Walter R. Cunningham, *University of Florida*
S. H. C. Du Toit, *Pretoria University*
Merrill F. Elias, *University of Maine*
Susan E. Embretson, *University of Kansas*
Harry F. Gollob, *University of Denver*
John W. Graham, *University of Southern California*
Fumiaki Hamagami, *University of Virginia*
Lisa L. Harlow, *University of Rhode Island*
Christopher Hertzog, *Georgia Institute of Technology*
John L. Horn, *University of Southern California*
Kenneth Jones, *Brandeis University*
Roderick J. A. Little, *University of California at Los Angeles*
John Loehlin, *University of Texas at Austin*
J. J. McArdle, *University of Virginia*
William Meredith, *University of California at Berkeley*
Bengt O. Muthén, *University of California at Los Angeles*
John R. Nesselroade, *Pennsylvania State University*
Charles S. Reichardt, *University of Denver*
Michael A. Robbins, *University of Maine*
Robert E. L. Roberts, *University of Southern California*
Donald B. Rubin, *Harvard University*
Judith D. Singer, *Harvard University*
Keith F. Widaman, *University of California at Riverside*
John B. Willett, *Harvard University*

FOREWORD

Federal research agencies stopped most support of investigator-initiated state-of-the-art research conferences in scientific psychology over a decade ago. During this period, however, scientific psychology has continued to grow, as well as to diversify into many new areas. Yet, there have been relatively few opportunities for investigators in new and promising research areas to convene in special settings to discuss their findings.

As part of its continuing effort to enhance the dissemination of scientific knowledge in psychology, the American Psychological Association (APA) has undertaken a number of initiatives designed to foster scientific research and communication. In particular, the APA Science Directorate established in 1988 the Scientific Conferences Program, from which this publication resulted.

The APA Scientific Conferences Program provides university- based psychological researchers with seed monies essential to organizing specialty conferences on critical issues in basic research, applied research, and methodological issues in psychology. Deciding which conferences to support involves a competitive process. An annual call for proposals is issued by the APA Science Directorate to solicit conference ideas. Proposals from all areas of psychological research are welcome. These are then reviewed by qualified psychologists, who forward substantive suggestions and funding recommendations to the Science Directorate. At each stage, the criteria used to determine which conferences to support include relevance, timeliness, comprehensiveness of the topics, and qualifications of the presenters. From its inception in 1988 to mid-1991, nineteen conferences have been funded, with a total outlay of more than $250,000. We expect to support several conferences annually in the future.

This program has two major goals. The first is to provide, by means of the conferences, a broad view of specific topics and, when appropriate, to encourage interdisciplinary participation. The second goal is to assure timely dissemination of the findings presented, by publishing carefully crafted scholarly volumes based, in part, on the conferences. The information thus reaches the broader psychological and scientific communities as well as the audiences at the conferences. Psychology and related fields thereby benefit from the most current research on a given topic.

This volume presents findings reported at an October 1989 conference entitled "Best Methods for the Analysis of Change," held at the University of Southern California. The major purpose of this conference was to identify significant problems of design and data analysis in research on change, and to explore the most appropriate methods for dealing with such problems. Conference presentations provided comprehensive examinations of what are considered to be the best methods to analyze change. Both substantive and methodological experts participated in this important meeting—producing an exciting marriage of ideas in an area critical to the continued development of psychological science.

The American Psychological Association is pleased to have supported this conference and now to make the research presented there available in book form. We hope you will enjoy and be stimulated by this volume and others to come.

A list of the conferences funded through this program follows:

Research Community Psychology: Integrating Theories and Methodologies, September 1988

The Psychological Well-Being of Captive Primates, September 1988

Psychological Research on Organ Donation, October 1988

Arizona Conference on Sleep and Cognition, January 1989

Socially Shared Cognition, February 1989

Taste, Experience, and Feeding, April 1989

Perception of Structure, May 1989

Suggestibility of Children's Recollections, June 1989

Best Methods for Analysis of Change, October 1989

Conceptualization and Measurement of Organism-Environment Interactions, November 1989

Cognitive Bases of Musical Communication, April 1990

Conference on Hostility, Coping/Support, and Health, November 1990

Psychological Testing of Hispanics, February 1991

Study of Cognition: Conceptual and Methodological Issues, February 1991

Cardiovascular Reactivity to Psychological and Cardiovascular Disease: A Conference on the Evidence, April 1991

Developmental Psychoacoustics, August 1991

Maintaining and Promoting Integrity in Behavioral Science Research, October 1991

The Contributions of Psychology to Mathematics and Science Education, November 1991

Lives Through Time: Assessment and Theory in Personality Psychology from a Longitudinal Perspective, November 1991

For the Science Directorate of the American Psychological Association:

Lewis P. Lipsitt, Ph.D.
Executive Director for Science

Virginia E. Holt
Manager, Scientific Conferences Program

ACKNOWLEDGMENTS

The editors are pleased to acknowledge the support, financial and otherwise, that we received from two major sources. The first is the American Psychological Association (APA) Science Directorate, which paid for half the expenses for the conference and the book. Virginia Holt of the APA Science Directorate was extremely helpful with both the conference and book, and Joan Buchanan of the APA Office of International Affairs provided important expertise at a time when we very much needed such help. The second major source of support is the University of Southern California (USC), which, largely through the generous work of Sylvester Whitaker (Dean of the Division of Social Sciences and Communication) and Gerald Davison (Chair, Department of Psychology), provided the major portion of the other half of the funding. We thank Syl Whitaker also for helping us through several awkward developments in arranging the conference and for making the welcoming remarks to the conference attendees.

We give our thanks for financial contributions also to the USC Department of Sociology (Carlfred Broderick, Chair), the Research Branch of the USC School of Gerontology (Vern Bengtson, Director), the USC Davidson Conference Center, the Pennsylvania State University College of Health and Human Development (Anne Petersen, Dean), and the University of Virginia Department of Psychology (Sandra Scarr, Chair).

We gratefully acknowledge the invaluable assistance of David Epstein, Laurel Fisher, Jacob Chung, and Jennie Noll; the conference could not have run smoothly without them. Additionally, we thank Jennie Noll for much help in the preparation of this book. Very special thanks go to our conference coordinator, Mary Vreeland. Besides keeping the conference matters organized, Mary served as a buffer between us and the world, handling with characteristic tact and intelligence, a multitude of problems that came up.

Finally, we wish to thank John and Matthew Graham and Penny Trickett, who provided constant support throughout the entire process of planning and executing the conference and editing this volume. We dedicate this book to them.

PREFACE

This book is based on presentations given at the conference "Best Methods for the Analysis of Change," held at the University of Southern California on October 29–31, 1989. The conference was inspired by a previous, seminal conference organized by Chester Harris and held in Madison, Wisconsin, in 1962. (One of the present book's editors, John L. Horn, attended that previous conference.) The Harris conference was a watershed in the history of psychological research. It brought together many of the foremost methodologists and scientists who were then studying issues related to the analysis of change. It signaled that the study of change raises important challenges that must be met in a science dedicated to understanding development. The book based on that conference (Harris, 1963) distilled the state of the art at the time, and is still frequently cited today. In the field of social science methods, it is a classic.

Given the importance of the Harris conference and book and the interest they generated, one might have thought that many similar efforts would follow, yet they did not. Why? It is not because the study of change is unimportant in modern research. The number of longitudinal studies has increased exponentially in the decades since the Harris conference; today, such studies are found in a wide variety of substantive domains. It is not because there is a dearth of innovative methodological work in this area. Articles and chapters in leading journals and books in the social sciences attest to the fact that research on analysis of change has remained active. Nor is it because all the important methodological questions have been answered. The Harris book helped to answer some important questions and raised many others that have since been addressed, but the answers it provided have been swamped by a flood of new methodological issues pouring forth from studies undertaken since that early work appeared. We must look elsewhere for the reasons why there have been no follow-ups to the Harris conference and book.

One reason seems to be that Harris's "act" is so difficult to follow! When we—Jack McArdle, Bill Meredith, John Nesselroade, and the two editors of this volume—first considered the idea of a conference on methods for the analysis of change, we thought that probably one or more follow-ups of the Harris work had been done already. When we could not find any, we reasoned that no one had mounted such an effort because it seemed unlikely that another conference in this area could be as important as the Harris conference or have its historical significance. We did not ask for that comparison when we designed our conference, nor do we welcome it now.

In company with Harris's work, however, we aimed to bring forth an overview of major strategies and methods for analyzing change: We sought strategies and methods regarded as most applicable today. Additionally, we aimed to explore the state of the art by hearing about the most pressing unsolved methodological problems in today's research. These objectives led us to seek conference presenters and discussants who were actively engaged in substantive work centering on questions about change or who were actively engaged in methodological work dealing with such questions (or both).

Announcements of the conference uncovered wide interest; nearly 200 people attended the conference. Many more applied but, regrettably, had to be turned away because we did not have enough space to accommodate them. Although attendance at the conference was too large to be optimal for discussion, presenters and discussants were met with an unusual number of stimulating questions from the attendees, and group discussion was carried out at a level usually seen only in much smaller meetings. Exchanges continued into the breaks and into the lunch and dinner hours. Much of this vibrancy cannot be retained in written work, of course, and rightly so. But the writers contributing to this volume have been able to use what they learned at the conference to revise and polish what they said. The writings that resulted—chapters and comments—thus provide the reader with an efficient, if somewhat muted, account of the conference.

We have kept the title of this book essentially the same as the title of the conference. Rather grandly we had entitled the conference "Best Methods for the Analysis of Change," and we received some good-natured ribbing from our colleagues for this. In response, we have added a subtitle, *Recent Advances, Unanswered Questions, Future Directions* to show that the book is intended to raise issues and stimulate thought in a field that is still changing dynamically more than a quarter of a century after the Harris conference. Editing this volume has proved to be thought-provoking for us; we hope you find reading it to be the same.

Linda M. Collins
John L. Horn

ORGANIZATION OF THIS BOOK

The chapters making up this book represent a rich offering of current research on the analysis of change. When we thought about how best to order these chapters, we concluded that there was no single best order. If one's purpose were pedagogical, for example, the optimal order would be different from what it would be if one were using the presentations to help design a study and needed to specify alternatives for analyzing data; this order, in turn, could be different from the order of study one would use if the aim were to develop alternatives for analyzing data already in hand. Given these possibilities, we reasoned that it would be best to suggest some unifying themes for organizing the chapters, thereby allowing the reader to choose the course of reading. Outlined in Table 1 are the unifying themes that we selected.

In Table 1 we have indicated one or more categories into which each chapter is seen to fall. Each of these categories is discussed in greater detail in the following sections. In addition, we begin each chapter with an editors' introduction, which contains a brief discussion of the aspect of change that is addressed, remarks on how the chapter adds to or enlarges our understanding, and a note directing readers to other chapters that examine related themes.

Several of the chapters end with a comment, and two end with replies to the comments. This format is an outgrowth of the conference setting from which this volume evolved. We hope that this format will stimulate the reader to move from perspective to perspective and expose him or her to much of the best and most significant research in the ever expanding area of methodologies for the analysis of change.

DESCRIPTIVE GROUPS

Issues in Applied Settings (APP)

These chapters discuss methodological issues that have arisen in substantive applications. In chapter 2 Cohen, speaking from a behavioral epidemiology per-

Table 1

CHAPTER CATEGORIES

	Descriptive Category				
Chapter/Author	APP	PDP	D&A	NEW	LVM
1 Muthén		•	•	•	•
2 Cohen	•		•		
3 Cliff		•		•	
4 Browne and Du Toit		•	•	•	•
5 Jones			•	•	
6 Nesselroade			•		
7 Cunningham		•	•		•
8 Bock		•	•	•	
9 Collins		•	•	•	
10 Meredith				•	•
11 Roberts and Bengtson	•	•	•		•
12 Embretson		•		•	
13 Widaman			•		
14 Loehlin	•		•		•
15 Gollob and Reichardt			•		•
16 Elias and Robbins	•				•
17 McArdle and Hamagami			•	•	•
18 Willett and Singer			•	•	

spective, raises an important issue that has been all but ignored in the methodological literature: the timing of the measurement of a covariate. Elias and Robbins (chapter 16), who study hypertension and its consequences, talk about the problems presented by vanishing samples in long-term studies. In chapter 11, Roberts and Bengtson discuss problems in distinguishing changes within people and differences between people across three generations. Loehlin (chapter 14) looks at decomposing the variance in change, per se, into genetic and environmental components.

Psychometric and Distributional Properties of Variables (PDP)

Addressed in these chapters are some of the special problems presented by the measurement of change. Cliff (chapter 3) discusses fundamental issues having to do with level of measurement, and presents new ordinal approaches to measurement. Collins (chapter 9) considers the correspondence between one's theory about change and the operationalization of measures of change. Establishing that the same latent variable has been measured in different samples or different times is a topic taken up by Cunningham (chapter 7), Embretson (chapter 12), and Roberts and Bengtson (chapter 11). Browne and Du Toit (chapter 4), Bock (chapter 8), and Muthén (chapter 1) discuss the assumptions that can be made about the distributions of variables and errors.

Design and Analysis (D&A)

Chapters in this group explore important factors to consider in designing good studies to measure change, and in analyzing data. Nesselroade (chapter 6) examines the problems of adequately sampling variables, occasions, and subjects. Cunningham, Browne and Du Toit, Roberts and Bengtson, Loehlin, Muthén, and McArdle and Hamagami (chapters 7, 4, 11, 14, 1, and 17, respectively) all discuss models (latent and manifest) for variables, for determinants, and for change. The amount of time allowed, or assumed to elapse, between an identified cause and the measure of its effect is shown by Cohen (chapter 2) and by Gollob and Reichardt (chapter 15) to have a potentially profound effect on results. McArdle and Hamagami (chapter 17) consider how to build a basis for inference when data are missing, a matter also considered in discussions by Rubin and Little (chapters 17 and 2). Chapters in this group also consider whether change is qualitative or quantitative (Widaman, Collins, and Cunningham; chapters 13, 9, and 7, respectively), whether it is monotonic or fluctuating (Cohen, Jones, Bock, and Brown & Du Toit; chapters 2, 5, 8, and 4, respectively), and when it can be thought of in terms of survival and hazard functions (Willett & Singer, chapter 18).

New Methodologies (NEW)

As might be expected in a conference of this type, quite a few of the chapters fit in this category. A number of these chapters involve some aspect of growth curves. Bock (chapter 8) discusses growth curves most directly; he deals with the problem of predicting human adult height by modeling growth. Browne and Du Toit, Meredith, and Muthén (chapters 4, 10, and 1, respectively) discuss latent variable approaches to growth curve analysis. The new methods of Meredith (chapter 10) and McArdle and Hamagami (chapter 17) indicate ways to compare longitudinal and cross-sectional data. New measurement methodologies are presented in three chapters: In chapter 3 Cliff discusses ordinal measurement; in chapter 9 Collins discusses measurement theory for dynamic latent variables, and in chapter 12 Embretson applies item response theory to measurement of change. Methodologies new to the social sciences are introduced by Willett and Singer (chapter 18) who present survival analysis, and Jones (chapter 5) who reviews recent developments in time series analysis.

Latent Variable Modeling (LVM)

A number of the chapters touch on various aspects of latent variable modeling. Both Roberts and Bengtson (chapter 11) and Cunningham (chapter 7) deal with the invariance of factors. Latent variable growth curve approaches are presented by Browne and Du Toit, Meredith, and Muthén (chapters 4, 10, and 1, respectively). McArdle and Hamagami (chapter 17) consider models for relations that represent change. Elias and Robbins (chapter 16) and Loehlin (chapter 14) discuss latent variable models in applied settings. Gollob and Reichardt (chapter 15) talk about temporal effects in latent variable models, and the pitfalls of using cross-sectional designs.

OMISSIONS

We must acknowledge that in spite of our best efforts to be comprehensive, fate conspired to prevent us from including several topics we know to be important and had hoped to include. In particular, there is no chapter devoted to growth curve models, as such, although models for functions that can represent growth are discussed by Bock, Browne and Du Toit, McArdle, Meredith, and Muthén (chapters 8, 4, 17, 10, and 1, respectively). Similarly, there is no thorough treatment of the age, cohort, and time (ACT) models or the repeated analysis of variance methods that have been discussed so much in the literature on adult development and aging. Hierarchical and higher order models generally are also not systematically discussed in any single chapter. It is likely that there are other omissions of important topics. We regret the omissions. We want to make it clear, too, that they in no way indicate our evaluation of a topic's importance.

CHAPTER 1

ANALYSIS OF LONGITUDINAL DATA USING LATENT VARIABLE MODELS WITH VARYING PARAMETERS

BENGT O. MUTHÉN

Editors' Introduction

Random effects growth models are currently an exciting topic in quantitative methods (Longford, 1989; Raudenbush & Bryk, 1988; Rogosa & Willett, 1985b). In these models one simultaneously fits individual growth models, estimating parameters for curves of change for individuals, and models for the group(s), estimating parameters that indicate the "typical" change in a classification of people. The idea that researchers should make this kind of distinction among individuals, types of individuals, and groups is one that Ledyard Tucker presented (and excited with) back in the days when the Harris book on methods for studying change aroused the field of developmental methodology. Chapter 1 by Muthén is a good representation of this kind of model. Important improvements and additions to such models are also provided.

This chapter has several particularly noteworthy features. First, Muthén gives an example of the use of one of the programs for random effects

This research was supported by Grant No. SES-8821668 from the National Science Foundation. I thank Mike Hollis, Gilbert Fitzgerald, Kathy Wisnicki, Jin-Wen Yang, and Tammy Tam for research assistance. I thank my fall 1989 Research on Methodology seminar group for valuable comments.

growth models, VARCL (Longford, 1989), which will be useful to substantive researchers who wish to apply this new technique in their own
work. Second, Muthén's incorporation of random effects growth models
into the framework of latent variable modeling furthers the understanding
and utility of both procedures. Third, Muthén shows how to perform random effects growth analyses using LISCOMP (Muthén, 1987), a widely
available latent variable modeling program. (Control language for this is
included in an appendix to the chapter.) An advantage of LISCOMP is that
one need not assume that the variables of the analysis are multivariate normal. The analyses Muthén proposes thus are directly relevant for research
on change; they are likely to be useful in many future studies.

   The models Muthén discusses are for interindividual differences in intraindividual growth, which is precisely what many contributors to this
book state we must carefully analyze if we are to understand change better.
It is interesting to compare and contrast Muthén's models with those of
Browne and DuToit (chapter 4) and Meredith (chapter 10). In some ways
this chapter is an application of Nesselroade's thinking (chapter 6).

This chapter attempts to bridge two different traditions in the analysis of longitudinal data to describe individual differences in change: random effects modeling
and structural equation modeling. Random effects modeling uses both fixed and
random parameters and describes the data as T replicated observations on p variables. A primary focus is on differences in parameter values across individuals.
Conventional structural equation modeling provides fixed effect techniques and
describes a set of p variables observed at T time points by means of a model for
pT variables. A primary focus is on differences in parameter values across time.
Conventional structural equation modeling has been criticized for being insensitive
to individual differences in change (see, e.g., Rogosa, 1987). The possibility of
incorporating random effects into the framework of structural equation modeling
is considered here. The aim is to provide modeling that combines the special
strengths of each tradition.

A REGRESSION MODEL WITH RANDOM EFFECTS

Consider the model for $i = 1, 2, \ldots; I$ individuals observed at $t = 1, 2, \ldots;$
T time points

$$y_{it} = \alpha_i + \beta_i x_{it} + \epsilon_{it}, \tag{1}$$

$$\alpha_i = \alpha + \gamma_\alpha z_i + \delta_{\alpha i}, \tag{2}$$

$$\beta_i = \beta + \gamma_\beta z_i + \delta_{\beta i}, \tag{3}$$

where y, x, and z are observed variables, α, β, and γ are (fixed) parameters, and
ϵ and δ are random errors, adding the further parameters $V(\epsilon)$, $V(\delta_\alpha)$, $V(\delta_\beta)$, and

$\text{Cov}(\delta_\alpha,\delta_\beta)$. Whereas y and x vary over both individuals and time, z is a time-invariant variable describing differences between individuals.

In terms of studies of growth, the x variable is often a time-related variable, such as age. In studies of growth it is natural to assume that the mean of the x variable increases with time, inducing an increase in the mean of the ys. The preceding model covers the special case of straight-line growth with across-individual variation in initial status α_i and growth rate β_i.

Analysis of the type of models outlined in Equations 1–3 can be handled by computer software such as VARCL (Longford, 1989) and HLM (Raudenbush & Bryk, 1988), where the parameters of α, β, and γ; the variances of ϵ and δ; and the covariances among the δs are estimated by maximum likelihood analysis. These programs also provide empirical Bayes estimates of each individual's regression coefficients, that is, the estimates of the α_i and β_i in Equation 1. Such an analysis recognizes that longitudinal data are obtained in a hierarchical fashion, with correlated observations obtained for independently observed individuals. Analogous data structures are found in educational data with students observed within classrooms or schools. The latter application has given rise to the name "multilevel" analysis for such situations (see, e.g., Bock, 1989b).

An Example

Muthén (1983) analyzed the stability of neuroticism measures. These data were obtained as a random sample of Canberra, Australia, electors interviewed 4 times at 4-month intervals in 1977 and 1978 (see Henderson, Byrne, & Duncan-Jones, 1981, for further details). Complete data were available for 231 individuals. The indicators at each time point are four dichotomous items intended to measure "neurotic illness," arising as the yes or no answers to the following questions: "In the last month have you suffered from Anxiety? Depression? Irritability? Nervousness?"

Four variables provide a measure of "life events" (L) that the respondent has experienced in the 4 months prior to each interview. The Neuroticism (N) scale from the Eysenck Personality Inventory is used to measure long-term susceptibility to neurosis. N is here taken as the average score from Occasions 2 and 4. Sex is also recorded. Table 1.1 gives descriptive statistics. For simplicity, a neuroticism score is created as the sum of the four yes or no responses.

In contrast to the aforementioned growth perspective, this example is such that no growth or other mean trend is expected in either y or x. Neuroticism is expected to go both up and down across time. (Note, however, the downward trend in Table 1.1.) The object of the longitudinal analysis in this case is not growth but change or stability. However, the statistical framework of a regression model with random effects is still useful.

Table 1.1

NEUROTICISM (N = 231) MEAN SCORES AND VARIANCES

	Time 1	Time 2	Time 3	Time 4
Neuroticism				
Mean score	1.17	0.81	0.78	0.75
Variance	1.65	1.29	1.24	1.17
Life events				
Mean score	3.86	3.17	2.58	2.42
Variance	6.54	5.89	4.90	5.27
N scale				
Mean score	9.31			
Variance	20.66			

In the neuroticism example the time-varying x variable of Equation 1 corresponds to the life event variable L. The time-invariant z variable of Equations 2 and 3 corresponds to the N scale and sex. Randomly varying intercepts over individuals implies that without stressful life events, different individuals are expected to have different levels of measured neuroticism. The differences in such levels can to some extent be explained by the individual-specific N and sex variables. Variations in the slopes across individuals implies that the L variable has different predictive strength for different individuals. For example, a person with a high N score may react more strongly to stressful life events, corresponding to a positive γ_β.

To illustrate, I shall analyze the neuroticism data by the random coefficient regression program VARCL (Longford, 1989). I will apply a model with random variation in both intercepts and slopes and attempt to explain this parameter variation by N and sex, where sex is a 0/1 variable scored as 1 for female subjects. The results are as follows for a sequence of increasingly complex models. The model number is prefixed by the letter R for random parameters.

Model R1

The first model specifies a random intercept and fixed slopes. No time-invariant, individual-specific variables are used. The VARCL maximum likelihood estimate of the intercept variance obtains a clearly significant value.

Model R2

The second model is the same as Model R1, except that the intercept variation is expressed as a function of N, in line with z of Equation 2. In Equation 2, the regression of the individual intercepts on N (or z) obtains a positive slope estimate of 0.107, with a standard error of 0.011. This regression coefficient is therefore significant. The remaining intercept variance is still significantly different from zero.

Model R3

The third model is the same as Model R2 except that sex is added to explain the intercept variance. The estimated slope in the regression of the intercepts on N is 0.106, with a standard error of 0.011, and the sex slope is 0.099, with a standard error of 0.101. We conclude that N is still a significant predictor, but sex is not. The residual intercept variance is still significant.

Model R4

Model R4 adds a random slope specification to the random intercepts and takes the intercept variation to be predicted by N, while no individual-level variable is used to predict the slope variation. The intercept-related slope for N obtains the estimate 0.104, with a standard error of 0.011, and is therefore still significant. The variance of the slopes is estimated as 0.002 and is not significant. Note, however, that the introduction of random slopes in addition to random intercepts adds not one but two parameters—the variance of the slopes and the covariance between the intercept and the slope residuals. A likelihood ratio test of Model R4 versus Model R2 is the appropriate way to test whether random slopes are warranted (given that the absence of influence from sex is accepted). This test gives a chi-square value of 7.75 with 2 degrees of freedom, which is significant on the 5% level, although not on the 1% level. This indicates a need to include a random slope specification in addition to random intercepts as is done in Model R4, although the nonsignificant variance estimate does not appear to reflect this. If there is a slope variation, it is not very large.

Model R5

The fifth model keeps the specification of random intercepts and random slopes. The intercept variation is still described in terms of N. Compared with Model R4, Model R5 adds N as a predictor of the slope variation. Although N is still a significant predictor of the intercept variation, it is not found to be an important predictor of the slope variation. The coefficient in the regression of the slopes on N is estimated as 0.0060, with a standard error of 0.0033. The ratio of 1.82 does not indicate significance on the 5% level. The estimated mean of the slopes is 0.036 with an estimated variation in the slope of 0.037 (the variance of N is

20.66). According to this model, N explains only 2% of the slope variation. If the nonsignificance is ignored, the positive slope estimate indicates that increasing N increases the strength with which L predicts the neuroticism score.

Model R6

The final model maintains Model R5 features except that sex replaces N as predictor of the slope variation. Sex is not found to have a significant influence, however.

Given this sequence of model estimation and testing, Model R4 is deemed to be the most appropriate for the data. Note, however, that Model R2 gives very similar results. Model R4 specifies that the intercepts vary across individuals as a function of N. The slopes also vary, but they are not explained by individual-level variables such as N and sex. Recall that the amount of slope variation appears ignorable. The estimated R4 model can be summarized as follows. The variance in the intercepts explained by N is estimated as 38%. The estimated intercept variance is 0.59, and it is of interest to compare this variance to that of the dependent variable of the neuroticism score. The estimated variance in the dependent variable at each of the four time points is 1.37, 1.35, 1.34, and 1.35, so that the variation in intercepts across individuals corresponds to about 44% of the total variation.

STRUCTURAL EQUATION MODELING OF REGRESSIONS WITH RANDOM INTERCEPTS

Structural equation modeling of longitudinal data such as the data analyzed above considers a "strung out" data vector for pT variables. In terms of the neuroticism data, the one y and one L observed at four time points then gives eight variables, to which the N and sex variables are added. Interestingly enough, it turns out that such an approach can in fact be used to analyze a model such as that of Equations 1 and 2 (a random intercept model).

The key to such an analysis is to specify a time-invariant factor

$$\eta_{0i} = \alpha + \gamma z_i + \delta_i \qquad (4)$$

corresponding to the random intercept of Equation 2. The random intercept notion may then be reconceptualized. In the neuroticism example, we may instead view η_0 as a person-specific latent predisposition toward neuroticism, which can to some extent be predicted by N.

To capture the model of Equations 1 and 2, the structural equation analysis uses a mean and covariance structure model with equality restrictions on the slopes and residual variances over time, while allowing the means, variances, and covariances of N and the Ls to be unrestricted parameters. The structural modeling path diagram corresponding to such an analysis is given in Figure 1.1. This analysis also provides a chi-square test of fit to the restrictions imposed by the model used in sections 2 and 3 and enables straightforward relaxations of such restrictions.

This technique was applied to the neuroticism data using the LISCOMP structural equation modeling program of Muthén (1987). In line with the earlier results we use the four y variables, the four L variables, and the N variable (nine variables in all). A chi-square value of 59.9 with 29 degrees of freedom was obtained for the random intercepts model, Model R2. Hence, this model does not fit well ($p = 0.0006$) when tested against the model of no structure imposed on the means and covariances of the nine variables. Inspection of the distributions of the variables shows strong skewness as might be expected. The normality assumption, imposed for the residuals in Equations 1 and 2, is therefore not tenable and may explain part of the large chi-square. Browne's "asymptotically distribution free" (ADF) estimator (Browne, 1984; Muthén, 1987) was also applied, but it reduced the chi-square to only 50.0. The sample size of 231 may be too

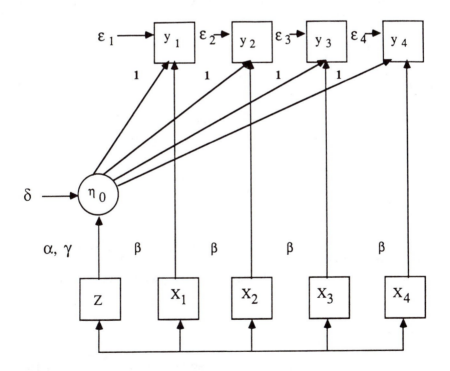

Figure 1.1 Random intercept as a person component in structural modeling.

small to rely on this ADF chi-square value. Below we will work with chi-square differences in models in which it is assumed that non-normality plays a lesser role.

Certain model assumptions can be relaxed in a straightforward fashion in the structural modeling framework. For example, the slopes for L and the residual variances in y need not be equal over time. Table 1.2 describes chi-square statistics for a series of increasingly relaxed models estimated by maximum likelihood. The prefix S refers to structural models. We note that Model S1 is the same as Model R2 (the S counterpart of R1 could be estimated but is not, given the significant influence of N).

The sequence of models in Table 1.2 relaxes the different types of restrictions in the basic model of S1 (R2) in the following order: Equal L slopes over time, equal residual variances in y over time, and uncorrelated residuals over time. For each such model, an alternative specification with cross-lagged influence of L on y is also tested. This means that L at Time 1 is allowed to influence y at Time 2, L at Time 2 is allowed to influence y at Time 3, and L at Time 3 is allowed to influence y at Time 4. R_0^2 refers to the explained portion of variation in the latent predisposition variable η_0, R_1^2–R_4^2 refer to explained variation in the ys, and P_1–P_4 refer to the ratio of estimated variance in the predisposition variable relative to the ys.

Model S1

The basic model of S1 (R2) does not fit well even with lagged L effects. The R^2 and P statistics will, however, be of interest for comparisons with subsequent models.

Model S2

Allowing the slopes for L to be different at different time points gives a significant reduction in chi-square compared with Model S1 (59.95–40.82 with 29–26 degrees of freedom). The drop is also significant if one adopts the lagged model.

Model S3

Model S3 allows both slopes and residual variances to differ across time. This also gives a significant drop in the chi-square level compared with any of the previous models.

Table 1.2

STRUCTURAL EQUATION MODELING

Parameter	Model S1 Basic	Model S1 + lagged L[a]	Model S2 Unequal slopes	Model S2 + lagged L	Model S3 Unequal slopes and residual variances	Model S3 + lagged L	Model S4 As S3, correlated residuals	Model S4 + lagged L	Model S5 As S4, unequal intercepts	Model S5 + lagged L
X^2	59.95	54.32	40.82	38.95	31.75	29.84	28.20	26.73	23.92	21.80
df	29	26	26	23	23	20	20	17	17	14
Probability	.0006	.0009	.0324	.0201	.1055	.0725	.1046	.0621	.1216	.0828
R_0^2	.403	.413	.406	.401	.392	.387	.394	.390	.394	.389
R_1^2	.519	.525	.550	.553	.495	.498	.518	.519	.501	.500
R_2^2	.511	.509	.507	.509	.500	.504	.530	.531	.534	.539
R_3^2	.509	.509	.509	.512	.570	.573	.575	.576	.586	.585
R_4^2	.512	.509	.505	.507	.526	.525	.522	.521	.526	.525
P_1	.443	.452	.434	.426	.388	.381	.408	.401	.434	.427
P_2	.450	.467	.475	.470	.446	.462	.494	.488	.496	.484
P_3	.452	.467	.472	.466	.527	.520	.532	.525	.530	.519
P_4	.449	.466	.476	.471	.494	.486	.490	.484	.492	.484

[a]Life events variables.

Model S4

Longitudinal data would appear to result frequently in residuals that are correlated over time as a result of the effects of omitted predictors. Model S4 tests this, but when the results are compared with those of Model S3, such correlated residuals are found insignificant in this application.

Model S5

So far, the models have implied that the means of the ys may differ over time only as a function of mean changes in L. In technical terms, the specification of a nonzero intercept in the regression of η_0 on N implies equal intercepts in the (reduced-form) regressions of the ys on the Ls and N. As a final test, Model S5 relaxes this restriction. Technically, this is done by allowing the intercepts in the equations for y at Time points 2–4 regressed on L and η_0 to be different from a zero intercept for y at Time 1. A significant improvement in model fit is not achieved.

In conclusion, it appears that Model S3 without lagged L effects is the most parsimonious model that fits well ($p = .11$). Allowing for differences in L slopes and residual variances across time appears warranted. The estimates (and standard errors) of the slopes at the four time points are .125 (.017), .061 (.018), .070 (.020), and .054 (.021), whereas the results for the residual variances are .802 (.087), .660 (.074), .502 (.060), and .592 (.068). Time point 1 appears different from the other time points (this is also seen in Table 1.1). In this model the amount of variation in the intercepts explained by N is 39%. The estimated variation in η_0 is 0.62, whereas the estimated variances of y at each of the four time points are 1.59, 1.32, 1.17, and 1.25. It is interesting to compare Models R4 and S3 with respect to the estimated ratio of η_0 variance to y variance. The η_0 variance is interpreted as variance in predisposition in the structural modeling framework of Model S3 and as intercept variance in the random coefficient framework of Model R4. Whereas Model R4 (which is close to R2 or S1) obtained a ratio of about 44%, Table 1.2 shows that the ratio for Model S3 varies across time and ranges from 39% at Time 1 to 53% at Time 3. The LISCOMP setup for Model S3 is given in the appendix (a LISREL setup would be similar).

STRUCTURAL EQUATION MODELING WITH LATENT VARIABLES

Figure 1.2 shows a path diagram for the structural model for neuroticism of Muthén (1983). Here, multiple indicators are used to capture latent variable constructs in order to avoid distortions of measurement errors. The original four dichotomous

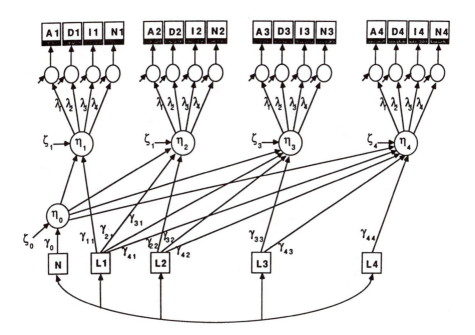

Figure 1.2   Neuroticism model of Muthén. From "Latent Variable Structural Equation
Modeling With Categorical Data" by B. Muthén, 1983, *Journal of Econometrics, 22*, p. 57. Copyright 1983 by Elsevier Sequoia. Reprinted by
permission.

variables are used as indicators. Certain features are typical of many structural
equation models for longitudinal data:

1. Measurement errors in the outcome variables are of primary concern
   and multiple indicators are used to define a factor. This gives rise to
   multivariate response at each time point.
2. The issue of time-invariance of the factor-analytic measurement model
   used is of primary concern. This assumption, although natural since
   the same measurement instrument is use, is however not necessary
   and can be tested.
3. The issue of variations over time in factor means and variances is of
   interest. The hypothesis of invariance of these parameters can be
   tested.
4. The specification of how variables correlate across time is of primary
   concern but little agreement has been reached in the field on how to
   specify such correlations.

5. Differences in parameters across groups of individuals can be studied by simultaneous multiple-group analysis.

It is interesting to relate these conventional structural equation models to the random effects models. Points 1 and 2 are not of concern in the random effects model, in which a single, error-free outcome measure y is studied. The dependent variable factor in Figure 1.2 takes the role of this y variable.

Point 4 is of particular interest in this chapter. The partial regression coefficient for the path between the factors at two time points was taken to describe the "stability" of the factor by Wheaton, Muthén, Alwin, and Summers (1977), but this idea was criticized by Rogosa (1987) from a growth-modeling perspective. In Figure 1.2, the factors have no such direct effects between them. Instead, the path diagram in Figure 1.2 specifies a latent random variable η_0, which affects each factor with equal weight 1. Muthén (1983) motivated the role of η_0 by generalizing econometric variance component modeling for the pooling of cross-section and time-series data to the latent variable context. As shown above, this component captures intercept variation. The observed indicators may also be correlated as a result of measurement errors' being correlated over time; this could also be added to Figure 1.2.

Random Parameters in Structural Equation Models With Multiple Indicators

Random parameters in structural equation models have been proposed in recent work by Goldstein and McDonald (1988), Muthén (1989), and Schmidt and Wisenbaker (1986). These authors considered data for students observed within classrooms or schools. To clarify the ideas, I shall use a factor analysis model proposed in Muthén (1989). In line with the discussion of regression models with random effects, the notion of classrooms can be translated to individuals and students can be translated to observations across time. As one example, Muthén (1989) considered a factor analysis model in which factor means and measurement intercepts were allowed to vary randomly across classrooms. Again, let i represent individuals (the classrooms of Muthén, 1989), with $i = 1, 2, \ldots, I$, and let t represent the time points (the students of Muthén, 1989), $t = 1, 2, \ldots, T$. For p observed indicators y and m factors η,

$$y_{it} = \nu_i + \Lambda\eta_{it} + \epsilon_{it}, \tag{5}$$

$$\eta_{it} = \alpha_i + \omega_{it}, \tag{6}$$

$$\alpha_i = \alpha + \delta_{\alpha i}, \tag{7}$$

$$\nu_i = \nu + \delta_{\nu i}, \tag{8}$$

where ϵ, ω, and the δs are random residuals, not correlated with each other. Equations 6 and 7 are written to mimic the random intercept formulation of Equations 1 and 2 with η taking the place of y and with no counterpart to x. Equations 5 and 8 express a random intercept model for the indicators of y, with η taking the role of x in Equation 1. With appropriate assumptions, we obtain

$$V(y) = \Sigma_W + \Sigma_B, \tag{9}$$

where

$$\Sigma_W = \Lambda V(\omega) \Lambda' + \Theta, \text{ and} \tag{10}$$

$$\Sigma_B = \Lambda V(\delta_\alpha) \Lambda' + V(\delta_\nu), \tag{11}$$

where Θ and $V(\delta_\nu)$ may be taken to be diagonal. Σ_W gives the covariance matrix for the p y variables holding the individual constant. Σ_B gives the covariance matrix resulting from variation across individuals.

In line with conventional structural equation modeling for longitudinal data, the analysis vector is of length pT,

$$\mathbf{d}'_i = (y'_{i1}, y_{i2}, \ldots, y'_{iT}). \tag{12}$$

The model assumes time invariance (student invariance in Muthén, 1989) of the mean vector and covariance matrix for the p y variables, so that

$$\mu'_d = [\mathbf{1}'_T \otimes \mu'_y] \text{ and} \tag{13}$$

$$\Sigma_d = \mathbf{I}_T \otimes \Sigma_W + \mathbf{1}_T \mathbf{1}'_T \otimes \Sigma_B, \tag{14}$$

where $\otimes$ denotes the Kronecker product, $\mathbf{I}_T$ denotes an identity matrix of dimension $T \times T$, and $\mathbf{1}_T$ denotes a vector of T unit elements.

Assuming multivariate normality and independent observations on $\mathbf{d}$, Muthén (1989) pointed out that this model can be estimated by existing software for structural equation modeling using covariance matrices that are only of order $p \times p$. A simultaneous analysis of two groups is required, in which the maximum-likelihood fitting function may be written as

$$F = I \{\log | T^{-1} \Sigma_W + \Sigma_B | + \text{tr} [(T^{-1} \Sigma_W + \Sigma_B)^{-1} S_B]\}$$
$$+ (I \cdot T - I) \{\log | \Sigma_W | + \text{tr} [\Sigma_W^{-1} S_{PW}]\}, \tag{15}$$

where

$$\mathbf{S}_B = I^{-1} \sum_{i=1}^{I} (\bar{\mathbf{y}}_i - \bar{\mathbf{y}}) (\bar{\mathbf{y}}_i - \bar{\mathbf{y}})' \text{ and} \tag{16}$$

$$\mathbf{S}_{PW} = (I \cdot T - I)^{-1} \sum_{t=1}^{I} \sum_{t=1}^{T} (\mathbf{y}_{it} - \bar{\mathbf{y}}_i)(\mathbf{y}_{it} - \bar{\mathbf{y}}_i)', \tag{17}$$

where $\bar{\mathbf{y}}_i$ is the individual-specific mean of the p dimensional $\mathbf{y}$ vector taken across time points and $\bar{\mathbf{y}}$ is the p-dimensional vector of total means. The $\mathbf{S}_B$ matrix is a sample covariance matrix for each individual's mean vector, and the $\mathbf{S}_{PW}$ matrix is a pooled within sample covariance matrix, adjusting for individual differences in means. The first group (Equation 16) is viewed as having I observations and the second group (Equation 17) is viewed as having $(IT - I)$ observations. The two groups have certain parameters in common.

We may also note that the mean and covariance structural model implied by Equations 13 and 14 can be viewed as a model for pT variables, in line with the approach to longitudinal data taken by conventional structural equation modeling exemplified above. For example, for three time points we would have

$$\mu_d' = (\mu_y', \mu_y', \mu_y') \text{ and} \tag{18}$$

$$\sum_d = \begin{bmatrix} \Sigma_W + \Sigma_B & & \text{Symm.} \\ \Sigma_B & \Sigma_W + \Sigma_B & \\ \Sigma_B & \Sigma_B & \Sigma_W + \Sigma_B \end{bmatrix} \tag{19}$$

This model can be analyzed in a single-group structural equation model with both the mean and covariance structure imposed on the pT-dimensional variable vector. The appropriateness of the Kronecker structure for the mean vector and the covariance matrix can be tested, even before the factor analysis structure is imposed on μ_y, Σ_W, and Σ_B. Assuming for simplicity's sake a single-factor model, the corresponding path diagram for the covariance structure part of the model of Equations 5–11 could therefore be drawn as in Figure 1.3. This model is clearly identifiable because it describes a standard one-factor model at both the "between" and "within" levels (see Equations 10 and 11). The formulation of random factor means and random measurement intercepts provides a clear rationale for how the factors and the indicators correlate over time. The random factor means part of the model gives rise to the individual-specific δ_α factor in Figure 1.3.

Breaking out an individual-specific component of η_{it}, δ_i, provides a different way to define "stability" than was done by Wheaton et al. (1977). The stability of the vector may be taken as that part of the variance of the factor which is due to δ_i, giving a notion of how much of the factor variance comes from the variation in the personality trait as opposed to time-specific variation. If the time-specific residual component is allowed to have varying variance across time, the stability value will differ over time.

So far in this section, we have assumed stationarity of the factor distributions across time. In growth applications of mixed effects models such as Equations 1 and 2, this assumption is naturally not made. However, in the neuroticism example,

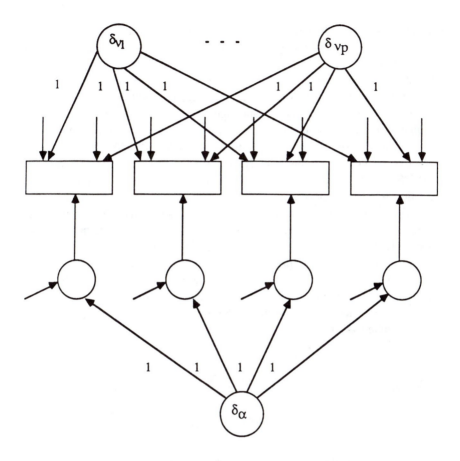

Figure 1.3   Person components of factor and measurement error correlations.

growth over time is generally not expected, but the levels may go up and down in a largely random fashion. Nevertheless, the stationarity assumption may be relaxed and the factors expressed as functions of time-invariant and time-varying observed predictors. This is in line with Figure 1.2 in which the mean of the neuroticism variable is assumed to vary with the life event variable, which in turn is not necessarily stationary in terms of means or variances. Our previous discussion indicates that the path diagram of Figure 1.2 in fact corresponds to a model with random structural regression intercepts for the regressions of η on L at each time point and where this intercept variation is in part predicted by the N variable. Hence, this modeling of longitudinal data does in fact represent a mixed effects model. This particular type of model can be fitted by existing conventional software for structural equation models. Correlated measurement errors could be added to this particular model. As in the study by Muthén (1983), the indicators need not be multivariate normal but can be dichotomous. The LISCOMP program of Muthén (1987) is particularly suited to this task. Simultaneous analysis of several groups of individuals may also be carried out.

It is interesting to compare the results of the neuroticism Model S3 with that of Muthén (1983). The Muthén (1983) model allowed for different effects of L across time, as does Model S3, although the residual variances were taken to be equal over time. Cross-lagged effects of L appeared small. The percent variation in the predisposition variable relative to the dependent variable factors were estimated at about 68%, a considerably higher value than the 39%–53% range of Model S3. The difference may result from the more proper treatment of the neuroticism measures in Muthén (1983).

This chapter does not address the case of structural models with randomly varying slopes, such as Equation 3. Given this limitation, structural equation software provides more flexibility than is presently given by random coefficients software such as VARCL and HLM. We may easily handle multivariate responses at each time point and formulate factor-analytic measurement models that avoid the influence of measurement errors. Correlated measurement errors over time can also be handled. Multiple-group analysis gives a flexible way to study differences among groups of individuals. Finally, the variables need not be normally distributed.

APPENDIX 1.1

Input to the Computer Program LISCOMP

```
TI  LONGITUDINAL ANALYSIS OF NEUROTICISM
TI  A SINGLE Y REGRESSED ON A SINGLE X AT 4 TIME POINTS
TI  IN A RANDOM INTERCEPT MODEL WITH ONE Z WITHOUT
        STATIONARITY OF X.
TI  NOTE: FIRST 4 ETAS REPRESENT THE YS, NEXT FOUR THE XS,
        THE NINTH ETA REPRESENTS Z (OR N), AND THE TENTH ETA
        REPRESENTS THE LATENT PREDISPOSITION VARIABLE (OR
        RANDOM INTERCEPT) (HENCE AL(5) - AL(8) REPRESENT X
        MEANS)
DA  IY = 9 IX = 0 NO = 231
MO  MO = SE P1 P3 NE = 10 NU = FI AL = FI LY = FI PS = FI TE = FI BE = FI
VA  1.0 LY(1,1) LY(2,2) LY(3,3) LY(4,4) LY(5,5)
        LY(6,6) LY(7,7) LY(8,8) LY(9,9)
FR  AL(5) AL(6) AL(7) AL(8) AL(9) AL(10)
FR  PS(1,1) PS(2,2) PS(3,3) PS(4,4) PS(5,5) PS(6,6)
        PS(7,7) PS(8,8) PS(9,9) PS(10,10)
```

```
FR   PS(6,5) PS(7,5) PS(7,6) PS(8,5) PS(8,6) PS(8,7)
       PS(9,5) PS(9,6) PS(9,7) PS(9,8)
VA   0.5 PS(1,1) PS(2,2) PS(3,3) PS(4,4) PS(5,5) PS(6,6) PS(7,7)
       PS(8,8) PS(9,9)
VA   1.0 BE(1,10) BE(2,10) BE(3,10) BE(4,10)
FR   BE(1,5) BE(2,6) BE(3,7) BE(4,8)
FR   BE(10,9)
OU   MN PT ES SE
RA   FO UN=8
(4F2.0,5F3.0)
```

CHAPTER 2

A SOURCE OF BIAS IN LONGITUDINAL INVESTIGATIONS OF CHANGE

PATRICIA COHEN

Editors' Introduction

Chapter 2 is a startling reminder that in longitudinal research, no data analysis approach, however well established or widely used, can be assumed to be fully effective in a particular setting. Instead, careful scrutiny must be given to every application. Cohen gives the reader who uses covariates— practically every reader who analyzes empirical data—plenty to scrutinize. This chapter raises the problem of the "premature covariate," which arises when a covariate is changing over time. Cohen shows that, quite apart from any measurement error considerations, if a covariate is not measured at the time it exerts its causal influence, it may not be an effective covariate; that is, the statistical analysis may not partial out all of the effect of the covariate on the dependent variable. The consequences can be substantially biased estimates of effects. The argument and example given in this chapter involve reciprocal causation, but the general idea holds whenever a covariate or dependent variable is dynamic.

Two comment sections follow this chapter. In the first, Collins and Graham outline the general problem of timing of measurements as a design consideration. They argue that this issue is relevant to most large-scale longitudinal studies. In the second comment section, Little frames this as a missing data problem, where the covariate at the time it exerts its effects constitutes an array of missing data. Together, chapter 2 and the two comment sections provide a new look at one of the social sciences' most commonly used statistical procedures.

This chapter addresses what appears to be a neglected problem in studies of naturally occurring change in human characteristics and behavior. The perspective of these investigations is social or psychological epidemiology, by which I mean that changes in population characteristics are observed over time without any attempt to influence the phenomena. The object of the research is to understand the natural history of the phenomena, including secular or age-related increase, decrease, and fluctuation. Such understanding requires a determination of the influences on this natural history, including factors affecting onset, growth, recovery, persistence, and decline. The inferences drawn from these observations are supported by confirmation of theoretical predictions (e.g., as in geology or astronomy), based on presumed causal mechanisms.

Including the term *epidemiological* in the method implies that the data are based on large random samples from some specifiable population and that the purposes include identification of the natural history of some "pathological" phenomenon and of the factors that may influence this natural history. A central problem in this research is the difficulty in empirically confirming effects involving variables for which reciprocal mechanisms of causation are theoretically expected; that is, where it is expected that X produces effects in Y and Y produces effects in X.

Ideal circumstances for such studies include an explicit matching of the interval of longitudinal investigation to the time required for a change in X to produce a change in Y, where X and Y are defined so that the time for the $X \rightarrow Y$ effect is equal to or shorter than the time for the $Y \rightarrow X$ effect when effects in both directions can be expected. (The term *effect period* will be used to refer to that minimum period over which the predominant effect of a change in one variable on change in another takes place and equilibrium may be said to have been reached. Gollob and Reichardt (1987) and Heise (1975) have useful discussions of dynamic considerations in causal analysis.) However, in practice, there are a number of reasons why equilibrium periods will not match the longitudinal interval, even when approximate equilibrium periods can be theoretically specified.

WHY LONGITUDINAL STUDIES ARE NOT GENERALLY DESIGNED THE WAY THEY SHOULD BE

For many reasons (see chapter 15, by Gollob and Reichardt, this volume), the ideal design would include repeated measures at many closely spaced intervals. If one is not certain about what interval is needed, or if the effect period varies from one set of investigations within a study to another, it is clearly best to use the shortest likely interval over which effects take place. Then assessment can be repeated until the longest likely interval is also spanned.

However, for several reasons, this design imperative is hardly ever followed. First, under conditions in which a large sample must be followed repeatedly for phenomena having a weekly, monthly, quarterly, or even annual effect period, it is often too difficult and too expensive to cover all matches between the longitudinal intervals and the various effect periods of interest. In addition to the expense and logistical difficulties, short intervals often produce unacceptable subject attrition, so that the resulting sample on which effects are actually estimated is biased in unknown and potentially serious ways. Furthermore, frequent repeated assessments tend to be too reactive and often lead to a deterioration of the quality of the responses, or even a psychological restructuring of the phenomena under investigation.

If assessment at closely spaced intervals is not possible, one alternative is to use assessment procedures that include estimates of intermediate values, such as event histories. However, there is much evidence that memory loss and telescoping effects tend to seriously bias accounts over more than a short span of time, even when the phenomena covered are discrete, concrete events such as the use of services or life events. Furthermore, the evidence suggests that event timing is even more inaccurately reported than event occurrence. A generally accepted solution to the problem of unreliability of retrospective reporting is to confine reports to a brief recent period to maximize their dependability. Such periods over which the events are to be recorded, however, must be balanced carefully between the need for adequate statistical power and the need for adequate validity. When intervals are too short, one may get too few intervening events or have too little change in the targeted variables to allow for statistically powerful estimation of effects.

Some examples of this problem are as follows. Current empirical investigations include estimation of the effect of life events on measures of psychopathology, the effect of treatment that occurs between two assessments of pathology and the effects of change in health-relevant behaviors on health status. In all of these cases, it must be assumed that prior pathology may increase the likelihood that the intervening event or behavior will occur. The goal of the research is to determine the effect of the event on the natural history of the pathology. For example, in studying the effect of routine checkup visits to a physician on long-term health outcome, researchers must allow for the possibility that an increase in minor symptoms will increase the probability that the subjects will make such "routine" visits. If one could make observations at frequent intervals, one could see which came first, the increase in symptoms or the visit. However, it is generally not feasible or desirable to assess symptoms at too closely spaced intervals because of the problems of sample attrition, response quality, and reactivity noted above. Concern for reliability of the independent variables (e.g., life events, treatment, or health behaviors) often leads to measurements that cover only the most recent interval, thus including only a portion of the period over which change in the pathology measure is assessed. In fact, this is the recommended procedure with regard to life events or treatment histories, for example, where it is often advocated that data be collected on the previous 3 or 6 months or, at most, 1 year in spite of there being a longer longitudinal interval since baseline data on the dependent variable of interest. However, this recommendation may produce a seriously biased estimate of effects. The remainder of this chapter is devoted to the demonstration of bias associated with this problem, which will be termed the problem of the *premature covariate* (see Judd & Kenny, 1981, p. 125–127, for a related discussion). In the absence of an analytic method for correcting this bias, a systematic investigation using simulated data is proposed.

THE PROBLEM OF THE PREMATURE COVARIATE

The problem of the premature covariate may be illustrated by an investigation of the effect of a stressful life event (or a particular set of such events) on psychopathology. Because it is not ethical to administer stressful events to human subjects, we usually depend on the fact that such events will occur to some but not all of the members of an observed sample in a study in which regression or structural equation models are applied to longitudinal data. Thus, we have measures of current psychopathology (e.g., depression) at T_1 and, in a follow-up, collect data on whether a stressful event (e.g., divorce or loss of employment) has occurred in the interim. In the follow-up interview, we also assess current psychopathology. The simplest analysis would examine the effects of the event on regressed change (or raw change) in depression, controlling for any other variables deemed crucial in eliminating bias or error from the equation because they may be confounders (common causes).

However, we know that this analysis is likely to be wrong. The likelihood that a subject would experience a stressful life event was itself probably not independent of the level of psychopathology. There are both theoretical and empirical reasons for expecting that individuals with higher levels of psychopathology are more prone to experience stressful life events. Furthermore, with regard to these data, this dependence will have been a function not of the level of psychopathology at the T_1 assessment but rather a function of the level of psychopathology just before the event occurred. This point will typically have been some time after the T_1 assessment, and the relevant interval will vary from one respondent to another. Use of the T_1 assessment as a proxy will lead to biased estimates of the effects of life events, such that any real tendency for psychopathology to increase in response to stressful life events will be made larger because we have failed to take into account the change in psychopathology occurring between the event and the postevent assessment. It should be noted that this problem is solely a consequence of the premature covariate—if we had been able to assess psychopathology just prior to the event for each individual, and then again at a standard interval following the event, no bias would be present.

A more dramatic effect is likely to occur when the direction of causal effects is not congruent. Consider, for example, the case in which the probability of a subject's entering treatment increases with increases in psychopathology, but the level of psychopathology decreases in response to treatment. When longitudinal data are used to assess the effects of treatment occurring during some substantial interval, such as a year or two, the bias attributable to the premature covariate may make it appear that treatment actually increased psychopathology.

Parameters That Affect the Magnitude of the Bias

Let Y represent the variable on which we wish to assess change between two assessment points $(T_1$ and $T_2)$, X represent the intervening event, and its influence on Y be the target of the investigation. The period between T_1 and T_2 can further be expressed as subdivided into smaller time units, each of which is defined as an effect period in which the level of Y will affect the probability of X.

The extent of the bias in the estimate of the effect of X on change in Y will be a function of

1. The average rate of change over time units in Y; the autoregressive effect of Y,
2. The strength of the effect of Y on X,
3. The strength of the conditionality of X on Y,
4. The number of time units covered by the T_1–T_2 interval.

Although it is not difficult to identify logically relevant elements, a simulation was devised to demonstrate that bias would in fact result under these circumstances.

Demonstration of the Problem in a Simulated Example

Consider, for example, a research study investigating the effects of stressful life events (X) on psychopathology (Y). Suppose that in reality stressful life events have no effect on psychopathology, but rather their association results entirely from the fact that the presence of psychopathology increases the probability of occurrence of a stressful life event. The following simulated data were devised to model this example.

Y at T_1 consisted of a standard normal random variable with $n = 500$. Y_2 was constructed by adding to Y_1 for each case $+ .25$, $- .25$, or 0, as determined by another random variable; the three change values were equiprobable. Y_3 was created from Y_2 in the same manner, and the procedure was repeated over 24 consecutive time units. This process yielded an average empirical correlation that went from .99 for two consecutive time units (Y_i and Y_{i+1}) to .76 over a span of 24 units (Y_1 and Y_{25}). Depending on the substantive problem, appropriate time units might be minutes, days, months, quarters, years, or even longer. In this example, let us assume that we are examining change in depressive symptoms and the occurrence of life events at monthly intervals.

X (e.g., a relevant life event) either occurred (1) or did not occur (0) in any given time unit for each case. The probability of X for each unit of time was determined by a Markov process, with probability increasing as a function of the level of the contemporaneous Y. Probabilities used increased from 0 for those with current Y less than -1.00 to .25 for those with current scores of 1.5 or greater. The values used yielded an average contemporaneous correlation of .17 between X and Y, and an average correlation of .28 between Y and the likelihood of X's occurring in the preceding 5-unit period. Again, note that no effects of X on Y were included in the model.

The estimates of the effects of X were obtained from the equation estimating Y_{i+t} from X_i when Y_1 was included as a covariate. Two sets of X_i variables were used; the first was whether X occurred at any time between the initial assessment Y_1 and the current assessment Y_{i+t}, and the second was whether X occurred at any time in the 5 time units immediately preceding Y_{i+t}.

Findings are given in Table 2.1. As can be seen, when X was measured over a 5-unit span coinciding with the measurement of pre- and postmeasures in Y, no bias in the estimate was apparent ($B = .01$). This is in keeping with our expectation that when the timing of the premeasure of Y is appropriate, our

Table 2.1

REGRESSION ESTIMATES OF EFFECTS OF THE OCCURRENCE OF X ON CHANGE IN Y IN SIMULATED DATA ($N = 500$)

Effect	B	SE
Apparent effect of the occurrence of X since the premeasure of Y		
After 5 time units	.010	.050
After 10 time units	.116	.063
After 15 time units	.252	.074
After 20 time units	.236	.088
After 25 time units	.261	.098
Apparent effect of the occurrence of X during 5 time units prior to the postmeasure of Y		
After 10 time units	.205	.071
After 15 time units	.361	.085
After 20 time units	.335	.099
After 25 time units	.604	.105

estimates will be unbiased. However, as the number of effect periods increased, even when the entire span was included, a bias appeared such that X's estimated effect on Y ranged from .12 to .26.

When the occurrence of X in the 5 units prior to the post-Y measure was used as the independent variable, bias in all estimates was substantially larger than it was in the earlier analyses, ranging from .20 to as much as .60. Note that this simulation is analogous to the situation in which measurement is limited to a recent interval in order to minimize unreliability; as previously noted, this is commonly recommended.

Additional analyses in which the "effect" of X_1 was also removed by including it in the equation yielded essentially the same results and thus were also insufficient to remove the bias that resulted from the premature covariate. Of course, in this simulation unreliability is not included as a parameter, and the findings would apply to perfectly reliable data. Measurement error will, of course, reduce the autocorrelation in Y, and also the correlation between X and Y, the consequences of which will be the same as for correlations of the same magnitude arising for any other reason. However, estimates of reliability of assessment may be incorporated into any empirically based correction of real data.

Discussion and Extension of the Identified Problem

One solution to the problem of inappropriate timing of longitudinal assessments when reciprocal causation is plausible may be to model the data under alternative assumptions of Y (and possibly X) autoregression and magnitudes and effect periods for the $Y \rightarrow X$ effect. Methods such as those described by Little and Rubin (1989) may be adapted to produce unbiased estimates if some of the relevant parameters can be estimated or imputed, providing that it can be shown analytically or by modeling that the problem is completely formulated as a function of the aforementioned parameters.

A further extension of this work involves generalization to graduated (multivalued) as well as binary X variables. For example, suppose we follow up a sample of 50-year-old subjects at age 65 to determine the effects of various levels of poor physical health on mental health. Assume that the 50-year-old subjects were mostly healthy and that the negative effects of mental illness on physical health did not amount to much before this vulnerable period. Now we assess physical health in the 5-year period prior to age 65 on some graduated scale and use mental health (or illness) assessed at age 50 as a covariate. We will have the same problem of the premature covariate as we had in the binary X example presented earlier.

Of course, the identified problem exists only in circumstances in which effects of Y on X are present. Unfortunately, it is likely that in many of the most interesting and important problems in the observational sciences, reciprocal causation is plausible if not certain. It is hoped that new work may determine magnitudes of $Y \rightarrow X$ effects, ratios of effect periods for $Y \rightarrow X$ relative to $X \rightarrow Y$, and perhaps other parameters within which this bias will be negligible.

Another potential use for work on this problem is in determining the appropriate parameters that need to be considered in selecting an interval for longitudinal investigation of a problem. Developmentalists have been concerned about appropriate interval duration, but as yet there is no clear formulation of the parameters on which the interval selection should depend. Consideration of the parameters that are part of the current conceptualization may assist in the development of clearer criteria for longitudinal assessment intervals. Of course, there will be residual difficulties in implementing an identified optimal interval, both because of practical considerations previously discussed and because an interval that is appropriate to one aspect of the investigation may be inappropriate to another.

Proposed Future Investigation

Neither the current author nor other colleagues interested in the assessment of change have as yet produced an analytic formulation of this problem. However, my proposal for a systematic investigation of the factors influencing bias in effect estimation as a function of the presumed relevant parameters, using a range of plausible values on simulated data, appears promising to several experts. It is hoped that this work can be carried out in the near future.

COMMENTS ON "A SOURCE OF BIAS IN LONGITUDINAL INVESTIGATIONS OF CHANGE"

LINDA M. COLLINS AND JOHN W. GRAHAM

Cohen's chapter illustrates a point that is developed in some detail by Gollob and Reichardt in chapter 15 of this book: Relations between variables do not occur in a temporal vacuum. The relation between a causal variable and its effect may look considerably different, depending on whether the causal variable is measured a day before the effect, a month before, a year before, or over a longer interval. The reason for this is that a causal relation is always defined in terms of two periods of time: Time X, during which the cause occurs, and (even if causation is almost instantaneous) subsequent Time Y, during which the effect occurs. The most accurate picture of the relation is obtained if measurement of the cause is taken over Time X and measurement of the effect is taken at the completion of Time Y. Any measurement taken before or after Time X is not a measure of the causal variable; rather, it is a temporal proxy.

For example, theory predicts that in an adolescent population, friends' alcohol use is an important determinant of subject alcohol use. As is true of many theories in the behavioral sciences, this one does not specify how much time elapses between cause and effect. What is usually meant in statements of this kind is that friends' use of alcohol during some unspecified time (Time X) is an important determinant of adolescent alcohol use during Time Y. Suppose that in a school-based study, adolescent use of alcohol is measured every September and January, that friends' use of alcohol in September is used to predict subjects' use in January, and that only a weak relation emerges. Two equally plausible conclusions can be drawn: (a) the relation between friends' use and subjects' use is

26

in fact weak, or (b) the relation between adolescent use in January and friends' use during Time X is strong, but September is not Time X. Implicit in the study as conducted is an assumption that friends' alcohol use in September is either friends' use at Time X, or a potent temporal proxy for this causal variable.

The problem with using a temporal proxy is that it is not the causal variable and probably is not as predictive of an effect as is the causal variable during Time X. This is the central problem Cohen raises. She shows that an important consequence of using a temporal proxy as a covariate, even if measurement is perfect, is that it becomes impossible to partial out all of the variance resulting from the causal variable. How validly a temporal proxy in fact represents the causal variable at Time X depends on how highly correlated it is with that true cause. This in turn depends on two factors, discussed below.

INTERINDIVIDUAL HETEROGENEITY OF DEVELOPMENT

If the causal variable is unchanging over time, the issue of the validity of a temporal proxy is moot because the correlation between the proxy and the variable is always unity. It may be tempting to conclude on this basis that the speed with which the causal variable changes over time affects the correlation between a temporal proxy and the causal variable, with temporal proxies tending to be more highly correlated with slowly changing causal variables. However, there is only an indirect relation between speed of change of the causal variable and its correlation with a temporal proxy. A direct effect on the correlation between a causal variable and its temporal proxy is exerted by the amount of interindividual heterogeneity in growth rate. Even if change on the causal variable is very rapid, the causal variable and its temporal proxy will be perfectly correlated if all individuals change at the same rate and in the same direction between the temporal proxy and Time X. Conversely, even very slow change will cause rapid decay in the correlation between a causal variable and its temporal proxy if there is considerable interindividual heterogeneity in growth rate. This is true whether growth is linear or curvilinear. Usually the amount of heterogeneity in growth rate in a study is not under the investigator's control.

AMOUNT OF ELAPSED TIME

A related factor affecting the correlation between a causal variable and its temporal proxy is the amount of time elapsed between them. All else being equal, the closer the temporal proxy is to Time X, the stronger the correlation between the causal variable and the proxy will be. Unlike the degree of interindividual heterogeneity in growth rate, this factor is under the researcher's control. The maximum amount of time allowed to elapse between a causal variable and its temporal proxy is

controlled directly by the spacing of observations. The more frequently observations are taken, the smaller is the maximum amount of time that is allowed to
elapse between the temporal proxy and the causal variable, the larger is the
correlation between them, and the more useful is the proxy as a substitute for the
causal variable.

SPACING OF OBSERVATIONS AS A DESIGN CONSIDERATION

Thus, Cohen raises an issue that is of fundamental importance to the study of
change, yet has received little or no attention in the methodology literature: the
temporal spacing of repeated observations. Cohen has shown how temporal spacing
of observations can have a profound effect on the validity of the statistical conclusions (Cook & Campbell, 1979) of a study, clearly indicating that the spacing
of observations should be one of the design considerations that researchers think
through when a longitudinal study is being planned. In order to maintain adequate
validity of statistical conclusions, researchers must give careful consideration to
selecting a measurement design that ensures that the correlation between the proxy
and the causal variable will not reach an unacceptably low level.

Unfortunately, in the conduct of longitudinal research, observation periods
tend to be scheduled more according to the convenience of the investigators than
with regard to the fundamental factors just outlined. Rare indeed are descriptions
of longitudinal studies in which the Methods section includes justification in terms
of substantive theory for the spacing of observational periods or statements that
the periods chosen were designed for purposes of testing specific hypotheses.
Rather, the choice of observational periods is often defended on grounds of logistics
(e.g., "We made a single yearly sweep of data collection during the yearly first-
day assembly"). There is little reason to suppose that such blind sampling will
hit on a good, or even reasonable, approximation to observational periods for
which findings can be robust. Neglect of this important design consideration is a
serious problem affecting the entire longitudinal research field.

PROBLEMS INTRODUCED BY TAKING FREQUENT
OBSERVATIONS

Consideration of the questions Cohen raises leads to the conclusion that study
designs should involve more frequent observations than have been considered
adequate. But there are impediments to taking frequent observations, several of
which are noted by Cohen. Expense is one. "To keep expenses manageable" is
frequently given as a major reason justifying the common data collection strategy
of large longitudinal studies, such as school-based studies, where measures are
taken infrequently but on as many subjects as possible. This strategy often effec-

tively prevents researchers from obtaining an accurate picture of causal relations, so it should be reconsidered. Where resources are limited, it may be necessary to measure fewer subjects in order to obtain more frequent observations. The tradeoff between number of subjects and frequency of observations is a difficult one, and considerations of statistical power must be thought through carefully. Power may become unacceptably low if too few subjects are involved in a study, but it may also become unacceptably low if observed effect size is diminished through the use of temporal proxies.

Frequent observations can change the character of what is being measured. The measurement itself may even become a treatment. An example of this is found in dietary studies, in which frequent measurement causes people to focus on the amounts and types of foods they are eating, directly leading some to reconsider their habits. The problem in general is pervasive and important because it threatens the ecological validity of many studies. There are ways to address this problem, however. The effects of measurement can be controlled for if the researchers employ a missing-data design in which individuals are randomly assigned to a frequent-measurement or infrequent-measurement condition. Under some circumstances, part or all of the missing data in the infrequent-measurement condition may be replaced by means of the procedures developed by Little and Rubin (1987), as discussed by Little in his comments on Cohen's chapter.

Attrition can also be a cost associated with making frequent observations. Subjects on whom heavy measurement demands are made are likely to feel imposed on and leave the study in consequence, temporarily or permanently. A compromise plan that can help to avoid such problems is to have relatively few full-blown data collection sessions interspersed with numerous shorter data collection sessions, wherein data are collected on only those variables central to the study. The many brief sessions should take only small amounts of time and, ideally, should be done in a manner maximally convenient for the subjects, such as over the telephone.

WHEN FREQUENT OBSERVATION IS IMPOSSIBLE

There will always be research problems in which observations cannot be made as frequently as the researcher would like. Under such circumstances, it is important to be aware of the limitations presented by the design. This means being cautious when one interprets the size of effects. If observations in a study are spaced far apart, the relation observed between the temporal proxy and the effect may be considerably smaller than the relation between the actual causal variable and the effect. As Cohen makes abundantly clear, particular caution is needed when a temporal proxy is used as a covariate. There is a real danger of failing to partial out adequately the variance due to the causal variable. Gollob and Reichardt (chapter 15, this volume) provide a useful way of making a set of assumptions and then estimating what certain effects would be if the assumptions are met. This approach can effectively help researchers interpret their results in studies in which the interval between observations is longer than the ideal.

COMMENTS ON "A SOURCE OF BIAS IN LONGITUDINAL INVESTIGATIONS OF CHANGE"

RODERICK J. A. LITTLE

Cohen presents an interesting and important problem. The statistical literature on causality by Rubin, Holland, and others (e.g., Holland, 1986; Rosenbaum & Rubin, 1983; Rubin, 1974, 1977) teaches us the difficulties in drawing causal inferences from observational studies; hence I think we should be circumspect about how we analyze such data. Fancy analytical techniques are no substitute for a well-designed study, and I do not think we should take the attitude that we can be bailed out of any mess by writing down and fitting a clever mathematical model. Sometimes we should admit that the problem is with the problem, not with the lack of sophisticated mathematical tools for addressing the problem.

One example of what I regard as overoptimism about the power of mathematical models is in a research proposal I recently read, in which an investigator suggested that panel data with measurements at two or more time points would allow him to estimate "bidirectional effects" of two variables. Another is the widespread use of "Heckman" corrections for selectivity (Heckman, 1976), which are inevitably based on untestable assumptions about the characteristics of the unselected units (Little, 1985; Little & Rubin, 1987; Roberts & Bengtson, chapter 11 of this volume).

Although models cannot solve inherently insoluble problems, they are still very useful provided one views them with a healthy dose of skepticism. One use

Research for this comment was supported by Grant USPHS MH37188 from the National Institute of Mental Health.

of modeling in information-deficient problems is to display sensitivity of answers to a range of assumptions about the data, and this is the approach to Cohen's problem that I wish to propose. I shall present the general line of attack, avoiding too many details of the model because they depend on the context of the specific example. The precise nature of the models would be driven by the treatment assignment mechanisms, which are very context specific.

In the statistical literature on causation, Cohen's problem might be termed *potentially nonignorable treatment assignment*. Let Y_1 be the measure of psycho-pathology at the baseline time point T_1, and let Z_1 be other recorded covariates at that time; let Y_D be the (unobserved) measure of psychopathology at time $T_D > T_1$, when a treatment decision was made. Suppose one of two treatments is administered, denoted by the value (1 or 2) of treatment variable X. If the effect of a life event rather than an intervention is of interest (as in Cohen's simulated example), I choose to regard the event as a form of treatment; thus let $X = 1$ denote occurrence of the life event and $X = 2$ denote nonoccurrence.

It is useful to distinguish the outcomes that would occur under the two treatments, even though only one of the two possible outcomes is actually observed for each subject. Thus let Y_2 be the measure of psychopathology at time $T_2 > T_D$ if the treatment given is $X = 1$, and Y_2^* be the measure of psychopathology at time T_2 if the treatment given is $X = 2$.

The treatment assignment is called ignorable given covariate C if outcomes Y_2 and Y_2^* are independent of treatment assignment, given C:

$$(Y_2, Y_2^*) \text{ ind } X \mid C$$

where ind denotes "independent." Under this assumption, the causal effects of the treatments can be assessed simply by comparing the distributions of Y_2 when $X = 1$ and Y_2^* when $X = 2$, adjusting for the covariate C.

It may be reasonable to assume that treatment assignment is ignorable given $C = (Z_1, Y_1, Y_D)$, because this set of variables includes psychopathology at time T_D when the treatment decision or life event occurred—indeed, a simple model might suppose that treatment assignment depends only on Y_D. It is less likely that treatment assignment is ignorable given the observed covariates Z_1 and Y_1, because treatment assignment is likely to depend on Y_D even after conditioning on Z_1 and Y_1; because Y_D and Y_2 or Y_2^* are also likely to be related, this implies that treatment assignment is associated with outcome. Ignoring this association leads to the potential bias that concerns Cohen.

Given the values of Y_D, the analysis would be easy; however Y_D is not in fact observed. My proposed solution, similar in spirit to the work of Rosenbaum (1984), is to treat the values of Y_D as missing data and to formulate models for predicting missing Y_D given the observed data.

Models for predicting Y_D should be based on information about the nature of treatment assignment; more than one model might be considered to assess sensitivity 'to alternative specifications. For each model, sets of two or more imputes for each missing value of Y_D are obtained by drawing from their predictive distributions. The resulting multiply imputed data sets can be analyzed straightforwardly using multiple imputation methods (Rubin, 1987). For a recent nontechnical discussion of multiple imputation, see Little and Rubin (1989).

Specifically, draws of Y_D should be based on the predictive density:

$$p(Y_D \mid Z_1, Y_1, Y_2, X = 1), \tag{1}$$

for subjects with $X = 1$, and

$$p(Y_D \mid Z_1, Y_1, Y_2^*, X = 2), \tag{2}$$

for subjects with $X = 2$. If X denotes a life event, then these are control subjects who have not experienced the life event; if no such controls exist, then the control group analysis needs to be replaced by some assumption about the distribution of change in Y in the absence of the event, thus making the results more speculative.

DEVELOPING PREDICTIVE MODELS FOR Y_D

Predicting Y_D using Equation 1 or 2 requires estimates of these predictive densities, a difficult task given that Y_D is never observed. The naive covariate analysis that just uses deviations from the baseline measurements is effectively based on the assumption that $Y_D = Y_1$. More realistic models would reflect the fact that (a) $Y_1 - Y_D$ may tend to be negative when $X = 2$, and nonnegative when $X = 1$, if an increase in psychopathology motivates the introduction of the new treatment or increases the likelihood of the life event; and (b) var($Y_1 - Y_D$) may be positively correlated with $T_1 - T_D$, because one would expect deviations to be smaller when the time from baseline to treatment assignment is small. The process of developing a predictive distribution for Y_D might involve statistical analysis of the time course of Y values among controls, as well as informal information from discussion with the people assigning the treatments. Thus the analysis has a rather informal Bayesian flavor. However, I would argue that the formulation in terms of prediction of Y_D allows a realistic reflection of uncertainty about Y_D, which is a key feature of the problem.

CONCLUSIONS

My comment (a) refers to literature on causal inference from observational studies, and (b) proposes a strategy for the problem of the "premature covariate," based on introducing the "true covariate" as an unobserved variable, multiply imputing values of that variable, and then applying Rubin's multiple imputation methods to analyze the data. Use of a variety of imputation models is advocated to display sensitivity of answers to plausible alternative model specifications.

CHAPTER 3

ORDINAL METHODS IN THE ASSESSMENT OF CHANGE

NORMAN CLIFF

Editors' Introduction

Research on change often seems to call for elaborate designs and complicated statistical procedures. The models for analysis are often large, cumbersome, difficult to interpret, and laden with assumptions that are difficult to justify. At times it seems as though the trend in the social sciences is toward use of more such statistical machinery at the expense of conceptual thinking. One aim of this book is to counter such a trend.

Chapter 3 is a good example of thinking that does indeed counter excessive, thoughtless elaboration and complication of statistical analyses. Cliff brings discussion of change pointedly to consideration of basics. What level of measurement reasonably can be assumed for the variables under study, and what can be revealed dependably with different possible forms of analysis of these variables? Often the most reasonable conclusion must be that measures are at the ordinal level. Cliff points out that, consistent with this conclusion, researchers often seek to make only ordinal statements about findings even as they base these conclusions on analyses with interval statistics. It may be, for example, that all a researcher seeks to say about change, and all that can be said dependably, is that it is monotonic, even as analyses with linear (product-moment) correlation and its offshoots are used to provide a basis for the statement. Wouldn't it be more sensible, Cliff argues, to base ordinal statements on ordinal statistics? He gives several other good reasons why ordinal methods can be the methods of choice for studies of change. He points out that there are more powerful ordinal statistics than many researchers believe and briefly describes some of the procedures most appropriate for the study of change. Such alternatives to interval statistics are computationally simple but provide the researcher with a sound basis for drawing the kinds of inferences often sought in studies of change.

It is my conviction that ordinal methods are important to the study of change. In this chapter, I shall explain why and then describe some of the methods, or adaptations of them, that seem particularly relevant.

There are several reasons for using ordinal statistics and ordinal measurement theory, and some have special relevance to the study of change. After making a case for ordinal procedures, I shall mention some ordinal statistics, some of them familiar, some perhaps not. What will probably be less familiar is how these statistics can readily be adapted to provide descriptive information rather than being used to simply test null hypotheses, which is how we most commonly encounter them. These hypothesis-testing applications will be examined to see how their usual rationale, which makes complete randomization the null hypothesis, can be expanded; the expansion is to a sampling conception that is much more like the way we use parametric statistics. Then I shall briefly touch on some of the recent work on the formulation of an ordinal psychometric theory.

REASONS FOR USING ORDINAL METHODS

At some point in our research training, most of us get some introduction to ordinal methodology, and we may use it on occasion in our research. A number of years ago, there was a flurry of interest in such methods, and they briefly became methods of choice in some instances or with some researchers. Sidney Siegel's book (Siegel, 1956), which has recently come out in a new edition (Siegel & Castellan, 1988), was both the result of, and a stimulus to, this interest. (Interest waned, but I shall not attempt to analyze the reasons here.)

Perhaps the most often cited reason for using ordinal statistics is that they and, more importantly, the inferences based on them, are "distribution free" in the sense that it is not necessary to make any assumption about the nature of the distribution the observations are sampled from, such as assuming univariate or multivariate normality. This is a desirable property, but it applies more or less equally to all contexts, not just to the study of change. Therefore, I will not say much about it other than to note that, on the one hand, work such as that by Rand Wilcox (Wilcox, 1987) shows that the form of the distribution has a greater effect on parametric inference than we have been led to believe. On the other, the ordinal tests are often distribution free in a more limited sense than we might like.

A second reason, the one I think is more relevant to the concerns of this book, is that ordinal methods do not have to assume that the scales of measurement are at the interval level. Work on abstract measurement theory, epitomized by Krantz, Luce, Suppes, and Tversky (1971), has demonstrated in considerable detail what needs to be true if an interval scale is to be defined. Let me summarize these ideas in a simple statement: To define an interval scale, there must be an empirically nontrivial sense in which score differences at one point on the scale can be equated with nominally equal differences at other points on the scale. If there is not an interval scale in this sense, then our conclusions, whether descriptive or inferential, may be overthrown under a legitimate transformation of the scale, unless we use ordinal methods. True, there are arguments (Abelson & Tukey, 1963; Labovitz, 1967) that say that such effects are small or unlikely, but there is reason to believe these views may be overly optimistic. Besides, why not treat data the way they should be treated?

Clearly, change involves score differences, so it seems to me that we face this problem everywhere: What reason does one have to say that a change from a score of 4 to a score of 5 is the same as a change from 9 to 10? Yet we do what amounts to this all the time. Even in research on response time, which seems to have excellent credentials as an interval scale, it can be asked, "What do conclusions about changes in response *time* have to say about changes in response *rate*?" Changing from response time to response rate, or bits per second, say, is an example of a nonlinear transformation, sometimes radically so. This is only one of many examples of the general problem. One *can* make statements about "quicker than" and have them translate directly into "at a faster rate" but only if the information is provided directly by the statistics not by some possibly erroneous implication based on distributional or transformational assumptions.

Another reason for using ordinal methods is one that is less often cited, but I am going to argue that it is important: The conclusions we make from our data, particularly when they are presented in summary form, are almost always ordinal. We say that children respond more quickly as they become older, or that children who are better at arithmetic than other children at one age are likely to be better at another age. These are statements of ordinal relations, but they are usually made on the basis of parametric statistics: mean differences, Pearson correlations, and the like. Because there is an almost inevitable mistranslation of interval information to ordinal, is it not better to make ordinal statements about change on the basis of ordinal statistics?

Related to this reason is researchers' frequent observation of monotonic but nonlinear trends either across time or over the course of treatment. These are typically studied with Pearson correlations or linear contrasts. Surely it is preferable to use statistical methods, which do exist, for expressing the monotonicity without introducing erroneous implications of linearity or even more misleadingly, adding quadratic trend terms.

The reasons discussed so far have to do with the statistical treatment of data as we observe them, but there is also another realm in which ordinal methods are important. Much of the measurement we do in studying change involves psychometrically based instruments, what we broadly call "tests," including in that term instruments of the questionnaire and checklist type. Such instruments, at least the better ones, are developed on the basis of psychometric theory. Yet virtually all of psychometric theory assumes interval scales. This assumption is, let me say, either demonstrably wrong, as in classical test theory of the Gulliksen–Lord–Novick type (Gulliksen, 1950; Lord & Novick, 1968), or arbitrary, as is true of the current manifestations of item response theory (Lord, 1980). There are various discussions of this issue (e.g., Cliff, 1989a; Mislevy, 1987; Yen, 1986). Even proponents of item response theory (IRT) are coming to the same conclusion, but it does not seem to be widely understood. An ordinally based psychometrics seems to be as desirable as ordinal statistical analysis if these difficulties are to be avoided.

Let me close this section by anticipating a bit. There is much more ordinal methodology in existence than most of us are aware of, and more is being developed.

SOME ORDINAL STATISTICS

Kendall's τ

In discussions of ordinal statistics, it is a good idea to start with the index of correlation called Kendall's τ (Kendall, 1938, 1970). One reason is that it is such a useful descriptive statistic. Given observations on two variables, Kendall's τ is the difference between the proportion of pairs of subjects that is in the same order on both variables and the proportion that is in the opposite order.

$$\tau_{xy} = \Pr\left[(x_i > x_h) \cap (y_i > y_h)\right] - \Pr\left[(x_i > x_h) \cap (y_i > y_h)\right], \qquad (1)$$

where i and h are individuals. That strikes me as a very direct translation of the kind of statement made above that we like to use to summarize a correlation. Thus τ has a much more literal and direct interpretation than, say, a Pearson r. Later, I show how some group comparison statistics can be transformed to give τ-like interpretations. Spearman's ρ, on the other hand, involves all the interpretational convolutions of a Pearson r, with the added complication of applying them to ranks.

Inferences about τ can follow one of two paths, which introduces us to a distinction that is important to making ordinal methods more broadly useful. In the discussion of τ in standard texts, the formula given for the variance of τ is a simple function of the number of cases, n, and the sample τ. This usual version of the standard error gives a test of the independence or complete randomization hypothesis; that is, given the order on one variable, all possible permutations of values on the other variable are equally likely. Analogous hypotheses are involved in various other statistics discussed later.

This limits the range of inferences we can draw. It could easily be that the τ between two variables is zero even though not all permutations are equally likely, as, for example, a U-shaped trend. The probabilities indicated by the standard all-possible-permutations test may well be in error if that is the case. We also want to be able to construct confidence limits for τ, or compare two different τs, and do everything we can with a Pearson r.

We broaden the range of inferences if we think about τ in a different way, one more in line with what we do with other correlations. That is, we assume that the observations in the sample are from a bivariate population in which there is some true parameter value for the τ, and we are trying to draw inferences about what that parameter is. There is a second formula, also by Kendall (1970), for the variance of the sample τ that is appropriate in the latter case, which I think is the more common. It allows us not only to test hypotheses about the population τ in a more generally applicable way but also to calculate confidence intervals for τ. The formula is somewhat more complicated than the usual one, but not much more; further, a computer will perform the calculations. It is derived from the fact that the formula for τ is a statement about the proportions of pairs that are in congruent or incongruent relations. If we have a sample, the sample proportions of each kind should be similar to, but not the same as, the population proportions, and the standard error of τ should reflect the expected size of the discrepancy. The general formula for the standard error of τ must take into account the fact that we sample individuals, not pairs, and that individuals will vary in the proportion of their relations that are congruent. Using this formula, we can, for example, establish a confidence interval for τ.

Using the same approach, we can go quite a bit further. We can test the hypothesis that τ is the same in two different groups, such as the elderly and the young, and proceed, if we wish, to establish a confidence interval for the population difference. Using extensions of Kendall's formula by Cliff and Charlin (in press), we can draw inferences about the difference between τs computed in the same sample, a situation that is more important in the change context. For that, we need expressions for the covariances between different τs in the same sample, and these are given by Cliff and Charlin (in press). For example, suppose we are conducting a longitudinal study and want to know whether the correlation between, say, vocabulary and digit span changes between ages 17 and 37. As another example, suppose we measure a variable on three occasions and want to know if the correlations between Time 1 and Time 2 and between Time 2 and Time 3 are the same. These formulas allow us to draw inferences of the usual kind about such differences. Note that we can also use this whenever we want to know whether two predictors correlate equally with a criterion.

τ can also be extended so that it resembles an ordinal version of multiple regression. This was first suggested in the 1970s in the sociological literature (Smith, 1972) and independently revived by Reynolds and Suttrick (1986), but it fell out of favor in sociology for several reasons. One was the problem of interpreting the "regression" weights as partial regression coefficients (e.g., Somers, 1976). Another was certain ambiguities in the interpretation of just what was being predicted (Somers, 1974), a problem that is especially acute when there are ties on the criterion variable.

Recently, Cliff (1989b) seems to have found a way to formulate the problem that circumvents all these problems. It does so at the cost of abandoning any partialing or structural interpretations of the weights; they are just the best weights for predicting ordinal relations. Some of the inferential, as opposed to descriptive, aspects of this procedure have been worked out, but we are not ready to publish anything about that yet.

There is, by the way, such a thing as a partial τ (Kendall, 1970), but I caution the reader to be very careful of it. Its definition is subtly different (Somers, 1976) from that of an ordinary partial correlation, even though the formula looks just like a partial correlation. Failure to recognize this difference (Cliff, 1989a; Hettmansperger, 1984, p. 208) can lead to erroneous conclusions.

Thus, Kendall's τ can do many of the things we want a correlation coefficient to do and in many respects do them better than a Pearson r does. Given that the variables we use have only ordinal justification, it seems that Kendall's τ should receive wider use than it does.

Location Comparisons

It is probably safe to say that most of the time when people speak of change they are looking at means, either between groups or within subjects. It has already been suggested that the goal of these analyses is actually ordinal, to a large extent, and that the means are computed on ordinal scales. There are some ordinal statistics that compare locations of distributions in much the same descriptive and inferential ways we compare means, at least if they are adapted somewhat.

Perhaps the main thing we should look at in studying change is consistency in the direction of change. Linda Collins (chapter 9, this volume; Collins & Cliff, 1985, in press) has emphasized the monotonicity criterion in defining developmental consistency and assessing it. In the latter paper, and in Collin's other work, there are indices of consistency that depend on several characteristics of the data. However, I would like to focus on just some simple aspects of how to look at this, aspects that are related to standard nonparametric statistical methods.

First, consider longitudinal or other within-subject designs. Figure 3.1 shows several sets of data for four individuals on three occasions, and the identity of the individuals is identified by connecting the points. In Figure 3.1A, every curve goes up from left to right, and they go up considerably. In Figure 3.1B, the changes are smaller, but still every individual increases across each interval. In Figure 3.1C, the situation looks more complex because the people are in different orders on different occasions, but still every one of them increases each time. Figure 3.1D shows a far more complex situation, in which most curves go up, but some go down, and there is some mixing of orders on different occasions.

Another way to structure this kind of data is shown in Figure 3.2, which can be called a *dominance matrix*. A plus sign ($+$) indicates that the column element ranked ahead of the row element, and a minus sign ($-$) the reverse. A zero (0) indicates a tie, although the only ties illustrated here are that each score is tied with itself.

The matrix is organized by occasions, the different boxes representing different combinations of occasions. Within the boxes, the principal subdiagonals are highlighted because they identify comparisons of an individual to himself or herself on different occasions.

The data in Figure 3.2 correspond to Figure 3.1D, the mixed relations case. Looking at the upper right section of the matrix in Figure 3.2, we can see quite readily in the highlighted diagonals that there is a preponderance of plus signs, indicating positive change, and a few minus signs. We can (a) count how many there are of each in the three subdiagonals (Time 1 vs. Time 2, Time 2 vs. Time 3, and Time 1 vs. Time 3), (b) subtract the number of minuses from the number of pluses, and then (c) divide by the total possible. Call this ratio v, to have a way to refer to it.

$$v = \frac{\#\ (x_{i2} > x_{i1})\ -\ \#\ (x_{i2} < x_{i1})}{nT\ (T\ -\ 1)\ /\ 2}, \tag{2}$$

where $\#$ means "the number of" and $i\ =\ 1,\ 2,\ \ldots,\ n$. In these data, v is $(10\ -\ 2)\ /\ 12\ =\ .67$. This number is the probability that a person changed in the positive direction between any two times minus the probability of a change in the negative direction.

In the case of two times, v is the proportion that is the basis of the well-known sign test. With more than two times, it is the average within-individual τ between score and time. Even in non-null cases, such averages have readily estimable sampling characteristics, so we can make inferences about v. One might often prefer information such as v to some kind of mean difference on a scale whose units permit little interpretation.

The interested researcher may wish to consult a small monograph by George Ferguson (Ferguson, 1965), which suggests a number of ways of analyzing re-

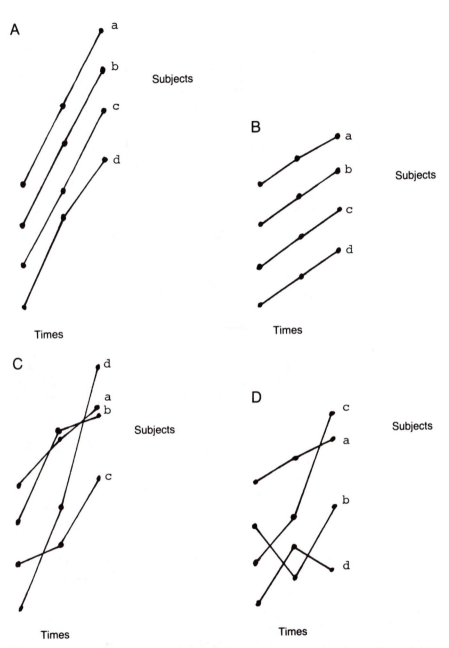

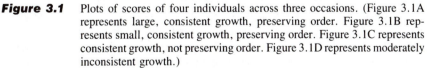

Figure 3.1   Plots of scores of four individuals across three occasions. (Figure 3.1A represents large, consistent growth, preserving order. Figure 3.1B represents small, consistent growth, preserving order. Figure 3.1C represents consistent growth, not preserving order. Figure 3.1D represents moderately inconsistent growth.)

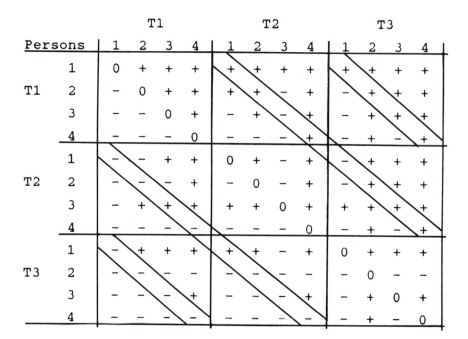

Figure 3.2   Dominance diagram for the data shown in Figure 3.1D. Boxes denote occasions. A plus sign (+) indicates that the column element ranked ahead of the row element and a minus sign (−) the opposite, and 0 indicates a tie. Outlined subdiagonals represent relations for the same person at different times.

peated measures data by ordinal methods. It is quite worth reading, although I would quibble with some of the details.

The sign test, in spite of its humble nature, has some attractive theoretical properties (Hettmansperger, 1984; Randles & Wolfe, 1979). One is that it is truly distribution free as far as inferences are concerned, as Hettmansperger and Randles and Wolfe demonstrate, unlike some other tests, which share this property in only a limited sense. The major difficulty of the sign test, though, is that it uses and conveys only a limited amount of information. Our quantity v is the same in Figure 3.1A as in Figure 3.1B, in spite of the much larger movement that takes place in the latter. Statistical procedures that make use of more of the data are more informative, and generally they permit stronger inferences.

There is also a second procedure to apply in this context. Consider any above-diagonal block in Figure 3.2. If it consists of all pluses, this means that all the scores of all the persons at the column time ranked ahead of the scores of all the persons at the row time. If there is a mixture of pluses and minuses in a block, we can conclude that some scores at one time ranked ahead of scores at another, and sometimes the reverse was true. The same kind of index as t or v

can be obtained by simply counting the pluses and minuses and then dividing by n^2. Call it m.

$$m = \frac{\#\ (x_{ij} > x_{hk})\ -\ \#\ (x_{ij} < x_{hk})}{n^2 T\ (T\ -\ 1)\ /\ 2}, \tag{3}$$

where i and h refer to individuals, j and k refer to occasions, and $j > k$ and T is the number of occasions. It is the probability that a score sampled from one time is higher than a score sampled from an earlier time, minus the reverse probability. The difference between m and v is that here we are considering the ordinal relations between all the persons at one time to all those at another. With v, we were just considering each person relative to himself or herself.

What about inferences? An answer is available, but it is not as complete as I would like. Again, the available part has been around for a long time; with a small modification, it is Wilcoxon's Signed Rank test (WSRT). In the WSRT, one takes the differences between the raw scores on two occasions and ranks them in absolute value. The signs of the differences are then attached to the ranks. There is then a well-established procedure for testing the null hypothesis that the differences in direction of change result from chance.

One can use this procedure directly on the data as they are given, but there would be a problem because the procedure would be applied to the differences in the *raw* scores, and we are not supposed to take differences of raw scores if the scale is ordinal. The solution to the problem is to rank the *original* scores and obtain the differences in the ranks for each person. It is these differences in ranks that relate directly to the quantity m. Then the inferential theory that applies to the WSRT can be used here as well.

What is missing in the inferential part is anything beyond the test of the hypothesis of pure randomization. It would be preferable to be able to set up confidence intervals in the non-null case. I think that would be possible, using adaptations of the methods used with t, but it remains to be worked out.[1]

Not all change is studied in the within-person context. Sometimes we want to make group comparisons in a between-group design, for example, comparing different age groups in a cross-sectional design or comparing one or more treatments with a control. Again, there is a familiar way to do this, as well as adaptations of it that amplify the interpretability, broaden the inferential possibilities, or both.

The familiar method is the Mann-Whitney-Wilcoxon U Test (MWW-U; Mann & Whitney, 1947; Wilcoxon, 1945). This is a well-known alternative to the ordinary t test for independent groups. Given two groups of subjects, the researcher ranks the complete set of scores and sums the scores in the smaller group. This gives the statistic U, which can be compared with tabled values or,

---

[1] I have recently derived a method for this purpose, but it is too new to try to describe here.

for a moderate-sized n, converted to an approximate normal deviate. This is used to test the randomization hypothesis (i.e., that the ranks are assigned to the two groups at random).

In this, its usual form, the MWW-U has utility, but only of a limited sort. We can test a null hypothesis of complete randomization, but that is all, and concluding that there is some difference or effect is a very small conclusion in the overall research picture.

Why, then, might one do such a study? One response might be "to find out if people who take this pill have better memories than people who don't." A between group design employing a placebo control, say, could be used, and a memory measure given after a few weeks. The typical way to analyze the data is the familiar independent-group t test of the hypothesis that the means are equal. The investigator might report the two means, perhaps the respective variances, and the significance level of the mean difference, and draw a conclusion about the research question posed.

Notice two things. One is that it is a virtual certainty that the memory measure can be given only ordinal justification; there is no way to equate differences at different points along the scale. Notice also the discrepancy between the conclusion about a difference between means and the research question, which was framed in terms of the *probability that an experimental subject has a better memory than a control*. One cannot come close to estimating that probability from the information usually given. First, doing the estimation is an exercise beyond the capabilities of most of us, and second, it can be done only by making arbitrary, and probably erroneous, assumptions about the nature of the distributions involved.

An answer to the question asked is readily available from the MWW-U. The test in this case is still based on the sum of the ranks in one group. All we have to do is take that sum, subtract from it a simple function of the size of that group, and divide it by the product of the groups' sizes, and we have the appropriate proportion. That proportion tells us the probability that if we select an experimental subject at random and a control subject at random, the experimental subject will score higher than the control: just what we were looking for. We can subtract the complementary proportion and get a -1 to $+1$ scale.

$$d = \frac{2\Sigma R\,(x_{i1}) - n_1\,(n_1 + 1)}{n_1 n_2}, \tag{4}$$

where $R(x_{i1})$ refers to the overall rank of score i in Group 1. This procedure is actually quite well established in the statistical literature. See, for example, Agresti (1984, p. 166), who calls the corresponding population quantity delta (Δ), and Hettmansperger (1984, p. 158). These authors show that the proportion we are talking about is a perfectly respectable statistic in the sense that it has not only a ready interpretation but rather straightforward sampling properties.

Hettmansperger (1984) in particular shows how to use the MWW-U to go beyond the usual test of randomization. One can do such things as constructing confidence intervals for Δ and even take into consideration the ordinal analogue of greater heterogeneity in one group than the other. Fligler and Policello (1981) found this to be about the most robust of the methods they evaluated in their study of the effects of non-normality and variance differences on between-group comparison statistics. So it seems reasonable to suggest that we report this statistic. It seems to me to tell us very directly what we want to know, and it has good inferential properties. Both m and Δ, by the way, are readily translatable into τs between *score* and *time*.

In this section, I have suggested some of the possible ways to apply ordinal statistics to research situations, and I hope that some of the readers will consider using this approach in their work. Unfortunately, there seems to be no readily available source for this information other than the statistical literature itself, for example, Hettmansperger (1984). Probably the best practical source is still Conover (1980), but as far as I know there is no nontechnical source that explains the use of the ordinal statistics described here.

ORDINAL PSYCHOMETRICS

Virtually without exception, psychometric instruments are developed with interval scale models, even though only ordinal ones are justified. A major reason is the paucity of alternative models that are only ordinal. Although there have been a few notable exceptions to this statement—names such as Guttman (1944), Loevinger (1947, 1948), Mokken (1971), and Cliff (1977, 1979) come to mind—the problem with these attempts is that they are data descriptive in the sense that they describe the consistency of scores on a set of observed items. There is no latent variable invoked as what is measured by the whole collection, as there is in classical test theory or IRT.

In the past few years, a few people have been working on ordinal psychometric models that are more like the interval ones in this respect. One direction is the work of Linda Collins on dynamic latent variable models (chapter 9, this volume). A second direction is my own. Briefly, one study (Cliff, 1989a) attempted to formulate a model, analogous to classical test theory, that was based on a sort of local ordinal uncorrelatedness. This model has attractive properties, but it exhibited flaws when confronted with data (Donoghue & Cliff, in press). The problems stem from the peculiar nature of Kendall's partial τ, mentioned earlier.

Recently, another attempt (Cliff, 1990) has been, I think, more successful in that it seems to agree well with what we find in data. One of the original formulations of test theory relied on a kind of item-sampling approach. The items on a test represent a sample of the items in a universe of actual or possible items, and test validity represents the correlation between test score and universe score. From an ordinal point of view, it is the order on the universe that we are trying to estimate with the order on the test.

It turns out that, when the concepts involved in the ordinal multiple regression mentioned earlier (Cliff, 1989b) are used, it is possible to estimate the τs of each item with the universe order using the τ correlations among the items. These in turn can be used to estimate the τ of the test score with the universe order. An interesting sidelight is that the model readily gives the probability that individuals who differ in observed score by a certain amount, say, three items, differ in the same direction on the true order. So far this model agrees very well with both real and simulated data. There are other psychometric developments of an ordinal nature (e.g., Loevinger, 1947, 1948; Mokken, 1971) that can help us analyze our data in a realistic and appropriate way, but space precludes a discussion of them.

CONCLUSIONS

There are three main reasons why data should be studied using ordinal methods in the context of change: (a) their distribution-free aspects, (b) their invariance under monotonic transformation, and (c) the fact that they often provide what we want to know from our data more accurately than parametric statistics do. A major ordinal tool is Kendall's τ, with its attractive, simple interpretation as a correlation index. Recent developments have broadened its usefulness inferentially and multivariately. Statistics ordinally reflecting change within individuals or by comparing groups are also available. Those such as the WSRT and the MWW-U statistic can be altered in simple ways that reflect the proportion of scores within one set that are higher than scores in another. Their inferential aspects can be broadened also, making them more widely useful. Psychometric theory can be formulated in ordinal ways as well, and developments in this regard promise to make it possible to develop and assess instruments in a way that realistically reflects their ordinal nature.

CHAPTER 4

MODELS FOR LEARNING DATA

M. W. BROWNE AND S. H. C. DU TOIT

Editors' Introduction

Browne and Du Toit's contribution to this volume is unusual. Chapter 4 allows the reader to compare three different statistical treatments of a single empirical data set. Rarely does the reader have such an opportunity. The data are measures of learning obtained six times in a sample of 137 adults. The three models on which the statistical treatments are based are described in a concise overview by Harlow in her comment at the end of this chapter. Harlow's figures are particularly useful in indicating the nature of the analyses; in fact, the reader might well turn to Harlow's comment before tackling this chapter.

The three models can be briefly described as follows: The first model, the time series model, is a first-order, autoregressive moving average time series. In such a model the measures at each time are a function of the measures at the just-previous time and the residual of that previous time—the part not predicted from the measures before that. In the second model, the stochastic parameter learning curve model, growth is approximated by means of a monotonic nonlinear equation with an estimate for each person of asymptote (highest level reached), increase from the first to the last trial, and rate of change (growth). In the third model, the latent curve model,

We are indebted to Robert Cudeck for regenerating our interest in this topic with his enthusiasm and helpfulness, and to Ruth Kanfer and Phillip Ackerman for providing us with details about their work and making their carefully collected data available to us. We are also indebted to the editors, Linda Collins and John Horn, for their particularly detailed and helpful comments, which have had a substantial influence on this chapter.

measures at each time are a function of three common factors that summarize basic features of the nonlinear equation that represents growth. These
basic features are similar to those of the second model. One factor represents the asymptote, one the increment in growth, and one the rate of
growth. Growth is not assumed to be monotonic in the third model, however, whereas this assumption is a part of the second model. Covariates can
be included in any of the models. These allow one to introduce an element
of control (mathematical control) of factors such as educational level or
gender differences.

   Brown and Du Toit discuss estimation and goodness-of-fit indices for
such models in general and for the three models considered. They warn
against use of "wastebasket" parameters—that is, parameters that have no
substantive importance but are included simply to improve the fit of the
model. They develop and argue for goodness-of-fit indices that reward parsimony.

   As noted in the introduction to chapter 8 and in chapter 3, one should
think very carefully about level of measurement in fitting nonlinear functions such as those of the Browne-Du Toit methods. In considering the role
of the covariate in their models, one will want to consider where the influences represented by a covariate should occur, as discussed most fully by
Gollob and Reichardt (chapter 15). In her comment on this chapter, Harlow
considers these and other issues important to researchers who wish to apply
the methods of Browne and Du Toit.

In this chapter, we consider situations of the following type. Each of a sample of
N subjects is measured T times at regular intervals on a learning task yielding
measurements x_t, $t = 1, \ldots, T$. An additional measurement, c, an ability measure,
is also taken on each subject. The aim of the analysis is to summarize the data
in such a manner as to isolate interindividual differences in intraindividual learning
characteristics and to relate the individual learning characteristics to performance
on the concomitant ability measure.

   Three models are considered. The first takes as a starting point a single
fixed learning curve, with variability about this fixed curve represented as an
ARMA(1,1) (autoregressive moving average) time series (Du Toit, 1979). In this
model there is one stochastic individual differences term representing the initial
state of the time series; the remaining terms are parameters describing growth and
do not vary across individuals. The second model is a stochastic parameter learning
curve model (Du Toit, 1979). It deals with interindividual variability by means
of three stochastic individual differences terms describing various aspects of a
monotonic individual learning curve. The third model (cf. Meredith & Tisak,
1990) involves latent growth curves that are not necessarily monotonic. This model
expresses an individual learning curve as a weighted sum of three "basis" curves,
in which the weights vary across individuals but the basis curves do not. All three
models incorporate a concomitant variable.

THE DATA

We used a data set of Kanfer and Ackerman (1989) as the basis for our comparison of the three models. Subjects were U.S. Air Force enlisted personnel. Each of the 137 subjects carried out a computerized air traffic controller task developed by Kanfer and Ackerman (1989, pp. 666–669). They were instructed to accept planes into their hold pattern and land them safely and efficiently on one of four runways (varying in length and compass direction) according to rules governing plane movements and landing requirements. Feedback concerning the success of each landing was given. Each subject performed a series of six 10-minute trials. The measurement employed was the number of correct landings per trial, yielding six scores. The Armed Services Vocational Aptitude Battery (ASVAB) (Wilfgong, 1980) was also administered to each subject. A global measure of cognitive ability was obtained from the sum of scores on the 10 subscales. This is employed as the concomitant ability measure in our analyses.

Table 4.1 shows the sample means, standard deviations, and correlation matrix. Both the trial means and standard deviations show clear monotonic increasing trends, whereas the trial correlation matrix has a pattern of decreasing elements usually associated with a Guttman simplex model. However, as Rogosa and Willett (1985a) pointed out, the usual simplex model is not the only model that results in a correlation pattern of this type. It is also noticeable that the ASVAB ability measure correlates most strongly with the first trial and that the correlations show a tendency to decrease as the number of trials increases.

Mean scores are plotted in Figure 4.1A. It can be seen that these means closely follow a smooth monotonic increasing curve tending toward an asymptote. The curve shown is a Gompertz curve, fitted by least squares. Individual trends

Table 4.1

SAMPLE MEANS, STANDARD DEVIATIONS, AND CORRELATIONS

	Trial 1	Trial 2	Trial 3	Trial 4	Trial 5	Trial 6	ASVAB[a]
M	11.77	21.39	27.50	31.02	32.58	34.20	0.70
SD	7.60	8.44	8.95	9.21	9.49	9.62	5.62
Correlation matrix							
Trial 1	1.00						
Trial 2	0.77	1.00					
Trial 3	0.59	0.81	1.00				
Trial 4	0.50	0.72	0.89	1.00			
Trial 5	0.48	0.69	0.84	0.91	1.00		
Trial 6	0.46	0.68	0.80	0.88	0.93	1.00	
ASVAB	0.50	0.46	0.36	0.26	0.28	0.28	1.00

[a]U.S. Armed Services Vocational Aptitude Battery.

are not so smooth. Three individual trends are shown in Figures 4.1B, 4.1C, and 4.1D superimposed on the mean curve. The subject scores in Figure 4.1B could be approximated fairly closely by a smooth monotonic increasing curve tending toward an asymptote. In Figure 4.1C, however, there is no evidence that an asymptote is being approached before Trial 6, and in Figure 4.1D, a continual decline in scores occurs after Trial 3.

MODELING IN THE SOCIAL SCIENCES

We regard all models as approximations to reality. It is unrealistic to think that any statistical model we use can ever be entirely correct. Consequently, a statistical test of a null hypothesis that the model is completely "true" or "correct" does not make practical sense. Other ways of assessing the usefulness of a model are necessary.

There are two main requirements of a model. First, a model should make sense. The values of the model's parameters should convey meaningful information. This requirement cannot be formulated in objective terms; it can only be assessed subjectively. Because this makes agreement difficult, the requirement has often been disregarded, but that does not reduce its importance. In particular, in models for repeated measurements, it is desirable that parameter values be required to follow smooth trends over time and not fluctuate wildly. This applies to both factor loadings and error variances. It is difficult to understand wild fluctuations in parameter values from one trial to another. Also, because it is easier to assign meaning to a few parameters than to many, a model should not have too many parameters. Meaningless wastebasket parameters employed only to make a model appear to fit well should be avoided.

Second, a model should be appropriate to the data. It should fit the data reasonably well, although one cannot expect the fit to be perfect. It is also desirable that measures of fit take the number of parameters into account favoring few parameters over many.

Fitting a Model

We use the following approach when formulating a model for learning data. First, we specify a data model, explaining trial scores in terms of unobservable or latent variables. An example of this approach is the well-known factor analysis model, which reappears later in our discussion as a latent curve model. Here $x = \Lambda y + e$, where the vector variate x represents manifest variables, y represents latent variables, e represents errors, and Λ is a parameter matrix. Assumptions concerning the distribution of latent variables are made, for example:

$$\mathscr{E}(y) = \xi, \; \mathscr{E}(e) = 0, \; \text{cov}(y, y') = \Phi, \; \text{cov}(e, e') = D_\psi, \; \text{and} \; \text{cov}(y, e') = 0.$$

The data model generates a "moment structure" for the manifest variables, for example:

$$\mathscr{E}(\mathbf{x}) = \boldsymbol{\mu} = \boldsymbol{\Lambda}\boldsymbol{\xi}, \text{ and } \text{cov}(\mathbf{x}, \mathbf{x}') = \boldsymbol{\Sigma} = \boldsymbol{\Lambda}\boldsymbol{\Phi}\boldsymbol{\Lambda}' + \mathbf{D}_{\psi}. \tag{1}$$

We shall consider structures for the manifest variable mean vector, $\boldsymbol{\mu}$, and covariance matrix, $\boldsymbol{\Sigma}$, only. This may involve some loss of information if the manifest variables do not have a normal distribution.

The moment structure is fitted by choosing parameter values so as to minimize the discrepancy between the sample mean vector, $\bar{\mathbf{x}}$, and covariance matrix $\mathbf{S}$ and the fitted mean vector, $\boldsymbol{\mu}$, and covariance matrix $\boldsymbol{\Sigma}$. The discrepancy is represented by a discrepancy function: $F(\bar{\mathbf{x}}, \mathbf{S}; \boldsymbol{\mu}, \boldsymbol{\Sigma})$. In the examples described in this chapter, we chose parameters (e.g., $\boldsymbol{\Lambda}, \boldsymbol{\Phi}$, and $\mathbf{D}_{\psi}$ in Expression 1) so as to minimize the usual normal theory maximum likelihood discrepancy function:

$$F(\bar{\mathbf{x}}, \mathbf{S}; \boldsymbol{\mu}, \boldsymbol{\Sigma}) = (\bar{\mathbf{x}} - \boldsymbol{\mu})' \boldsymbol{\Sigma}^{-1}(\bar{\mathbf{x}} - \boldsymbol{\mu})$$

$$+ \ln|\boldsymbol{\Sigma}| - \ln|\mathbf{S}| + tr[(\mathbf{S} - \boldsymbol{\Sigma}) \boldsymbol{\Sigma}^{-1}]. \tag{2}$$

Minimizing it will yield consistent parameter estimates. These estimates will also be asymptotically efficient if the manifest variables are normally distributed (and under some circumstances even if they are not; see Browne, 1989).

Once the model parameters have been estimated, it is desirable to assess model fit. In the present chapter, two alternative measures of fit are used: the root mean square error of approximation (RMSEA) (Steiger & Lind, 1980) and a cross-validation index (CVI) (Browne & Cudeck, 1989). Both these measures satisfy the requirement of parsimony mentioned above.

RMSEA

The RMSEA is based directly on the discrepancy function. We denote the minimized sample discrepancy function value by $\hat{F}$:

$$\hat{F} = \min_{\boldsymbol{\mu}, \boldsymbol{\Sigma} \in \mathscr{L}} F(\bar{\mathbf{x}}, \mathbf{S}; \boldsymbol{\mu}, \boldsymbol{\Sigma}),$$

where $\mathscr{L}$ is the set of mean vectors and covariance matrices ($\boldsymbol{\mu}, \boldsymbol{\Sigma}$) satisfying the structural model under consideration (e.g., that specified in Expression 1). This discrepancy function value gives an indication of the fit of the structural model to the sample mean vector $\bar{\mathbf{x}}$ and covariance matrix $\mathbf{S}$. It is relevant to have an indication of the fit of the structural model to the mean vector $\boldsymbol{\mu}_0$ and covariance matrix $\boldsymbol{\Sigma}_0$ of the population from which the sample was drawn. This is provided by the minimized population discrepancy function value F_0:

$$F_0 = \min_{\boldsymbol{\mu}, \boldsymbol{\Sigma} \in \mathscr{L}} F(\boldsymbol{\mu}_0, \boldsymbol{\Sigma}_0; \boldsymbol{\mu}, \boldsymbol{\Sigma}).$$

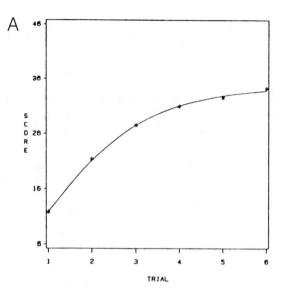

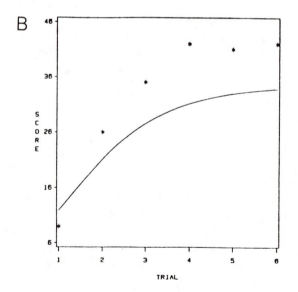

Figure 4.1   The data of Kanfer and Ackerman (1989). (Figure 4.1A represents sample means. Figure 4.1B represents Case 35.)

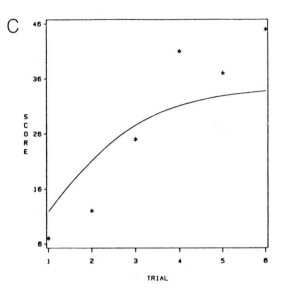

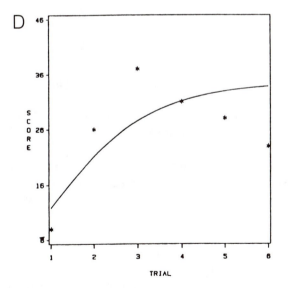

Figure 4.1
(continued)   The data of Kanfer and Ackerman (1989). (Figure 4.1C represents Case 115. Figure 4.1D represents Case 95.)

This discrepancy function value is always greater than or equal to zero; the value is zero only when ($\boldsymbol{\mu}_0$, $\boldsymbol{\Sigma}_0$) satisfy the structural model exactly. Thus F_0 may be regarded as a measure of badness of fit. There are two difficulties to be overcome before F_0 is employed. First, the values of $\boldsymbol{\mu}_0$ and $\boldsymbol{\Sigma}_0$ are not known, so that, unlike $\hat{F}$, it is not possible to compute F_0. It can, however, be estimated. Let p represent the number of variables (including trials and the concomitant variable), q the number of parameters in the model, and d the degrees of freedom [$d = \frac{1}{2}p(p + 3) - q$]. An estimate of F_0 is given by $\hat{F} - d/N$ (cf. McDonald, 1989). (This will be asymptotically unbiased when [cf. Steiger, Shapiro, & Browne, 1985] the asymptotic distribution of $N\hat{F}$ is noncentral chi-squared with d degrees of freedom and noncentrality parameter NF_0.)

The second difficulty with F_0 is that it decreases, indicating better fit, if parameters are added to the model, even if they are superfluous. Consequently, it is not consistent with our desire to favor few parameters over many. In order to overcome this problem, one may consider the RMSEA (Steiger & Lind, 1980):

$$\text{RMSEA} = \frac{F_0}{d}, \tag{3}$$

which can increase, indicating poorer fit, if unnecessary parameters are added to the model. (A finding by Shapiro (1985), showing that any discrepancy function can be expressed as a quadratic form, justifies the terminology used here.) A point estimate of the RMSEA is given by

$$\text{Estimate (RMSEA)} = \sqrt{\frac{(\hat{F} - d/N)}{d}}. \tag{4}$$

An interval estimate may be obtained from a confidence interval on the noncentrality parameter of a chi-squared distribution (Steiger & Lind, 1980); we use a 90% confidence interval. If the lower limit of the confidence interval on the RMSEA is zero, this implies that the corresponding test of fit of the model $N\hat{F}$ as the test statistic) would *not reject* the null hypothesis that the model is "correct" (H_0: RMSEA = 0) at the 5% level. The confidence interval on the RMSEA, however, is less open to misinterpretation than the test of fit, because a nonzero upper limit is a reminder that the model should not be accepted as correct.

CVI

The CVI indicates to what extent a fitted moment structure derived from one sample can be expected to fit another sample of the same size from the same population. Two samples of the same size are considered: a calibration sample C, and a validation V. Suppose that $\hat{\boldsymbol{\mu}}_C$ and $\hat{\boldsymbol{\Sigma}}_C$ have been obtained by fitting the model using C, and that $\bar{\mathbf{x}}_V$ and $\mathbf{S}_V$ are the mean vector and covariance matrix, respectively, of V. A cross-validation measure of the model fit is given by the discrepancy, $F(\bar{x}_V, S_V; \hat{\mu}_C, \hat{\Sigma}_C)$, between the fitted model from C and the data from V. The disadvantage of this measure is that two samples are required. One can avoid this, however, by regarding $F(\bar{x}_V, S_V; \hat{\mu}_C, \hat{\Sigma}_C)$ as an estimate of its expected value and then estimating the same quantity from a single sample. Assuming that the discrepancy function is correctly specified for the distribution of the data, and taking expectations over both calibration samples and validation samples, we obtain the expected cross-validation index,

$$\text{CVI} = \underset{CV}{\mathscr{E}\mathscr{E}} \, F(\bar{x}_V, S_V; \hat{\mu}_C, \hat{\Sigma}_C) \approx F_0 + (d + 2q) / N, \qquad (5)$$

which may be estimated (Browne & Cudeck, 1989) from a single sample, using

$$\textit{Estimate (CVI)} = \hat{F} + 2q / N \qquad (6)$$

If maximum likelihood estimation is employed, as it is here, the point estimate (Expression 6) of the CVI is linearly related to the Akaike information criterion (Akaike, 1973) and will therefore lead to the same conclusions.

It can be seen that a penalty for the number, q, of parameters is added to $\hat{F}$ in Expression 6). If N becomes very large, however, the effect of this penalty becomes negligible. Again, an interval estimate of the CVI in Expression 5 can be obtained from a confidence interval on the noncentrality parameter of a chi-squared distribution. For purposes of comparison, it is convenient to look at the CVI of the saturated model where no structure is imposed on μ and Σ:

$$\textit{CVI (Saturated Model)} = p(p + 3) / N$$

The two measures of fit of the model have different purposes. The RMSEA indicates how well the model, with unknown parameter values, would fit the population mean vector μ_0 and covariance matrix Σ_0. The number of parameters is taken into account, but no term involving sample size, N, appears in Expression 3. The CVI takes inaccuracy in parameter estimates obtained from a sample of specified size into account, and N does appear in Expression 5. It gives an impression of how many parameters to include in a model if estimate values obtained from a sample of limited size are to be considered relevant to observations outside the sample.

THREE MODELS FOR LEARNING DATA

We now consider three models for learning data. These are fitted to the Kanfer-Ackerman data, using the normal theory discrepancy function Expression 2. This may not be the best discrepancy function to use in all three cases, but it was desirable to use the same discrepancy function for all three models for comparative purposes. In addition, a computer program for this function was available, and there is some doubt about any advantages of an asymptotically distribution-free analysis (Browne, 1984) in the present situation because the sample size is quite small ($N = 137$). The computational method uses numerical derivatives and is described in Browne and Du Toit (1987).

Fixed Learning Curve with Time Series Deviations

We shall assume that the learning trial means μ_t, $t = 1, \ldots, T$ lie on a smooth monotonic increasing curve tending to an asymptote. The deviations of a person's trial scores from the mean curve are assumed to follow a first-order autoregressive time series with first-order moving average residuals, that is, an ARMA(1,1) process. The deviation from the mean on trial t, then, is related to the deviation from the mean on the previous trial, and the change in performance on trial t is related to the change in performance on the previous trial. Different persons' deviations from the mean are regarded as different realizations of the same time series. We then have a repeated time series model instead of the usual single time series model. There are a number ($N = 137$) of independent observations on a short time series ($T = 6$) instead of one observation on a long time series. The stationarity assumptions usually made in order to be able to estimate parameters from a single observation on the time series are not necessary here. Some restrictions on parameters are imposed for model parsimony, however.

We employ the Gompertz curve for the learning trial means:

$$\mu_t = \theta_1 \exp\left[-\theta_2 \exp\left\{-(t-1)\theta_3\right\}\right], \quad t = 1, \ldots, T. \tag{7}$$

A Gompertz curve fitted by least squares to the trial means is shown in Figure 4.1A. Other members of the Richards (1959) family, such as the exponential and logistic curves, would also be suitable. The parameters are interpretable as follows: θ_1 ($\theta_1 \geq 0$) is the asymptote, θ_2 ($\theta_2 \geq 0$) governs the distance from the asymptote on the first trial, and θ_3 ($\theta_3 \geq 0$) represents the rate of learning. Parameter values that yield the curve in Figure 4.1A are as follows: $\hat{\theta}_1 = 34.58$, $\hat{\theta}_2 = 1.07$, and $\hat{\theta}_3 = 0.77$.

Autoregressive weights are assumed to have the same value, α, from one trial to another and moving average weights the same value, β. The data model for observations after the first is

$$x_t - \mu_t = \alpha(x_{t-1} - \mu_{t-1}) + u_t + \beta u_{t-1}, \quad t = 2, \ldots, T,$$

where the u_t, $t = 1, \ldots, T$, are disturbances, distributed independently with $\mathscr{E}(u_t) = 0$ and $\mathrm{var}(u_t) = v_{tt}$, $t = 1, \ldots, T$, and the means μ_t follow the trend in Expression 7. Because no observations have been made prior to x_1, the initial state latent variable,

$$s = \alpha^* (x_0 - \mu_0) + \beta^* u_0,$$

is introduced (Du Toit, 1979, chapter 4) to replace observations and disturbances before the first trial. We do not necessarily require that $\alpha^* = \alpha$ or that $\beta^* = \beta$. The model for the first observation, then, is

$$x_1 - \mu_1 = s + u_1, \tag{8}$$

where $\mathscr{E}(s) = 0$, $\text{var}(s) = \sigma_s^2$, and s is distributed independently of $u_1, \ldots, u_T$.

In matrix notation, the data model may be written as

$$T_\alpha (x - \mu) = I_{T, 1} s + T_\beta u,$$

where $I_{T, 1}$ is a vector formed from the first column of the identity matrix I_T,

$$T_\alpha = \begin{bmatrix} 1 & 0 & 0 & \cdots \\ -\alpha & 1 & 0 & \cdots \\ 0 & -\alpha & 1 & \cdots \\ \vdots & \vdots & \vdots & \ddots \end{bmatrix} \text{ and } T_\beta = \begin{bmatrix} 1 & 0 & 0 & \cdots \\ \beta & 1 & 0 & \cdots \\ 0 & \beta & 1 & \cdots \\ \vdots & \vdots & \vdots & \ddots \end{bmatrix}.$$

To allow for relations between the concomitant ability variable, c, and performance on the learning task, we allow s to be correlated with c. Thus the latent variable, s, which directly affects a person's initial performance (cf. Expression 8), and indirectly affects performance on subsequent trials through the autoregressive process, is assumed to be correlated with ability, c. Let $\mathscr{E}(c) = \mu_c$, $\text{var}(c) = \sigma_c^2$, and $\text{corr}(s, c) = \rho_{sc}$, with

$$-1 \leq \rho_{sc} \leq 1. \tag{9}$$

Because few changes in performance occur after the learning task has been mastered, we shall require that the disturbance variate variances v_{tt} follow a two-parameter monotonic decreasing exponential trend tending to an asymptote of zero:

$$v_{tt} = \gamma_1 \exp\{-(t-1)\gamma_2\}, \quad t - 1, \ldots, T, \gamma_1 \geq 0, \gamma_2 \geq 0. \tag{10}$$

Let D_v be the diagonal matrix with v_{tt} as typical diagonal element.

The data model generates the following moment structure for the $p = T + 1$ manifest variables. For the Kanfer-Ackerman data, $T = 6$ and $p = 7$. The mean vector is

$$\mu = \begin{bmatrix} \mu_x \\ \mu_c \end{bmatrix},$$

where μ_x is a $T \times 1$ vector valued function of $\theta = (\theta_1, \theta_2, \theta_3)'$ and μ_c is a scalar parameter. Elements of μ_x satisfy the Gompertz curve (Expression 7). The covariance matrix is

$$\Sigma = \begin{bmatrix} \Sigma_{xx} & \sigma_{xc} \\ \sigma'_{xc} & \sigma_{cc} \end{bmatrix},$$

where

$$\Sigma_{xx} = T_\alpha^{-1} (I_{T,1}\sigma_s^2 I'_{T,1} + T_\beta D_v T_\beta') T_\alpha^{-1'}$$

$$\sigma_{xc} = T_\alpha^{-1} I_{T,1}\sigma_s\sigma_c\rho_{sc}, \quad \sigma_{cc} = \sigma_c^2.$$

There are 11 parameters to be estimated in the model: θ_1, θ_2, θ_3, μ_c, α, β, σ_s, σ_c, ρ_{sc}, γ_1, and γ_2.

Parameter estimates obtained from the Kanfer-Ackerman data are shown in Table 4.2. The estimate of the autoregressive weight α is close to 1, indicating a substantial influence of one trial on the next, and the estimate of the moving average weight is negative but near zero. This indicates a small negative effect of the disturbance from trial $t - 1$ on trial t. The estimate of the correlation ρ_{sc} between initial state and the ASVAB concomitant variable lies on the upper bound of 1 in Expression 9. This is in keeping with the higher correlations of ASVAB with initial trials than with later trials evident in Table 4.1, but it is larger than would be anticipated. The model is not very informative concerning the nature of interindividual learning differences. There is only one latent variable, s, which characterizes differences in learning and can be related to the concomitant ability variable, c. The number of initial state variables could be increased by considering an ARMA(k, l) process yielding max(k, l) initial state variables (Du Toit, 1979, chapter 4). Because of the very good fit of the time series (TS) model to the Kanfer-Ackerman data, which can be seen in Table 4.6, it would not be easy to justify the corresponding increase in the number of parameters.

Table 4.2

TIME SERIES MODEL: PARAMETER ESTIMATES

Parameter	Estimate
θ_1	34.83
θ_2	1.07
θ_3	0.77
μ_c	0.76
α	0.96
β	−0.12
σ_s	3.76
σ_c	5.62
ρ_{sc}	1.00
γ_1	40.42
γ_2	0.23

Stochastic Parameter Learning Curves

The stochastic parameter learning curve (SPLC) model assumes that a person's true scores on the learning trials lie on a smooth curve increasing monotonically to an asymptote. Unlike the fixed learning curve with time series deviations, this true score curve varies from one person to another but always retains the property of increasing monotonically to an asymptote. The data model (Bock, 1983; Du Toit, 1979) is:

$$x_t = f(t, y) + e_t, \, t = 1, \ldots, T, \tag{11}$$

where $f(t, y)$ is a smooth monotonic increasing function of t tending to an asymptote, y is a latent vector variate representing learning curve characteristics that vary from one person to another, and e_t is an error variate. For example, the Gompertz curve used for the fixed mean curve in Expression 7 may now be employed for the true score curves:

$$f(t, y) = y_1 \exp\left[-y_2 \exp\{-(t - 1) y_3\}\right], \tag{12}$$

where $y = (y_1, y_2, y_3)'$ and y_1 $(y_1 \geq 0)$ is the asymptote, y_2 $(y_2 \geq 0)$ governs the distance of the first trial from the asymptote, and y_3 $(y_3 \geq 0)$ governs the learning rate.

We assume that $\mathscr{E}(e) = 0$, $cov(y, e') = 0$, and $cov(e, e') = D_\psi$. Because few fluctuations in scores are observed after a learning task has been mastered, the diagonal error covariance matrix D_ψ is required to have diagonal elements that follow the two-parameter monotonic decreasing exponential trend,

$$\psi_{tt} = \gamma_1 \exp\{-(t - 1) \gamma_2\}, \, t = 1, \ldots, T, \tag{13}$$

like the disturbance variances in Expression 10.

The model in Expression 12 may be regarded as a confirmatory nonlinear factor analysis model (McDonald, 1983) with three factors. One possibility would be to estimate the factor scores y separately for each person, yielding estimated scores $\hat{y}$. There are two main disadvantages to this approach. First, $corr(\hat{y}, \hat{y}') \neq corr(y, y')$, and $corr(\hat{y}, c) \neq corr(y, c)$, so that it is difficult to accurately investigate relations between different learning factors and between learning factors and the concomitant variable. Second, there are cases in which it would be difficult to choose y when fitting Expression 12 to trial scores because many values of $\hat{y}$ would yield almost the same fit, and none would give a good fit. An example is given in Figure 4.1D.

The data model in Expressions 11 and 12 generates structures for μ and Σ. These structures cannot be expressed in closed form and are not given here. They involve multiple integrals that may be evaluated numerically (Du Toit, 1979, chapter 7) by means of a Gaussian quadrature. The elements, μ_t, of the mean vector do not exactly follow the Gompertz curve of Expression 12.

Because the data model is nonlinear in the latent variables, the structure of μ and Σ depends on the distribution chosen for the learning factors. In this respect the SPLC model differs from the TS model and the latent curve (LC) model, both of which are linear in the latent variables. It is mathematically convenient to choose a normal distribution for the latent variables. It is not plausible, however, to assume that the learning factors y_1, y_2, and y_3 in Expression 12 are normally distributed, because they must be nonnegative. We therefore make use of the reparameterization $\mathbf{y} \rightarrow \mathbf{z}$, where $\mathbf{z} = (z_1, z_2, z_3)'$ and

$$
\begin{aligned}
y_1 &= \exp(z_1), & -\infty < z_1 < \infty, \\
y_2 &= \exp(z_2), & -\infty < z_2 < \infty, \\
y_3 &= \ln\{1 + \exp(z_3)\} & -\infty < z_3 < \infty.
\end{aligned}
\tag{14}
$$

Because z_1, z_2, and z_3 are unbounded, it is now plausible to assume that their joint distribution is multivariate normal.

There are other choices of reparameterization to normally distributed factors, however, and the fit of the structure of μ and Σ to $\bar{x}$ and S will depend on the choice of reparameterization. In particular, if y is retained unchanged and assumed to have a normal distribution, a poorer fit to the Kanfer-Ackerman data is obtained.

The normally distributed learning factors now are z_1, which governs the asymptote or maximum performance; z_2, which governs the distance from the asymptote on Trial 1; and z_3, which governs the rate of learning. There are 16 parameters in the model: the learning factor means μ_{z_1}, μ_{z_2}, and μ_{z_3}; the concomitant variable mean μ_c; the factor standard deviations σ_{z_1}, σ_{z_2}, and σ_{z_3}; the concomitant variable standard deviation σ_c; the factor intercorrelations ρ_{z_1,z_2}, ρ_{z_1,z_3}, ρ_{z_2,z_3}; the correlations of the learning factors with the concomitant variable $\rho_{z_1,c}$, $\rho_{z_2,c}$, and $\rho_{z_3,c}$; and the error variance trend parameters γ_1 and γ_2.

Parameter estimates obtained from the Kanfer-Ackerman data are shown in Table 4.3. It can be seen that the "distance from the asymptote on Trial 1" factor, z_2, has a negative correlation with the ASVAB score, c, which is greater in absolute value than the correlation of the "asymptote" factor, z_1, with ASVAB. The negative correlation is due to the fact that distance from the asymptote rather than distance from zero is reflected by z_2, whereas the rank order of the estimates of the absolute correlations $|\rho_{z_1,c}|$ and $|\rho_{z_2,c}|$ is in keeping with the rank order of trial–ASVAB correlations in Table 4.1. The correlation of the asymptote factor, z_1, with the "rate of learning" factor, z_3, is negative but not large. Other factor correlations are sufficiently small to be disregarded. Measures of fit of the SPLC model are shown in Table 4.6 (later in this chapter).

For comparability with the results presented in previous sections, the discrepancy function of Expression 2 was minimized to provide the estimates and measures of fit reported here. This discrepancy function is not strictly appropriate

Table 4.3

STOCHASTIC PARAMETER LEARNING CURVES: PARAMETER ESTIMATES

Parameter	Estimate
μ_{z_1}	3.54
μ_{z_2}	0.13
μ_{z_3}	0.27
μ_c	0.63
σ_{z_1}	0.28
σ_{z_2}	0.51
σ_{z_3}	0.66
σ_c	5.62
ρ_{z_1,z_2}	0.04
ρ_{z_1,z_3}	-0.33
ρ_{z_2,z_3}	0.00
$\rho_{z_1,c}$	0.25
$\rho_{z_2,c}$	-0.51
$\rho_{z_3,c}$	-0.10
γ_1	10.27
γ_2	0.10

under the assumption of normal distributions for z and e, because x will then not have a normal distribution. Alternative methods for fitting stochastic parameter growth curve models are available. Du Toit (1979, chapters 6 & 7) has developed and applied a generalised least squares (GLS) method for obtaining parameter estimates of the mean vector and covariance matrix of z and the covariance matrix of e, and testing the fit of the model. The weight matrix of the GLS discrepancy function is appropriate if normal distributions are assumed for z and e. Bock (1983, Section 4), also assuming normal distributions for latent variables, has suggested an expectation-maximization (EM) algorithm for obtaining marginal maximum likelihood parameter estimates.

Structured Latent Curve Models

Latent curve (LC) models were first proposed independently by Rao (1958), Tucker (1958) and Meredith in an appendix to Scher, Young, and Meredith (1960). Models of this type have been employed by McArdle (1988), and a careful recent treatment is given by Meredith and Tisak (1990). The model employed here is a modification of previous work and will have the additional property that the "basis curves" involved are parameterized parsimoniously in terms of a small number of parameters.

Like the SPLC model, this LC model assumes that a person's true scores on the learning trials lie on a smooth curve. Also, like the SPLC model, this true score curve is assumed to vary from one person to another, but it is no longer required to be monotonic. As in the TS model, the trial means are required to have a curve of a specified form. For consistency with previous sections, the Gompertz curve is employed. However, the methods used here can easily be applied to other learning curves.

The data model for the vector of learning trial scores is

$$\mathbf{x} = \boldsymbol{\Lambda}\mathbf{y} + \mathbf{e},\tag{15}$$

where $\mathbf{y}$ is a $m \times 1$ latent vector variate representing learning factors and $\mathbf{e}$ is an independently distributed error variate with $\mathscr{E}(\mathbf{e}) = 0$ and $\mathrm{cov}(\mathbf{y}, \mathbf{e}') = 0$. This model is very much like the usual linear factor analysis model, but the columns of $\boldsymbol{\Lambda}$ represent m "basis" curves evaluated at each of the T time points. In the present example, $m = 3$. A true score curve, then, is a weighted sum of the common basis curves with weights that vary from one person to another.

Let $\mathscr{E}(\mathbf{y}) = \boldsymbol{\xi}$, $\mathrm{cov}(\mathbf{y}, \mathbf{y}') = \boldsymbol{\Phi}$ and $\mathrm{cov}(\mathbf{e}, \mathbf{e}') = \mathbf{D}_\psi$. The error covariance matrix $\mathbf{D}_\psi$ is diagonal, and its diagonal elements may again be required to follow the monotonic decreasing trend of Expression 13. The data model in Expression 15 generates the moment structure

$$\boldsymbol{\mu}_x = \boldsymbol{\Lambda}\boldsymbol{\xi} \qquad \boldsymbol{\Sigma}_{xx} = \boldsymbol{\Lambda}\boldsymbol{\Phi}\boldsymbol{\Lambda}' + D_\psi.\tag{16}$$

The following approach is used to generate smooth basis functions to provide the columns of $\boldsymbol{\Lambda}$: As was done with the TS model, the elements of $\boldsymbol{\mu}_x$ are required to follow a smooth monotonic increasing trend, $\mu_t = f(t, \theta)$, $t = 1, \ldots, T$. True score curves close to the mean curve will have a similar shape, but those some distance away can differ appreciably in shape and need not be monotonic. This suggests the use of a first-order Taylor series to represent a person's true score curve as a deviation from the mean curve. The Gompertz curve in Expression 7, with the other members of the Richards (1959) family has the property

$$f(t, \theta) = \theta_1 f_1'(t, \theta),\tag{17}$$

where $f_i'(t, \theta) = (\partial/\partial\theta_i)f(t, \theta)$, $i = 1, \ldots, 3$. We then obtain the latent curve model

$$x_t = y_1 f_1'(t, \theta) + y_2 f_2'(t, \theta) + y_3 f_3'(t, \theta) + e_t,\tag{18}$$

where y_1, y_2, and y_3 are learning factors, with $\mathscr{E}(y_1) = \theta_1$, $\mathscr{E}(y_2) = 0$, and $\mathscr{E}(y_3) = 0$. In matrix notion, Expression 18 is of the form of Expression 15, where $\boldsymbol{\Lambda}$ is a $T \times 3$ matrix with columns given by

$$\lambda_{t1} = f_1'\ (t,\ \theta) = \exp\ [-\theta_2\exp\{-(t\ -\ 1)\ \theta_3\}],$$

$$\lambda_{t2} = f_2'\ (t,\ \theta) = -\theta_1\exp\{-(t\ -\ 1)\ \theta_3\}\lambda_{t1}, \qquad (19)$$

$$\lambda_{t3} = f_3'\ (t,\ \theta) = -(t\ -\ 1)\ \theta_2\lambda_{t2},$$

for $t = 1,\ \ldots,\ T$, and the factor mean vector is

$$\xi = (\theta_1,\ 0,\ 0)'.$$

Because of Expression 17, the trial mean vector $\mu_x = \Lambda\xi$ satisfies the Gompertz curve in Expression 7.

Learning factors are interpreted similarly to those of the SPLC models presented above: y_1 is the person asymptote, y_2 governs the distance from the asymptote on Trial 1, and y_3 governs the learning rate.

To accommodate the concomitant variable, we replace Expression 15 by

$$\begin{bmatrix} x \\ c \end{bmatrix} = \begin{bmatrix} \Lambda & 0 \\ 0' & 1 \end{bmatrix} \begin{bmatrix} y \\ c \end{bmatrix} + \begin{bmatrix} e \\ 0 \end{bmatrix}$$

and augment ξ, Φ, and D_ψ in Expression 16 accordingly. Because correlations are easier to understand than covariances, we shall parameterize the elements of Φ in the form $\upsilon_{y_i,y_j} = \sigma_{y_i}\sigma_{y_j}\rho_{y_i,y_j}$. The parameters of the model correspond closely to those of the SPLC models. They are the mean trend parameters θ_1, θ_2, and θ_3; the concomitant variable mean μ_c; the factor standard deviations σ_{y_1}, σ_{y_2}, and σ_{y_3}; the concomitant variable standard deviation σ_c; the factor intercorrelations $\rho_{y_1,y_2}, \rho_{y_1,y_3}$, and ρ_{y_2,y_3}; the correlations of the learning factors with the concomitant variables $\rho_{y_1,c}$, $\rho_{y_2,c}$, and $\rho_{y_3,c}$; and the error variance trend parameters γ_1 and γ_2.

Parameter estimates obtained from the Kanfer-Ackerman data are shown in Table 4.4. Also shown are estimates obtained when the trend (Expression 13) on error variances was not imposed.

Imposing the error variance trend (Expression 13) has not made much difference to the estimates of the other parameters shown in Table 4.4. The largest difference is 0.17 in the estimates of ρ_{y_2,y_3}.

The estimates of the mean trend parameters θ_1, θ_2, and θ_3 are similar to those of the TS model in Table 4.2. Estimates of the error variance trend parameters γ_1 and γ_2 are similar to those of the SPLC model in Table 4.3. Learning factor correlations, and correlations between the learning factors and concomitant variables are also similar to those of Table 4.3; they can be interpreted in the same way as was done in the SPLC model. Learning factor standard deviations, however, differ between the two models because a reparameterization corresponding to Expression 14 has not been necessary here.

The basis curves, from the latent curve analysis (with the trend on the error variances), are plotted in Figure 4.2A. It can be seen that an initial quick rate of

Table 4.4

LATENT CURVE MODEL: PARAMETER ESTIMATES

Parameter	Estimate	
	Restricted	**Unrestricted**
θ_1	34.70	34.52
θ_2	1.09	1.08
θ_3	0.76	0.77
μ_c	0.61	0.66
σ_{y_1}	9.65	9.54
σ_{y_2}	0.51	0.55
σ_{y_3}	0.30	0.35
σ_c	5.62	5.62
$\rho_{y_1 y_2}$	-0.00	-0.03
$\rho_{y_1 y_3}$	-0.18	-0.18
$\rho_{y_2 y_3}$	0.03	0.20
$\rho_{y_1 c}$	0.26	0.25
$\rho_{y_2 c}$	-0.50	-0.44
$\rho_{y_3 c}$	-0.09	-0.04
γ_1	10.90	—
γ_2	0.11	—

increase in performance followed by a decline can be allowed for by giving a substantial positive weight to the rate curve. Similarly, an initial decrease in performance followed by an increase can be allowed for by assigning a substantial negative weight to the rate curve. As the number of trials increases, the initial distance and rate curves approach zero. Results of fitting a weighted sum of the basis curves by linear least squares to the three sets of subject scores from Figure 4.1 are shown in Figures 4.2B, 4.2C, and 4.2D. Reasonably good fits are obtained in all three cases, including the case in Figure 4.2D, in which a steady decrease in performance occurs after the third trial. The monotonically increasing Gompertz true score curve would not be appropriate for this case.

Error variance estimates obtained from the two latent curve analyses, with and without a trend on error variances, are shown in Table 4.5.

It can be seen that the differences are substantial, particularly on the first trial, in which the small error variance of the unrestricted solution seems counterintuitive. Measures of fit of the two latent curve models are given in Table 4.6.

DISCUSSION

As shown in Table 4.6, the point estimates of the RMSEA yield the same ranking of models as point estimates of the CVI. The TS model gives the best fit, followed

Table 4.5

LATENT CURVE MODEL: ERROR VARIANCE ESTIMATES

	Estimate	
Error variance	Restricted	Unrestricted
ψ_{11}	10.90	0.55
ψ_{22}	9.81	14.11
ψ_{33}	8.82	7.48
ψ_{44}	7.93	7.55
ψ_{55}	7.13	5.27
ψ_{66}	6.41	8.61

Table 4.6

FIT MEASURES

Model	No. of parameters	df	Point estimate	90% Confidence interval	Point estimate	90% Confidence interval
	Root mean square error of approximation				**Cross-validation index**	
TS	11	24	0.054	(0.000 ; 0.094)	0.407	(0.336 ; 0.549)
SPLC	16	19	0.065	(0.001 ; 0.108)	0.454	(0.372 ; 0.593)
LCT	16	19	0.078	(0.035 ; 0.119)	0.489	(0.395 ; 0.639)
LCF	20	15	0.068	(0.000 ; 0.115)	0.470	(0.401 ; 0.599)
SAT	35	0			0.511	

Note: TS = time series model, SPLC = stochastic parameter learning curve model, LCT = latent curve model with an exponential trend on error variances, LCF = latent curve model with free error variances, and SAT = saturated model.

by the SPLC model, the latent curve model with free error variances (LCF), and the latent curve model with a trend on error variances (LCT). Differences in point estimates of fit indices are small relative to the widths of the interval estimates. The ordering of models should therefore be regarded with caution. All the models considered here yielded a point estimate of the CVI that was smaller than the CVI for the saturated model. The interval estimates of RMSEA for the TS and LCF models have lower limits of zero, indicating that the null hypothesis of perfect fit would not be rejected at the 5% level. We are reminded by the nonzero upper limits, however, that we cannot accept either of these models as "correct."

Comparison of Models

Because all these models fit the Kanfer-Ackerman data reasonably well, plausibility and interpretability of a model become more important criteria for evaluation

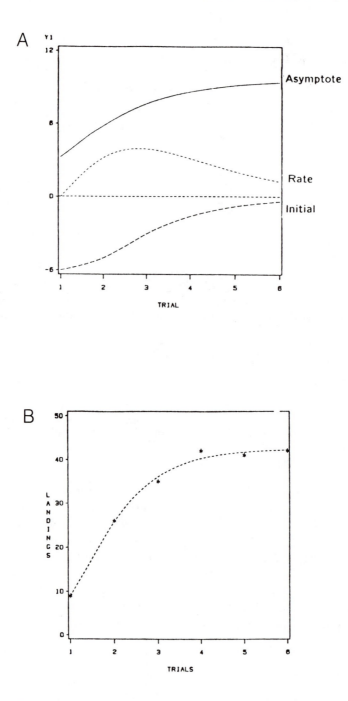

Figure 4.2   Latent curve analysis. (Figure 4.2A represents latent curves. Figure 4.2B represents Case 35.)

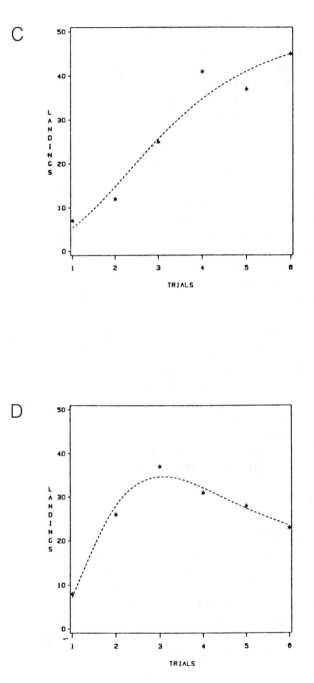

**Figure 4.2
(continued)** Latent curve analysis. (Figure 4.2C represents Case 115. Figure 4.2D represents Case 95.)

in a comparison of models. Differences beween the LCT and LCF models are minor, so we shall consider only the LCT model.

The TS and LCT models have the same mean curve and differ in covariance structures only. The TS model gives less information about the situation under consideration than the SPLC and LCT models do because it has only one latent variable, not three, to explain individual differences in learning. This latent variable represents initial performance. The estimate $\hat{\rho}_{sc} = 1$ on the upper bound for the correlation between the initial performance latent variable and the ability manifest variable in the TS model is disturbingly high.

The SPLC and LCT models have the same number of parameters and provide very similar information. They are both types of the factor analysis model but differ in that the SPLC model is *nonlinear* in the factors, whereas the LCT model involves a *linear function* of factors. The learning factors in the two models are interpreted in a similar manner: The first factor represents a person's asymptote or maximum attainable performance; the second, the distance from the asymptote on the first trial; and the third, rate of learning. Of these, the second factor corresponds most closely in interpretation to the single initial performance factor of the TS model.

In the SPLC model, the true score curve is always monotonic. This seems inappropriate for data such as those in Figure 4.2D. The LCT model permits a nonmonotonic true score curve if the asymptote factor score, y_3, is large in absolute value. It is worth bearing in mind that the LCT model involves substantially less computation than the SPLC model, and it is thus easier to apply in situations in which there are more factors. In the development of an SPLC model, the choice of the parameterization of a curve affects the fit of the model. This is not the case for a latent curve model. Reparameterization of the mean curve, $f(t, \theta)$, will not affect the fit of the covariance structure developed from Expression 18.

CONCLUSIONS

We do not wish to say, at this point, that any model is "best." Far more experience must be gained in applying the models before such conclusions can be drawn. Further, different users will have different opinions. Also, none of the models can be regarded as "correct." It is to be expected that other models will be developed, possibly by amalgamating models considered here. One approach worth consideration would be a latent curve model with a TS structure for the error variates. It may also be necessary to make use of learning curves with more than three parameters when the number of trials of the learning task is large.

COMMENTS ON "MODELS FOR LEARNING DATA"

LISA L. HARLOW

Browne and Du Toit present three covariance structure models to assess the pattern of growth or change over time. I shall briefly describe each model, suggest considerations researchers may have when applying these models, and outline some major contributions of these models.

THREE MODELS OF CHANGE

All three models assume that individuals are assessed at p time points (at least three or more) on a variable of interest, such as a learning task, and an additional concomitant variable, c. Output from the models provides the following information:

1. The asymptote, a, representing the final score for an individual;
2. The increment in growth, b, between the initial state and the final score; and
3. The rate of growth or change, r, over time.

For all models, the errors of measurement or residuals can have a specified structure. Usually this takes the form of a decreasing pattern of error variances over the p time points, such that the error variance at each time point is smaller than that of the previous time point. For each model, estimation is based on information from a sample mean vector and sample covariance matrix.

Excellent suggestions on the contributions of these models, offered by Robert Cudeck, are gratefully acknowledged. Thanks and appreciation are also extended to Michael Browne, who provided valuable feedback on the summary and figures. This project was supported in part by Grant CA50087 from the National Cancer Institute to the Cancer Prevention Research Center, University of Rhode Island.

Fixed Learning Curve With Time Series Deviations

The first model is a first-order autoregressive moving average [ARMA(1,1)] time series (TS), and it incorporates relations with an additional concomitant variable (i.e., covariate), c. Although Browne and Du Toit discuss the addition of only a single concomitant variable, it would be possible to extend this model to consider several concomitant variables to assess the initial state of a person. A person's score at the first time point, x_1, depends on the initial state, s, and a white noise variable, u_1. The latent initial state variable, s, is correlated with the observed concomitant variable, c. Subsequent scores are a function of the previous observation, x_{t-1}, indicated by a first-order autoregressive parameter, α, as well as the previous white noise residuals, u_{t-1}, indicated by a first-order moving average parameter, β. In order to maintain a parsimonious model with a limited number of parameters, the autoregressive parameter, α, is restricted so as to be equal across time points, and so is the moving average parameter, β. A diagram of this model with three time points is shown in Figure 4.3.

Stochastic Parameter Learning Curves

The second model is a stochastic parameter learning curve (SPLC) model. The learning curve for each person is the focus interest. In this model, a person's score at each time point is a nonlinear function of the three learning parameters, a, b, and r.

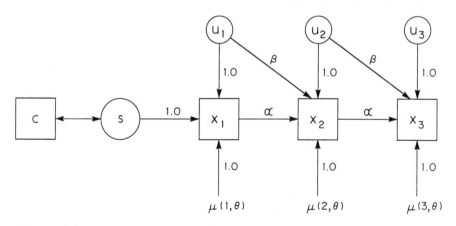

Figure 4.3   The time series model. A fixed learning curve model with ARMA(1,1) time series deviations, in which c is a concomitant variable related to the initial state (s) of a person; x_t is an observation at time t; $\mu(t, \theta)$, is the nonstochastic mean, which is a function of time t and the parameter vector, $\theta = (\theta_1, \theta_2, \theta_3)'$; β is a moving average parameter; μ_t is a latent white noise variable at time t; and α is an autoregressive parameter.

Correlations among the three stochastic parameters and a covariate variable, are also examined. This model is depicted in Figure 4.4 with three time points.

Structured Latent Curve Models

The third model is a latent curve (LC) model. At each time point, a score is derived from three underlying basis curves that are largely functions of the asymptote, a; the incremental growth in a person's score over time, b; and the rate of growth, r, plus error. The model is similar to a factor analysis model that includes a mean vector, in which the measured variables are scores at the p time points. The m factors are the three basis curve latent variables for a, b, and r, respectively.

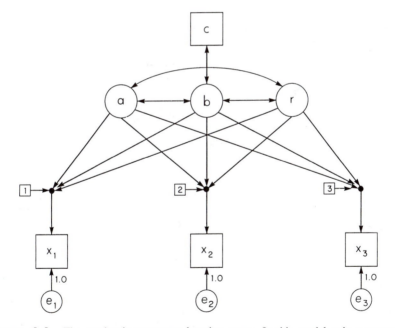

Figure 4.4 The stochastic parameter learning curve. In this model c is a measured concomitant variable; a is a latent variable that yields the asymptote or final score for a person; b is a latent variable representing the increment in growth from the first trial to the last; r is a latent variable that measures the rate of growth for each person; the fixed variable $\boxed{t}$ stands for time, $\bullet$ represents a nonlinear function that combines the effects of a, b, and r; x_t is an observation at time t; and e_t is a latent error variable at time t.

Correlations among these m latent variables, and the concomitant measured variable, c, are examined. A diagram of this model is given in Figure 4.5.

APPLICATION CONSIDERATIONS

A number of practical concerns must be considered to apply these models. The main considerations are:

1. *Computing Facilities.* Browne and Du Toit have written a computer program using maximum likelihood (ML) estimation to analyze these three models. The program can currently run on an IBM 386 PC with 640K RAM. It is estimated that small models, with six time points and one concomitant variable, would take at most five minutes of

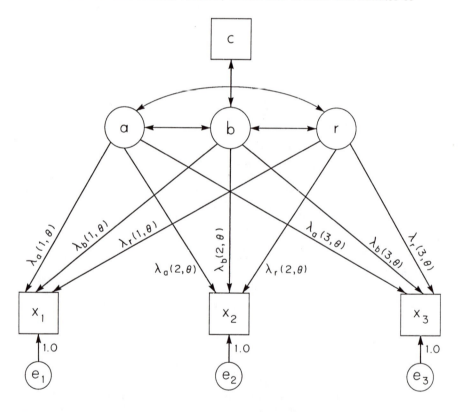

Figure 4.5   The latent growth curve model. In this model c is an observed concomitant variable; a, b, and r are latent variables representing the asymptote, increment in growth, and rate of growth, respectively; x_t is an observation at time t; e_t is a latent error variable at time t; and λ_i (t, θ) is a factor loading on latent factor i at time t and is a function of t and $\theta = (\theta_1, \theta_2, \theta_3)$.

CPU time. The TS model and the LCT model take much less time than the SPLC model does because they do not entail the numerical evaluation of multiple integrals required for the SPLC model.

2. *Number of Time Points.* In order to use any of these models, the researcher should collect at least three time points, in addition to one or more covariates. It is preferable, however, to have at least six time points, or even more, in order to provide stable estimates of the parameters; this enables the pattern of growth over time to be modeled more reliably.

3. *Number of Subjects.* Considerations regarding sample size are comparable to those for other covariance structure models. Boomsma (1983) recommends samples of at least 200 subjects in order to minimize convergence problems and to provide stable parameter estimates for moderate size models with multivariate normality.

4. *Assumption of Normality.* Currently, only ML estimation is available, which assumes multivariate normality. Robustness studies (e.g., Boomsma, 1983; Harlow, 1985; Muthén & Kaplan, 1985) suggest that ML may provide unbiased estimates with moderate size models with skewness of less than 1 or 2 and kurtosis of less than 6. With larger models and more extreme nonnormality, ML estimates, standard errors, and chi-squared values tend to be biased.

5. *Reliability of Scores.* Because the models currently allow only one score or measured variable at each time point, it is important to choose reliable measures. This is also true of the covariate or concomitant variable, although the possibility of using more than one covariate somewhat alleviates this concern.

6. *Applications of the Models.* As with any new set of procedures, it is of practical interest to know how each model can best be used and when one model is to be preferred over another. The researcher will want to know, for example, the complexity of each model, the degree to which each model depends on knowledge of previous theory, and whether all three models are expected to fit a data set equally well or whether there are specific uses for each of the three models. Because guidelines for these concerns are not yet available, researchers will have to make their own decisions based on criteria that are relevant to their research questions. For instance, because th TS model has fewer parameters (12 vs. 17 for the SPLC and latent curve models), computation should be easy and quick. Browne and Du Toit expect that the latent curve model and the TS model will use a comparable amount of CPU time (about 30 seconds) because they both have mean and covariance structures in closed form. Phenomena such as substance use, which can potentially be modeled by knowing the previous substance use of an individual, plus the

previous residuals may be adequately estimated with the TS model. More specific suggestions should become available as researchers gain more experience with these models using actual data and when simulation studies for these models are conducted.

Contributions

Browne and Du Toit present a versatile set of models for assessing change over time. These models offer five main contributions:

1. *Unified General Approach.* Together, the models provide a unified, general approach that takes into account intraindividual (e.g., individual growth curve parameters for each person) as well as interindividual information (e.g., group means, variances, and covariances), providing a rigorous evaluation of growth or change in a phenomenon. The latent curve model can handle decreases or fatigue trends that yield curvilinear patterns, as well as monotonic increases for growth data. Thus, a wider variety of phenomena can be modeled than is possible with traditional monotonic increasing learning data; for example, complex phenomena such as substance abuse and AIDS preventive behavior change (with relapse) can be examined.
2. *Covariate.* The addition of a covariate or concomitant variable allows assessment of the relation between this variable and the characteristics of the growth curve.
3. *Model Fit.* Model fit focuses more on indices of relative fit for comparing models, as opposed to indices of absolute fit, such as chi-square. Two indices of fit are used: the Steiger-Lind root mean square error of approximation (RMSEA) and the Cudeck-Browne expected cross-validation index (CVI).
4. *Multimethod Approach.* In the spirit of Campbell and Fiske (1959), Browne and Du Toit offer several methods to validly assess growth or change, providing more flexibility and choice.
5. *Error Variance Structure.* These models take covariance structures to a new level of specification by allowing structure on the error variances, as well as the loadings and means. For example, error variances can be structured to decrease in value over time, thereby providing a more realistic model of the behavior.

CONCLUSIONS

Browne and Du Toit offer three versatile models for assessing change over time. Future work could provide guidelines for general use, as well as more options for nonnormal estimation and multiple indicators at each time point. The introduction of these models is expected to have a positive impact on the field and should stimulate better models of change.

CHAPTER 5

THE APPLICATION OF TIME SERIES METHODS TO MODERATE SPAN LONGITUDINAL DATA

KENNETH JONES

Editors' Introduction

In this chapter, Jones first invites consideration of the familiar data box (proposed by Cattell many years ago) in which times (of measurement) are represented along the depth dimension of the box, subjects are represented along the height dimension, variables are represented along the width dimension, and measurements are in cells, like the cells of an egg carton, within the box. He then introduces the reader to methods of analysis based on a ''tray'' of data (like a tray of eggs) such as one would have if a single row of data were selected—m measurements obtained at t times for a single subject. Such data are said to represent a time series. Just as in the usual data gathering of m measurements for N subjects one might calculate the summary statistics, intercorrelations, factors, and so on, for m variables, so one might calculate such quantities for m measurements over t times with time series data. Cattell reasoned that major parts of the same reality reside in all the data trays and that therefore we should be able to gain important understanding of reality by analysis of each kind of data tray that can be sliced from the data box. In particular, analyses of time series data should indicate some of the same things about reality that are indicated by analyses of other, more usual, data trays from the data box, as Jones discusses.

It is likely that social scientists who have some understanding of time
series analysis gained part of it from the writings, more than a decade ago,
of McCain and McCleary in the much-cited Cook and Campbell (1979)
book. McCain and McCleary concentrated on autoregressive integrated
moving average (ARIMA) models, with tests for models of intervention effects. There are many more possibilities for considering time series data
besides ARIMA models, and Jones introduces the reader to many of these.
He concisely states assumptions on which such analyses are based, indicates regularities one might reasonably expect (model) in time series data,
and identifies major anomalies and artifactual effects one should be on
guard to detect. In the comment section following this chapter, Reichardt
provides a fascinating comparison of the bases for causal inference that can
be derived from time series analysis in contrast to the more usual analyses
of longitudinal data.

THE DATA MODEL

The problem of the prediction of change is conceptually related to the general
issue of forecasting time series. Nevertheless, with notable exceptions (Anderson,
1978, 1985; Brillinger, 1973), the psychometric literature does not abound in
methodological or applications studies relating to the developments in engineering
and econometrics that have addressed the issue of change over time. A major
contributing factor appears to be the modest length of psychometric time series
data. In fact, these data often are referred to as *repeated observations* or *longitudinal data*, rather than the equally applicable term *time series*. The purpose of
this chapter is to outline the principal approaches to the prediction of time series
and to explore ways in which these could enhance the data analysis in psychometric
longitudinal studies, with their shorter lengths of time.

Cattell presented a formulation of data called the "data box" (Cattell,
1966b). The three axes of the model represent the observations (persons), variables, and time (occasions) aspects of the data. In the time series literature, the
multivariate profile of a single observation is referred to as a realization of a
process. The concept of a realization is analogous to that of a sample from a
population. Often data collected in a particular study occupy only one face of this
scheme. Cross-sectional data rest in one time slice of the front face, whereas time
series typically occupy one observational slice of the time (occasions) by variable
face. Cattell referred to analyses of the correlations based on the columns (variables) of this face as the P technique and analyses of the correlations over columns
(variables) of the former cross-sectional data face as the R technique. Each of the
three unique faces of the data box gives rise to two possible correlation matrices;
hence there are six possible techniques involved in the scheme, Q being the obverse
of R, and O the obverse of P. The other two matrices give rise to S and T

techniques. Though creative and logically attractive, these techniques are informationally inefficient when the data contain variance distributed along all three design axes (Molenaar, 1985).

If one is fortunate enough to have data collected over each of the three axes, this array might be referred to as the data, or observational, tensor, just as the Persons × Variables array is referred to as the data matrix. Analogously, just as two associational matrices for the cross-sectional face may be computed, three associational tensors for the data tensor also may be computed. Because it is of immediate interest to observe the evolution of variable relations over time, the correlations of each variable with its own past values (lag relations), or the past values of other variables (cross-lagged relations) are of major interest. This would be a Rank 4 tensor of order—Variables (v) × Time (t) × Variables × Time.

The rank of a tensor describes the number of organzing axes in contrast to the definition of the term when it is applied in the context of matrix algebra. The so-called contraction of a Rank 3 tensor by its transpose yields a Rank 4 tensor. The contraction of a tensor is simply column × row multiplication of the two tensors, using the last row of the first and the first column of the second. When the tensors are matrices, the contraction is their cross-product. This calculation may be carried out by tensor manipulations, as provided in *Mathematica* (Wolfram, 1988).

However, the same result may be obtained by regarding each time instance of a variable as a new variable; hence, instead of having a Rank 4 tensor of ($v \times t \times v \times t$), there is a matrix of order ($m \times m$) where $m = vt$. If the correlations over the variables are computed, a supermatrix similar to that represented in Table 5.1 will result. This supermatrix represents all of the coincident and cross-lagged correlations appropriate to this particular view of the data tensor. When the number of observations (n) is moderate to large and the number of time intervals (t) is relatively small, approaches involving canonical correlations have been tried (Carroll, 1968; Horst, 1961a, 1961b; Kettenring, 1971; McDonald, 1968). However, these methods do not take into consideration specifically the issue of the constancy of the canonical factors over time; that is, in general the latent variables may vary in composition from set to set. Later work has addressed this issue (Meredith & Tisak, 1982; Millsap & Meredith, 1988; Tisak & Meredith, 1989).

It is possible to look at this matrix from a different perspective in which the number of cases is small (in particular, 1) and the number of time intervals is quite large (e.g., greater than 50). Many economic data are of this type. There is only one observation for each variable, such as the Producer Price Index (PPI) for the month of August 1989. It is, of course, impossible to estimate the lagged cross-correlation supermatrix of Table 5.1 from data of one observation without further assumptions. In order to determine if there are aspects of the mainstream

Table 5.1

THE TIME VARIABLE CORRELATION SUPERMATRIX

							Realizations					
	1	2	3	4	5	6	7	8	9	10	11	12
Time 1												
V1	1.00	-0.13	-0.15	-0.04	0.03	-0.03	-0.33	-0.01	0.06	-0.01	-0.09	-0.06
V2	-0.13	1.00	-0.19	0.05	-0.30	-0.07	-0.09	-0.20	0.03	0.31	-0.08	0.19
V3	-0.15	-0.19	1.00	-0.24	-0.11	0.06	-0.02	-0.02	-0.43	-0.25	-0.06	-0.03
V4	-0.04	0.05	-0.24	1.00	0.00	0.07	-0.25	-0.04	0.22	0.03	-0.14	0.07
Time 2												
V1	0.04	-0.30	-0.11	0.00	1.00	0.16	-0.05	0.19	0.27	-0.17	0.23	-0.04
V2	-0.04	-0.07	0.06	0.07	0.16	1.00	-0.03	-0.08	0.03	0.06	0.01	-0.17
V3	-0.33	-0.09	-0.02	-0.25	-0.05	-0.03	1.00	0.11	-0.05	-0.06	-0.01	-0.11
V4	-0.01	-0.20	-0.20	-0.04	0.19	-0.08	0.11	1.00	0.08	-0.24	0.13	-0.01
Time 3												
V1	0.06	0.03	-0.43	0.22	0.27	0.03	-0.05	0.08	1.00	-0.11	-0.02	-0.13
V2	-0.01	0.31	-0.25	0.03	-0.17	0.06	-0.06	-0.24	-0.11	1.00	-0.03	-0.10
V3	-0.09	-0.08	-0.06	-0.14	0.23	0.01	-0.01	0.13	-0.02	-0.03	1.00	-0.07
V4	-0.06	0.19	-0.03	0.07	-0.04	-0.17	-0.11	-0.01	-0.13	-0.10	-0.07	1.00

Note: Random data are used. There are 50 realizations, four variables, and three time spans. V1 = variable 1, V2 = variable 2, and so forth.

methodologies of time series analysis that have anything to contribute to the analysis of data from the generally shorter longitudinal studies, it is helpful to examine the assumptions on which these methods are based.

Assumptive Perspective

Measurement level

The data should be measured at the interval or ratio level. This assumption is needed for any analysis in which means are to be used as summary statistics. It is appropriate for all parametric procedures (e.g., t-test).

Stationarity

The major assumption about an observed time series is that it is stationary over time. This assumption implies that the probability distribution of its observations is constant over time (strong stationarity). A weaker form implies that the observations are deviating from a mean value that is constant over time and that the variance attached to each observation is also constant over time. Though even the weak form is rarely true for observed series, usually the series in question can be made to appear stationary by transformation and differencing. The latter process consists of taking the first or second difference between adjacent observations as the new variable. In other words, changes or invariables are analyzed rather than levels of variables. Usually the first differencing of a series is sufficient to make it appear stationary in the mean. If the differenced variable is then not stationary in variance, sometimes it is transformed prior to differencing, but this situation is difficult to handle. Suggestions have been made by several researchers (Cartwright, 1984; Jones, 1983).

Ergodicity

If the series can be assumed to be stationary and if it is representative of (i.e., randomly drawn from) the hypothetical ensemble of possible realizations, then the ergodic theorem (Hannan, 1974; Robinson, 1959; Wiener, 1948) states that the autocross-covariances or autocorrelations computed by pairing an observation with its lagged neighbor, in time, will converge with those that would be computed across multiple realizations of the series, had such been available. The theorem implies that in the situations in which it applies, matrices such as that represented in Table 5.1 will have equivalent diagonal submatrices of correlation coefficients, and all submatrices in the bands inferior and superior to the diagonal will be equal. Such a matrix (Table 5.1) is said to be "block Toeplitz" in form. Each block is indicated by a box around its entries. The blocks are on the diagonal. Given such ergodicity, realization expectations may be replaced with time expectations and the means and covariances may be computed from a single realization of the process. Anderson (1978) describes several tests that may be applied to multiple realization situations to compare the equivalence of the submatrices shown in Table 5.1.

The characteristics of the ergodicity process imply that the autocorrelations will decrease with increasing lags. This is taken to be a sign of stationarity. These characteristics also imply that a "shock" (a model residual) to the data series will have an ever decreasing effect on future values. This is the so-called condition of invertibility. These conditions may be checked with respect to a given model imposed on the data.

THE USE OF TIME SERIES METHODS WITH MULTIPLE REALIZATION MODERATE SPAN LONGITUDINAL DATA

The use of the general methodologies for time series data analysis with longitudinal data rests on whether converting a data tensor of the form shown in Table 5.1 to block Toeplitz form is justified. There must also be enough discrete time points to enable resolution of the lag structure of the underlying model. This in turn is linked to the appropriateness of pooling the multiple realizations to estimate the cross-lagged correlation matrix. Assuming the researcher can rationalize the use of a covariance or correlation matrix of the block Toeplitz form and has enough time points, then it is possible to develop a time-dependent model using existing multiple time series approaches. The question of the number of time points has no precise answer, but it is a matter of concern in different ways. First, there must be sufficient data points to reliably estimate the lagged correlations. If there are multiple realizations, this concern is ameliorated. Second, there must be sufficient lags to properly represent the underlying process. This latter concern remains, no matter how many realizations are available to estimate the correlations. Generally speaking, even with seasonal data, 20 to 40 lags should be sufficient to estimate correlations; this is what I term "moderate span" because there are fewer data than usual for time series analyses.

An Overview of Time Series Methods

Figure 5.1 outlines the relations among some time series and cross-sectional methods. They are arranged hierarchically, with the most general at the top. State transition or state space analysis is the most general. It is capable of dealing with both time series and cross-sectional problems. It can encompass models that are nonlinear or that have nonconstant parameters. Below this, the methodologies divide into those primarily oriented toward cross-sectional or short longitudinal problems and those whose forte is the longer time series data. Under this division, there are three major methods for handling multivariate time series: spectral anal-

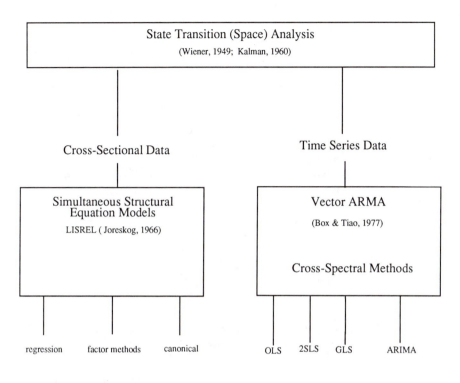

Figure 5.1　The relations among some data analytic methods. ARMA = autoregressive moving averages, ARIMA = autoregressive integrated moving averages, OLS = ordinary least squares, 2SLS = two stage least squares, GLS = generalized least squares.

ysis methods, vector autoregression-moving average (VARMA) methods, and the variants of regression analysis such as ordinary least squares (OLS), and so on. Figure 5.2 gives a more detailed map of the relations among several time series methods. Again the state space technique is at the head of the list. Under this is the VARMA, also known as ARMAX, which stands for autoregression-moving average with exogenous variables. This methodology is restricted to models that are linear and have constant coefficients. It has a mirror image in multispectral analysis. The Weiner-Khintchine-Wold theorem states that every covariance or correlation function has a spectral representation (Robinson, 1959, 1967). This means that time series data can be analyzed equivalently in the time domain or in the frequency domain with methods derived from the Fourier transformation of the data. For data in which periodicities or cycles are hypothesized, the frequency domain approach is attractive.

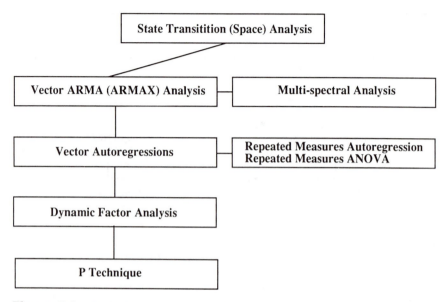

Figure 5.2   Methodologies for the analysis of multivariate time-dependent data.
ARMAX = autoregressive moving averages with exogenous variables,
ANOVA = analysis of variance.

Under the ARMAX method is listed the vector autoregression (VAR) method
which has a number of proponents (e.g., Litterman, 1980; Sims, 1980). The idea
is that the complexity of having a moving average component in the model can
be eliminated by taking advantage of Wold's decomposition theorem (Wold, 1954)
and the condition of invertibility. The theorem states that any process that is
stationary, even though it is nonlinear, can be represented by a moving average
model of perhaps infinite length. Because the invertibility condition states that
any moving average (MA) process can be represented as an autoregressive process
of perhaps infinite length, reasonably long autoregressive models will capture
most of the predictive information in a data set. Naturally, if the length of lags
becomes excessive with limited observations, serious inefficiencies in estimation
can complicate the picture. Runkle (1987) has noted several criticisms of this
approach. Longitudinal methods such as repeated measures analysis of variance
(ANOVA) are similar.

   In the VARMA approach and the VAR approach, the attempt is to fit a
model to the data in much the same manner as with cross-sectional structural
equation approaches such as LISREL. However, there may be no a priori model
or any causal ordering of the variables, but the objective may be to induce the
latent variables from the data, as in cross-sectional factor analysis. There have
been a number of approaches to this problem. One of the earliest was the aforementioned P technique of Cattell. However, this method ignores the lagged cor-

relation structure in the data. Other approaches that address this issue might be categorized as dynamic factor analysis because of inclusion in the input of information relating to lag structure.

The solution to the problem may be further subdivided into four strategies. The first is through the Fourier transform of the covariance-correlation supermatrix (Geweke, 1975, 1977; Geweke & Singleton, 1977, 1981; Priestly, Rao, & Tong, 1973, 1974; Singleton, 1980). This method takes advantage of the fact that the individual Fourier frequencies resulting from the transform are independent of one another. These may be reduced to principal components free of the complicating aspect of the nonindependence of rows in the data matrix. However, retrieving the latent time-dependent variables is difficult. A second approach involves formulating the issue in terms of a state equation (Engle & Watson, 1979, 1981; Watson & Engle, 1983; Watson & Kraft, 1984). This method concentrates on the manufacture of index numbers to represent underlying latent economic or social variables. A third approach might be termed the "canonical correlation" approach. Recognizing that the canonical correlation (Hotelling, 1935, 1936) uncovers an interbattery factor, some methodologists have proposed it as a method for Time 1 and Time 2 studies (Corballis & Traub, 1970; Nesselroade, 1972). Its extensions (Horst, 1961a, 1961b; Kettenring, 1971; McDonald, 1968; Meredith & Tisak, 1982; Tisak & Meredith, 1989) to several sets of variables can be applied to multioccasion data sets in a number of different ways. These approaches are capable of dealing with a multiple realization data tensor and a nonblock Toeplitz correlation supermatrix. Most allow the nature of the latent variables to change over time, but Meredith and Tisak (1982) suggest a solution to the problem of a constant factor definition over time. A fourth approach might be termed the "model-based" approach (Box & Tiao, 1977; Molenaar, 1985; Pena & Box, 1987). Here the search is for the latent factors that represent the underlying vector ARMA process. Although the goal is not reached in the same manner or with the same degree of fidelity in the various approaches described, the wealth and diversity of the methods reflect not only the importance of the problem but its difficulty.

Particular Approaches

Regression

Multiple regression has been adapted to the prediction and description of time dependent data by including in the linear equation terms representing lagged observations. These may be on the dependent variable itself and on the independent or exogenous variables. Time series variants of the regression technique form the core of the classic econometric model. The fact that the data are ordered in time usually means that adjacent observations have a degree of dependence. This is manifested in an autocorrelation function that usually decreases with increasing lag. It has long been known that this autocorrelation phenomenon can cause major disturbances in the standard errors of the parameters as estimated by the usual regression formulas. The Durbin-Watson statistic only partially measures this effect. Although numerous compensatory techniques are available to adapt multiple regression to time dependent data, as these become more encompassing, they approach the VARMA model. The classical regression model assumes independence of observations, among other things. In addition, multiple regression often is applied to nonstationary data with disastrous consequences (Pierce, 1977). When two time series are correlated with nonstationary means (trending), very high r-squares are likely to occur. Even two random walks, series whose increments are purely random, may show r-squares close to 1.0. Regression analyses applied to such data often show deceptively rosy results, which pass the wrong significance tests (Granger & Newbold, 1977, p. 202). When researchers deal with time dependent data, the goal of explaining deviations from the population mean must be replaced by the goal of prediction of the change. This change often appears to be a less "reliable" measure, and it is almost always much more difficult to predict. However, the concept of "Granger causality" (Granger, 1969; Pierce & Haugh, 1977) suggests that causally explanatory variance is that which may be attributed to an independent variable when that variance related to the dependent variable's own past is adjusted out. It seems reasonable to require that evidence be presented for variable stationarity over time regardless of whether two time intervals, moderate span longitudinal data, or classical time series data are being analyzed.

In addition to the aforementioned anomalies arising from nonstationarity of the data, three other effects of the time ordering of data can confound the investigator. These are discussed in the following sections.

The "Slutzky effect"

Slutzky (1927) explains the introduction of cyclical components into a time series simply through the arithmetical aggregation of adjacent observations prior to analysis. In his conclusion, Slutzky states:

> The summation of random causes generates a cyclical series which tends to imitate for a number of cycles a harmonic series of a relatively small number of sine curves. After a more or less considerable number of periods every regime becomes disarranged, the transition to another regime occurring sometimes rather gradually, sometimes more or less abruptly, around certain critical points. (1927, p. 27)

This means that many of the apparent periodic effects that have been observed, particularly in econometric data may well be artifactual and result from the various averaging processes applied to the time points.

The "Yule effect"

The Yule (1926) effect is related to the Slutzky effect, but it is somewhat more curious. The effect arises, once again, when observations are aggregated over time. This may be initiated by the investigator or by some aspect of the series generating process. It describes the counterintuitive fact that one will induce a correlation between two series by aggregating each of them in some manner over time. To put it another way, by aggregating series the researcher raises the standard errors associated with the cross-correlation coefficients. Small, insignificant cross-correlations between two series thus become amplified as larger time aggregations are taken.

The "Working effect"

Working (1960) found that if random data ("white noise") are aggregated and first differences are taken with moderate to large aggregation spans, an induced first order autocorrelation of 0.25 can be expected. Higher order autocorrelations remain zero. For weekly averages of daily data (5), the induced autocorrelation is 0.235.

Each of these three effects illustrates the fact that any "filter" applied to the data either prior to the investigator's participation or as part of the research effort becomes part of the model. It is important, therefore, that the methodology applied to time series data be capable of illuminating the several aspects of that which has caused the data to take on their observed characteristics. Regression analysis can do this to some extent, but with some difficulty compared with the other three methodologies.

Vector Autoregression-Moving Averages

As Tukey (1978) has suggested, VARMA might be better termed "auto-regressive-moving sums." It extracts from the lagged covariance matrix all the linear information available. Ideally, the residuals from the application of the model to the data are multidimensional white noise. In order to accomplish this, it is necessary to estimate parameters for both the stationary form of the lagged observed variables and the lagged residuals. The latter represent the moving average aspect of the analysis. Generally, in order to enable estimation of such models, one rules out instantaneous causality. Granger and Newbold (1977, p. 223) give three equivalent forms for the VARMA model. In this formulation all variables are potentially endogenous. The model is driven by the exogenous white noise series. The major drawback lies in the number of parameters that must be estimated in the absence of a priori fixing information. Recently, several researchers have suggested ways in which subsets of parameters can be identified prior to estimation (Jones, 1983; Koreisha & Pukkila, 1987; Liu & Hudak, 1983; O'Reilly, Hui,

Jones, & Sheehan, 1981; Tsay, 1989). This methodology offers potential for the fitting of structural equation models using either a priori full models or the building up of a model from partial hypotheses.

Multispectral Analysis

In multispectral analysis, instead of viewing the data through the cross-lagged correlation matrix, one takes advantage of the fact that the correlations may be transformed into a form describing their cyclical propensity. The most widely known method is the Fourier transform (Bracewell, 1989; Lanczos, 1966), but other transforms can accomplish this end (e.g., Bracewell, 1986). The general univariate method for deriving the frequency spectrum from the Fourier transform is described in Bloomfield (1976). Multivariate spectral analysis is less frequently described, but there are some good sources (Harvey, 1981; Koopmans, 1974; Priestly, 1981). In multispectral analysis, it is the coherence that assumes the role of the correlation in the time domain. The major difference is that the coherence, which is the frequency domain analog of the multiple correlation coefficient, takes on values at each of the frequencies that link the pairs of series. It is possible, therefore, not only to look at the overall correlation between series but also to observe if there are particular frequencies in which the series may be associated. The major drawback of this methodology is that often frequency is not a theoretically meaningful way to view the data unless it is inherently cyclical. In addition, in order to get a reasonable resolution of frequencies, fairly long lags are needed. Tukey (1978) suggests 100–300 time periods.

State Transition Analysis

State transition analysis is becoming much more attractive as it is better understood by economists and other social scientists. A new book by Aoki (1987) offers a good synthesis of the current methodology. In spite of the computer programs of Akaike and the procedure in Statistical Analysis System (SAS; SAS Institute, 1980), easy to use programs are not available. Nevertheless, the methodology offers the most flexible approach to the more complex problems. For example, given the proper data set, possibilities related to models whose parameters can vary slowly in time can be examined, or the method may be used to compensate for nonconstant variance (Cartwright, 1984). This latter problem is common when one is dealing with volatile auction markets. One can show that any VARMA model may be represented in state space form (Hannan, 1976; Jones, 1982; Mehra, 1974), but the reverse is not true; the state space model is the more general.

CONCLUSIONS

The methods described in this chapter clearly are designed for and appropriate to single realizations of a long span of perhaps 100 time points. Such length is necessary in order to estimate the lagged cross-correlations with some degree of precision. In addition, if one is to estimate a reasonable number of Fourier frequencies, a long span is required. If the series are stationary, then time lagged correlations can be substituted for ensemble correlations. However, if the lagged correlations are available from several realizations, they can be used to increase the precision of the lagged correlation matrix, provided they can be pooled legitimately. The question then becomes one of justifying the lagged cross-correlation supermatrix (Table 5.1) as a block Toeplitz form. If this is the case and there are sufficient lags available, perhaps 20, then a model of the VARMA type might be estimated. This could be either a full model in the fashion of Box and Tiao (1981), or if there are many variables in the model, two approaches could be taken. The first would be to use one of the previously mentioned variable selection procedures; the second would be to perform a latent variable discovery procedure using dynamic factor analysis. Molenaar (1985) has suggested a method that is adapted to rather modest time spans. The advantage of using time dependent data rather than cross-sectional data for modeling is that the temporal nature of the data may be used to restrict the models. In most situations there is no single model to be tested, but rather a few generalities are known. The hope is to infer much of the model from the data. If it is possible to order the data in time, the number of models is substantially restricted. Coupled with the use of approximate significance tests of the parameters, the use of time dependent data can lead to a suitable model in many cases. However, it is well known that models derived in this manner are not in general unique. Nevertheless, they will be optimal in terms of their predictive capacity. Inspection of the coefficients of such models can shed light on the possible underlying causal generating mechanisms. Sims (1977, 1980) has used this approach with great effectiveness. It is clear that, although such methods offer much in potentially increasing the understanding of moderate span longitudinal data, there are problems to be overcome. One of these is obtaining comparable data over enough time periods. Another is the appropriate choice of the time interval; the longer the time interval is, the more difficult it is to get the data. Of course, the interval must be linked to the expected change of the variables being investigated.

COMMENTS ON "THE APPLICATION OF TIME SERIES METHODS TO MODERATE SPAN LONGITUDINAL DATA"

CHARLES S. REICHARDT

In the preceding chapter, Jones draws a distinction between time series data and longitudinal data. In broad terms, time series data consist of repeated observations on a single individual or entity. It is often said that methods for the analysis of time series data require that the number of repeated observations be at least 50. In contrast, longitudinal data consist of repeated observations on many individuals or entities. With longitudinal data, the number of individuals or entities usually is far greater than the number of time points, and the number of time points is often less than 10.

Over the years, different methods have been developed for the analysis of time series and longitudinal data. Jones's purpose is to explore the possibility of using time series methods to analyze longitudinal data of moderate length. As I understand Jones's argument, the time series methods he considers require that the data be stationary. Stationarity requires that the means, variances, and covariances of the data at Time 1 are the same as at Time 2, Time 3, and all other time points. Stationarity also requires that the covariances between the data at time t and the data at time $t + k$ are the same for all values of t, for any given value of k. This means, for example, that the covariances between the data at Times 1 and 2 are the same as the covariances between the data at Times 2 and 3, Times 3 and 4, and so on.

I thank Harry F. Gollob for helpful comments on earlier drafts of this comment.

Longitudinal data generally do not satisfy the assumptions of stationarity and generally cannot be usefully transformed to satisfy these assumptions. Therefore, time series methods that require stationarity probably are not widely applicable to longitudinal data. Moreover, even when the data are stationary, the potential benefits of applying time series methods to longitudinal data are not made clear, in my view, by Jones.

But even if time series methods usually cannot be applied to longitudinal data, the methodological perspectives that have been developed for the analysis of time series data may be enlightening to longitudinal researchers. The purpose of this comment is to illustrate briefly three differences in perspective that have evolved within the separate traditions of time series and longitudinal data analysis, with the hope that such comparisons may provide insights helpful to researchers from both traditions.

THE DEFINITION OF CAUSALITY

What does it mean to say that variable X causes variable Y? In the time series literature, the most widely used definition is probably the one provided by Granger (1969). In this definition, X is said to cause Y if present values of Y can be predicted using past values of both X and Y better than by using past values of Y alone. This means that to estimate the effect of X on Y, researchers must first take account of the autoregressive effects of Y on itself. Further, X is said to cause Y simultaneously, if present values of Y can be predicted by using both past and present values of X better than by using only past values of X, assuming that past values of Y are used in both cases.

In the longitudinal literature, the meaning of "X causes Y" typically is left unspecified. However, when causality is defined, the most common definition is the counterfactualist one that specifies that a change in Y is caused by a change in X if the change in Y would not have occurred if the change in X had not occurred (Holland, 1986). Gollob and Reichardt (1987) have argued that this definition implies that the effect of X on Y should be estimated by taking account of the autoregressive effect of Y on itself, as in Granger's definition. But this suggestion has been controversial (e.g., Hertzog & Nesselroade, 1987). In addition, the counterfactualist definition would seem to rule out simultaneous causality (Reichardt, 1988).

CAUSALITY DETECTION

On the basis of Granger's definition of causality, a variety of procedures has been developed in the time series literature for detecting whether X causes Y, whether Y causes X, or whether both X causes Y and Y causes X (Pierce & Haugh, 1977).

To detect the effect of X on Y, the most obvious procedure with time-series data is to regress present values of Y on past values of Y and on both past and present values of X. The effect of X on Y can also be detected, somewhat counterintuitively, by regressing X on past, present, and future values of Y. In this procedure, X causes Y if and only if future values of Y appear in the regression of X on past, present, and future values of Y.

Alternatively, the effect of X on Y can be detected by transforming both X and Y to white noise. This means that present values of X are regressed on past values of X, and present values of Y are regressed on past values of Y. The residuals from these two regressions produce two white noise processes. With these data, X causes Y if and only if past or present values of the X white noise process predict present values of the Y white noise process. Further, on the basis of Granger's definition, it can be shown that X causes Y simultaneously if and only if Y causes X simultaneously (Pierce & Haugh, 1977). So if simultaneous causality exists, it must be bidirectional.

In contrast, such a variety of causality detection procedures has not been developed and used in the analysis of longitudinal data. In addition, longitudinal data analysts often estimate models with simultaneous causality that is unidirectional.

DETRENDING THE DATA

In the time series literature, it is widely assumed that the causal relations between X and Y can be assessed properly only after trends in the means of X and Y are removed because it is assumed that the causal processes that account for trends in the means are different from the causal processes that account for the covariances between detrended variables.

In the time series literature, it is also thought to be more appropriate to assume that trends in the means of a variable are nondeterministic than to assume that these trends are deterministic. Further, it is generally believed that nondeterministic trends can be better removed by differencing the data (i.e., by taking differences between adjacent time points) than by regressing the data onto variables representing time, time squared, and the like (cf. McCleary & Hay, 1980). Two of the presumed advantages of removing trends by differencing the data rather than by regressing the data onto variables representing time are that (a) differencing does not imply trends in the data beyond the time periods that are observed, and (b) differencing can more parsimoniously model irregular trends, such as in stock market prices.

In the longitudinal literature, it is also common to detrend the data before analysis, though in this case detrending is usually accomplished by using covariance or correlation matrices, which is equivalent to detrending by subtracting the means of the variables. However, there has been recent interest in using moment matrices in the analysis of longitudinal data so as to model trends in the means of the variables with the same latent (and perhaps causal) variables that are used to model the relations (i.e., covariances) between the detrended variables (e.g., McArdle & Epstein, 1987). Further, trends in longitudinal data are usually assumed to be deterministic and are modeled by means of polynomial regressions with variables to represent time rather than by differencing.

CONCLUSIONS

Researchers concerned with the analysis of time series data have confronted many of the same problems as researchers concerned with the analysis of longitudinal data. Perhaps the perspectives and conceptualizations that each group of researchers has developed can enlighten the other. The three issues discussed in this comment are some of the ones on which the two separate traditions might profitably interact.

CHAPTER 6

INTERINDIVIDUAL DIFFERENCES IN INTRAINDIVIDUAL CHANGE

JOHN R. NESSELROADE

Editors' Introduction

In this thought-provoking chapter, Nesselroade provides a system in which most of the chapters and major issues of this book can be organized. In this system one sees that (a) the phenomena of interest to behavioral scientists occur in an infinite universe of persons, variables, and occasions; (b) research always involves only fallible samples drawn from this universe; and (c) the quality of the research design, and the quality of inference one can derive from research results, is primarily and fundamentally dependent on the adequacy of the samples drawn. This adequacy rests not only on the sample of persons, as considered in most applications of statistics, but also on the sample of variables and, most critically for studies of change, on the sample of occasions. Too often convenience, rather than thoughtful consideration of possibilities, determines how these samples are drawn. But if important strides in scientific understanding are to be made, sampling from these domains must be done in ways that make it possible to distinguish influences and identify the effects of uncontrolled variables. Nesselroade describes the kinds of possibilities that must be considered in designs in order to obtain adequate sampling from these domains.

This implies that in order to draw strong inferences in the study of change, one should obtain repeated measures on particular individuals

I am grateful to the MacArthur Foundation Research Network on Successful Aging and the Max Planck Institute for Human Development and Education, Berlin, for support of this research.

and have an adequate basis for generalizing from idiographic analyses of individuals to regularities that characterize all individuals. There should be adequate samples of different possible durations (the time during which influences operate to produce the major effects of interest) and possible intervals (the spacing between repeated measures); see also chapter 2 (Cohen) and chapter 15 (Gollob & Reichardt) in this volume. There should be opportunity to distinguish among the "hum" of short-period fluctuations, the changes that develop and endure over long periods of time, and the stable individual differences that characterize people despite fluctuations and changes. These matters are thoughtfully analyzed by Nesselroade.

The study of change requires that one look carefully beyond the statics to the dynamics of phenomena. As West (1985) pointed out, in the development of science a good job of analyzing statics is a necessary precursor to a successful job of analyzing dynamics.

After decades of doing battle, involving both direct (e.g., Harris, 1963) and indirect attacks (e.g., Cronbach & Furby, 1970) on the problems of representing, measuring, analyzing, and interpreting change, the researcher finds that many of the challenges of studying change are still unanswered, and most of the objectives remain to be taken. The occasion of this volume testifies to a lack of resolution of issues. Happily, it also suggests that behavioral and social scientists remain committed to resolving them.

FOCUS

The goal of this chapter is not to provide a technical treatment of change scores but rather to identify and discuss a set of conceptual issues that have emerged in the context of a couple of decades of trying to study change, especially developmental change. The approach to studying change on which I focus involves simultaneous consideration of multiple persons, multiple variables, and multiple occasions of measurement. Indeed, as is evident in some of the other chapters in this volume, change can (and should) be defined across a complex of observations, the dimensionality and nature of which are carefully chosen to reflect the various phenomena of interest to the investigator. In this chapter, I distinguish (a) between change as it is discussed in most chapters of this volume and short-term variability, (b) between changes in the ordering of individuals over time and individual differences in changes, and (c) between change that characterizes most people and change that characterizes individuals as such. Two fundamental points to be advanced are: first, that change needs to be studied at the intersection of variation across persons, variables, and occasions, and, second, that change involves research design, measurement, and analysis considerations, collectively.

THE DISTINCTION BETWEEN CHANGE AND VARIABILITY

The focus of the developmental orientation around which this chapter is organized is the study of interindividual differences in intraindividual changes (Baltes, Reese, & Nesselroade, 1977). Conceptual and empirical research stemming from this orientation has fostered recognition of the potential value of integrating two kinds of systematic intraindividual change in the study of development. These are referred to as *intraindividual variability* and *intraindividual change* (Nesselroade, 1988; Nesselroade & Featherman, in press; see also Fiske & Rice, 1955).

Intraindividual variability identifies short-term, relatively reversible changes or fluctuations. Examples are moods and emotions. Such changes are often identified as states in descriptions of the state–trait distinction.

Intraindividual change designates long-term changes that usually are relatively not so reversible. Examples are changes associated with development, learning, and progressive organic damage.

These two kinds of intraindividual phenomena are often depicted superimposed on each other, as, for example, in an economist's trend line and fluctuations about that trend line. The fluctuations about the trend line (intraindividual variability) are emphatically not to be thought of as "error," which is random fluctuation that also occurs. Rather, intraindividual variability is a coherent, interpretable steady-state "hum" that describes the base condition of the individual (Nesselroade, 1988; Nesselroade & Featherman, in press; Nesselroade & Ford, 1985). Indeed, in some respects the trend line can be visualized as a modulation of the steady-state hum somewhat analogous to the amplitude modulation of a radio frequency carrier wave.

Both intraindividual variability and intraindividual change are manifested with respect to variables or dimensions. Both kinds of changes can be reflected in the same observed variables while representing quite different kinds of latent or unobserved variables. Thus, the characterization of a given individual at any given point in time involves the individual's status on intraindividual change (e.g., trait change) latent variables and his or her status on intraindividual variability (e.g., state) latent variables. In addition, the individual's standing on stable interindividual differences latent dimensions (e.g., traits) is involved. Differences among persons at any one point in time thus reflect at least three sources of variance: stable individual differences, intraindividual changes, and intraindividual variability (see Cattell, 1966a). That is, in addition to stable traits, both kinds of intraindividual change phenomena can contribute to the among-persons variance (interindividual differences) as it appears at a particular point in time.

Intraindividual changes are confounded with more or less stable interindividual differences at any one measurement occasion. The magnitude of the contribution of intraindividual variability and change to among-persons variance is in direct proportion to the extent to which the two are asynchronous over persons. Across time, both kinds of change and stable trait variation remain as potential sources of differences among individuals. Thus, both intraindividual change and intraindividual variability are proper raw material on which to investigate interindividual differences (and similarities).

In light of this, to the extent that some variables manifest increased amongpersons variability with increasing age, possible explanations include both increased interindividual differences in intraindividual changes (differential trajectories of intraindividual change) *and* increased intraindividual variability, asynchronous over individuals. In physiological attributes of the very old, for example, intraindividual changes might reflect the accumulated effects of different life histories of illness, and intraindividual variabilities might indicate increasingly errant homeostatic mechanisms.

CHANGE IN INDIVIDUAL DIFFERENCES VERSUS INDIVIDUAL DIFFERENCES IN CHANGE

Developmentalists have concerned themselves for some time with both intraindividual change and interindividual differences. Wohlwill (1972) was among the first to distinguish thoroughly between *developmental aspects of individual differences* and *individual differences aspects of development* (see also Cattell, 1950; Emmerich, 1968). Wohlwill identified the aspect of developmental change that involves the study of the individual differences that are reflected in developmental functions. He argued for the utility of expressing differences among individuals in terms of the quantitative parameters and qualitative characteristics of developmental functions for given variables. He pointed out that the differences in parameters of developmental functions can be used for descriptive purposes and can be related to other information about individuals. Wohlwill argued that the methodologically and conceptually more difficult topic to study is the developmental aspect of individual differences. It involves (a) the origin and developmental course of individual differences, (b) differentiation of psychological attributes as the person develops, and (c) the transformations with age of dimensions of individual differences.

Wohlwill's emphases are important. They continue to be manifested in the efforts of developmental researchers. Among the methodological innovations that have helped to clarify issues implied in Wohlwill's distinction between change in individual differences and individual differences in change are the "Tuckerizing" of growth and learning performance scores (Meredith & Tisak, 1984; Tucker, 1966), McArdle's (1988) exposition of the differences between curves of factors and factors of curves, and the analyses of individual growth curves (Rogosa, Brandt, & Zimowski, 1982; Rogosa & Willet, 1985b).

In Table 6.1, the three kinds of variability discussed to this point are summarized to help keep the reader oriented toward change (and stability) issues both in the remainder of this chapter and in other chapters of this volume.

INDIVIDUAL VERSUS GROUP INFORMATION

One long-lived and important distinction between research orientations is that between idiographic and nomothetic approaches (Allport, 1937). The idiographic approach focuses on the uniqueness of each individual; the nomothetic approach aims to establish lawful relations that apply across individuals. The idiographic/ nomothetic distinction draws attention to important methodological issues and figures prominently in the study of change.

Table 6.1

DISTINCTIONS AMONG KINDS OF VARIABILITY

Kind of variability	Change characteristics	Example label	Other key features
Intraindividual variability	Relatively rapid, more or less reversible changes	State, mood	Contributes to characterizing an individual at a given point in time, thus confounding intraindividual change and interindividual differences; can have relatively slowly changing or stable interindividual-differences aspects, such as rate and amplitude of changes
Intraindividual change	Relatively slow changes reflecting processes such as development and learning	Trait change	Contributes to characterizing an individual at a given point in time and across time, and thus can confound interindividual differences; central to the interests of developmentalists in respect to both levels or traits and parameters in intraindividual variability distributions
Interindividual differences	Highly stable, even over lengthy amounts of time	Trait	Important, but not the only source of among-persons variance at a given point in time

P-technique factor analysis (Cattell, 1952b, 1966) is directed at appreciating and understanding the individual; it is an idiographic method. The P-technique involves repeated measurements of a single experimental unit (person) with a battery of measurement devices, each device yielding one or more different variables. The variables are chosen to cover a domain of interest. A representation of the data box (Cattell, 1952; 1966b), highlighting the slice of data involved in the P technique, is shown in Figure 6.1. The variables are covaried over occasions of measurement, and the covariances are decomposed into factors that are interpreted as the dimensions of change for the particular experimental unit. Horn's (1972) research on patterns of intraindividual variability and stable interindividual differences in ability-based performance illustrates how P-technique factors differ from the more conventional R-technique factors. In the ability of visualizing, for example, the intraindividual variability factor was characterized by tasks indicating fluctuations in ability to concentrate, fluctuations that accompany changes in fatigue, and so forth, whereas the comparable R-technique factor was more prom-

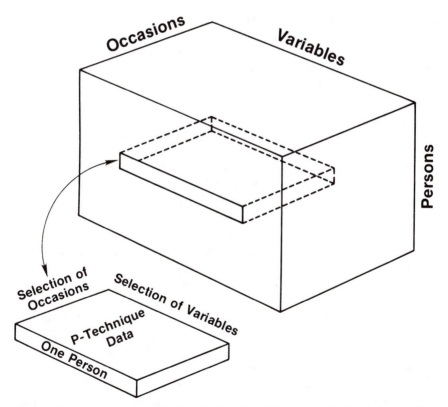

Figure 6.1   The data box, highlighting the slice of data targeted in P-technique studies.

inently marked by variables indicating relaxed ability to fix one's gaze on particular patterns.

Bereiter (1963) characterized P-technique factor analysis as "the logical way to study change." Zevon and Tellegen (1982) described how the P-technique can be used to define idiographic emphases at the level of intraindividual variability that, with multiple persons' data, could be put to the service of evolving more efficacious nomothetic representations encompassing both change and stability (see also Horn, 1972; Lamiell, 1981; Nesselroade & Ford, 1985).

Other recent and important work has incorporated this explicit focus on first "forming up" data at the individual level before trying to analyze the data for multiple individuals (e.g., Bryk & Raudenbush, 1987; Rogosa et al., 1982). Although this is an important gain in the study of change, this approach can place heavy demands on design, measurement, and the analysis resources of the researcher.

SELECTION AND GENERALIZABILITY IN THE DATA BOX

The distinctions of previous sections of this essay—different kinds of changes, interindividual differences in changes, idiographic and nomothetic approaches, and so on—point to a picture that involves a confluence of dimensions, all of which bear on the evaluation and interpretation of change. These multiple aspects of research place a large burden on the researcher seeking to develop adequate designs for data collection. The costs of not attending to demands for adequate design are measured in inadequate description and erroneous inference. These costs are high.

To formalize the nature of the demand for adequate design for developmental research, I have used Cattell's data box as a heuristic for specifying design features in terms of selection and selection effects (Nesselroade, 1983, 1988; see also Nesselroade & Jones, in press). The design and measurements that produce a set of data can be described as a set of selection operations that are performed on the data box to "extract" a set of observations for further analysis and interpretation. Because no one study can involve data on unlimited persons, variables, and occasions, the operations that define one's data also invoke *selection effects*. These selection effects restrict the generalizations that are possible from the selected data.

The three central modes of classification of the data box are *persons*, *variables*, and *occasions*. The selection effects of any set of data reflect two kinds of information: (a) the way variables are organized in nature, which is the information one is trying to apprehend; and (b) the nature of the selection operations defining the data. Research design and measurement operations will invariably involve greater selection along some modes of the data box than along others, while restricting selection in respect to others. Where selection is restricted, selection effects confound the estimates of the very relations in which one is interested.

The three basic modes of the data box are considered briefly in turn. Selection with respect to the occasions mode is emphasized because that aspect of selection can be linked most cogently to the study of change.

Person Selection

Selection of data with reference to the persons mode of the data box has received the most explicit and careful attention of methodologists and substantive researchers. With some exceptions (e.g., Brunswick, 1956; Cattell, 1952a; Humphreys, 1962), most discussions of "representative" sampling focus on this particular concern to the exclusion of concern for other modes. Rules and procedures for drawing samples of subjects (people) are relatively well worked out. Despite this knowledge about representative sampling of persons, "convenience" samples are the norm for most behavioral science studies. Data obtained from such samples are fraught with selection effects that affect estimates of the relations among variables being studied.

Practically speaking, representative sampling in its loftiest sense will remain an ideal except in rare instances. Therefore, researchers must continue to seek ways to make the best of the biased samples their data comprise. Thus, arguments that we must be as clear as possible about the design and sampling limitations of each data set so that we can explicitly attend to them in comparing outcomes across data sets are directly to the point (e.g., Donaldson & Horn, in press).

Variable Selection

The specific set of variables one *selects* to mark or indicate concepts is just that— a selection. It invites selection effects into the data as surely as convenience sampling of persons does. The threats due to selection of data with reference to the variables mode are becoming increasingly appreciated by researchers. This is manifested, in part, in the development of latent variable modeling, in which there is explicit concern for choosing manifest variables and constructing measurement models that validly reflect the latent variables of interest.

From a domain sampling viewpoint, some manifest variables must fall closer to the "centroid" of the concept's domain than others, so one's choice of markers will influence the measurement models and thus the estimates of interrelationships among concepts. This idea is illustrated in Figure 6.2. Work must be done to define precisely the effects of selection with respect to variables. If such definition is worked out, it will greatly aid our understanding of outcome differences when the "same" constructs are studied by means of "different" manifest variables.

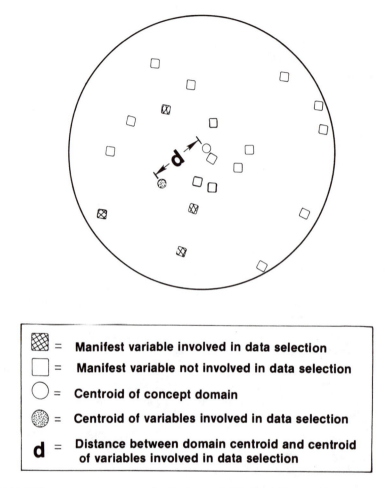

Figure 6.2   A representation of selection and selection effects with respect to the variables mode of the data box. From "Multimodal Selection Effects in the Study of Adult Development: A Perspective on Multivariate Replicated, Single- Subject, Repeated Measures Designs" by J. R. Nesselroade and C. J. Jones, in press, *Experimental Aging Research*. Copyright 1990 by Beech Hill Enterprises, Inc. Reprinted by permission.

Occasion Selection

Selection with respect to the occasions mode of the data box—that is, temporal selection (Nesselroade, 1983)—is at the core of the study of change. Change is defined across occasions of measurement. Statements that, with respect to (some) variables, persons are either stable or changing imply that one has information on two or more occasions of measurement. Both change and stability statements imply knowledge reflecting more than one occasion. The quality of one's generalizations regarding measurement occasions rests, in large part, on the nature of the temporal selection and selection effects characterizing one's data. In chapter 15, Gollob and Reichardt illustrate the point vividly with their discussion of the dependence of the magnitude of effects in structural models of longitudinal data on the magnitude of the interval between measurement of putative cause and measurement of outcome.

Temporal selection effects are illustrated by "sleeper effects" and the action of "slow viruses." Both of these phenomena involve the exposure of the organism to some event, the crucial aftermath of which occurs much later in time. In order for the "cause" and its "effect" to become linked by scientific investigation, the occasions dimension must be adequately represented in the nature of the data being collected. A too narrow sampling of occasions might pick up cause or effect but not both. This idea is illustrated in Figure 6.3 which shows putative cause, putative effect, and occasions as three intercorrelated variables. Narrow selection

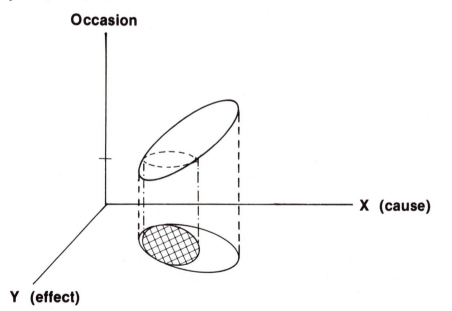

Figure 6.3 A representation of selection and selection effects with respect to the occasions mode of the data box. From "Multimodal Selection Effects in the Study of Adult Development: A Perspective on Multivariate Replicated, Single- Subject, Repeated Measures Designs" by J. R. Nesselroade and C. J. Jones, in press, *Experimental Aging Research.* Copyright 1990 by Beech Hill Enterprises, Inc. Reprinted by permission.

on the occasions variable attenuates the correlation (cross-hatched ellipse) between cause and effect, whereas more adequate representation of the occasion mode indicates the relation (open ellipse).

Sampling with respect to two different kinds of temporal units should be recognized. One type of temporal unit can be called *duration*. It is defined as the length of the observational period from the initial observation to the final one. This might be an hour or it might be 50 years. The second temporal unit is the *interval*. For example, 1-year or 5-year intervals might be used in a longitudinal study of 50 years' duration.

Setting values on the duration and interval is a research design consideration. Implementing the design involves occasion selection and thus introduces selection effects into one's data.

For students of change, the occasions mode is most important. Nevertheless, data are simultaneously characterizable by the other modes, too, so the data that bear on the analysis of change occur at the intersections of these various modalities of the data box.

This focus on the data box leads one to consider multiple individuals, occasions, and variables simultaneously. The multimodal nature of selection is thus seen to be inherent in empirical inquiry. Questions of generalizability explicitly involve attention to the several selection modes, as has been pointed out in discussions of generalizability by Campbell and Stanley (1967); Cattell (1966); and Cronbach, Gleser, Nanda, and Rajaratnam (1972).

MULTIVARIATE, REPLICATED, SINGLE-SUBJECT, REPEATED MEASUREMENT (MRSRM) DESIGNS

The most frequent criticism of P-technique research is that it involves only one individual. Indeed, one individual does represent a narrow selection along the persons mode of the data box. Such extreme selection invites strong selection effects. Concerns about the generalizability of findings based on one individual, or a small number of individuals, or even a large but unrepresentative number of individuals are pervasive in the research design and sampling literature. For this reason, some researchers (e.g., Horn, 1972; Lebo & Nesselroade, 1978; Zevon & Tellegen, 1982) have sought design and analysis schemes that enable one to extract information concerning intraindividual variability and change from data derived from multiple individuals. The strength of the P-technique is the generous selection of observations with respect to variables and occasions. To capitalize on this strength while avoiding or minimizing the penalties associated with a narrow selection of individuals, one can investigate intraindividual variability and change patterns simultaneously on multiple individuals (Horn, 1972; Lebo & Nesselroade, 1978; Nesselroade & Ford, 1985; Zevon & Tellegen, 1982).

A second line of criticism of the P-technique has centered on technical aspects of analyzing or modeling P-technique data (Holtzman, 1963; Molenaar, 1985). These include the failure of researchers who use the P-technique to account for serial dependencies in their data. In principle, this line of criticism is vitiated by developments in multivariate analysis during the past few years (e.g., McArdle, 1982; Molenaar, 1985), which provide for the explicit representation of serial dependencies in the factor-loading patterns, although these tools have yet to be applied routinely to this kind of data.

Substantive reviews of the literature on the P-technique and closely related studies (Jones & Nesselroade, in press; Luborsky & Mintz, 1972; Nesselroade, 1988) have demonstrated considerable support for the coherence of intraindividual variability in a wide variety of psychological attributes, including locus of control, temperament, work values, self-concept, depression, and even human abilities. This empirical evidence, along with the recognition of the existence of short-term fluctuations (intraindividual variability) by a wide variety of behavioral scientists (including proponents of classical test theory), has helped to reinforce the distinction between intraindividual variability and intraindividual change.

Combining the intraindividual variability and intraindividual changes, as is suggested in Figure 6.4, leads to a representation of the developing individual that accents the variable and occasion selection concerns described previously. Adding the identification of interindividual differences (and similarities) in intraindividual changes brings in the persons mode explicitly. Together, these modalities accentuate the complexities of developmental research.

To study interindividual differences (and similarities) in intraindividual change patterns creates a considerable demand on resources because it means extracting a multimodal selection of data from the data box. Moreover, design, measurement, and analysis concerns all are involved in defining the selected subset of data. Given the real-life constraints on research projects, that subset of actually collected data must, in turn, be of limited value because of selection effects. The best one can do is to try to shape the limits on the design in relation to the question being asked. Thus, in research design, trade-offs among modes become important. Developmental research requires more rather than fewer occasions, other things being equal. In the study of change, in general, it may be as important or more important to increase the number of occasions as the number of subjects when design constraints permit.

CONCLUSIONS

In light of a variety of concerns about the study of change phenomena, extant research and concepts have been organized and discussed in terms of three kinds of variability. These include short-term, more or less reversible changes (intrain-

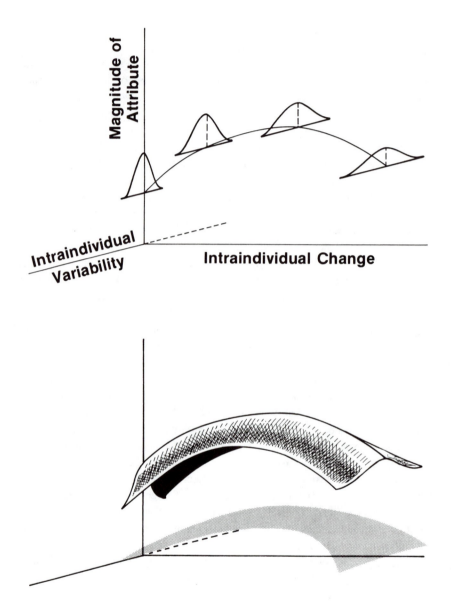

Figure 6.4   Combining intraindividual variability and intraindividual change to represent the fabric of development. From ''The Warp and the Woof of the Development Fabric'' by J. R. Nesselroade in *Visions of Development, the Environment, and Aesthetics: The Legacy of Joachim F. Wohlwill* edited by R. Downs, L. Liben, and D. S. Palermo, in press, Hillsdale, NJ: Erlbaum. Copyright 1990 by Lawrence Erlbaum Associates, Inc. Reprinted by permission.

dividual variability); slower, more regular changes, such as those involved in development and learning (intraindividual change), and relatively stable interindividual differences such as those labeled traits. The presence of the three kinds of variability can create serious design problems for researchers interested in one or another aspect of change (and stability). For example, at any given instance of measurement, these three sources of variability are confounded in estimates of interindividual differences. When one focuses on the person, at any given instance of measurement intraindividual variability and intraindividual change are confounded. Moreover, characteristics of intraindividual variability at the level of the individual (e.g., means, variances, periodicities, and so on) can be the substance for both intraindividual change and stable interindividual differences.

Thus, the study of change (and stability) is rich with possibilities that need to be disentangled from one another. This situation is further complicated by other well-known issues. One involves the integration of idiographic concerns, which emphasize understanding what is taking place at the individual level, with nomothetic concerns for developing general statements of lawfulness.

A second key issue is that of generalizability of one's research findings, whether they are focused on change or stability. The discussion of generalizability in this chapter has explicitly recognized the several different data classification dimensions described by Cattell (1952b, 1966b, 1988) in his data box heuristic and emphasizes how any set of manifest data is a selection from the vast data box of nature. Thus, collected data are subject to selection effects in relation not only to selection of persons but also to selection of variables and to selection of occasions of measurement. The latter includes both historical epochs and time intervals, for instance, and thus bears critically on matters of change and stability. The selection emphasis is intended to force researchers to confront the complexity (and the consequences) of the choices they must make about samples of persons, choice of measures, retest intervals, and so forth, in designing research.

The line of argument pursued here is that the study of change is properly construed in the context of selection and generalizability issues as defined in relation to the data box. Placing the study of change in the data box emphasizes systematic representation of the various dimensions that characterize data and their interrelations. It also underscores the point that the representation of change involves a complex of issues that cut across design, measurement, and analysis concerns. If we are to make progress in articulating better (if not yet the best) methods for the analysis of change, we will have to face these issues.

CHAPTER 7

ISSUES IN FACTORIAL INVARIANCE

WALTER R. CUNNINGHAM

Editors' Introduction

In chapter 7, Cunningham deals with a question that is basic to any statement about change: "What is it that changes? Is the change (thought to be) from one quality (e.g., *A*) to another (e.g., *B*), where *A* and *B* are fundamentally different, or is the change from magnitude *m1* to magnitude *m2* in a particular quality?"

There is little doubt that in science it is often useful to regard phenomena as changing qualitatively, for example, as water vapor changes to water and water changes to ice. But often, too, it is useful to regard change quantitatively, for example, as height increases with age in childhood (see Bock, chapter 8). Indeed, quantitative changes often provide a basis for describing qualitative change. For example, quantitative changes in different skeletal dimensions—length, width, and breadth of head, body, legs, and so on provide a basis for describing the qualitative change from infancy to adulthood in the figural shape of the human body. Similarly, to the extent that we can describe qualitative changes in what we refer to as human intelligence (as from concrete to logical operations), we do so in terms of changes we describe quantitatively, as in conversation, verbal comprehension, and fluid reasoning.

It is important to be clear about whether one is analyzing qualitative or quantitative change. Factors that need to be carefully considered in making this distinction are discussed in chapter 6 (Nesselroade), chapter 9 (Collins), and chapter 13 (Widaman). This chapter focuses on quantitative change.

Given that the aim is to describe change quantitatively, it is important that the same attribute be measured at the different points over which change is thought to occur. A description of quantitative change in height would be of little use if the measure were, at one point, toe-to-nose length; at another point, toe-to-navel length; and, at still another point, chin-to-nose length. Such a muddle is unlikely in the measure of height because the operations of measurement can be the same at different points in development, and that which is measured can be seen to be—calibrated to be—the same (Bock, chapter 8). But when the psychological attributes of humans are measured, often the operations of measurement are not, and cannot be, the same; even when they are the same, it is not immediately clear that they measure the same attribute.

Thus the fundamental issue Cunningham addresses is that of measurement invariance: When the operations of measurement are the same, how can we be clear about whether or not these operations produce measures of the same attribute when they are used at different points over which change is to be recorded?

Questions about factorial invariance, the principal focus of this chapter, are questions about measurement invariance because the factor measures implicit in factor analysis are linear composites, and linear composite measurement is the most common kind of measurement in the behavioral sciences. The logic and procedures for producing evidence in support of factorial invariance are, in principle, the same as the logic and procedures for demonstrating invariance in linear composite measures in general (Horn & McArdle, 1990; Horn, McArdle, & Mason, 1983). Thus, if measurements are obtained as linear composites, then when one asks if what is measured at one time is the same as what is measured at another time, one asks, in effect, if the same elements of the composite measure the same attribute in the same way under different conditions. This is the basic question of factorial invariance; Cunningham examines it in some detail.

Factorial invariance has long been an important issue within factor analysis. Invariance is also a fundamental topic in the study of change. The basic concept is the logical opposite of change—the consistency of results across variations in subjects and variables in factor analytic research.

The term *factorial invariance* is usually used in early writings (e.g., Thurstone, 1947) to indicate identical factor loadings, typically across different studies involving different samples of subjects. The term is also used in both a more restrictive sense and a less restrictive one. A very restrictive form of invariance requires identical factor variance/covariance matrices across samples of subjects. This implies equal uniquenesses and factor loadings. A less restrictive form of invariance requires only that the same loadings be salient across samples. Thus, the pattern of the simple structure would be the same across samples although parameter values need not be identical.

Another term sometimes used to indicate factor invariance (stability) of loadings over time within a sample is *stationarity*. However, stationarity is better used in the context of autoregressive models to refer to stability among sets of covariances.

EARLY INVARIANCE THEORIES

Early factorists regarded invariance as a criterion for the validity of the factor analytic method. Thurstone (1947) devoted a chapter to invariance in his classic book, *Multiple Factor Analysis*. It is essential to realize that Thurstone developed the concept of simple structure with the aim of providing a basis for obtaining consistent factor analysis results. His development of the conditions of invariance was motivated in part by critics of factor analysis. He recognized that factor loadings and factor covariances cannot be expected to be exactly invariant from one population to another (he used different age groups as an example), but he maintained that, if there were a simple structure, exact numerical invariance for loadings could be expected from several samples drawn from the same population, within the limits of sampling error. Thurstone hoped that simple structure criteria would lead to more invariant results.

Ahmavaara (1954) summarized the mathematical theory of invariance under selection. He showed that the selection formulas developed earlier by Aiken are equivalent to a linear transformation in the factor space. Ahmavaara offered a proof of Thurstone's claim regarding the invariance of simple structure under selection. He also showed that multivariate selection can always be reduced to successive univariate selections. Ahmavaara's research showed the importance of working with the variance/covariance matrix (rather than correlations). Further, his work showed that (except for very special selection cases), if a simple structure existed in the unselected analysis, that simple structure was generally invariant.

In two seminal papers, Meredith (1964a, 1964b) applied Lawley's selection theorem to subpopulations selected from a parent population. Assuming that selection did not occur directly on the observed variable and also that the selection did not reduce the rank of the solution, he demonstrated that a factor pattern matrix describing the regression of the observed factor variables in all subpopulations was invariant but that such a factor pattern was not unique. Also, Meredith showed that if a satisfactory simple structure could be determined in one subpopulation, the same simple structure could be found in any subpopulation derived by selection. The argument regarding invariance of loadings (regressions) assumed linearity and homoscedasticity of the regression of the observed variable on the selection variable.

Meredith's conclusions require that the same unit of measurement be used across subpopulations, which means that standardization within subpopulations must be avoided. The conclusions also require that factor comparisons be based on factor pattern matrices rather than on factor structure matrices. Mulaik (1972) provides a very clear presentation of this material.

Jöreskog's Model

Jöreskog (1971) presents a very general model for examining similarities and differences between factor structures in different groups. The model allows any parameter (factor loadings, factor variances, factor covariances, and unique variances) to be assigned arbitrary values or to be constrained to be equal to some other value. Given these specifications, the model can be estimated by the maximum likelihood method, and resulting large sample chi-squares can be obtained to indicate goodness of fit. This approach allows one to examine different degrees of invariance; also, it does not require that the number of variables or common factors be the same for all groups. The approach is applicable whether the population is derived by selection or not.

Jöreskog's procedure begins by a test of the hypotheses of equality of the covariance matrices. If this hypothesis is found to be tenable, all factor characteristics for all groups can be obtained from the pooled covariance matrix, and there is no need to analyze each group separately. If this hypothesis is found to be untenable (as in the vast majority of analyses), one can then test for the equality of the number of common factors. If this hypothesis is not rejected, one can then test the hypothesis of an invariant factor loading pattern and also the equality of the unique variances, the equality of factor variances, or other hypotheses. The hypothesis of equal unique variances is usually of primary interest to researchers focusing on the psychometric properties of variables.

The model requiring identical factor loadings and factor variance/covariances is often of interest. Because substantively oriented researchers often have theoretically derived hypotheses regarding increases or decreases in shared variance across groups, a commonly adopted model requires factor loadings and the factor variance/covariance matrix to be identical across groups. Some factors may be constrained to be orthogonal, whereas others are allowed to be oblique.

Extreme invariance requires identical uniquenesses as well as identical loadings and equality of factor variance/covariance matrices across groups, but this model is extremely demanding and is almost never consistent with real data obtained from different groups that vary in some systematic way. With regard to the statistical tests of fit, Jöreskog (1971) also commented,

> It should be emphasized that significance levels are unknown when a sequence of tests like these [is] carried out and that even if a chi-square is large, there may be reasons to consider the model. After all, the basic model with its assumptions of linearity and normality is only regarded as

an approximation to reality. The true population covariance matrix will not in general be exactly of the form specified by the hypothesis, but there will in general be discrepancies between the true population covariance matrix and the formal model postulated. These discrepancies will not get smaller when the sample size increases but will tend to give large chi-square values. Therefore, a model may well be accepted even though chi-square is large. Whether to accept or reject a model cannot be decided on a purely statistical basis. This is largely a matter of the experimenter's interpretations of the data, based on substantive theoretical and conceptual considerations. Ultimately the criteria for goodness of the model depends on the usefulness of it and the results it produces. (p. 421)

A key advance in Jöreskog's approach involves the investigator's latitude in constraining various parameters of the model, which pushes factor analysis distinctly further in the direction of a strict hypothesis testing procedure. A detailed application of Jöreskog's approach was given in McGaw and Jöreskog (1971).

Metric Invariance Versus Configural Invariance

Horn, McArdle, and Mason (1983) contrasted metric invariance of factor loadings (or other aspects of the factor model) with Thurstone's original idea of configural invariance, which requires only that the configuration of zero loadings and salient loadings remain the same. Horn et al. (1983) further argued that exact metric invariance, that is, identical loadings, across groups is scientifically unrealistic.

Researchers who analyze data across groups are quick to appreciate the reasonableness of Horn et al.'s (1983) position. Models requiring a very "rigid" invariance (all model parameters identical) are rarely supported by empirical data. When such rigid models show reasonable fits, they usually have a contrived character. In my experience (perhaps three dozen comparative factor analyses), such a model is usually rejected as a poor fit with the data. In a sizable minority of cases, exactly identical loadings are found. In relatively rare cases, even identical factor variance/covariances or uniquenesses are found. When more flexible configural constraints are employed, highly similar salient loadings usually result, with often trivial differences between groups and the same simple structure. Let me emphasize that good design is necessary to guarantee satisfactory simple structure.

These observations lead one logically to consider levels of invariance that are wider than those proposed by Jöreskog. These levels include various weaker forms of configural invariance. As a logical extension of Horn et al.'s (1983) arguments, it seems wise for researchers in invariance to think out carefully in advance what level of invariance is required to fulfill the goals of the research.

For example, in many theoretically oriented studies and even more so in applied research situations, strict metric invariance is not really needed: Key issues such as the generality of factorial validity across groups often are fully satisfied by configural invariance. On the other hand, if the researcher wishes to maintain strict operational consistency across groups or occasions of measurement, then more demanding forms of invariance are necessary. The point I wish to make is that the level of invariance depends on the hypotheses, goals, and objectives of the researcher.

If one thinks in terms of an expanded level of invariance to include relaxed forms of configural invariance, much of the discrepancy between Horn et al. and Meredith/Jöreskog disappears. When one considers these issues, a question naturally arises as to why these models requiring equal factor loadings are so often rejected. On the surface, Meredith's conclusions regarding selection seem to imply that equal factor loading patterns will often be found. This discrepancy can be resolved by observing that Meredith's mathematical reasoning is well in advance of the quality of most empirical data. Two assumptions underlying Meredith's arguments often are not met in practice: (a) linearity, and most important, (b) the homoscedasticity of the regression of observed variables on selection variables. Also, the normality of errors assumption may not be exactly met in practice.

Given the likelihood of modest violations of assumptions, the intuitive expectation would be approximate rather than exact invariance—one of the key points made by Horn et al. (1983). In the context of development and aging, one could also consider whether groups of different ages should be thought of as samples from the same parent population (in this context) or as members of different populations, which was an example Thurstone used.

Given these observations regarding levels, possible violations of assumptions underlying the reasoning about selection, and also the issue of age and sample-population relationships, the Horn et al. (1983) article is an extension of both Jöreskog's and Meredith's positions, and perhaps also a reminder of "old truths" alluded to by Thurstone decades ago.

STANDARDIZATION OF COVARIANCE MATRICES

Another interesting recent article by Robert Cudeck (1989) published in the *Psychological Bulletin* concerns the scaling of covariance matrices. It has been well known since the 1940s that correlation matrices standardized within several groups can create problems in multigroup studies of invariance. This makes it impossible for means and variances to vary from one group to another and distorts the covariances in consequence. A procedure that reduces the problems is standardizing across groups (rather than within groups). However, Cudeck points out that if in analyses a standardization is employed (across groups) that specifies a model with fixed unities for factors on the main diagonal of the factor variance/covariance—that is, the factors within groups are required to be in standard score form—

the resulting matrix results in a model that is not scale invariant. Cudeck argues that "structural models cannot be arbitrarily applied to a matrix of correlations" without risking problems, such as incorrect test statistics, standard errors, and incorrect parameter estimates. He cites 18 published articles by Jöreskog, other prominent researchers, and the present writer in which problems of this sort occur. Cudeck is right. His article is important reading in this area.

Invariance and Change

Two other recent articles in *Psychometrika* describe interesting new models for studying change that are pertinent because they involve variations in degree of invariance. Millsap and Meredith (1988) extend component analysis to both longitudinal and cross-sectional data. The model is particularly attuned to developmental studies in that a series of cohorts can be followed over time. The components can be derived with the restriction of invariance/stationarity of loading weights, but these constraints can also be relaxed. A two cohort longitudinal example is also presented.

In another important article, Tisak and Meredith (1989) describe a method for carrying out exploratory longitudinal factor analysis in multiple groups, obviously in response to the fact that many previously proposed longitudinal factor analysis approaches (such as LISREL) involve highly "structured" or confirmatory models. The analysis may be conducted with or without stationarity constraints. The approach clearly extends the realm of what is possible in many longitudinal studies of development.

Empirical Examples

As concrete examples of the kinds of hypotheses that might be tested, as well as possible results, some work from my research on factorial invariance is discussed next.

As an extreme example of dissimilarity of factorial structure, consider the results of a study by White and Cunningham (1987). This study concerned the structure of certain speeded cognitive ability factors as represented by four measures of simple and choice reaction time, six measures of Sternberg reaction time, and three measures of card sorting. It should be mentioned that the Sternberg reaction time measures consisted of two measures with verbal content, two with symbolic content, and two with figural content. Data were gathered on two groups: (a) 150 young adults ranging in age from 18 to 33 years, and (b) 150 older adults ranging in age from 58 to 73.

Results indicated that in the young adult, a three factor solution corresponding to the three types of task demands accounted well for the covariances among the variables. However, for the older adults, neither a three nor even a four factor solution was satisfactory. With a five factor solution, a satisfactory fit was obtained. Exploratory Promax rotations resulted in a solution in which three of the factors were very similar to the results with the young adult sample. One of the extra factors appeared to be an artifact of order in the older adult sample. However, in the older adult sample, a separate Figural Sternberg factor emerged, in contrast to the young adult sample, in which all six Sternberg tasks loaded on the same factor. These results illustrate a situation in which there are substantial differences in structure between old and young, and even the possibility of testing for equivalence of factor loadings is preempted by a change in the number of factors.

As a specific example of an unusually similar structure, consider an analysis carried out by Cunningham and Birren (1980), in which a group of college students tested with one of the original forms of the Army Alpha Examination in 1919 was contrasted with a group of college students tested with the Nebraska Edition of the Army Alpha Examination in the early 1970s. Very similar structures were obtained. The number of factors, the factor loadings, and even the factor intercorrelations were found to be identical even though the two groups from which the data were obtained differed in cohort membership by more than 50 years.

These two examples mark extremes in our experience in comparing ability structures in groups of different ages and cohorts. The most common result is a situation in which there are statistically significant differences in the exact values of factor loadings, but, after independent rotations, these differences in loadings tend to be quite small, and configural invariance is obtained. The next most common result is the situation where there are no significant differences in the exact values of factor loadings, but there are highly significant differences in factor variance/covariance matrices and the uniquenesses.

CONCLUSIONS

To summarize key points, it is clear that factorial invariance is an important issue in the study of change. Second, it seems useful to think in terms of levels of invariance. Third, only relaxed forms of invariance, such as configural invariance, are to be expected or needed with most data sets and many research objectives. Finally, it is critical to test for more stringent forms of invariance, because when they are found, they are often of considerable substantive interest and may be useful in quantification in the study of change.

COMMENTS ON "ISSUES IN FACTORIAL INVARIANCE"

JOHN L. HORN

Cunningham has described the intricacies of determining what it is about linear composites—factors—that might change, or not change (i.e., be "invariant"), when there is change in the situations in which the composites are obtained. These intricacies of determining factorial invariance are the intricacies of determining measurement invariance. Cunningham points to different levels of intricacy—different levels of factorial invariance—and suggests that the level of invariance sought, required, or assumed in a given study should be consistent with the objectives of the research. Let us consider these matters in overview and summary.

MEASUREMENT INVARIANCE

First, consider the notion that tests of factorial invariance are tests of measurement invariance. In this we might step back to get the broad perspective and see two basic kinds of evidence of measurement invariance: stability within subjects and invariance in linear composites. Analyses to show factorial invariance provide evidence of the second of these two kinds of invariance.

It is possible to establish stability within subjects if the same sample of subjects is measured on two or more occasions and the measured attribute is (assumed to be) a trait for which the order of magnitude of the measurements is perfectly stable over occasions. Under these conditions, a high correlation between the measurements taken on different occasions (high test–retest reliability) indicates that the same attribute is measured on these occasions; this evidence is not unequivocal, however, for reasons considered next.

If the measured attribute is not (assumed to be) order-of-magnitude stable, as in a trait, lack of retest correlation between measurements obtained on different occasions is not indicative of lack of invariance of measurement. Also, if different subjects are measured on different occasions, correlations over occasions cannot be obtained, so test–retest reliability cannot be calculated to provide evidence that the same attribute is measured on the different occasions.

Under these two conditions, if measurements are obtained as linear composites, the question of measurement invariance can be framed as one of factorial invariance. This is true because there is an equivalence in the logic and procedures for producing evidence for evaluating factorial and measurement invariance. The details of this equivalence are rather intricate (Horn & McArdle, in press; Horn, McArdle, & Mason, 1983), but one need not grasp all the details to understand the reasoning and arrive at the main conclusions. The main points can be summarized as follows:

1. The methods of factor analysis indicate relations, $\mathbf{P}_{kj}$, between factor measurements and variable measurements.
2. In factor analysis, the factor measurements, $\mathbf{X}_{ji}$, for person i on factor j, are (implicitly in the model and estimated in calculation) weighted (by $\mathbf{W}_{jk}$) linear combinations of the variable measurements, $\mathbf{Z}_{ki}$, of person i and variable (i.e., element) k, where in general there are $k = 1, 2, \ldots, n$ elements and $i = 1, 2, \ldots, N$ persons. This is summarized crisply in the following equation:

$$\mathbf{X}_{ji} = (\mathbf{W}_{j1})(\mathbf{Z}_{1i}) + (\mathbf{W}_{j2})(\mathbf{Z}_{2i}) + \ldots (\mathbf{W}_{jk})(\mathbf{Z}_{ki}) \ldots + (\mathbf{W}_{jn})(\mathbf{Z}_{ni}) \quad (1)$$

3. The $\mathbf{W}_{jk}$ weights usually are not literally the coefficients indicating the relations ($\mathbf{P}_{kj}$) between factors and elements, but they are derived directly from these relations, such that if the $\mathbf{P}_{kj}$ are invariant, so too are the $\mathbf{W}_{jk}$.
4. To demonstrate factorial invariance across different situations in which $\mathbf{X}_{ji}$ is measured—symbolizing this as $\mathbf{X}_{jis}$ to indicate $s = 1, \ldots, t$ situations—is to show, by testing a refutable hypothesis, that the $\mathbf{P}_{kjs}$ (hence $\mathbf{W}_{jks}$) obtained in different situations are not different. One statistical test of this kind is that of goodness of fit for a model in which corresponding $\mathbf{P}_{kj}$ in different samples are required to be equal. As Cunningham pointed out, other features of a factor analytic solution also might be required to be equal. The requirement for factor measurement invariance is that the $\mathbf{W}_{jkq}$ weights calculated in any one situation, q, yield essentially the same array of measurements when used in any other situation (i.e., to within a linear transformation of each other). In the summary solution of a factor analysis (the factor mea-

surements are usually not actually calculated), this requirement is that the $\mathbf{P}_{kjq}$ coefficients obtained in any situation, q, provide the same relational information in any other (sampled) situation. The requirement is essentially the same as the requirement of cross-validation (double cross-validation) in regression analysis. The measurements obtained in sample A with the weights of samples B, D, and so on must be perfect linear transformations of the measurements obtained with the weights of sample A.

5. Psychological measurements usually are linear composites obtained in the manner indicated by Equation 1, the elements being the item subscores (often simply "1" or "0") added to give the measure (e.g., the "number of right answers," "the number of turns in the maze," or "the sum of reaction times"). The element weights for different items in such composites, although often implicitly assumed to be the same (i.e., equal to unity), are different. The different items contribute more and less to the overall measures. This can be shown objectively with a factor analysis. Differences in factor coefficients indicate differences in the extent to which the subscores for each item, relative to the subscores for all other items, measure an attribute. Such differences indicate that different attributes are measured.

6. Thus, if the same items are combined in different situations to obtain measurements of the same (by hypothesis) psychological attribute, then these linear composites should satisfy the conditions (specified in Item 4) for factorial invariance. The element weights of measurement $\mathbf{W}_{ji}$ should not be different across situations, the weights for any situation should yield measures that are linear transformations of the measures obtained with the weights of any other situation, the relational coefficients $\mathbf{P}_{kj}$ indicating the weights should be the same to within a linear transformation in all samples, and it should be reasonable to retain the hypothesis of fit for a model requiring all corresponding $\mathbf{P}_{kj}$ weights to be equal (to within a linear transformation) in different situations.

A concrete example may be helpful at this point. Suppose that a researcher aims to show that self-esteem increases from 20 to 60 years of age and that self-esteem is (hypothesized) to be measured by adding the number of "yes" answers to the following three questions:

$\mathbf{Z}_1$: Do you feel you are as good-looking as the average person?
$\mathbf{Z}_2$: Do you feel you are every bit as smart as the average person?
$\mathbf{Z}_3$: Do you feel you are liked by others as much as the average person is liked?

Suppose, further, that the following are factor patterns (for a single factor) found for the items measuring self-esteem in large samples of 20-year olds and 60-year-olds:

$$X_{ji} = .6(Z_{1i}) + .3(Z_{2i}) + .4(Z_{3i}) \text{ for individuals } i \text{ in the sample of 20-year-olds,}$$

$$X_{ji} = .0(Z_{1i}) + .8(Z_{2i}) + .4(Z_{3i}) \text{ for individuals } i \text{ in the sample of 60-year-olds,}$$

where, in accordance with Equation 1, j represents self-esteem; i represents an individual; the X_{ji}s are measures of self-esteem; k is 1, 2, or 3 representing Items 1, 2, or 3, the Z_{ki}s are the item subscores; and the decimal numbers multiplying the Z_{ki}s are the weights (W_{jk}s) found in separate factor analyses in large samples.

These factor analytic results thus indicate that self-esteem is represented in a different way in the thinking of young and old people. In young people, it is indicated more by self ratings of "looks" (how one feels about one's looks, it might be assumed) than by self-ratings for smartness. In samples of older people the opposite is true: Self-ratings of looks do not enter at all into self-esteem. In the sample of 20-year-olds, a yes answer to Item 1 increases the self-esteem score by .6, but such a self-rating does not increase the self-esteem score at all in the sample of 60-year-olds. Thus, the self-esteem measured in the linear composite for young people is different from self-esteem measured in the composite for older people. This was discovered by factor analysis.

Such findings indicate qualitative differences in what is measured and call into question the logic of performing analyses designed to indicate quantitative differences or quantitative changes. For example, if one were to count the number of yes answers to all three items of the example under the assumption that one was measuring the same self-esteem in the two samples and then compared the means on this linear composite for the samples of young and the old people, one would be comparing means for different things. A difference in such averages would not indicate a quantitative difference, nor would it necessarily indicate a qualitative difference. It could indicate neither. Basically, the comparison is ambiguous. To compare qualitatively different things with quantitative analysis is to generate confusion.

In our example, differences in averages for the young and the old might falsely suggest that the young people had higher self-esteem than the older people, whereas in fact the two groups did not differ in self-esteem when the same thing was measured in the two groups. In one possible configuration of this outcome, the means for all items could be the same in the two samples. The results might look as follows:

For the young, $X_{ji} = .6(.5) + .3(.5) + .4(.5) = .65$.
For the old, $X_{ji} = .0(.5) + .8(.5) + .4(.5) = .60$

The means for all items are .5 in both samples. The young appear to have higher self-esteem because looks are weighted heavily in their thinking about self-esteem, whereas looks are not so weighted in the sample of older people. On Item 3, however, the one item that enters into self-esteem measures to the same extent in both groups (the evidence suggests), the groups do not differ. Thus, comparing averages for qualitatively different concepts would lead one quite falsely to the conclusion that the mean self-esteem for 20-year-olds is greater than the mean for 60-year-olds. As we have said, this would happen because the looks item contributes to the measure of self-esteem in young people, but not in older people.

On first consideration, one might think that if the mean on the looks item is substantial in the sample of older people—the same as in the sample of young people—the item should come into the concept of self-esteem in the sample of old individuals. But on further reflection, it becomes apparent that the averages for many things could be substantial in both samples, but that would not indicate whether those things are part of a concept of self-esteem. The average for "wearing or not wearing a tie," for example, could be the same in both groups, but knowing that would not help one determine if wearing a tie is part of a linear composite measure of self-esteem. The fact that the mean on the looks item is the same in the sample of 60-year-olds as in the sample of 20-year-olds does not threaten the assumption that the looks are not a part of a measure of self-esteem in the sample of older individuals: Correlation, the basic statistic indicating the extent to which elements contribute in a measurement, is not affected by the averages of variables.

We see, then, that if statements about quantitative change are to be unambiguous, it is important that the elements of composite measurements be invariant across the situations over which change is said to occur, and we also see that a hypothesis stipulating such invariance can be evaluated with the methods of factor analysis. Only one scale of measurement—one factor—was considered in the example, but questions about factorial invariance are usually addressed to a set of factors, that is, 1, 2, . . ., m factors.

MULTIPLE FACTOR ANALYSIS

A requirement of invariance simultaneously over several factors is in some ways more, and in some ways less, demanding than a requirement of invariance for a single factor (granted that the multiple factor requirement is more realistic, more indicative of the conditions under which research should be done). The requirement for multiple factors demands that a measure of a given factor be the same in different situations under conditions that allow the measurement contributions of elements to be distributed over several factors. This distribution is for "parted-out" contributions.

To describe the contributions as parted out is to recognize that in multiple factor analysis, the $\mathbf{P}_{kj}$ factor coefficients are similar to partial correlations: They represent the extent to which an element measures the kth factor when the effects of other $(m - 1)$ factors are partialed out. An element's contribution to measurement of one factor might thus be "taken" by another factor and thus be partialed out. This makes the requirement for invariance more demanding. But because elements that are not part of the attribute one seeks to measure can be removed by the partialing of factor analysis and thus be statistically controlled, the requirement for invariance in multiple-factor space is less demanding than if the requirement is imposed one factor at a time.

In sum, then, clear statements about change in quantity should be premised on evidence that the same attribute is measured under the different conditions over which change is assumed to occur. If there is no evidence, pro or con, indicating measurement invariance (which is most commonly true), then either change in quantity or no apparent change in quantity may reflect qualitative change. Statements about quantitative change under such conditions are misleading. This is true also if there is evidence indicating that measurement invariance does not obtain. When measurement invariance is lacking, differences between individuals and groups cannot be interpreted unambiguously. If measurement invariance is lacking, then differences between means can just as well be interpreted as indicating that different things are measured as that there are quantitative differences in one thing measured. A finding of no difference in means can be interpreted in the same way. Just as interpretations of differences between means are confused when measurement invariance is not known to obtain, so are interpretations of correlations and other results from analyses of measurements. Without evidence of measurement invariance, the conclusions of a study must be weak.

FACTORIAL INVARIANCE

A test of factorial invariance is an objective means of providing evidence that the same attribute is measured under different conditions. It is a test of measurement invariance. It is not the only test; test–retest correlations can also indicate measurement invariance in stable attributes (traits). A test of factorial invariance is not always appropriate; it works only for linear composite measures (but almost all measurements in the behavioral sciences are linear composites). It is not always necessary; assumption is adequate in some kinds of studies. But it is necessary for unambiguous interpretation of results under conditions of comparison of linear composite measurements—in particular, comparison over occasions to infer change. It behooves us, therefore, to study factorial invariance.

The different levels of factorial invariance Cunningham describes can be examined in terms of goodness of fit for different parts of a model based on the following equation:

$$\mathbf{Z}_{ki} = (\mathbf{P}_{k1})(\mathbf{X}_{1i}) + (\mathbf{P}_{k2})(\mathbf{X}_{2i}) + \ldots (\mathbf{P}_{kj})(\mathbf{X}_{ji}) + \ldots + (\mathbf{P}_{km})(\mathbf{X}_{mi}), \qquad (2)$$

where

> $\mathbf{Z}_{ki}$ is an observed score obtained for individual i on element k (i.e., item, subscore, or variable k), there being N individuals, $i = 1, \ldots, N$, and n elements, $k = 1, \ldots, n$.
>
> $\mathbf{X}_{ji}$ is a factor measurement of individual i on factor j, there being m factors, $j = 1, \ldots, m$. Depending on the model, m may or may not be equal to n.
>
> $\mathbf{P}_{kj}$ is a weight by which factor measurements are multiplied before being added to yield the scores of element k.

In the most common form of factor analysis—common-factor analysis—there is partitioning of the variance of the observed elements into common-factor and unique-factor measurements (often implicit, i.e., the measurements are not actually calculated) and corresponding common-factor and unique-factor weights. This partitioning is symbolized with the following equation:

$$\mathbf{Z} = \mathbf{P}_c\mathbf{X}_c + \mathbf{P}_u\mathbf{X}_u, \qquad (3)$$

where

> $\mathbf{Z}$ is the $n \times N$ matrix of $\mathbf{Z}_{ki}$ scores of N individuals on n elements,
>
> $\mathbf{X}_c$ is an $m \times N$ partitioning of X into m common-factor measurements,
>
> $\mathbf{X}_u$ is a $q \times N$ partitioning of X into the $q = n - m$ unique-factor measurements,
>
> $\mathbf{P}_c$ is the $n \times m$ part of $\mathbf{P}$ that contains the weights by which the m common factors are multiplied in the reproduction of the element scores, and
>
> $\mathbf{P}_u$ is the $n \times q$ part of $\mathbf{P}$ that contains the weights by which the q unique factors are multiplied in reproduction of the element scores.

Typically, in applications, the unique factors are put aside (although the unique factor coefficients are calculated), and only the common factors are considered in any detail. Typically, too, an initial solution is obtained and linearly transformed (rotated) to approximate a simple structure (for details, see Horn, 1967; Horn et al., 1983). A simple structure solution can be symbolized with the matrices of Equation 3, but usually one should suppose that the common factors may have intercorrelations different from zero. Allowing this possibility and considering common factors only, Equation 3 can be simplified thus:

$$\mathbf{Z} = [\mathbf{P}_c] \quad [\mathbf{X}_c] \text{ and}$$

$$
\begin{array}{c}
\begin{array}{ccccc} 1 & \ldots & i & \ldots & N \end{array}\\
\begin{array}{c} 1 \\ \\ \\ n \end{array}
\left[\begin{array}{c} \\ \mathbf{Z} \\ \\ \end{array}\right]
\end{array}
=
\begin{array}{c}
\begin{array}{ccc} 1 & \ldots & m \end{array}\\
\left[\begin{array}{c} \\ \mathbf{P}_c \\ \\ \end{array}\right]
\end{array}
\begin{array}{c}
1\\
\vdots\\
m
\end{array}
\begin{array}{c}
\begin{array}{ccccc} 1 & \ldots & i & \ldots & N \end{array}\\
\left[\begin{array}{c} \\ \mathbf{X}_c \\ \\ \end{array}\right]
\end{array}. \tag{4}
$$

$$n \times N \qquad\qquad n \times m \qquad m \times N$$

In tests of factorial invariance, the focus is on showing that features of the matrices in this representation of the model are invariant across $s = 1, 2, \ldots,$ t situations. This variation across situations can be symbolized as follows:

$$[\mathbf{Z}_s] = [\mathbf{P}_{cs}]'[\mathbf{X}_{cs}], \tag{5}$$

where the added subscript s in each case represents the variation in the matrices across different situations. To fit the models represented by Equations 3–5, one calculates what is called the "moment matrix" (average cross-product, covariance, or correlation matrix) for which the equations representing the model are derived and fitted. These equations are derived by multiplication of Equation 5 on the right by the transpose of $[\mathbf{Z}_s]'$. If the c subscript is then dropped to reduce clutter, the model for the moment matrices has the following form:

$$[\mathbf{M}_s] = [\mathbf{P}_s][\mathbf{Q}_s][\mathbf{P}_s]', \tag{6}$$

where

$\mathbf{M}_s$ is the $n \times n$ moment matrix for the element scores obtained under condition s. If the element scores happen to be in standard scores form, $\mathbf{M}$ would be a correlation matrix; if the element scores are in deviation-score form, $\mathbf{M}$ would be a covariance matrix; if the element scores are raw scores, as assumed here, $\mathbf{M}$ is a matrix of sums of squares (down the diagonal) and cross-products (in the off-diagonals), each usually divided by N.

$\mathbf{P}_s$ is $\mathbf{P}_{cs}$ without the c, but still representing common factor pattern weights. It is usually calculated to approximate a simple structure.

$\mathbf{Q}_s$ is the $m \times m$ matrix of variances and covariances for the common factors under condition s.

Each of the matrices in Equations 5 and 6 can, in principle, vary from one situation to another. The "levels of invariance" identified by Cunningham are specified in terms of which, and how many, of these matrices must be model invariant (to within chance) and which are allowed to vary freely across situations.

To put the matter of levels concretely, suppose s represents three conditions: $s = f$, g, and h. Questions about invariance (Do equalities hold?) can be raised with respect to each of the following sets of results:

The average cross-products matrices: $\qquad\qquad \mathbf{M}_f = \mathbf{M}_g = \mathbf{M}_h.$ (7)

The matrices of factor covariances and variances: $\mathbf{Q}_f = \mathbf{Q}_g = \mathbf{Q}_h.$ (8)

The off-diagonals of $\mathbf{Q}$s (factor covariances): $\quad \mathbf{C}_f = \mathbf{C}_g = \mathbf{C}_h.$ (9)

The main diagonals of $\mathbf{Q}$s (factor variances): $\quad \mathbf{V}_f = \mathbf{V}_g = \mathbf{V}_h.$ (10)

The factor correlations of $\mathbf{Q}$s: $\qquad\qquad\quad \mathbf{R}_f = \mathbf{R}_g = \mathbf{R}_h.$ (11)

The factor patterns: $\qquad\qquad\qquad\qquad\quad \mathbf{P}_f = \mathbf{P}_g = \mathbf{P}_h.$ (12)

The averages for factors: $\qquad\qquad\qquad\quad \mathbf{A}_f = \mathbf{A}_g = \mathbf{A}_h.$ (13)

Levels of invariance are defined by which of these sets of conditions of equality are required in the model one fits to the data. Tests for invariance at different levels are tests of goodness of fit for models in which different conditions of equality are imposed.

To require that the average cross-products matrices be equal—$\mathbf{M}_f = \mathbf{M}_g = \mathbf{M}_h$—is, in effect, to require all the other equality conditions of Equations 8–13. To test this model is to test an extreme of level of invariance.

Commonly, in the study of change, the aim is to show that averages for different situations are different. To reject a hypothesis that means are equal—$\mathbf{A}_f = \mathbf{A}_g = \mathbf{A}_h$—does not threaten hypotheses stipulating the equalities of Equations 8–12: All the equalities except those of Equation 7 can be required when means are allowed to vary.

Metric Invariance

A requirement that only the factor patterns be equal across situations—the conditions of Equation 12—is a test of measurement invariance. One coefficient is fixed in each column to identify the model. Factor correlations and variances can vary, which means that the $\mathbf{Q}$s may vary, across situations. This requirement, indicating metric invariance, is adequate to support an assumption that the same attribute is measured in different situations (Horn & McArdle, 1991; Horn et al., 1983).

Between the extreme of invariant average cross-products matrices and metric invariance is a requirement that factor patterns and factor variances be equal—conditions in Equations 12 and 10. Requiring factor variances to be equal corresponds to setting factor standard deviations equal to 1.0, seemingly a reasonable thing to do considering that the factors are latent variables for which the units of measure are unknown and, therefore, might well be set at a convenient value. But Cunningham emphasizes that although this condition is quite commonly imposed, Cudeck (1989) has shown that it results in a model in which the factors are not scale invariant. This means that evidence of invariance would not support a hypothesis that the same attribute is measured in different situations.

At a far extreme from the requirement that average cross-products matrices be invariant is the requirement that only a selected set of the pattern coefficients in the equivalent of $\mathbf{P}_f$, $\mathbf{P}_g$, and $\mathbf{P}_h$ be equal. Typically, investigators suggest that only corresponding salient loadings—the $\mathbf{P}_{jk}$ coefficients that are significant—should be equal across situations. The common (although often implicit) assumptions are those of a simple structure model in which only about one fourth of the elements in each column of $\mathbf{P}_f$, $\mathbf{P}_g$, and $\mathbf{P}_h$ are expected to be significantly different from zero (and equal across situations), and the relations for the other elements are expected to be only random—not literally zero, but varying from zero only as a function of chance.

Salient-Loading Invariance

Although salient-loading invariance logically has less stringent requirements than metric invariance, investigators sometimes impose tests that, in effect, make the requirements more stringent. This happens when the model tested (with LISREL or a similar algorithm) requires invariance in all the nonsalient coefficients in the equivalent of $\mathbf{P}_f$, $\mathbf{P}_g$, and $\mathbf{P}_h$. Most commonly, the requirement is that nonsalient coefficients be fixed at zero (i.e., the zeros are required to be invariant). The salient coefficients are left free to vary in estimation, under the constraint that corresponding coefficients be invariant across the $\mathbf{P}_f$, $\mathbf{P}_g$, and $\mathbf{P}_h$ situations. This is more demanding than the requirement in metric invariance that for each column of $\mathbf{P}$s all but one coefficient (fixed to identify the model) be free to vary, subject to a constraint that corresponding coefficients be invariant across situations.

To make the test for salient-loading invariance less stringent than the test for metric invariance, one can fix all nonsalient loadings at the values obtained in the model for test of metric invariance. This frees degrees of freedom (df) while still fitting the model just as well as when the nonsalient loadings are estimated. With this larger number of df (relative to the metric invariance test) a larger chi-square can be obtained and still not differ enough from the df to call for rejection of the hypothesis that the model fits the data.

Logically less stringent than salient-loading invariance (in which nonsalients must be zero) is a requirement that the salient loadings simply remain salient, not numerically invariant when nonsalients are required to be zero. This test can be made less stringent by fixing nonsalient loadings in each $\mathbf{P}$s at the values estimated.

The salient loadings in $\mathbf{P}_f$, $\mathbf{P}_g$, and $\mathbf{P}_h$ are allowed to vary. This is the form of invariance that Horn et al. (1983) referred to as "configural." A finding that only configural invariance obtains in data is a finding of qualitative change. Such a result suggests that a different attribute is measured in the factors identified in different situations. Under such conditions, comparison (across situations) of averages for linear composites is a dubious practice.

CONCLUSIONS

Often it is reasonable to suppose that all salient variable coefficients are equal— in which case they can, for convenience, be set to 1.0. The most stringent test under these conditions requires that all nonsalient coefficients equal zero. Less stringent is a test in which nonsalients are set equal to estimated values (and all salients are required to be 1.0). This test indicates measurement invariance when all items (only salients) are weighted the same. In sum, then, the levels of invariance described by Cunningham can be briefly identified as follows:

1. At the most stringent level, there is a test for the invariance of the average cross-products matrices. This is a very demanding model and rarely a good representation of reality.
2. If the element averages are subtracted from the average cross-products matrices, the resulting covariance matrices can be tested for invariance. Slightly less stringent because it does not require that element means be a part of the invariance package, this model, too, is very demanding and rarely appropriate.
3. A somewhat less demanding, often reasonable, model allows the factor variances—$\mathbf{V}_f$, $\mathbf{V}_g$, $\mathbf{V}_h$—to vary but requires the equalities of Equations 11 and 12 (factor correlations, hence covariances, and patterns). For example, it is not unreasonable in substantive theory to suppose that variance in self-esteem decreases systematically with increase in age in adulthood, whereas its correlations with other factors do not change.
4. At the next level, one can keep the requirement that factor patterns remain invariant but relax the requirement that corresponding factor correlations be equal. There might be conditions in which, mindful of the cautions of Cudeck (1989), one would keep a requirement that factor variances be equal. The factor covariances would still vary as a function of the (allowed) variation in factor intercorrelations.
5. Allowing factor variances and factor correlations to vary but retaining the requirement that factor patterns satisfy stringent equality constraints is a requirement for metric invariance (Horn et al., 1983). Invariance at this level provides support for a hypothesis of

measurement invariance. Invariance at this level is a reasonable ideal for research in the behavioral sciences. It is reasonable to suppose, for example, that with pattern invariance the variance on self-esteem and occupational role assumption increase as the correlation between them decreases with advancing age in adulthood. As with most ideals in life, this reasonable ideal invariance is a condition to be striven for, not one expected to be fully realized.

6. Measurement invariance is indicated, also, if there is good fit for a model in which salient loadings within each factor are required to be equal (say, to 1:0). The means that components (salient variables) in the linear composites are added with equal nominal weights.

7. Logically less demanding than factor-pattern (measurement) invariance, configural invariance of the most demanding form requires that corresponding salient pattern coefficients in $\mathbf{P}_{jk}$ remain numerically invariant across situations. Less demanding configural invariance requires only that salient loadings remain salient, which is a requirement that near-zero loadings (called *hyperplane loadings*) vary as if they were zero to within chance. Contrary to what is widely assumed (although the assumption is rarely examined), neither of these forms of invariance supports a hypothesis that the same attribute is measured in different situations. Evidence of such invariance, if adduced (as it only rarely is), does not support the very common practice of comparing means and other summary statistics (e.g., correlations) across groups that represent different situations. If based only on invariance at this level (assumed or demonstrated), generalizations about quantitative differences are ambiguous. Most of the science of psychology is based on such ambiguous statements, a conclusion that should lead one to think very seriously about the ideas Cliff presents in chapter 3.

CHAPTER 8

PREDICTION OF GROWTH

R. DARRELL BOCK

Editors' Introduction

In this chapter, Bock models human growth in stature by means of logistic equations. A logistic equation describes a particular nonlinear relation between two variables: The relation is roughly that of an S-shaped curve. For describing growth of stature, such an equation represents the notion that as age increases, height increases initially relatively slowly, then increases rapidly through adolescence, after which it gradually levels off until adult height is reached. Logistic equations have been used extensively to describe various kinds of biological growth. Bock and his colleagues have found that the relation between age and height is best described by linking together three logistic equations. Here Bock shows how such a triple-logistic model is defined and how it is used to describe and predict the growth in stature of individuals.

In thinking about applications of Bock's approach to studying change, we should keep in mind that we are making a "strong" assumption that the variables are measured at least at the interval level, in which a unit of scale difference represents the same magnitude of attribute difference anywhere along the scale. As Cliff points out in chapter 3, it is possible to make only a "weak" assumption of interval level measurement when we calculate linear relations using the product-moment correlation coefficient and its offshoots because we can interpret the linear relation as representing only

This research was supported in part by National Science Foundation Grant No. BNS 85-117674 and National Institute of Child Health and Development Grant No. HD-26031 to the University of Chicago.

monotonicity. But it makes little sense to fit precise nonlinear equations to data unless we feel comfortable interpreting inflections, accelerations, and peaks in the curves, which means that the measures must be regarded as numbers in the real number system.

Compared to most psychological phenomena, human stature is easily measured. Nevertheless, studies of the measurement and modeling of physical growth provide indications of problems likely to be encountered and solutions that might be effected in studies of change in psychological attributes, such as cognition, motivation, and social development. In addition, the remarkable predictive accuracy in Bock's analyses shows the benefits of explicit models of how change occurs within individuals.

As the growing child matures physically and behaviorally, the two realms of development mutually affect one another. There is ample evidence that physical size is a factor in social role and position, and environmental and emotional stress are well-known to influence growth rate in children. For these reasons, a child's growth in height has the continuing attention of parents, and it is the main index by which pediatricians monitor thriving during childhood. Thus, no study of development, even if it is psychologically or sociologically oriented, should exclude height as a variable of interest.

In addition, the study of growth in height is an excellent model for the investigation of other forms of growth. Any progress we make in measuring and modeling physical growth will serve us well when we attempt the more difficult task of describing cognitive, affective, or social development. Working with data from large-scale longitudinal studies has shown us, for example, that a curve based on cross-sectional group means may be a very poor description of the actual course of growth seen in any given child and that modeling of growth must therefore be carried out at the individual level. It has also shown us that measuring change within the developing child is possible only if we use a model that accounts for both the systematic and stochastic components of the observations.

Ultimately, the test of our success in modeling growth is our ability to predict future growth or mature attainment from the current state of the child. Prediction is of immense importance in pediatrics, where it is now possible to intervene medically to alter growth if the outcome of the treatment can be reliably foretold. Prediction of cognitive and emotional development could contribute in a comparable way to child psychiatry and behavioral modification programs. With respect to height, the prediction of growth is now fairly well advanced. There are a number of systems for this purpose, and they are widely used in pediatric medicine. Notable examples are the Bayley–Pinneau (1952) tables and the Tanner–Whitehouse (1975) and Roche–Wainer–Thissen (1975) regression equations.

For behavioral development, systems with the same general intent are the Geselle–Inhelder norms, the Bayley scale, and the Brazelton scale of infant development. At later ages, the various intelligence scales, such as the Stanford–Binet and the Wechsler Intelligence Scale for Children (WISC), serve much the same purpose. Not as highly developed as those available for prediction of height, these systems are equivalent to the most primitive approach to predicting height: namely, the growth channel method, in which the child is predicted to remain at the same percentile point of the population throughout development.

For a number of years, my students and I have been developing and testing methods for predicting growth in height using the superb collection of data contained in the Fels Institute Growth Study. I am indebted to Dr. Alex Roche for access to, and regular updating of, this large sample of longitudinal growth records begun at the Fels Institute in 1929. Because the Fels data include a great number of cases measured from birth to maturity, it is possible to evaluate the accuracy of the system by predicting growth at maturity from data recorded at any earlier stage of development. Included in these records is information required for the growth prediction system: namely, the child's sex; the height of first-degree relatives, especially parents; and estimates of the skeletal age of the child based on hand–wrist or knee radiographs.

MODELS FOR GROWTH

If the data are sufficiently detailed, it is possible to describe both physical and behavioral growth without the use of a functional model. Smoothing splines and kernel estimation have been used for this purpose to describe growth in height (Gasser et al., 1984; Largo et al., 1978), and the stage theory of Piaget is an ordinal description of cognitive development. Although these systems have the advantage of not imposing any preconceived form on the descriptors, they have the disadvantage, in the present context, of not providing a basis for statistical prediction. Conversely, prediction is possible without a model, as in the regression methods cited above, but regression methods do not provide a description of the course of development over the growth cycle. Both description and prediction are features of parametric models when the researcher applies the statistical methods described here. At present there are two well-known models capable of describing human growth throughout much of childhood: the Preese and Baines (1978) model and the triple logistic model of Bock and Thissen (1980). This chapter assumes the latter, although the proposed methods could be applied to either.

Bock and Thissen express the triple logistic model as

$$f(x) = \frac{a_1}{1 + e^{-b_1(x - c_1)}} + \frac{a_2}{1 + e^{-b_2(x - c_2)}} + \frac{a_3}{1 + e^{-b_3(x - c_3)}}, \tag{1}$$

where a_1, a_2, and a_3 are the contribution of the respective logistic components to mature stature; b_1, b_2, and b_3 are proportional to the maximum velocity of growth of the components; and c_1, c_2, and c_3 are the ages at which these maxima occur. Figure 8.1 illustrates how these components accumulate to represent the growth of a boy and girl with average parameter values in the Berkeley Growth Study (Tuddenham & Snyder, 1954).

There is a long history of logistic component models applied to description of growth. The single-component model serves fairly well to represent the growth of many organisms, exclusive of humans and the anthropoid apes, both of which exhibit an adolescent growth spurt. As early as 1908, Robertson suggested that additive combinations of logistic components could represent more complex growth, and Burt (1937) fitted a three-component logistic model to cross-sectional growth data. Bock et al. (1973) attempted to fit a two-component logistic model to data from the Fels study, but Bock and Thissen (1976) and El Lozy (1978) found that

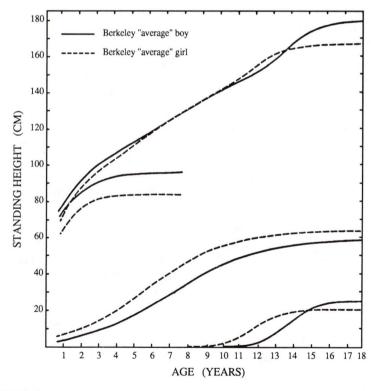

Figure 8.1   Triple-logistic growth curve of an ''average'' boy and girl in the Berkeley growth study.

a third component was essential to provide good fit over the range from 1 year to maturity. Bock and Thissen (1980) presented a first attempt at the statistical treatment of the triple-logistic model. Similar models and statistical approaches are now in use in animal husbandry (Grossman & Koops, 1988).

FITTING INDIVIDUAL GROWTH CURVES

The triple logistic model presented in Equation 1 is overparameterized; that is, variation in the patterns of growth of normal children can be fully described with fewer than nine parameters. Bock and Thissen (1980), using published data from the Berkeley Growth Study, found that the sample distribution of the nine growth parameters was under a linear restriction such that

$$\frac{a_2}{a_1 + a_2} = 0.851 + 0.041b_1 - 0.018c_1 - .0517b_2 - 0.042c_2. \tag{2}$$

In all their subsequent work with the model they assumed this restriction and estimated only the eight unrestricted parameters.

Mixture models such as Equation 1 cannot in general be fitted to data without stochastic constraints on the parameters. Without such constraints, the components can exchange roles, and the fitting process can become indeterminate. The method employed by Bock and Thissen (1980) to impose such constraints is a form of empirical Bayes estimation. In this procedure, the distribution of the eight unrestricted growth parameters is estimated in the target population to provide the empirical prior distribution for the Bayes procedure. For present purposes, the Fels data are treated as a calibrating sample from the population that provides the empirical prior. Data from the Berkeley Growth Study (Tuddenham & Snyder, 1954) or the Harpenden Study in England (cf. Tamer et al., 1975) could be used in a similar way.

In the prediction system described here, the growth parameters are assumed to be normally distributed, with mean μ and variance–covariance matrix Σ. In addition, the residuals from the fitted curves are assumed to be normally distributed, with mean zero and variance and autocorrelation function estimated as described below. The residuals and growth parameters are assumed to be mutually independent.

For clarity, I shall discuss first the estimation of a child's growth parameters from measures of height, then explain how other information, such as height of parents and the child's skeletal age, is used to improve these estimates. In the first of these methods, a child's growth parameters are estimated by the Bayes procedure, given the available measurements for the child. Because of the high dimensionality of the model, estimation of the posterior mean and covariance matrix is extremely laborious, so maximum a posteriori (MAP) estimation is employed instead. The MAP equation is

$$\sigma_\epsilon^{-2}\left[\frac{\partial f(x_i)}{\partial\theta}\right]\Lambda_i^{-1}\,[y_i - f(x_i)] - \Sigma^{-1}(\theta_i - \mu) = 0, \tag{3}$$

where θ is the vector of the eight free parameters of the model, σ_ϵ is the standard deviation of the residuals, μ and Σ are the population mean and covariance matrix, and Λ_i is the correlation matrix of the residuals implied by the autocorrelation structure. The solution of these equations estimates the mode, but because the posterior distribution of the parameters tends to multinormality as the number of observations increases, the mode and mean are consistent estimators of the same population value. The corresponding covariance matrix of the posterior distribution is estimated by the inverse of the posterior information matrix,

$$J_{\theta|y_1} = \sigma_\epsilon^{-2}\left[\frac{\partial f(x_i)}{\partial\theta}\right]\Lambda_i^{-1}\left[\frac{\partial f(x_i)}{\partial\theta}\right]' + \Sigma^{-1}. \tag{4}$$

In practical applications, the values of σ_ϵ^2, μ, and Σ required in Equations 3 and 4 are estimated in the calibrating sample by the marginal maximum likelihood method described in Bock (1989a, 1990) and Hedeker (1989). The estimation of Λ_i is described in Hedeker and Bock (1990).

Fitting of individual growth curves by the empirical Bayes method has a number of attractive properties. Given whatever data are available for the case, even as little as the child's sex and a single measurement of his or her current height, the estimator will select the model that is most probable for a child drawn from the specified population. When the estimated growth parameters for the child are substituted in the triple logistic model, it predicts (or postdicts) *growth*; that is, it predicts height at any age, not just at maturity. This feature of the model is illustrated by Figure 8.2, taken from Bock (1986), which presents the growth curve, based on one measurement at the age of 9.5 years, for the boy whose complete growth record is shown in Figure 8.3 (these displays were produced with the TRIFIT program of Bock and Thissen, 1983). Because this boy's growth is typical for the population, the curve fitted to a single point predicts mature height almost perfectly, as would even the growth channel method with this easy-to-predict case. Note that his skeletal development, as represented by the observed skeletal ages shown in the center of Figure 8.3, also follows closely the expected line for boys.

Nearly 90% of the Fels cases are as easy to predict as that in Figure 8.2. The remaining cases present a challenge, however. An example is the girl whose complete record is shown in Figure 8.4, also from Bock (1986). This girl is short but growing at a typical rate through 8 years of age. Yet during this period her skeletal age is increasing more rapidly than expected. At 10 years, she reaches a skeletal age of 12 years, and maximum adolescent growth occurs as expected in

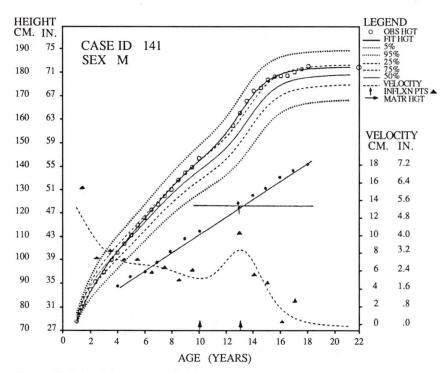

Figure 8.2 Triple-logistic model fitted to the complete growth record of a boy in the Fels study.

girls of that skeletal age. Her growth ceases soon thereafter, and she is thus quite short as a mature person. As a result, with height at 9.5 years as the only information used, the Bayes-fitted curve in Figure 8.5 is far wide of the mark at maturity. In the next section, we will see how the estimates of skeletal age can be used to improve prediction for this case.

CONDITIONED PREDICTION

The use of estimates of skeletal age prior to adolescence to condition the fitting of the triple logistic model can markedly improve prediction of mature height. The effect is illustrated for the girl represented in Figure 8.4 by the fitted curve shown in Figure 8.6, based on a measurement of height at age 9.5 and a determination of bone age at age 10. The effect of this conditioning is primarily to improve the estimation of the age of the adolescent growth maximum and thus to bring the fitted curve into better alignment with the measured heights shown in Figure 8.4. Prediction of mature height is much improved as a result and agrees almost exactly with a similar prediction, also using skeletal age, based on the Tanner–Whitehouse (TW2) regression equation.

Skeletal age determinations can be used either as first-stage covariates, as in the study by Goldstein (1989), or as second-stage covariates, as in the Bock (1990) study. In the latter role, they condition the estimation of the growth parameters, and in so doing they change the shape of the predicted growth curve, as illustrated in Figure 8.6. Other case-level information, such as height of parents, can similarly improve prediction when used as second-stage covariates. Height of parents is especially valuable at early ages, before the child's rate of skeletal development accurately predicts the timing of maximum adolescent growth.

CONCLUSIONS

As others have pointed out (Laird & Ware, 1982; Strenio, Weisberg, & Bryk, 1983), the combination of first-stage empirical Bayes estimation of individual growth parameters and second-stage estimation of population parameters provides a nearly ideal methodology for the description and prediction of growth and

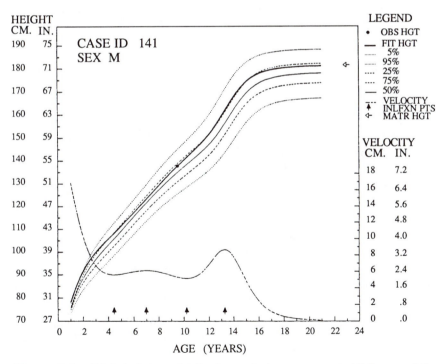

Figure 8.3   Triple-logistic model fitted to a single measurement at 9.5 years of the boy in Figure 8.2.

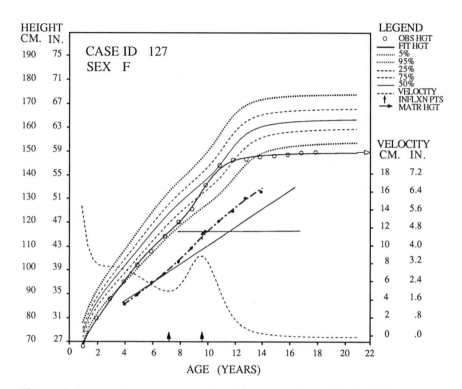

Figure 8.4 Growth record and fitted model for an atypical girl in the Fels study.

development. When data are limited or irregular at the first stage, as they often
are in both clinical and longitudinal studies, the Bayes procedure uses the population information to strengthen prediction; when second-stage data are extensive,
as they are in large-scale longitudinal studies, the large-sample properties of
consistency and efficiency in marginal maximum likelihood estimation are available to the investigator for estimating the population parameters. The present
chapter sketches the extension of these methods to the case of nonlinear models
with second-stage covariates. The provision for second-stage covariates is extremely important in growth studies, not only to improve prediction at the first
level but also to justify the multinormal assumptions at the second level. Human
populations are often mixtures of subpopulations that differ primarily in their mean
levels. Because of nutritional and health care effects, ethnic and social class
differences generate such subpopulations with respect to height (Tanner, 1986).
If the differences are sufficiently great, the population distributions can even appear
multimodal. Fortunately, if midparent stature is included as a covariate, these
differences, as well as any change in means between generations, are almost
entirely absorbed in the model (assuming the environments in which the parents

and offspring have been raised are substantially correlated). Conditional multi-normality of the distribution of the growth parameters thus becomes a much more reasonable assumption than it would be unconditionally. The extension of existing statistical methods to this case is straightforward and computationally manageable. A more detailed discussion of this approach to the description and prediction of human variation is in preparation.

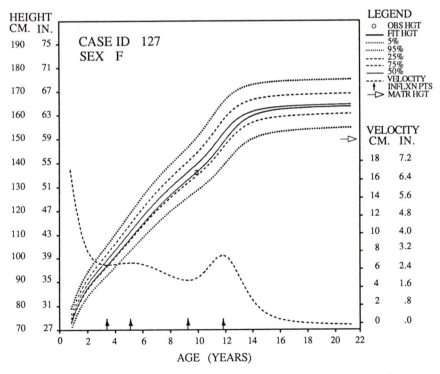

Figure 8.5   Estimated growth curve fitted to a measurement of the girl in Figure 8.4 at 9.5 years of age.

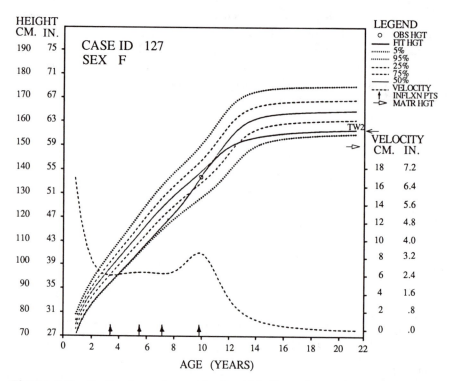

Figure 8.6   Predicted growth curve for the girl in Figure 8.4, adolescent peak height
velocity conditional on skeletal age at 10 years.

CHAPTER 9

MEASUREMENT IN LONGITUDINAL RESEARCH

LINDA M. COLLINS

Editors' Introduction

A major conclusion developed in this chapter is that we should not continue to think about change in ways that we have thought about measuring static individual differences: Different theories, different models, and different procedures are needed to conceptualize and study change. In making this point, Collins first shows that models and methods developed for measurement of static variables—interindividual differences at particular points in time—involve assumptions that are not appropriate for measurement of dynamic variables—intraindividual change over time. For example, items that generate no variance on particular occasions, and thus contribute nothing to reliability of measurement on those occasions, can be the best indicators of change over time. Because interindividual differences and intraindividual differences are logically independent, evidence indicating construct validity for one of these forms of measurement does not necessarily indicate construct validity for the other. Fundamentally, this means that one should have a clear theory about change for measurement of a dynamic variable, and this theory will differ in notable respects from the kind of theory most commonly put forth for the measurement of static variables.

In preparing this chapter, I have benefited from conversations with Ngar-Kok (Jacob) Chung, Norman Cliff, Clyde W. Dent, John W. Graham, and Stuart E. Wugalter. The work discussed here was supported by National Science Foundation Grant BNS8403126 and National Institute on Drug Abuse Grants DA3673 and DA04111.

> Collins presents two kinds of models that are appropriate for measure-
> ment of dynamic latent variables. The first model is an extension of the
> familiar Guttman scale (in which persons and items are jointly ordered) to a
> scale in which times and items are jointly ordered, and the order is consis-
> tent across persons. This model is appropriate for change that is cumula-
> tive, unitary, and irreversible. The second model, derived from latent class
> theory, can represent a wider range of conditions. For this model, change
> need not be cumulative, unitary, or irreversible. Latent Markov models of
> change can be specified in accordance with the strictures of this model.
> Collins summarizes procedures for evaluating each kind of model, indicates
> the limitations of each, and points to areas in which further work is needed
> to develop improved methods for studying change.

There is growing awareness that new approaches to data analysis are needed for
longitudinal studies; this is what motivated the conference on which this book is
based, "Best Methods for the Analysis of Change." Yet, when it comes to
measuring change, most people are still using the familiar traditional approaches.
At first glance, it seems eminently reasonable to assume that an instrument of
demonstrated reliability and validity will be a good measure of change. However,
one of the primary points of the present chapter is that this assumption is not
justified; we cannot be so sanguine about measuring change.

When thinking about measurement in the context of longitudinal research,
it is important to draw a distinction between two varieties of latent variables: static
and dynamic. Dynamic latent variables are those involving systematic intraindividual change over time. In contrast, static latent variables do not make reference
to change, either because change is hypothesized not to occur or because it is not
of interest in a particular study. Because studying change is a primary objective
of longitudinal research, dynamic latent variables figure prominently in this area,
although they are usually not identified as such. Traditional approaches to measurement fall short when applied to dynamic latent variables because these approaches were developed with static latent variables in mind. Much of the rationale
behind traditional measurement approaches is based on the idea of unchanging
true scores, with any change in observed scores directly attributable to measurement error. This does not apply, however, when the aim is to measure a dynamic
latent variable.

Because of their emphasis on static latent variables, traditional approaches
aid the researcher in developing instruments that are sensitive to interindividual
differences at one particular point in time. But a researcher studying change is
usually interested in intraindividual differences—for example, in the difference
between a particular individual's ability at one time and that same individual's
ability at some later time. Little in traditional measurement theory is of any help
to those who desire an instrument that is sensitive to intraindividual differences.

In fact, applying traditional methods to the development of a measure of a dynamic latent variable amounts to applying a set of largely irrelevant criteria.

PROBLEMS WITH TRADITIONAL APPROACHES

Collins and Cliff (1990) have outlined the problems that can arise when traditional approaches to developing an instrument are applied to dynamic latent variables. One problem is the inappropriate removal of items from a scale, particularly items that show across-time intraindividual variability but no within-time interindividual variability. Collins and Cliff (1990) used the example of a hypothetical instrument that measures mathematics skill development. The instrument is made up of items from four domains—addition, subtraction, multiplication, and division—and is administered on two occasions separated by about a year. On the first occasion, none of the children passes the division items because no one has sufficient mathematics skill yet to do them; on the second occasion, none of the children fails the addition items because everyone has sufficient skill to do them.

This situation creates problems for traditional approaches. Although the addition and division items reflect individual change over time, they are constants at one occasion of measurement. Because constant items exhibit no interindividual variability, they are routinely discarded in test development. They reduce Cronbach's alpha, and they cannot be included in factor analysis. But if the constant items are discarded, does the resulting measure remain as reflective of individual change? When one constructs a measure of individual change, does it make sense to discard items that reflect intraindividual variability across time because they do not reflect interindividual variability within time?

Perhaps an even more fundamental problem has to do with the definition of reliability. Most researchers agree that maximizing reliability is a desirable goal, and they think of reliability as an indication of the "precision" of a test, as do Lord and Novick (1968). Reliability is traditionally defined as follows:

$$\rho_{xx} = \frac{\sigma_t^2}{\sigma_x^2}. \tag{1}$$

In words, this is the ratio of (within-time interindividual) true score variance to total (within-time interindividual) variance. A number of authors (Cattell, 1964; Collins & Cliff, 1990; Cronbach, Gleser, Nande, & Rajaratnam, 1972; Rogosa, Brandt, & Zimowski, 1982) have pointed out that this definition does not involve across-time intraindividual variability; that is, that it has nothing to do with change over time.

A consequence of this definition is that, given the same nonzero error variance, a population with a small interindividual variance will yield a higher reliability than a population that is relatively homogeneous. This means that in situations in which, for example, a single cohort of about the same age is being followed over time, the lack of within-time interindividual variability can make it very difficult to show good measurement reliability. It should be stressed that this is not an artifact; according to the definition of reliability, such measures really are less reliable, although they may or may not be less precise measures of change.

Some readers might respond that the problem can be solved by making certain that one draws samples with sufficient interindividual heterogeneity. But this misses the point, which is that intraindividual differences occur independently of interindividual differences. Criteria for building and evaluating instruments based on interindividual differences are not useful for building and evaluating instruments to measure intraindividual differences. Increasing interindividual variability will not make the criteria any more relevant. Instead, new approaches to measurement theory are needed, approaches that evaluate instruments in terms of criteria that are directly relevant to intraindividual change over time.

NEW MEASUREMENT THEORIES RELEVANT TO DYNAMIC LATENT VARIABLES

What are we to look for in new approaches to measurement theory? A good starting point is the following quote from Coombs (1964): "A measurement or scaling model is actually a theory about behavior, admittedly on a miniature level, but nevertheless theory" (p. 5). This suggests that any measurement theory for dynamic latent variables must stem directly from a substantive theory about human development. However, with all the different ways that human development can take place, and all the different theories there are about human development, it seems unlikely that there will ever be one single measurement theory that will suit every longitudinal situation. Instead, when dynamic latent variables are involved, it is essential to have a well-defined theory about the latent variable's change. Only then can the appropriate approach to measurement be selected. Thus, the first step on the way to building a measurement theory for dynamic latent variables is a theory about the development undergone by the latent variable of interest.

Of course, there is an almost infinite number of forms of development. When the researcher is specifying the development of a particular dynamic latent variable, it is helpful to consider the following questions:

1. *Is development cumulative or noncumulative?* Development is cumulative when an ability (or skill, attitude, strategy, and so forth) is gained and all previously gained abilities remain, or when an ability is lost and all previously lost abilities remain lost. When development is cumulative, at any given observation for each individual, there is a level

of ability denoting a point above which no abilities are possessed and below which all abilities are possessed.

2. *Is development unitary or mult-path?* Is the latent variable best represented by one path, or do some individuals take a "detour"? Stage skipping is considered a detour.

3. *Is development reversible?* Is development always in one direction, or can setbacks, or restoration of lost ability occur?

4. *Is growth a continuous, quantitative phenomenon, or is it characterized by movement through a series of qualitatively different stages?*

Two measurement approaches that have been developed recently for dynamic latent variables are described below. One is for continuous dynamic latent variables undergoing cumulative, unitary, irreversible development. This model is called the longitudinal Guttman simplex (Collins, in press; Collins & Cliff, 1985, 1990; Collins, Cliff, & Dent, 1988). The other model is for stage-sequential dynamic latent variables that may take any of a variety of forms of development (Collins, in press; Collins, Chung, & Wugalter, 1991).

Longitudinal Guttman Simplex Model

The longitudinal Guttman simplex (LGS) model is an extension of the more familiar Guttman simplex model (Guttman, 1950) to three-set data. Whereas the ordinary Guttman simplex involves persons and items, the LGS involves persons, items, and times.

The concept of joint order is important for both the traditional Guttman simplex and the LGS. A traditional Guttman simplex is a joint order of items and persons. This means that in ability testing, for example, persons provide a difficulty order for the items, and the items provide an ability order for persons. This consistency allows persons and items to be ordered simultaneously in a Guttman scale, that is, persons relative to items and items relative to persons. This is what is meant by a joint order. In contrast, the key feature of the LGS model is that for each person there is a joint items–times order and that this order is consistent across persons. That is, in an LGS, a person's responses to a set of items at each of several times provide a difficulty order for the items and a temporal order for the times. This consistency allows items and times to be ordered jointly—items relative to times and times relative to items—and, in addition, this joint items–times order is consistent across persons.

An illustration of an LGS appears in Table 9.1. These are hypothetical data on two schoolchildren who took a mathematics skills measure on three occasions. First, it is evident that each child's data form a joint items–times order and that these orders are consistent with each other. For both Child A and Child B, the times provide an order for the items, and the items provide an order for the times;

Table 9.1

HYPOTHETICAL EXAMPLE OF A LONGITUDINAL GUTTMAN SIMPLEX
(LGS) MODEL

	Mathematics test results			
Individual	Addition	Subtraction	Multiplication	Division
Child A				
Grade 1	Pass	Fail	Fail	Fail
Grade 2	Pass	Pass	Pass	Fail
Grade 3	Pass	Pass	Pass	Fail
Child B				
Grade 1	Fail	Fail	Fail	Fail
Grade 2	Pass	Pass	Fail	Fail
Grade 3	Pass	Pass	Pass	Pass

Note: From "Using the Longitudinal Guttman Simplex as a Basis for Measuring Growth" by L. M.
Collins and N. Cliff, 1990, *Psychological Bulletin, 108*, p. 130. Copyright 1990 by the American
Psychological Association. Reprinted by permission.

that is, the items can be ordered according to the number of times each item was
failed. The item failed the most times is most difficult, the item failed the fewest
times is least difficult, and so on. In the example in Table 9.1, each subject orders
the items such that division is the most difficult item, then multiplication, then
subtraction, and finally addition. Likewise, the times can be ordered according
to the number of items passed at each time. The time when the most items have
been failed is the most difficult, the time when the fewest items have been failed
is the least difficult, and so on. Also, the two children's joint orders are consistent
with each other. For both children, the task order is that addition is learned first,
then subtraction, then multiplication, and finally division. For both children, the
times order is that Grade 1 is most "difficult," that is, the time when the least
mathematics ability is shown.

Table 9.1 also shows why a joint items–times order consistent across persons
reflects cumulative, unitary development. The data are cumulative because, as
the ability to perform a task is gained, previously gained abilities are retained.
For example, in Grade 3, Child B has gained the ability to perform multiplication
and division, and has retained the previously learned abilities of addition and
subtraction. The data are unitary because the two children are gaining skills in
the same order: first addition, then subtraction, then multiplication, and finally
division.

Table 9.1 illustrates two additional features of the LGS model. First, the
model allows heterogeneity in developmental rate both between individuals and
within individuals. At Grade 1 and again at Grade 2, Child A clearly performed
better on the mathematics test than Child B. However, between Grades 2 and 3,
Child B gains a great deal of ability and surpasses Child A. Although the ability

order of the two children changes over time, the data form a perfect LGS. In general, any amount of intra- or interindividual heterogeneity in developmental rate can be exhibited in an LGS as long as there is an items–times joint order that is consistent across persons. It is interesting to note that where there is substantial interindividual heterogeneity in developmental rate, across-occasion correlations will be low or even negative. This is independent of whether the data are consistent with the LGS model.

The second feature of the LGS model illustrated by Table 9.1 is how the model treats so-called constant items. Notice that each of the four items is a constant on at least one occasion. Such constant items do not present a problem for the LGS model as long as they show change across time.

LGS Procedures

Two procedures have been developed to help the researcher who is interested in using the LGS model to construct a measure of a cumulative, unitary developmental process. Briefly, the procedures are as follows:

1. The researcher who identifies a dynamic latent variable undergoing ir-reversible, cumulative, unitary development and wishes to construct an instrument to measure it has available a special item analysis procedure for LGS models, called LGSINDEX (see Collins & Dent, 1986; Collins et al., 1988).
2. Collins et al. (1988) have introduced an exploratory procedure developed especially for longitudinal data, LGSCLUS, which explores empirical data for longitudinal Guttman scales, that is, for sets of items that form irreversible, cumulative, unitary developmental sequences. LGSCLUS (Collins et al., 1988) is an extension of BINCLUS (Cliff, McCormick, Zatkin, Cudeck, & Collins, 1986), an agglomerative, nonhierarchical clustering procedure.

Approaches for Stage-Sequential Dynamic Latent Variables

This section discusses extending latent class theory to stage-sequential dynamic latent variables. Recall that latent class measurement theory postulates a static latent variable that divides the population into two or more latent classes. For example, several questionnaire items might be indicators of a "political conservatism" latent variable that divides individuals into three latent classes: "conservative," "liberal," and "middle-of-the-road." Now in contrast, consider a model starting with a dynamic latent variable that can be represented by a stage sequence. Markov models are the most widely used representation of such a stage sequence. Then, in addition to estimating latent class probabilities, the model estimates a latent transition probability matrix. This provides a more general model than the LGS, applicable to situations involving noncumulative, multipath, reversible development.

Consider a stage-sequential latent variable: early adolescent substance use onset, as depicted in Figure 9.1. According to this model, young people start out trying alcohol and tobacco in either order. They then progress to an experience with drunkenness, after which they may go on to advanced use, which may involve any of a number of substances. This model, taken from Graham, Collins, Wugalter, Chung, and Hansen (1991) is not an exclusively cumulative, unitary, irreversible model. First, both an alcohol–tobacco and a tobacco–alcohol sequence are featured in the model. If development were unitary, only one such sequence would be involved. Second, in the model depicted in Figure 9.1, development is partly reversible; the possibility exists of moving out of the advanced use stage and returning to the previous stage.

Each stage in the process can be thought of as a latent variable that divides individuals into latent classes. Then each individual has an array of latent class memberships–each individual is or is not a member of the "has tried alcohol" latent class, is or is not a member of the "has tried tobacco" latent class, is or is not a member of the "has experienced drunkenness" latent class, and is or is not a member of the "has engaged in advanced use" latent class. This array of

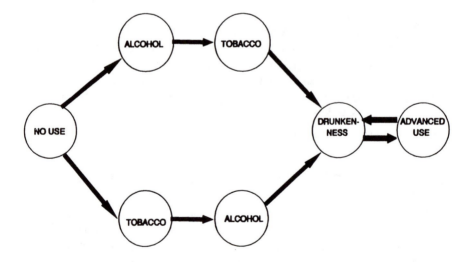

Figure 9.1   A stage-sequential model of adolescent substance use onset. From "Modeling Transitions in Latent Stage-Sequential Processes: A Substance Use Prevention Example" by J. W. Graham, L. M. Collins, S. E. Wugalter, N. K. Chung, and W. B. Hansen, 1991, *Journal of Consulting and Clinical Psychology, 59*, p. 49. Copyright 1991 by the American Psychological Association. Reprinted by permission.

latent class memberships is called a *latent status*. In this example, the model involves six possible latent statuses:

1. has never used a drug;
2. has tried alcohol only;
3. has tried tobacco only;
4. has tried both alcohol and tobacco;
5. has tried alcohol and tobacco, and has been drunk; and
6. has tried alcohol and tobacco, has been drunk, and has engaged in advanced use.

We are interested in modeling transitions from one latent status into another occurring between one occasion of measurement and another. These transitions are expressed by means of transition probabilities, parameters representing the probability of making a transition from, say, latent status A to latent status B, given membership in latent status A at the first occasion of measurement. It is customary to arrange these parameters in a transition probability matrix. In this case, the matrix is square and has a row and a column for each latent status. Each entry represents the probability of membership in the column latent status at Time 2, given membership in the row latent status at Time 1. (The exact meaning of the transition probability matrix varies slightly, depending on whether the process is considered to take place in continuous time or discrete time.) In our example, the transition probability matrix would be the one depicted in Table 9.2. For example, the fourth element in the second row represents the probability of being a member of the fourth latent status, "has tried both alcohol and tobacco," at the second occasion conditional on membership in the second latent status, "has tried alcohol only," at the first occasion. An element representing a transition

Table 9.2

TRANSITION PROBABILITY MATRIX

	Time 2 latent status					
Time 1 latent status	1	2	3	4	5	6
1. No use	$P(1\|1)$	$P(2\|1)$	$P(3\|1)$	$P(4\|1)$	$P(5\|1)$	$P(6\|1)$
2. Alcohol only	0	$P(2\|2)$	0	$P(4\|2)$	$P(5\|2)$	$P(6\|2)$
3. Tobacco only	0	0	$P(3\|3)$	$P(4\|3)$	$P(5\|3)$	$P(6\|3)$
4. Alcohol and tobacco	0	0	0	$P(4\|4)$	$P(5\|4)$	$P(6\|4)$
5. Alcohol, tobacco, and drunkenness	0	0	0	0	$P(5\|5)$	$P(6\|5)$
6. Alcohol, tobacco, drunkenness, and advanced use	0	0	0	0	$P(6\|5)$	$P(6\|6)$

Note: $P(1\|1)$ = probability of membership in latent status 1 at Time 2, conditional on membership in latent status 1 at Time 1.

that is not consistent with a model may be set to a value of zero. For example, the third element in the second row of Table 9.2 is zero because it is impossible to change from the second latent status to the third latent status, that is, it is impossible to change from "having tried alcohol" to "having tried tobacco only" (and "not having tried alcohol"). Note that the fifth element in the sixth row is nonzero, indicating that it is possible to move out of advanced use. Of course, a different model would involve a different transition probability matrix. When a model involves only cumulative, unitary development, the transition probability matrix may be set to be either upper triangular or lower triangular. A full transition probability matrix allows movement in either direction from any latent status.

The model estimates three groups of parameters. The first group of parameters is made up of the elements of the latent transition probability matrix, as described above. The second group of parameters estimates the proportion of individuals in each latent status at the first occasion of measurement. The third group of parameters estimates the relation between the latent statuses and the items, that is, the measurement quality of the items. There is a measurement parameter for each item response/item/latent status combination, representing the probability of a particular response to a particular item conditional on a particular latent status membership.

Suppose a researcher wishes to develop a measure of the dynamic latent variable depicted in Figure 9.1. The measure is made up of four items: (a) "Have you ever tried alcohol?", (b) "Have you ever tried tobacco?", (c) "Have you ever been drunk?", and (d) a logic variable taking on a value of unity if the subject has engaged in heavy alcohol use *or* any marijuana use *or* heavy tobacco use. The measure is administered to a group of young adolescents on one occasion and again some months later. This measure can be evaluated by estimating the parameters described above. Estimation is carried out by means of the Expectation-Maximization (EM) algorithm (see Collins et al., 1991). Two pieces of information returned by the procedure are of particular interest in this context. The first is the goodness-of-fit test. On the basis of the usual goodness-of-fit statistics, the Pearson X^2 or the likelihood ratio G^2, this test addresses whether the model of development that has been chosen is a reasonable representation of the observed data. If the model is rejected, it may be necessary to question the construct validity of the measure. The second aspect of interest is the measurement parameters. The closer these parameters are to zero or one, the better is the measurement of the latent variable. If we examine the measurement parameters it may be possible to identify and eliminate certain poorly performing items. Of course, this procedure can be followed in order to test a model of stage-sequential development.

Once it has been established that the model fits the data reasonably well and that the measurement parameters are satisfactory, the researcher can turn to the really interesting part of the results, found in the two remaining sets of parameters: the latent status probabilities on each occasion and the latent transition probability matrix. The latent transition probability matrix is particularly interesting because it offers a great deal of information about the movement between latent statuses undergone by the sample, in other words, about stage-sequential growth.

AREAS NEEDING MORE WORK

There are many interesting areas in which more work is needed. This section will briefly discuss a few of them.

More Measurement Theories

First, and perhaps most obvious, there is a need for more measurement theories. The models discussed in this chapter are not suitable for every type of dynamic latent variable. In particular, there is a need for measurement theories to handle continuous nonmonotonic development. But there is a need for other measurement theories as well.

Interindividual Variability

In this chapter, I have emphasized that there is no guarantee that instruments sensitive to interindividual variability are sensitive to intraindividual variability. The measurement theories described here emphasize the latter. However, there is also no guarantee that instruments sensitive to intraindividual variability are sensitive to interindividual variability. The many studies that are devoted to investigating interindividual differences in growth need measurement that is sensitive to both intra- and interindividual variability.

It may be conceptually clearest to separate these two aspects of measurement; that is, to evaluate an instrument separately on how sensitive it is to intraindividual differences and how sensitive it is to interindividual differences. However, it is important to remember that intraindividual differences may or may not be accompanied by significant interindividual variability and to try to determine a priori whether such differences are expected in a particular situation. Interindividual variability in growth can take on many different forms. For example:

- Individuals may follow the same growth curve but initiate the process at different times.
- Individuals may be undergoing growth described by the same basic equation, but there may be individual differences in growth curve parameters.

☑ Different paths in essentially the same processes may be followed by subgroups of individuals. For example, in a stage-sequential process, some individuals may skip an important stage, or some individuals may reach a certain stage and then stop, whereas others go on.

In order to develop measures that are sensitive to these or other manifestations of individual differences in growth, it is as important to have a theory about this as it is to have a theory about growth itself.

Exploratory Procedures

Often in behavioral research there is a need for exploratory procedures that will identify dynamic latent variables. We need a procedure similar to factor analysis, but one that starts with longitudinal data and ends with measures sensitive to change.

There are at least two distinctly different varieties of such an exploratory procedure. A procedure directly analogous to factor analysis would involve coexisting latent variables: One set of observed variables would be indicators of a dynamic latent variable representing, say, reading development, whereas another set would form a dynamic latent variable representing, say, mathematics development. Contrast this with an approach aimed at distinguishing subsets of individuals sharing similar growth characteristics. For example, such a procedure might identify groups of individuals, each characterized by a different growth curve or a different stage sequence. This would be more like a longitudinal version of cluster analysis. McArdle (1988) has made a similar distinction. In this volume, Meredith (chapter 10), Browne and Du Toit (chapter 4), and Bock (chapter 8) discuss aspects of this issue.

To my knowledge, relatively little work has been done to develop purely exploratory procedures for multiwave longitudinal data (with the notable exceptions of Millsap & Meredith, 1989, and Tisak & Meredith, 1989). As mentioned previously, Collins et al. (1988) have developed LGSCLUS, a procedure that explores longitudinal data for the presence of longitudinal Guttman scales. However, this procedure is limited in that it will find only longitudinal Guttman scales, not any other kind of dynamic latent variable.

CHAPTER 10

LATENT VARIABLE MODELS FOR STUDYING DIFFERENCES AND CHANGE

WILLIAM MEREDITH

Editors' Introduction

As you enter Meredith's chapter, get set to step up the ladder of abstraction to a very general, and heady, conception of change and difference. Begin with the familiar notion that for each individual of a sample of subjects, there are measures of several different qualities or attributes (e.g., abilities, motives). Think of the individual differences (variances) and interrelations (covariances) for these variables. Now suppose that the variables could be obtained either at different times or, alternatively, in different samples of subjects, and think of the variances and covariances for these cases. Meredith describes variance–covariance models for change and stability over time under the heading of ''latent change analysis;'' he describes such models for distinct groups under the heading of ''latent differences analyses.'' When there is change over time for individuals of different groups, Meredith describes latent change and difference analyses. The distinct groups of these models could be those formed by assignment in a controlled experiment, those obtained by selection, or both. Each permutation of a group and a time presents the researcher with a variance–covariance sample; the different possible and meaningful permutations identify several such samples for analyses. In Meredith's models, the observed similarities

This work was supported by National Institute of Aging Grant NIAG0316403 to William Meredith.

and differences of these samples—representing between-group differences and across-time changes as well as the lack of change and difference—are assumed to result from three separate sets of influence and thus are partitioned into three main classes of latent variables: (a) individual differences that are stable over time, across groups, or both; (b) individual differences of changes over time, differences between groups, or both; and (c) random error. Meredith demonstrates relations to canonical correlation and shows that tests of the goodness of fit of specified models, along with multivariate analysis of variance and discriminant function analysis, provide powerful means for describing data and drawing inferences about change under different conditions.

It is useful to think of the sampling conditions of Meredith's models in terms of the design concepts discussed in Nesselroade's chapter of this book (chapter 6). The procedures, as such, can be usefully compared with those described by McArdle and Hamagami (chapter 17), Muthén (chapter 1), and Browne and Du Toit (chapter 4).

Two latent variable models are developed in this chapter. The first, called latent difference analysis (LDA), is oriented toward establishment and interpretation of differences between groups. The second, called latent change analysis (LCA), studies change over occasions. The two models can be combined, yielding latent change and difference analysis (LCDA). This approach explicitly introduces individual differences by way of latent variates that explain differences between groups in means, variances, and correlations or latent variates that explain change in means, variances, and correlations over occasions, and cross-occasion correlations. In contrast to univariate analysis of variance (ANOVA) and multivariate analysis of variance (MANOVA) approaches, individual differences enter in the analysis as the primary sources of change and group differences instead of as a strictly additive, invariant source of noise.

In LDA the groups being studied might be (a) naturally occurring groups such as males and females; (b) selected subgroups from a parent population, such as age subgroups; (c) groups resulting from random assignment to treatment conditions in a controlled manipulative experiment; or (d) some combination of a, b, and c. In LCA the occasions of interest could arise in (e) a longitudinal study of some sample of individuals or (f) a repeated measures controlled manipulative experiment. In LCDA, a, b, c, or d are combined with e or f as, for example in a cohort sequential longitudinal design, or a controlled manipulative experimental design in which there are repeated measures nested within groups.

Suppose we are interested in studying a family of tasks related to fluency of verbal production. Tasks such as naming states, cities, mammals, things that are round, words that begin with ''s'' and end in ''p,'' have a long history in psychological research. Related tasks involve solving anagrams, inventing titles for supplied plots, sentence completion, and finding words that link unrelated words such as *beginner–grass* (*green*). Psychometric tests have been developed that are based on such tasks, and various experimental approaches have employed related measures. Time limits are imposed, and the variable of interest is typically the number of responses produced in a short time interval, although interresponse latencies may be recorded as well.

An oversimplified model for the measures (numbers of responses in a short time period) obtained from such tasks supposes that two latent variables—lexicon size and rate or speed of accessing the lexicon—determine an individual's score, and that these two factors enter additively. Now, different tasks surely invoke different lexicon sizes in different people, and different tasks are surely relatively distinct in access rate. But we might suppose some common factor underlies individual differences in task-specific lexicon sizes and that another single common factor accounts for individual differences in task-specific access speediness. This leads to a factor analytic model $x_{ij} = \beta_{j_1} z_{i1} + \beta_{j_2} z_{i2} + \alpha_j + e_{ij}$, where x_{ij} is the observed outcome for subject i on measure j, z_{i1} and z_{i2} are that person's values for the "lexicon factor" and "speediness factor," respectively, and e_{ij} is "error." The parameters β_{1j}, β_{2j}, and α_j are characteristic of the particular task chosen for study.

Developmental studies, either cross-sectional or longitudinal, of such tasks might turn out as follows. During late childhood, adolescence, and college years, individuals' lexicon factor scores would probably increase in magnitude with age but at different rates for different persons, whereas most persons' speediness factors would change very little, if at all. The result would be increasing means, variances, and so forth, for the observed measures. In late midlife and beyond the speediness factor scores would probably decline with age, but at different rates for different persons, whereas individuals' lexicon factor scores would change little, if at all. This would result in declining means and increasing variances for observed measures. The basic observation would be that performance increases earlier in life and declines later, and that variation increases, stabilizes, then increases again; however, the fact that entirely different mechanisms are involved would not be obvious.

An experimenter studying performance on such tasks might manipulate features such as practice on related tasks, instructional set, and strategy training that might affect lexicon size, access speed, or both differentially for different subjects. This could take place in an independent group or repeated measures framework. The net result would be differences in means, variances, and so on, but without clear evidence as to which factor, lexicon or speediness, was being altered by a particular treatment condition.

The purpose of LDA, LCA, and LCDA is to provide specific information about what factor is changing or differing in a given study and how it differs or changes. Like factor analysis, these analyses require a battery of measures (i.e., a multivariate manifest variable) such that there is a differential pattern of the β_{jk} elements. That is, some measures should depend mostly on the lexicon factor (e.g., sentence completion) and some mostly on the speediness factor (e.g., naming states, constructing simple anagrams) in our example. Furthermore, all three approaches are explicitly exploratory. Fundamentally, they examine differences (changes) in mean vectors and in variance–covariance matrices simultaneously and attempt to identify factors that account for the differences, not factors that account for the data.

For another example, suppose that we are interested in understanding individual differences in physiognomy (as in Horn's, 1985, metaphorical representation of intelligence). Several dimensions (latent variables) characterize these differences in any sample of individuals, and a person's facial appearance varies over age from youth to old age. Some features of the face change only slightly, and thus support judgments that the face is the same, even over long periods of time, whereas other features change rather much, and thus support judgments that the person has changed considerably (e.g., has become old, has been sick, etc.). During the period from young adulthood to old age, for example, the bone structure underlying the face probably changes little relative to the changes in musculature and skin. The question is, How can we identify those features that mainly indicate change and difference and distinguish them from those features that mainly indicate underlying structure that does not change? The LDA, LCA, and, particularly, LCDA models for analysis are directed at answering this question.

LDA has roots in the work of Pearson (1903), Aitkin (1934), Lawley (1943), and Meredith (1965). Of course, both LCA and LDA have their conceptual foundation in the rich tradition of factor analysis (see Bartholomew (1987) for a development of factor analysis similar to the approach employed in this chapter).

For LDA and LCA, the basic model is essentially the same. Differences between the two stem from the fact that different, and presumably independent, classes of individuals are studied in LDA, whereas in LCA data from the same subjects on different occasions (hence dependent) provide the basis for model fit and evaluation.

THE BASIC MODEL

Using the example of fluency, let X denote a column vector of p measures of fluency made on a single person. Or, using the example of physiognomy, let X denote a column vector of facial measurements made on a given individual. We have a theory that group differences or individual changes in X result from differences or changes in q $(< p)$ unmeasured latent variables. Imagine that these q variables are arranged in a q-dimensional column vector, Z, for a given individual. We stipulate a linear regression function for the manifest variable on the latent variable, or, using $\mathscr{E}$ to denote (conditional) expectation,

$$\mathscr{E}(X|Z) = \beta Z + \alpha. \tag{1}$$

In Equation 1 the $p \times q$ matrix β and the $p \times 1$ vector α will be assumed to be invariant over groups and stationary over occasions. We also assume that errors of measurement occur when X is measured, as is surely inevitable. Conventional assumptions about measurement error are made, namely, additivity of measurement error and "true" value, zero expected value for error, independence of errors and true values, and mutual independence of measurement errors.

Let U denote the column vector of p measurement errors for a given individual. We can then write

$$X = Y + \beta Z + \alpha + U, \tag{2}$$

where $Y + U$ is a vector of p regression residuals, that is,

$$Y + U = X - E(X|Z). \tag{3}$$

Finally, we assume homoscedasticity for the regression residual, namely,

$$\text{Disp}(Y + U|Z) = \Omega + \Delta, \tag{4}$$

where Disp( ) denotes a (conditional) dispersion matrix; Ω the unconditional dispersion matrix of Y; and Δ, diagonal, the unconditional dispersion matrix of U.

For a given individual, the vector Y is assumed to be stationary over occasions of measurement. We also assume that Ω is invariant over groups. Thus group differences in the distribution of X are entirely the result of group differences in Z and U. The only possible group differences in U are differences in the magnitudes of error variances. Similarly, changes over occasions in X are entirely the result of changes over occasions in Z and U; relative to U, only the magnitudes of error variances can change.

The Y part of Equation 2 thus represents the idea of some unvarying component of X, unvarying over occasions in LCA for a given person. In LDA individual differences occur in Y but with mean vector zero and a constant dispersion matrix over groups.

We remind the reader that Equation 2, coupled with the assumptions made in the foregoing paragraph (e.g., stationarity, invariance, and so forth), is a model for changes or differences in X. What happens to X in reality is another matter, and that is a question of fit of the model. Although any simple model such as the one proposed is almost surely falsifiable in the final analysis (e.g., given a sufficiently large number of subjects), a satisfactory fit of such a model is parsimonious if q is small, β is simple, or both. The aim of fitting such a model is to guide our understanding of the sources of variation in groups and over occasions.

The mathematical developments in this chapter provide the details for estimating the parameters of the LDA, LCA, and LCDA models. Each can be specified in terms of FIGMODES (McArdle & Horn, in press) of the kind that have become the hallmark of J. J. McArdle, the discussant of this chapter. Computer programs such as LISREL, EQS, or COFAM can be used to estimate the parameters of the models and evaluate the fits. An example is presented in a later section of this chapter to illustrate a particular application.

LATENT DIFFERENCE ANALYSIS

In the ith group, denote the mean vector of $\mathbf{X}$ by μ_i, the dispersion matrix by Σ_i, the mean vector of $\mathbf{Z}$ by v_i, the dispersion of $\mathbf{Z}$ by Φ_i, and the (diagonal) dispersion of $\mathbf{U}$ by Δ_i. The basic model implies that for $i = 1, \ldots, g$,

$$\mu_i = \beta v_i + \alpha, \tag{5}$$

and

$$\Sigma_i = \Omega + \beta \Phi_i \beta' + \Delta_i, \tag{6}$$

which can be combined into a single equation for the augmented moment matrix. For example, in Group 1 we would have

$$\begin{bmatrix} \Sigma_1 + \mu_1\mu_1' & \mu_1 \\ \mu_1' & 1 \end{bmatrix} = \begin{bmatrix} \Omega + \Delta_1 & 0 \\ 0 & 0 \end{bmatrix} + \begin{bmatrix} \beta & \alpha \\ 0 & 1 \end{bmatrix} \left[\begin{pmatrix} v_1 \\ 1 \end{pmatrix} \begin{pmatrix} v_1' \\ 1 \end{pmatrix} \right.$$
$$\left. + \begin{pmatrix} \Phi_1 & 0 \\ 0 & 0 \end{pmatrix} \right] \begin{bmatrix} \beta' & 0 \\ \alpha' & 1 \end{bmatrix}. \tag{7}$$

Note the following identification problems. Let v_0 be any vector of the same dimension as v_i, and let Φ_0 be any symmetric matrix of the same dimension as Φ_i. We may rewrite Equations 5 and 6 as

$$\mu_i = \beta (v_i - v_0) + (\alpha + \beta v_0) \tag{8}$$

and

$$\Sigma_i = (\Omega + \beta \Phi_0 \beta') + \beta (\Phi_i - \Phi_0) \beta' + \Delta_i. \tag{9}$$

This identification problem can be resolved by several strategies, for example, by letting $v_0 = v_1$, and $\Phi_0 = \Phi_1$. The implication of this is that we can obtain information only about differences between the mean vectors v_i and the dispersion matrices Φ_i. Furthermore, identification of β must be performed by setting q of the rows of β equal to some nonsingular matrix. Group differences in error variances can readily be accommodated or suppressed.

What we have here can be formulated as a linear structural relations model for multiple groups with structured means (Jöreskog, 1982, 1979; Jöreskog & Sörbom, 1979, 1984; Sörbom, 1982, 1974). Under normality assumptions, maximum likelihood estimates of β, $(v_i - v_0)$, $(\alpha + \beta v_0)$, $(\Phi_i - \Phi_0)$, $(\Omega + \beta \Phi_0 \beta')$, Δ_i, and chi-square measures of fit for a given q and identification scheme can be obtained by submitting the sample counterparts of the augmented moment matrices to the LISREL program (Jöreskog & Sörbom, 1984; see also Meredith & Tisak, 1990). Generalized least square (GLS) and unweighted least square (ULS) options are also available in LISREL.

It is clearly desirable to have estimation and fit evaluation procedures that are invariant or scale free (Anderson, 1984). By an invariant procedure, we mean that replacement of $\mathbf{X}$ by $\mathbf{TX} + \mathbf{C}$, where T is a nonsingular matrix and $\mathbf{C}$ a conformable vector, produces no alteration in the value of the fit function or test statistic. Furthermore, parameter estimates for $\mathbf{X}$ can be readily obtained by a one-to-one transformation of parameter estimates determined using $\mathbf{TX} + \mathbf{C}$. For a scale-free procedure, $\mathbf{T}$ is restricted to be diagonal. It can readily be shown that for LDA, normal theory maximum likelihood estimates and likelihood-ratio-based fit functions are invariant if $\Delta_i =$ constant and scale free otherwise, as are pseudo-maximum-likelihood procedures (Arminger & Sobel, 1987; Satorra & Bentler, 1986; Schoenberg, 1987). Generalized least square procedures are also invariant or scale free. LISREL can produce pseudo-maximum-likelihood estimates.

LATENT CHANGE ANALYSIS

Consider a single population measured on occasions $s, t = 1, \ldots, r$. Subscripting random variables that vary over occasions for a fixed individual, we have

$$\mathbf{X}_t = \mathbf{Y} + \beta \mathbf{Z}_t + \alpha + \mathbf{U}_t. \tag{10}$$

Let the dispersion matrix of $\mathbf{U}_t$ be Δ_t, diagonal. Now denote the mean of $\mathbf{X}_t$ by μ_t and its dispersion by Σ_{tt}; denote the mean of $\mathbf{Z}_t$ by ν_t and its dispersion by Φ_{tt}. Let Σ_{st} and Φ_{st} be the respective matrices of cross-occasion covariances. Our assumptions imply

$$\mu_t = \beta \nu_t + \alpha, \tag{11}$$

$$\Sigma_{tt} = \Omega + \beta \Phi_{tt} \beta' + \Delta_t, \tag{12}$$

and

$$\Sigma_{st} = \Omega + \beta \Phi_{st} \beta'. \tag{13}$$

Equations 11, 12, and 13 can be assembled into a single equation for the augmented moment matrix, which we illustrate for $r = 2$. The extension to more than two occasions is immediate and obvious.

$$\begin{bmatrix} \Sigma_{11} + \mu_1 \mu_1' & \Sigma_{12} + \mu_1 \mu_2' & \mu_1 \\ \Sigma_{21} + \mu_2 \mu_1' & \Sigma_{22} + \mu_2 \mu_2' & \mu_2 \\ \mu_1' & \mu_2' & 1 \end{bmatrix} = \tag{14}$$

$$\begin{bmatrix} I & \beta & 0 & 0 \\ I & 0 & \beta & 0 \\ 0 & 0 & 0 & 1 \end{bmatrix} \left[\begin{pmatrix} \alpha \\ \nu_1 \\ \nu_2 \\ 1 \end{pmatrix} \begin{pmatrix} \alpha' \\ \nu_1' \\ \nu_2' \\ 1 \end{pmatrix} \begin{pmatrix} \Omega & 0 & 0 & 0 \\ 0 & \Phi_{11} & \Phi_{12} & 0 \\ 0 & \Phi_{21} & \Phi_{22} & 0 \\ 0 & 0 & 0 & 0 \end{pmatrix} \right] \begin{bmatrix} I & I & 0 \\ \beta' & 0 & 0 \\ 0 & \beta' & 0 \\ 0 & 0 & 1 \end{bmatrix}$$

$$+ \begin{bmatrix} \Delta_1 & 0 & 0 \\ 0 & \Delta_2 & 0 \\ 0 & 0 & 0 \end{bmatrix}.$$

This is another linear structural relations model with structured means. Given the assumption of normality, maximum likelihood estimation and evaluation of fit can be performed using LISREL, as can GLS and ULS estimation and fit evaluation. Maximum likelihood, GLS, and pseudo-maximum-likelihood procedures are scale free but not invariant.

Note that there is an identification problem analogous to that described in connection with LDA. It can be solved in an analogous fashion by letting $\Phi_0 = \Phi_{11}$ and $\nu_0 = \nu_1$, say, and estimating differences between means and between dispersion and covariance matrices, and so forth; we actually will estimate β, $(\nu_t - \nu_0)$, $(\alpha + \beta \nu_0)$, $(\Phi_{st} - \Phi_0)$, $(\Omega + \beta\Phi_0\beta')$, and Δ_t. The matrix β must be identified by setting q rows equal to a nonsingular matrix. The option of requiring Δ_t to be constant is available.

LATENT CHANGE AND DIFFERENCE ANALYSIS

LCDA is a straightforward combination of LDA and LCA. Suppose groups $i = 1, \ldots, g$; occasions s and $t = 1, \ldots, r$. Let $\mu_{t,i}$ and $\nu_{t,i}$ denote the mean vectors for $\mathbf{X}_t$ and $\mathbf{Z}_t$ in group i, let $\Sigma_{tt,i}$ and $\Phi_{tt,i}$ denote the respective dispersion matrices, and let $\Sigma_{st,i}$ and $\Phi_{st,i}$ denote the cross-occasion covariance of $\mathbf{X}_s$, $\mathbf{X}_t$ and $\mathbf{Z}_s$, $\mathbf{Z}_t$ in group i. Finally, let $\Delta_{t,i}$ be the diagonal matrix of error variances for group i on occasion t. We have

$$\mu_{t,i} = \beta\nu_{t,i} + \alpha, \tag{15}$$

$$\Sigma_{tt,i} = \Omega + \beta \Phi_{tt,i} \beta' + \Delta_{t,i}, \tag{16}$$

and

$$\Sigma_{st,i} = \Omega + \beta \Phi_{st,i} \beta'. \tag{17}$$

Identification can be carried out by letting $\nu_0 = \nu_{1,1}$ and $\Phi_0 = \Phi_{11,1}$, for example, and specifying q rows of β equal to a nonsingular matrix.

Equations 15, 16, and 17 lead to g equations of the form of Equation 14, one for each group. Estimation and evaluation of fit can be carried out by submitting the g sample augmented moment matrices to LISREL and setting up a multiple-group model with structured means with appropriate identification. The scale-free properties of maximum likelihood (ML), pseudo-maximum likelihood (PML), and GLS procedures carry over from LCA and LDA.

Furthermore, constraints may be imposed across groups and occasions on the $(v_{t,i} - v_0)$ and $(\Phi_{tt,i} - \Phi_0)$. For example, in a cohort sequential design we would probably want something like $v_{2,1} = v_{1,2}$, $v_{3,1} = v_{2,2} = v_{1,3}$, and so on, and $\Phi_{22,1} = \Phi_{11,2}$, $\Phi_{33,1} = \Phi_{22,2} = \Phi_{11,3}$, unless period effects were present. Error variances may be equated over groups, over occasions, or over both.

RELATION OF THE PRESENT ANALYSES TO CANONICAL VARIATE ANALYSIS

In LDA, if $\Phi_1 = \Phi_2 = \ldots = \Phi_g$ and $\Delta_1 = \Delta_2 = \ldots \Delta_g$, we have $\Sigma_1 = \Sigma_2 = \ldots \Sigma_g$, and the conditions assumed for one-way multivariate analysis of variance (MANOVA) are met. Let M denote the $p \times g$ matrix of sample mean vectors expressed as deviations from the grand mean vector and S the pooled within-group sample dispersion matrix. Let $S = AA'$, with rank $(A) = p$, be an arbitrary factoring of S, and let N denote a diagonal matrix of subgroup sample sizes. Finally, let $A^{-1}MN^{1/2} = VDH$ represent the singular value decomposition of the $p \times g$ matrix $A^{-1}MN^{1/2}$. It can be shown that $A^{-1}V$ is an estimate of the matrix of canonical variate (CV) weights and that the first $q < g - 1$ columns of $A^{-1}V$ provide the weights for the q "most discriminating" CVs. It can also be shown that the first q columns of AV (which is both a canonical "structure" and "pattern" matrix) provide a maximum likelihood estimate of β in LDA for q latent variates. If Φ_i or Δ_i, or both $\neq$ constant, the foregoing is not true and a satisfactory q could exceed $g - 1$. It is also possible that the misapplication of MANOVA with canonical variates could lead to more "significant" CVs' being required than latent variates needed in fitting LDA. Note that the foregoing suggests that the matrix composed of the first q column of AV (possibly rescaled by diagonal matrices) is the logical candidate for rotation to simple structure in canonical variate analysis (CVA). Also note that the identification problem for v and Φ is not solved because the CVs are not the latent variates of the model. The CVs are analogous to factor score estimates in ordinary factor analysis, given the homogeneity assumptions made in the opening sentence.

In LCA, if Φ_{tt} is constant, Δ_t is constant, $t = 1, \ldots, r$, and $\Phi_{st} = \Phi_{ts}$ is constant for all s, t, it can easily be shown that the condition of multivariate compound symmetry is met. This condition is frequently invoked in repeated measures MANOVAs with all occasions (conditions) nested within subjects. Let M denote the $p \times r$ matrix of sample mean vectors expressed as deviations from the grand mean vector, and let W denote the $p \times p$ dispersion matrix of Subject $\times$ Occasion interaction effect vectors. Let $W, = AA'$, rank $(A) = p$, be an arbitrary factoring of W, and $A^{-1}M = VDH$ represent the singular value decomposition of $\mathbf{A}^{-1}\mathbf{M}$. Then $\mathbf{A}^{-1}\mathbf{M}$ is an estimate of CV weights, and the first $q < r - 1$ columns of $\mathbf{A}^{-1}\mathbf{M}$ furnish the q "most discriminating" CVs. As in LDA, it can also be shown that the first q columns of $\mathbf{AV}$ provide a maximum likelihood estimate of β given the compound symmetry assumption. Remarks similar to those made at the close of the preceding paragraph apply; that is, that rotation is possible and that the CVs are analogous to factor score estimates.

As with LDA and LCA, homogeneity and symmetry constraints imposed on LCDA can provide conditions that are usually assumed in two-way MANOVAs with one factor nested within subjects. The situation is complicated, however, by the fact that separate CVAs would be carried out for "row" effects, "column" effects, and "Row × Column interaction" effects. The three matrices of canonical weights bear no obvious relation to β in LCDA.

TWO APPROXIMATIONS

In LDA, let $\Gamma_i = \beta\Phi_i$ be the matrix of covariances of $\mathbf{X}$ with $\mathbf{Z}$ in the ith group. The matrix of regression weights for predicting $\mathbf{Z}$ from $\mathbf{X}$ then becomes $\Sigma_i^{-1}\Gamma_i = \Sigma_i^{-1}\beta\Phi_i$ from which it follows that the dispersion matrix of regression estimates of $\mathbf{Z}$ in the ith group is $\Gamma_i^{-1} \Sigma_i^{-1}\Gamma_i = \Phi_i\beta' \Sigma_i^{-1}\beta \Phi_i = \tilde{\Phi}_i$. Then $(\beta' \Sigma_i^{-1}\beta)^{-1} = \Phi_i(\tilde{\Phi}_i)^{-1} \Phi_i$ (Meredith, 1965). Assuming that Φ_i and $\tilde{\Phi}_i$ are not too different, we may take $(\beta'\mathbf{S}_i^{-1}\beta)^{-1}$ as an approximate estimate of Φ_i, where β is an obtained estimate of β and $\mathbf{S}_i$ is the sample dispersion matrix of $\mathbf{X}$ for group i. A reasonable improvement on the foregoing procedure using the LISREL estimates of $(\Phi_i - \Phi_0)$ is available, by forcing the approximations to have the same differences.

In LCA, we can improve on the procedure because an estimate of Δ_i, the diagonal matrix of error variances, is available, and we can consider the regression of $Z_1, Z_2, \ldots, Z_r$ jointly on $X_1 - E_1, X_2 - E_2, X_r - E_r$ jointly. The situation for $r = 2$ can be illustrated as follows:

Let

$$\beta^* = \begin{bmatrix} \beta & 0 \\ 0 & \beta \end{bmatrix}, \tag{18}$$

and

$$\phi^* = \begin{bmatrix} \phi_{11} & \phi_{12} \\ \phi_{21} & \phi_{22} \end{bmatrix} \tag{19}$$

$$\Sigma^* = \begin{bmatrix} \Sigma_{11} - \Delta_1 & \Sigma_{12} \\ \Sigma_{21} & \Sigma_{22} - \Delta_2 \end{bmatrix}. \tag{20}$$

By direct analogy we have

$$\Phi^* \, (\tilde{\Phi}^*)^{-1} \, \Phi^* \;=\; [(\beta^*)' \, (\Sigma^*)^{-1} \, \beta^*]^{-1} \qquad (21)$$

where $\tilde{\Phi}^*$ involves predictions of Z_1 and Z_2 from $X_1 - E_1$ and $X_2 - E_2$. An estimate of an approximation to Φ^* can be obtained substituting estimates of β and Δ and the sample dispersion matrix into the right side of Equation 21. The generalization of the foregoing to LCDA is obvious.

AN EXAMPLE

We present an example of latent change and difference analysis employing data taken from the archives of the Institute of Human Development (IHD) of the University of California at Berkeley. We used Wechsler Performance subtest scores for 165 males who were assessed twice and were divided into two age cohorts. The subjects were male participants of the ongoing longitudinal studies at IHD and male spouses of female participants of the ongoing longitudinal studies at IHD. Of the participants, 71 were tested at an average age of 39.5 and again at an average age of 53.5, and 38 were tested at ages 48 and 61. There was little variation around these age averages for the participants. The 71 younger participants were augmented by 19 male spouses of female participants ranging in age from 50 to 57 at the second assessment and the 38 older participants were augmented with 37 male spouses ranging from 57 to 67 years in age at the second assessment. All subjects were tested with the Wechsler Adult Intelligence Test (WAIS) in 1967–1972 and with the Wechsler Adult Intelligence Test-Revised (WAIS-R) in 1981–1984. The scores utilized here are based on only those items common to the WAIS and WAIS-R. The WAIS-R items were scored according to WAIS criteria. These subjects were bright and well educated. Their mean IQ was approximately 120 and the majority had 16 or more years of education. (For more details see Sands, Meredith, & Terry, 1988.)

Table 10.1 contains the augmented moment matrix for the performance subtests for both groups with the younger group depicted below the main diagonal and the older group depicted above the main diagonal. The variables are picture completion (PC), picture arrangement (PA), block design (BD), object assembly (OA), and digit symbol (DY). The last row and column contain the means. The data has been standardized with respect to the means and standard deviations of the younger group at the first assessment.

In the LISREL analyses we employ ML estimation and chi-squares. By requiring that $\nu_0 = \nu_{1,1}$ and $\Phi_0 = \Phi_{11,1}$, $\nu_{t,i}$ is expressed as a deviation from the mean of Z for the younger group on the first occasion. Similarly, $\Phi_{st,i}$ is expressed as a deviation from the dispersion matrix of Z for the younger group on the first occasion.

Table 10.1

AUGMENTED MOMENT MATRICES

	PC1	PC1	PA1	BD1	OA1	DY1	PC2	PA2	BD2	OA2	DY2	Mean
PC1	100	101	44	37	46	34	67	54	30	58	42	-12
PA1	27	100	116	74	67	58	67	89	69	89	77	-33
BD1	43	41	100	157	112	77	70	75	131	149	110	-49
OA1	30	41	60	100	193	54	83	64	111	147	84	-54
DY1	20	33	34	26	100	154	59	77	85	81	149	-37
PC2	35	24	29	18	15	80	131	80	60	80	79	-30
PA2	23	34	33	35	22	36	85	159	82	97	116	-67
BD2	41	32	80	68	42	24	44	131	192	146	130	-85
OA2	37	25	64	69	21	24	58	80	119	262	130	-82
DY2	26	35	41	32	89	24	36	79	47	151	209	-90
M	00	00	00	00	00	-20	-12	-37	-26	-49		
	PC1	PA1	BD1	OA1	DY1	PC2	PA2	BD2	OA2	DY2		

Note: The younger group is below the diagonal and the older group above the diagonal. Decimals are omitted; entries should be divided by 100. PC = Picture Completion, PA = Picture Arrangement, BD = Block Design, OA = Object Assembly, and DY = Digit Symbol, all Performance subtests of the Wechsler Adult Intelligence Scale.

A one factor LCDA model yields a chi-square $= 91.34$, $df = 78$, and $p = .143$. Equating error variances over groups and occasions (i.e., $\Delta_{t,i} = $ constant) gives a chi-square $= 123.97$, $df = 93$, and $p = .018$. The subtractive chi-square is 32.43, $df = 15$, and $p = .006$, so we can conclude the hypothesis of equal error variances, and, hence, a MANOVA model is unacceptable.

The ages of the two cohorts and similarity of their background suggests there should be little if any differences between the younger group at the second occasion and the older group at the first occasion. Consequently the following conditions were imposed on the one factor model: $v_{2,1} = v_{1,2}$, $\Phi_{22,1} = \Phi_{11,2}$, and $\Delta_{2,1} = \Delta_{1,2}$. For this constrained model chi-square $= 99.62$, $df = 85$, and $p = .133$. The subtractive chi-square against the unconstrained version is 8.28, $df = 7$, and $p = .309$.

Table 10.2 contains the maximum likelihood estimates of β, α, Ω, and Δ. This factor does not appear to be the factor usually found for the performance subtests in conventional factor analyses of the WAIS. A reasonable interpretation of this factor is that it involves speed of processing and response.

Table 10.3 consists of estimates of $\Phi_{st,i} - \Phi_0$ and $v_{t,i} - v_0$ for the two groups and two occasions. Note the decreasing means over occasions and cohorts and increasing variances over occasions and cohorts. We can infer from these

Table 10.2

ESTIMATES OF β, α, Ω, AND Δ

Subtest	β	α	Ω					$\Delta_{1,1}$	$\Delta_{2,1}=\Delta_{1,2}$	$\Delta_{2,2}$
PC	.280	−.049	.467					.621	.453	.499
PA	.785	.034	.360	.454				.627	.404	.533
BD	1[a]	−.048	.316	.339	.793			.247	.248	.506
OA	.816	−.081	.339	.376	.681	.794		.297	.536	.813
DY	1.235	.028	.251	.299	.403	.260	.903	.133	.253	.121

Note: PC = Picture Completion, PA = Picture Arrangement, BD = Block Design, OA = Object Assembly, DY = Digit Symbol, all performance subtests of the Wechsler Adult Intelligence Scale.
[a] Fixed for identification.

Table 10.3

ESTIMATED DISPERSION DIFFERENCES AND MEAN DIFFERENCES OF THE FACTOR IN EACH GROUP

	Younger subjects		Older subjects	
	Dispersion	Mean	Dispersion	Mean
Z_1	0[a]	0[a]	.125[b]	−.369[b]
Z_2	.021 .125[b]	−.369[b]	.136 .134	−.778

[a] Fixed for identification.
[b] Equated.

Table 10.4

APPROXIMATE FACTOR DISPERSION MATRICES

	Younger subjects	Older subjects
Z_1	.287	.308
Z_2	.275 .361	.221 .105

results that the factor(s) which account(s) for change and difference is (are) highly correlated over occasions within each group.

The procedure outlined in the previous section was implemented to compute the approximate factor dispersion matrices. These matrices are found in Table 10.4. There is clearly a problem here inasmuch as the approximate correlation across occasions exceeds unity in the older cohort, and the variance for the second occasion is too small in light of Table 10.3. These results are probably due to some estimated error variances being too large.

Repeated measures MANOVA applied to the data utilized in this study, with the usual homogeneity assumptions, yields highly significant cohort and occasion effects, and an insignificant cohort by occasion interaction. However inspection of the discriminant functions does not suggest that a single factor would account for age change both longitudinally and cross-sectionally, nor do post-hoc tests performed on variable subtests.

IDENTIFYING Φ AND ν

We first consider latent difference analysis. Suppose that there are group differences in error variances so that $\theta = \Omega + \Delta_i$, and that Ω admits of a factor analytic decomposition, $\Omega = \Lambda\Lambda' + \psi$. For simplicity of presentation, and without loss of generality, we shall choose uncorrelated factors. This can easily be overcome if substantive considerations so dictate. Therefore,

$$\mathbf{F} = \begin{bmatrix} \Lambda & \beta & \alpha \\ 0 & 0 & 1 \end{bmatrix}, \tag{22}$$

$$\mathbf{M}_i = [0 \ \nu_i \ 1], \tag{23}$$

$$\mathbf{V}_i = \begin{bmatrix} \mathbf{I} & 0 & 0 \\ 0 & \phi_i & 0 \\ 0 & 0 & 0 \end{bmatrix}, \tag{24}$$

and

$$\mathbf{D}_i = \begin{bmatrix} \psi + \Delta_i & 0 \\ 0 & 0 \end{bmatrix}. \tag{25}$$

Then it can be shown that the augmented moment matrix in the ith group is equal to $\mathbf{F} (\mathbf{M}_i\mathbf{M}_i' + \mathbf{V}_i) \mathbf{F}' + \mathbf{D}_i$ and there is no identification problem insofar as Φ_i and ν_i are concerned so long as the rank of $\mathbf{F}$ is equal to its column dimension.

For latent change analysis we again assume that $\Omega = \Lambda\Lambda' + \psi$. For two occasions let

$$\mathbf{F} = \begin{bmatrix} \Lambda & \beta & 0 & \mathbf{I} & 0 \\ \Lambda & 0 & \beta & \mathbf{I} & 0 \\ 0 & 0 & 0 & 0 & 1 \end{bmatrix}, \tag{26}$$

$$\mathbf{M}' = (0 \ \nu_1' \ \nu_2' \ \alpha' \ 1), \tag{27}$$

$$\mathbf{V} = \begin{bmatrix} \mathbf{I} & 0 & 0 & 0 & 0 \\ 0 & \phi_{11} & \phi_{21} & 0 & 0 \\ 0 & \phi_{12} & \phi_{22} & 0 & 0 \\ 0 & 0 & 0 & \psi & 0 \\ 0 & 0 & 0 & 0 & 0 \end{bmatrix}, \tag{28}$$

and

$$\mathbf{D} = \begin{bmatrix} \Delta_1 & 0 & 0 \\ 0 & \Delta_2 & 0 \\ 0 & 0 & 0 \end{bmatrix}. \tag{29}$$

It can readily be shown that the augmented moment matrix is equal to $\mathbf{F}$ ($\mathbf{MM}'$ + $\mathbf{V}$) $\mathbf{F}'$ + $\mathbf{D}$. The extension to more than two occasions is self-evident. No identification problem involving Φ_{st} and v_t arises so long as α does not lie in the column space of Λ and the rank of $[\Lambda, \beta]$ is equal to its column dimension. Thus, the extension to LCDA is obtained by subscripting $\mathbf{M}$, $\mathbf{V}$, and $\mathbf{D}$ with $i = 1$, . . ., g for different groups.

The potential user of this extension is cautioned that there is an ever-present danger of "factor collapse" (i.e., that the rank of $[\Lambda, \beta]$ is less than its column dimension). In other words, some columns of β might lie in the column space of Λ or vice versa. This event can create serious analytic difficulties.

Generally speaking, one would expect that the columns of Λ and of β would be such that even though the rank of $[\Lambda, \beta]$ might be equal to its column dimension the super matrix would be nearly degenerate. In practice, this will lead to real problems in fitting and estimation. Nor can one simply factor the estimate of Ω to get a look at Λ since Ω will be contaminated by $\beta\Phi_0\beta'$ because of the identification. The application of some joint constrained factor model (Tisak & Meredith, 1989) to the matrices $\Sigma_{st, i}$, s, $t - 1$, . . ., r, $i = 1$, . . ., g, as the case may require, might be helpful in understanding problems encountered but bear in mind the dispersion matrices are contaminated by β and Φ.

CONCLUSIONS

These approaches lend themselves to the development of randomization procedures for evaluation of the fit criterion. In LDA one would randomly assign N_1 subjects to Group 1, . . ., N_g subjects to Group g and compute estimates and evaluate the fitting function. This can be repeated a large number of times (say 1,000) and approximate empirical randomization standard errors. Also the approximate empirical randomization distributions of the fit function (e.g., likelihood ratio chi-square) can be determined for evaluation of goodness of fit and significance testing.

For each subject in LCA, occasions would be randomly allocated; that is, the vectors of observation X_t, $t = 1$, . . ., r would be randomized keeping the integrity of the subject. In LCDA the two randomization procedures would be combined.

In practice this will require the implementation of some more rapid procedures for estimation and fitting than is provided by LISREL and similar programs. Perhaps some scale-free alternative along the lines of the methods developed by Meredith (1965) would do.

COMMENTS ON "LATENT VARIABLE MODELS FOR STUDYING DIFFERENCES AND CHANGE"

J. J. McARDLE

Unlike the usual MANOVA models for dealing with differences and changes, Meredith's models have latent variables as common factors rather than canonical variates, and the focus is on change factors. Meredith presents these models in the elegant simplicity of matrix algebra using vector notation. The presentation is clear and concise; the WAIS-R example is particularly instructive. For those not highly conversant with matrix algebra, it may be helpful to translate his algebraic presentations into path diagrams (see Figure 10.1).

THE LCDA MODEL

The path diagram in Figure 10.1 highlights the major features of Meredith's latent change and latent difference (LCDA) model. Here it can be seen that the model contains multiple time points s and t, and multiple independent groups, f and g. Any of the parameters can be constrained to be invariant over several groups. This model is a multiple group factor model with the following particular features:

1. the common factors represent differences;
2. there is no factor model for the Y variables;
3. the first difference factor in the first group is constant, with no variance and no mean estimated; and
4. there is flexible organization for testing hypotheses about development.

This work was supported in part by a grant from the National Institute of Aging (AG07137).

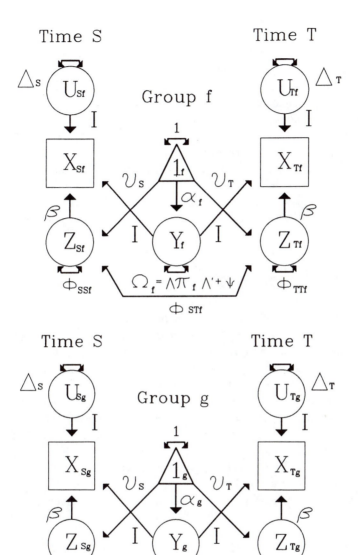

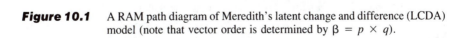

Figure 10.1   A RAM path diagram of Meredith's latent change and difference (LCDA) model (note that vector order is determined by $\beta = p \times q$).

Meredith points out that this model can be fitted using LISREL. One should be especially cautious in this fitting for several reasons. First, the model is complex and therefore is difficult to specify properly. I fit the diagrammed model for his data and was able to get correct values, but it took me more than an hour. The LISREL-VII setup that I used for this purpose is provided at the end of this section. Part of the difficulty of fitting the model stems from correctly specifying unique-nesses: There is a fixed variance $\Phi(1, 1) = 0$ with a free covariance $\Phi(1, 2) > 0$. With other data sets, other identification schemes may work better than the one shown here. There are also likely to be problems with analyses of average cross-products matrices in LISREL. Even for a unity scaled matrix, such as the one listed by Meredith, numerical optimization with LISREL requires that the start values be close to the final solution values. Thus, good prior knowledge is required.

ADDITIONAL MODEL FITS

I fitted several other models to study Meredith's idea about the difference between the average and the difference factor patterns. First, I fitted a one-factor model to the stationary Y variables (i.e., the Ω matrix). In this model, the average Y and difference $Z(t)$ common factors were free to vary. I obtained a likelihood ratio (LRT) of 116.83 ($DF = 77$). I then tested the hypothesis that the two factors had identical loadings. I constrained the factor loadings (L) to be invariant, but allowed the factor variances (V) to be free to vary over groups. The results were as follows: $L = [.45, .51, 1.00^*, .48]$, $V(g) = [.63, .69]$, and the LRT was 121.5 ($DF = 82$, $p = .003$). In comparison with the full-covariance model, there is a loss for this fit, with $dLRT = 30.17$ ($DF = 4$). The results, thus, indicate a poor fit for the invariant average and difference loadings. This is precisely the outcome that Meredith predicted: Factors of change are not the same as factors of level.

CONCLUSIONS

The LCDA model provides an integration of previous research. J. R. Nesselroade (personal communication, 1989) pointed out that the LCDA model is a combination of Harris's (1963) canonical changes model and a general linear dynamic model. The LCDA model has far fewer parameters than the usual MANOVA model for repeated measures. That it provides a flexible structural model for the analysis of change data is a main benefit of the LCDA. The model is, in this sense, very much like the invariant simultaneous equations of Haavelmo, who received a Nobel prize for his contributions. For his lifetime of contributions, perhaps we should award Meredith a Nobel prize as well.

LISREL PROGRAM

This is the LISREL setup used to run Meredith's model:

```
INPUT FOR LISREL-VII FOR MEREDITH'S LCDA MODEL
DATA NI = 11 NG = 2 N0 = 90 MA = MM
LABELS
Y__PCI Y__PAI Y__BDI Y__OAI Y__DY1 Y__PC2 Y__PA2 Y__BD2 Y__
OA2 Y__DY2 Y__M
MMATRIX
 1.00
  .27  1.00
  .43   .41  1.00
  .30   .41   .60  1.00
  .20   .33   .34   .26  1.00
  .35   .24   .29   .18   .15   .80
  .23   .34   .33   .35   .22   .36   .85
  .41   .32   .80   .68   .42   .24   .44  1.31
  .37   .25   .64   .69   .21   .24   .58   .80  1.19
  .26   .35   .41   .32   .89   .24   .36   .79   .47  1.51
  .00   .00   .00   .00   .00  − .20  − .12  − .37  − .26  − .49  1.00
MO NY = 11 NE = 9 TE = DI,FI LY = FI BE = FU,FI PS = SY,FI
FR[BETA1] LY 1 1 LY 2 1 LY 3 1 LY 4 1 LY 5 1
FR[BETA2] LY 6 2 LY 7 2 LY 8 2 LY 9 2 LY 10 2


EQ[BETA1__BETA2] LY 1 1 LY 6 2
EQ[BETA1__BETA2] LY 2 1 LY 7 2
EQ[BETA1__BETA2] LY 3 1 LY 8 2
EQ[BETA1__BETA2] LY 4 1 LY 9 2
EQ[BETA1__BETA2] LY 5 1 LY 10 2
FR[ALPHA1] LY 1 3 LY 2 3 LY 3 3 LY 4 3 LY 5 3
FR[ALPHA2] LY 6 3 LY 7 3 LY 8 3 LY 9 3 LY 10 3
EQ[ALPHA1__ALPHA2] LY 1 3 LY 6 3
EQ[ALPHA1__ALPHA2] LY 2 3 LY 7 3
EQ[ALPHA1__ALPHA2] LY 3 3 LY 8 3
EQ[ALPHA1__ALPHA2] LY 4 3 LY 9 3
EQ[ALPHA1__ALPHA2] LY 5 3 LY 10 3


FR[DELTA1] TE 1 1 TE 2 2 TE 3 3 TE 4 4 TE 5 5
FR[DELTA2] TE 6 6 TE 7 7 TE 8 8 TE 9 9 TE 10 10
FR[PHI1] PS 1 1
```

FR[PHI2] PS 2 2
FR[PHI12] PS 1 2
FR[NU1] BE 1 3
FR[NU2] BE 2 3

ST[SETUP__Y1] 1 LY 1 4 LY 2 5 LY 3 6 LY 4 7 LY 5 8
ST[SETUP__Y2] 1 LY 6 4 LY 7 5 LY 8 6 LY 9 7 LY 10 8

FR[OMEGA] PS 4 4 PS 5 5 PS 6 6 PS 7 7 PS 8 8
FR[OMEGA] PS 4 5 PS 5 6 PS 6 7 PS 7 8
FR[OMEGA] PS 4 6 PS 5 7 PS 6 8
FR[OMEGA] PS 4 7 PS 5 8
FR[OMEGA] PS 4 8

ST .5 ALL
ST 0 PS 1 2
ST 0 PS 4 5 PS 5 6 PS 6 7 PS 7 8
ST 0 PS 4 6 PS 5 7 PS 6 8
ST 0 PS·4 7 PS 5 8
ST 0 PS 4 8

ST[CONSTANT] 1 LY 11 3
FR[CONSTANT] PS 3 3
ST[CONSTANT] 1 PS 3 3

FI[FACTOR__ID] LY 3 1 LY 8 2
ST[FACTOR__ID] 1 LY 3 1 LY 8 2
FI[NU1] BE 1 3
ST[NU1] 0 BE 1 3
FI[PHI1] PS 1 1
ST[PHI1] 0 PS 1 1

FI[OMEGA] PS 4 5 PS 5 6 PS 6 7 PS 7 8
FI[OMEGA] PS 4 6 PS 5 7 PS 6 8
FI[OMEGA] PS 4 7 PS 5 8
FI[OMEGA] PS 4 8
FR[IOTA] PS 9 9
ST[IOTA] 1 PS 9 9
FR[PI] BE 4 9 BE 5 9 BE 6 9 BE 7 9 BE 8 9
FI[PI__ID] BE 6 9
ST[PI__ID] 1 BE 6 9

OU TO NS ND = 3 SE TV AD = OFF

Comment on Meredith: LCDA Model: Older Group Second
DATA NI = 11 NO = 75 MA = MM

LABELS
O_PC1 O_PA1 O_BD1 O_OA1 O_DY1 O_PC2 O_PA2 O_BD2
O_OA2 O_DY2 O_M
MMATRIX
1.01
.44 1.16
.37 .74 1.57
.46 .67 1.12 1.93
.34 .58 .77 .54 1.54
.67 .67 .70 .83 .59 1.31
.54 .89 .75 .64 .77 .80 1.59
.30 .69 1.31 1.11 .85 .60 .82 1.92
.58 .89 1.49 1.47 .81 .80 .97 1.46 2.62
.42 .77 1.10 .84 1.49 .79 1.16 1.30 1.30 2.09
− .12 − .33 − .49 − .54 − .37 − .30 − .67 − .86 − .82 − .90 1.00

MO TE = PS LY = IN BE = PS PS = IN

fr[phi2] ps 1 1 ps 2 2 ps 1 2
fr[constant2] ps 3 3
fr[nu2] be 1 3 be 2 3

fr[iota] ps 9 9
eq[pi] be 4 9 be 1 4 9
eq[pi] be 5 9 be 1 5 9
eq[pi] be 6 9 be 1 6 9
eq[pi] be 7 9 be 1 7 9
eq[pi] be 8 9 be 1 8 9

fr ps 4 4 ps 5 5 ps 6 6 ps 7 7 ps 8 8

OU

CHAPTER 11

ASSESSING FAMILIAL AND NONFAMILIAL SOURCES OF PARENT-CHILD ATTITUDE RESEMBLANCE OVER TWO MEASUREMENT OCCASIONS

ROBERT E. L. ROBERTS AND VERN L. BENGTSON

Editors' Introduction

Over a 14-year period, Roberts and Bengtson have obtained repeated measures data on samples of parents in their advanced years of adulthood, the middle-aged children of these parents, other adults of about the same age, and the children of the middle-aged adults. Such data provide a very interesting basis for studying change and invariance within individuals and within the circumstances in which individuals exist.

Roberts and Bengtson used structural equation modeling analyses to describe how variables that are interrelated at one point in time are associated with similar interrelated variables at a later time. Three important classes of problems must be thought through in modeling analyses under these conditions: (a) the separation and interpretation of influences associated with change in the society (period and birth cohort influences) and change

Funding for this research was provided by Grant R37-AG-07977 from the National Institute on Aging. We wish to thank John L. Horn and Linda Collins for their contributions to the development of this chapter. We would also like to thank Linda Hall and Christopher Hilgeman for their expert technical assistance in preparing the manuscript.

within individuals (aging influences); (b) the question of factorial invariance: Are the factor measurements obtained at one time, in individuals at
one stage of adult life, the same as the factor measurements obtained at
other times and in individuals at other stages of life?; and (c) the problems
that inevitably arise because the models we can specify are not, and never
can be, fully adequate—the problems of misspecification.

The results Roberts and Bengtson obtained are indicative of what to expect in the imperfect conditions under which research must be conducted. It
is particularly useful to read this chapter in the context of studying chapter
7 by Cunningham (and its introduction and comment) and chapter 15 by
Gollob and Reichardt.

This book has two main purposes: to identify major problems of design and
data analysis in research on change, and to indicate the most appropriate methods for dealing with such problems. This chapter primarily focuses on the
former. In our longitudinal study of attitude development and change in three-
generation families, we have come face to face with several major problems
endemic to substantive research on change. Moreover, the problems of understanding change in our research are in many respects different from those
met in most studies of development in psychology. This puts us in a good
position to raise important and distinct methodological questions about measurement, data analysis, and inference that arise when substantive interest and
available data come together in less than perfect ways. In raising these questions
we open doors to those who have become expert in developing methods designed to deal with questions about change.

To facilitate this discussion, we focus on one substantive interest of our
research project: assessing the extent to which one's family of origin accounts for
the genesis and continuance of important social attitudes in adulthood. In particular, we describe one approach for estimating the degree to which earlier patterns
of parental influence may account for the attitudes of adult children two decades
later. Two specific attitudes are examined: intolerance toward unemployment
insurance and belief in the social efficacy of religion.

THEORETICAL MODEL

Theories of early socialization acknowledge that individuals develop attitudes
under the press of influences operating within the family of origin as well as
influences external to that family (Glass, Bengtson, & Dunham, 1986). Early in
life, the impact of familial influences, relative to those coming from outside the
family context, is assumed to be great. As one ages, nonfamilial influences (e.g.,
teachers, school peers, spouses, and co-workers) become more salient and are
assumed to increase in relative importance. However, earlier familial influences

may endure because of the tendency for an individual's attitudes to persist over time and thus shape the attitudes he or she manifests at a later time. The aim of our research is to assess the extent to which familial influences continue to be important, both as immediate and ontological forces, in determining attitude stability and change in adulthood.

Figure 11.1 depicts a theoretical model for our theory of individual, familial, and nonfamilial influences on a child's attitude. We employ this model in our research. At any Time t, a child's attitude is expected to be a function of three influences:

1. his or her attitude at a previous time, Time $(t - k)$;
2. familial influences at Time t; and
3. nonfamilial influences at Time t.

Moreover, earlier familial and nonfamilial influences on a child's attitude (i.e., Time $[t - k]$) are expected to be reflected in the child's attitude at Time t as a function of the stability of the child's orientation between Time $(t - k)$ and Time t.

If one has appropriate data, the model in Figure 11.1 can be evaluated using covariance structure analysis techniques (as described in, e.g., Horn & McArdle, 1980; Jöreskog, 1979; McArdle & McDonald, 1984). Correlations between family members' attitudes (e.g., parents and children) can be employed to mirror familial influences. To mirror nonfamilial influences, one should find variables whose correlations with child's attitude would represent these influences. Lacking this, one can treat these effects as reflected in the residuals of the regression of child's attitude on parent's attitude for each measurement occasion. These residuals contain error, of course, in addition to nonfamilial influences, so one must be cautious when employing them in prediction.

The parameters F_1 and N_1 in Figure 11.1 refer to the direct effects of familial and nonfamilial experiences on an individual's attitude at Time $(t - k)$. The parameter S_C measures the distributional stability of a child's attitude. F_2 and N_2 represent the direct effects of familial and nonfamilial influences at Time t, respectively—the net of individual distributional stability. S_F and S_N refer to stability in earlier familial and nonfamilial influences, respectively, over time.

One can also use the model parameters to decompose the covariance between earlier familial influences and child's attitude at Time t into that portion that is mediated by stability in the child's attitude ($F_1 \times S_C$) and that portion due to stability in family influences ($S_F \times F_2$). Similarly, the covariation of earlier nonfamilial influences and later attitude can be broken down into that portion mediated by individual stability ($N_1 \times S_C$), and that portion due to stability in nonfamilial influences ($S_N \times N_2$).

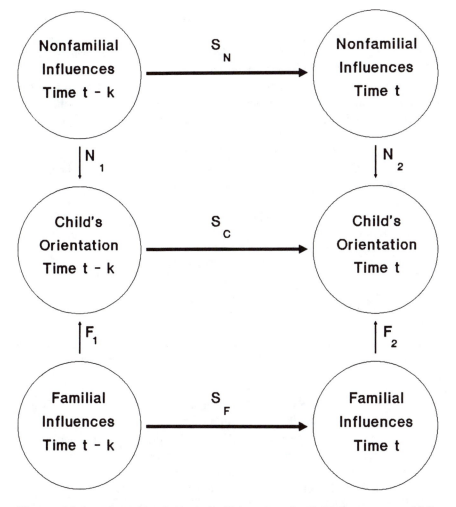

Figure 11.1   Model of individual, familial, and nonfamilial influences on a child's attitude. (S_N = stability of nonfamilial influences, N_1 = nonfamilial influences at Time 1, N_2 = nonfamilial influences at Time 2, S_c = stability of child's attitude, F_1 = familial influences at Time 1, F_2 = familial influences at Time 2, S_F = stability of familial influences.)

METHODOLOGICAL CHALLENGES

The conceptual model in Figure 11.1 poses several challenges for design and analysis. At a minimum, one needs to measure the attitudes of a number of parents and children on two separate occasions.

The data gathered in our three-generation study meet this minimum requirement. These data are unique compared to those usually found in developmental studies in that they include baseline and 14 year followup attitude measures from adult children, their parents, and grandparents. Because the young adult children and their parents really represent two groups of children, one group currently in their 30s and one group well into middle age (50s–60s), we can assess the extent of lagged parental influences through middle age by comparing results across the two sets of children.

Several potential problems need to be addressed before meaningful estimation and interpretation of a model like the one in Figure 11.1 can be accomplished. We shall address three of the most salient of these problems:

1. confounds among the effects of secular trends, birth-cohort membership, and aging;
2. measurement inconsistency over time; and
3. specification error.

Confounds in Secular Trends

Generational differences in observed patterns of familial influences and intraindividual consistency can reflect the operation of one or more of the following effects:

- ☑ *Group reproduction effects* or influences common to people who share membership in a distinct social unit such as a family (e.g., the influences of shared genes and socialization), workplace (e.g., shared activities and experiences), or social class/stratum (e.g., shared opportunity structure). Reproduction effects lead to intragroup homogeneity and intergroup attitude heterogeneity over time.
- ☑ *Period influences* (also called secular trends), which lead to changes over time in orientations (attitudes) that are reflected among most members of a society, regardless of age (e.g., influences of war, economic depressions, and natural disasters).
- ☑ *Birth cohort influences* operating at and through particular points in historical time (e.g., influences of growing up during the Great Depression, World War I, World War II, and the baby boom).
- ☑ *Aging influences*, which lead to individual change over the life course (e.g., change due to biological maturation, age-based social role transitions, and accumulation of injuries/pathology).

The conceptual thrust in our specification of models is to assess the extent to which group reproduction effects common to membership in one's family of origin extend into adulthood. It is tempting to view differences between model parameters obtained from separate groups of adult children, each representing a different age range (such as afforded by our data), as changes in the magnitude of family reproduction effects over the life course. However, such observed differences could be due to the operation of either aging or cohort effects. Because, by definition, all members of society would have been exposed to the same period influences between measurements, this class of influences should not result in differences in parameters across groups. Nevertheless, interactions between period influences and aging and/or cohort influences could result in intergroup differences. Thus, unless one effect or another can be ruled out logically or as being otherwise implausible, the interpretation of differences in model estimates across the two (or more) groups should classify them as due to aging/cohort or aging/cohort × period influences and not as due to any single effect exclusively.

Measurement Consistency

One must ensure consistency of measurement across generations and measurement occasions. As Horn, McArdle, and Mason (1983) have emphasized, one question that must be dealt with early in any analysis of change is whether the same attributes—or in our case, attitudes—are measured at different points in time and at different ages. Longitudinal data might reveal time-based differences in the relevance and meaning of some items used to measure an attitude. In addition, identical items may also have different meanings for members of different generations. Meaningful analyses of change or stability cannot be accomplished if one is measuring different attributes on each occasion.

Specification Error

One needs to specify as accurately as possible all relevant effects in the model. Ideally, one's theory should identify which variables are to be measured. In addition, one's data should contain measures of as many of these variables as possible. If one is not aware of, much less does not have, all of the variables representing all of the influences, there are bound to be errors in interpreting the results. How one brackets and minimizes the influence of such errors is a fundamental question that can be dealt with only partly in the analysis stage. One's ability to minimize this type of error is limited primarily by one's theory and one's ability to acquire appropriate data.

A particularly vexing version of this problem is described by Gollob and Reichardt in chapter 15 as the *time-specific* problem. In essence, the problem is that unless one specifies the time or age differences very precisely in terms of one's theory, results can be quite misleading. Often, however, one cannot know precisely over what time span an influence is expected to have an effect. In such circumstances, as in all others, one must live with the fact that a model is misspecified and try to make the best of this by developing evidence that indicates boundaries for influences and effects.

In the following empirical example, we first test the degree to which measures of two attitudes are consistent over a 14-year measurement interval and between parents and children in each of two parent/child samples drawn from our respondent pool. Then, we estimate parameters corresponding to those in the Figure 11.1 model for each set of parents and children. Finally, we attempt to demonstrate the kinds of biases that may occur when one fails to specify effects in a model such as the one in Figure 11.1.

METHODS

Subjects

The data are from the responses of 767 pairs of parents and children, representing three different generations, obtained at two points in time (Time 1 = 1971; Time 2 = 1985). Detailed descriptions of the overall sample and design (University of Southern California Longitudinal Study of Generations) have been published elsewhere (see Richards, Bengtson, & Miller, 1989; Roberts & Bengtson, 1990). We used the terms G_1, G_2, and G_3 to refer to each generation of respondents. G_1 was a group of 154 parents. The mean age of this sample in 1985 was approximately 78 years. One G_2 sample, G_{2a}, was a group of 154 middle-aged children of the G_1s. The mean age for this sample in 1985 was approximately 58 years. A second G_2 sample, G_{2b}, was a group of 613 middle-aged parents. The mean age of these parents in 1985 was approximately the same as the mean age of the G_{2a} children (58 years). (The G_{2a} sample was a subsample of the G_{2b} sample.) The G_3 sample was a group of 613 of the young-adult children of the G_{2b} sample of parents. The average age for the G_3 group in 1985 was approximately 33 years.

Measures

Measures included four multiple-choice items, two of which were hypothesized to tap intolerance toward unemployment insurance (ITUI) and two of which were hypothesized to measure belief in the social efficacy of religion (BSER); all were included in both the 1971 and 1985 surveys. The four items were:

1. It is a person's duty to work; it is sinful to be idle,

2. Most people on welfare are lazy; they just won't do a good day's work and so cannot get hired,

3. This country would be better off if religion had a greater influence in daily life, and

4. Every child should have religious instruction.

Responses to the first two items were expected to reflect ITUI; the last two items were expected to reflect BSER. Respondents chose either "strongly agree," "agree," "disagree," or "strongly disagree" to indicate their degree of ascribing to each of these attitudes. A preliminary factor analysis of the items was carried out using LISREL 6 (Jöreskog & Sörbom, 1986). A Procrustes rotation to a two-factor solution corresponding to our notion that ITUI and BSER are distinct constructs reflected in the attitude items provided a reasonable fit to the data.

Analysis

We first set out to assess the degree to which the same attitudes were being measured across parent–child generations and over time. One approach, developed most fully by Horn et al. (1983), is to specify each attribute as a multiple-indicator latent variable and test for invariance of the measurement model for this variable at the different points in time and different generations (i.e., to require factorial invariance, as discussed by Cunningham in chapter 7).

The question of factorial invariance of ITUI and BSER was tested by fitting LISREL models in eight subsamples of our data: G_1 and G_{2a} for measures obtained in 1971 and 1985 (each of these analyses was based on a sample size of 154); and G_{2b} and G_3 for measures obtained in 1971 and 1985 (each analysis was based on a sample size of 613). The following three models were estimated within each parent–child generational configuration: M_1 = a two-factor (correlated) model with the pattern matrix constrained to be equal across all groups; $M_2 = M_1$, with the additional constraint that the measurement error variance matrix is constrained to be equal across groups; and $M_3 = M_1$, plus an equality constraint on the factor variance/covariance matrix across groups. The test of factorial invariance consisted of assessing the significance of the χ^2 statistic associated with the fit of models M_1, M_2, and M_3.

The second set of analyses involved estimating with LISREL a model that conformed to the conceptual model in Figure 11.1. Figure 11.2 is a FIGMODE (Short, Horn, & McArdle, 1984) representation of the specification used to estimate the model parameters. In the FIGMODE, the boxes labeled "Var. 1" to "Var. 8" refer to the responses to the two empirical indicators of either ITUI or BSER (the model was estimated separately for each attitude). Thus, parent's and child's attitudes were treated as latent variables accounting for variance in the

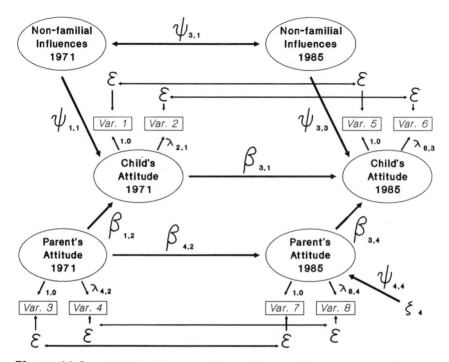

Figure 11.2   A FIGMODE representation of the specification used to estimate the model parameters. (Var. = variable.)

empirical indicators. A matrix of structural equation coefficients (β) representing directed relations between the latent attitude variables was estimated. The FIGMODE parameters $\beta_{1,2}$, $\beta_{3,1}$, $\beta_{4,2}$, and $\beta_{3,4}$ thus correspond to the Figure 11.1 parameters F_1, S_C, S_F, and F_2, respectively. LISREL also allows estimation of a variance/covariance matrix (ψ) for the residuals in the estimations of the structural relations between the latent variables. N_1 in Figure 11.1 was estimated as the square root of the variance of the residuals in the regression of child's attitude factor in 1971 on parent's attitude factor in 1971 (i.e., the square root of $\psi_{1,1}$); N_2 was given by the square root of the residual variance of the regression of child's 1985 attitude factor on child's 1971 and parent's 1985 attitude factors (i.e., the square root of $\psi_{3,3}$). The parameter S_N was estimated as the square of the correlation between the two sets of unmeasured variables, that is, ($\psi_{3,1}/N_1 \times N_2)^2$.

The model parameters were estimated twice for each attitude. In the first estimation, the parameter $\psi_{3,1}$ was constrained to be zero; in the second, $\psi_{3,1}$ was freely estimated. Thus, S_N would be zero in the former estimation and free in the latter estimation to reflect the directed relation between nonfamilial influences over time. In general, error in specifying relevant influences of an attribute could lead to the case in which part or all of the true S_N was treated as if it was zero, when in fact it was not. We estimated the model under each of these specifications in order to demonstrate the extent to which error in specifying and measuring relevant variables could bias one's results.

RESULTS

Table 11.1 presents summary statistics for the test of factorial invariance for the G_1–G_{2a} dyads. A hypothesis of fit for the model in which factor patterns alone are constrained to be equal need not be rejected. However, a model requiring that the factor variances and covariances be equal across generations does not fit the data (i.e., must be rejected: χ^2 [df = 19, N = 154, and p = .192]). The basic requirement of metric invariance, as specified by Horn et al. (1983), thus is achieved. The measurement model is similar enough across groups to warrant estimating the Figure 11.2 model for the data on parents and children. Table 11.2 contains the factor pattern matrix and interfactor correlation from the M_3 estimation.

Table 11.1

SUMMARY OF RESULTS FOR TESTS OF HYPOTHESES OF EQUALITY IN FACTOR STRUCTURES, ERROR VARIANCES, AND FACTOR VARIANCES OVER TIME AND ACROSS GENERATIONS (G_1–G_{2a} DYADS)

Model	Hypothesis	X^2	N	df	p	Decision
M_1	Equal factor structures	4.09	154	10	.943	Accepted
M_2	M_1 + equal error variances	47.34	154	22	.001	Rejected
M_3	M_1 + equal factor variance/covariances	24.11	154	19	.192	Accepted

Table 11.2

PATTERN MATRIX FOR MODEL WITH FACTOR LOADINGS AND FACTOR VARIANCES CONSTRAINED TO BE EQUAL ACROSS GENERATIONS AND MEASUREMENTS (G_1–G_{2a} DYADS)

	Factor[a]	
Item	Intolerance Toward Unemployment Insurance	Belief in Social Efficacy of Religion
Duty to work	.698	0
Welfare lazy	.475	0
More religion	0	.750
Religious instruction	0	.502

[a]Factor correlation = .586.

The results of the test of factorial invariance for the $G_{2b}-G_3$ sample of parents and children are presented in Table 11.3. The models, M_1, M_2, and M_3, do not fit the data (in each case, $p < .05$). Thus, a conclusion of factorial invariance—a prerequisite for estimating the Figure 11.2 model—was not supported.

Thus we have mixed results: a fit indicating factorial invariance in the G_1-G_{2a} dyads, but evidence of lack of fit in the $G_{2b}-G_3$ comparison. Given the nonerror influences that must operate to force nonfits for highly specified models (as discussed by Horn & McArdle, 1980), the fit for model M_1 in the $G_{2b}-G_3$ dyad is not all that bad. Also, these data meet the less stringent condition of configural invariance (Horn et al., 1983), with zero and nonzero loadings remaining zero and nonzero in a statistical sense over time and across generations (see Table 11.4). The factor patterns (standardized solution from LISREL) given by estimating the measurement model with no constraints on loadings, factor variances and covariances, or measurement error variance over time or across generations are presented in Table 11.4.

Table 11.3

SUMMARY OF RESULTS FOR TESTS OF HYPOTHESES OF EQUALITY IN FACTOR STRUCTURES, ERROR VARIANCES, AND FACTOR VARIANCES OVER TIME AND ACROSS GENERATIONS ($G_{2b}-G_3$ DYADS)

Model	Hypothesis	X^2	N	df	p	Decision
M_1	Equal factor structures	25.56	613	10	.004	Rejected
M_2	M_1 + equal error variances	130.34	613	22	.001	Rejected
M_3	M_1 + equal factor variances/covariances	57.53	613	19	.000	Rejected

Table 11.4

FACTOR PATTERNS FOR TWO-FACTOR MODEL OF ITUI[a] AND BSER[b] WITH NO EQUALITY CONSTRAINTS ON HYPOTHESIZED PATTERN MATRIX, FACTOR VARIANCES AND COVARIANCES, OR MEASUREMENT ERROR VARIANCES ACROSS GENERATIONS AND MEASUREMENT OCCASIONS ($G_{2b}-G_3$ DYADS)

	G_2 generation				G_3 generation			
	1971		1985		1971		1985	
Item	ITUI	BSER	ITUI	BSER	ITUI	BSER	ITUI	BSER
Duty to work	.741	0	.917	0	.753	0	.737	0
Welfare lazy	.464	0	.425	0	.520	0	.458	0
More religion	0	.653	0	.659	0	.710	0	.962
Religious instruction	0	.643	0	.611	0	.754	0	.670

[a]Intolerance toward unemployment insurance.
[b]Belief in social efficacy of religion.

We estimated the Figure 11.2 model parameters for the G_{2b}–G_3 sample. Because metric invariance was not supported, one should be cautious in interpreting the results of the subsequent model estimations. In practice, one might want to refocus the analysis on the single attitude items themselves, not the factors hypothesized to account for variability in the multiple items (for a discussion of issues in assessing stability and change in single items over time see, e.g., Heise, 1969; Wheaton, Muthén, Alwin, & Summers, 1977; Wiley & Wiley, 1970).

Table 11.5 contains parameter estimates (standardized, from LISREL) and chi-square tests of the fit of the Figure 11.2 model applied to BSER over time. A hypothesis of a model fit for the data cannot be rejected when the model is estimated for the G_1–G_{2a} sample. The model fit was much worse for the G_{2b}–G_3 sample (in each case, $p < .001$). Differences in the model fit are due in part to the measurement inconsistency shown previously in tests of factorial invariance (as already reported), but other reasons for the discrepancies are likely too (e.g., violations of distributional assumptions and differences in sample size). In chapter 4, Browne and Du Toit deal with some of the issues in assessing goodness or badness of fit of models.

The estimates in Table 11.5 indicate that the G_2 children were more stable (S_C) in BSER than the G_3 children over the 14 years (i.e., depending on the specification of $\psi_{3,1}$, $S_C = .949$ or $.907$ for the G_{2a} children and $S_C = .492$ or .275 for the G_3 children). However, earlier familial influences (F_1) and stability

Table 11.5

MAXIMUM LIKELIHOOD ESTIMATES OF PARAMETERS IN MODEL OF FAMILIAL AND NONFAMILIAL SOURCES OF STABILITY AND CHANGE IN A CHILD'S BELIEF IN THE SOCIAL EFFICACY OF RELIGION BETWEEN 1971 AND 1985

Parameter	G_{2a} children[a]		G_3 children[b]	
	$S_N = 0$	$S_N = 0$	$S_N = 0$	$S_N = 0$
S_c	.949	.907	.492	.275
F_1	.542	.543	.592	.593
N_1	.840	.839	.806	.806
S_F	.853	.851	.858	.861
S_N	—	.006	—	.062
F_2	−.168	−.146	.210	.329
N_2	.467	.469	.780	.797
X^2	16.83	16.81	38.93	37.68
df	15	14	15	14
p	.329	.266	.001	.001

Note: S = stability, F = familial, N = nonfamilial, C = child's attitude, 1 = Time 1 (1971), 2 = Time 2 (1985).
[a]$N = 154$.
[b]$N = 613$.

in those influences (S_F) were fairly constant across the two groups of children (i.e., exhibiting ranges from .542 to .593 and .851 to .863, respectively). Generational differences in the degree of persistence of earlier familial influences ($F_1 \times S_C$) largely result from differences in the stability of the child's orientation over time. Note that S_C was overestimated when S_N was constrained to be zero for each of the two groups, and estimates of the persistence of parental effects would thus also have been overestimated. The overestimation was especially acute for the G_{2b}–G_3 sample and reflects the greater stability in nonfamilial influences (S_N) over time.

Table 11.6 contains the parameter estimates and model fit statistics for the ITUI analysis. Again, the model fit the data well for G_1–G_{2a} sample ($p = .566$ and .498) and poorly for the G_{2b}–G_3 sample ($p < .001$ for both estimations). The most interesting development in Table 11.5 corresponds to the large negative coefficient corresponding to S_N in the G_1–G_{2a} estimation. Because N_2 reflects the influence of nonfamilial variables on the child's attitude in 1985 (the net of attitude stability over time) this finding suggests that change in levels of the nonfamilial variables that accounted for the child's attitude in 1971 were associated with change in the child's position in the distribution of this attitude over time. This suggests that there was high stability in the particular nonfamilial variables important in determining the G_{2a} child's attitude over the 14 years. The pattern of model estimates across specifications of $\psi_{3,1}$ for the G_{2b}–G_3 sample is similar to

Table 11.6

MAXIMUM LIKELIHOOD ESTIMATES OF PARAMETERS IN MODEL OF FAMILIAL AND NONFAMILIAL SOURCES OF STABILITY AND CHANGE IN A CHILD'S INTOLERANCE TOWARD UNEMPLOYMENT INSURANCE BETWEEN 1971 AND 1985

Parameter	G_{2a} child[a]		G_3 child[b]	
	$S_N = 0$	$S_N = 0$	$S_N = 0$	$S_N = 0$
S_c	.588	2.039	.632	.547
F_1	.373	.380	.707	.711
N_1	.928	.925	.708	.703
S_F	.969	.964	.837	.837
S_N	—	−.762	—	.015
F_2	.123	−.422	.104	.156
N_2	.766	1.547	.715	.713
X^2	13.48	13.37	47.73	47.59
df	15	14	15	14
p	.566	.498	.000	.000

Note: S = stability, F = familial, N = nonfamilial, C = child's attitude, 1 = Time 1 (1971), 2 = Time 2 (1985).
[a]$N = 154$.
[b]$N = 613$.

those found in the BSER analyses, with S_C being overestimated when S_N was unmodeled.

CONCLUSIONS

The foregoing analysis has illustrated some of the difficulties often faced by researchers interested in substantive research on attribute development, maintenance, and change. We have presented a model of individual, familial, and non-familial influences on a child's attitude over time and discussed difficulties associated with testing the model with actual data. Our suggestion is that researchers interested in modeling relational influences of individual attributes over time should be especially attentive to three issues. First, they need to acknowledge the historical character of attribute development and must attend to confounded historical/biographical influences. In the present example, main effects of period can be ruled out, but confounds remain between aging and cohort effects as well as interactions between aging/cohort and period. Second, investigators must assess the extent to which they are measuring the same thing over time and across relevant comparison groups. In our example, a case for metric invariance over time and generation in the two attitude factors could be made (albeit weakly) for only one of the two groups (G_1–G_{2a}). Finally, a researcher's estimates are really only as good as his or her theory and the variables for which he or she has data (echoing a research axiom, the implications of which may be ignored too often in the conduct of actual research). Our results demonstrate that stability in influences unaccounted for by one's model or measures may greatly bias the estimates one obtains from that model.

CHAPTER 12

IMPLICATIONS OF A MULTIDIMENSIONAL LATENT TRAIT MODEL FOR MEASURING CHANGE

SUSAN E. EMBRETSON

Editors' Introduction

In this chapter, Embretson describes a method whereby the ability assumed to produce observed performance, termed the *individual's effective latent ability*, is a sum of several subabilities. One of these subabilities is the ability one has before change is observed. Each of the remaining learning abilities represents an increment in effective ability between two successive measurements.

The model Embretson develops has a number of features that make it interesting for both methodological and substantive research. One feature is the model's conceptual clarity; when the model properly fits the data, item and scale comparability is provided. Thus using this approach enables one to construct comparable instruments containing varied measurement devices for use on different occasions. This is a very important feature, because there are many kinds of studies in which it is desirable to have different, but comparable, measures of the same attribute. For example, in studies in which subjects are intensively and frequently measured, it is desirable to have alternate forms of a measurement instrument. Several contributors to this volume (e.g., Cohen, Collins and Graham, Gollob and Reichardt, and Nesselroade) have argued that often it is desirable in longitudinal research to obtain frequent, repeated measures of individuals, provided one can circumvent problems of artifactual dependence. Having comparable alternate forms for remeasurement helps one deal with these problems. Similarly, when individuals are measured repeatedly across the life span it is often necessary that different sets of items be used. Embretson's approach can help provide assurance that the same attribute is being measured. It is interesting to compare this approach with the approaches of Cunningham (chapter 7) and of Meredith (chapter 10).

Measuring ability from the actual progress of learning has had theoretical appeal since the beginning of modern ability measurement. At the first major conference on intelligence, many participants stressed capacity for learning as the major aspect of intelligence. But, even then it was noted that " . . . most tests in common use are not tests of the capacity to learn, but are tests of what has been learned" (Dearborne, 1921, p. 195). Interest in the direct measurement of learning continues in contemporary research and theory on intelligence. Resnick and Neches (1984) pointed out that viewing static tests as measures of learning ability is based on the (probably faulty) assumption that "the processes required for performance on the tests are also directly involved in learning" (p. 276).

Despite the continuing interest, early attempts to measure individual differences in learning ability were largely unsuccessful. A brief review of the literature (presented below) suggests that both substantive problems and psychometric problems led to the failure to measure learning ability. Fortunately, contemporary developments in both cognitive psychology and psychometric methods can provide a new foundation for measuring learning ability.

In this chapter I describe a multidimensional Rasch model for measuring learning and change (MRMLC) that is based on item response theory (Embretson, in press). This model specifies a structure that relates item performance in a specified measurement condition or occasion to initial ability and one or more learning abilities. With certain constraints on the item discrimination parameters, the model belongs to the family of multidimensional Rasch (1961) models.

MEASURING LEARNING ABILITY

Substantive Approaches

Woodrow's (1938) early research on learning ability indicated that individual differences in changes over practice were specific to the learning task and were not valid predictors of learning in an educational setting. Although Woodrow's studies had a negative impact on learning ability research, it should be noted that certain aspects of the research design were biased for negative findings. Woodrow measured learning ability on simple perceptual tasks that do not predict school learning (see Wissler, 1901). Furthermore, practice on the tasks continued to asymptotic levels in which performance levels were converging. Thus, changes in performance were highly correlated with initial performance levels.

Contemporary approaches to measuring learning ability differ in several respects from Woodrow's (1938) early studies. First, learning ability is measured on complex tasks, such as ability test items, that do predict school learning. Second, the measurement conditions are designed to attribute performance changes to specific cognitive processes rather than to the unknown impact of practice. Contemporary cognitive studies on ability (e.g., Sternberg, 1985) have provided theories to understand the sources of cognitive complexity in items and, further, methods to manipulate the difficulty of these underlying sources. Thus, learning abilities are referenced to the sources of cognitive complexity that are influenced by the problem-solving cues or training (see Lidz, 1987, for several examples) that accompany the measurement condition. Third, changes in performance levels are not highly related to initial performance levels. By measuring change on complex tasks with a high ceiling, and by giving only a few replications, individual differences do not converge to a common level.

Psychometric Approaches

Appropriate psychometric models for measuring learning processes have also been difficult to develop. Earlier attempts to measure learning and change (e.g., Harris, 1963) led to many seemingly irresolvable conflicts. For example, Bereiter (1963) noted that measuring change by difference scores had three problems: (a) The reliability of change is inversely related to the reliability of the tests, (b) change may not be measured on the same scale for persons at different initial score levels, and (c) change scores have a spurious negative relation to initial scores. For the latter, Lord (1963) showed how the negative correlation of the pretest with change arises from the regression effect, even when no real change has occurred. Thus, these various difficulties seem irresolvable when change measurements are conceptualized within classical test theory. That is, both the mean level of change and the meaning of change (assessed by correlations) depend on the distribution of initial scores, which is population specific.

Some of these seemingly irresolvable problems can be resolved by conceptualizing change measurement within item response theory. Fischer (1976) proposed a linear logistic latent trait model with relaxed assumptions (LLRA) to simultaneously model performance at all measurement occasions by including both trend and treatment effects. The trend and treatment parameter estimates have the advantage of specific objectivity in that they do not depend on ability distributions. However, LLRA is not applicable to measuring individual differences in learning because the treatment or trend effects are assumed to be equal for all persons who receive the same treatments conditions (or time intervals).

Measuring individual differences in growth has also been examined with item response theory. Such an approach requires curve fitting, as in Bock's (1976) application of an item response model to fit growth curves. Unfortunately, however, Bock suggested that fitting mental growth curves may be difficult because the reliability of individual observations typically is too low to test hypotheses about trends. Furthermore, obtaining sufficient measurement replications to test higher order trend components may be impractical.

Finally, Anderson (1985) presented a multidimensional Rasch model for the repeated testing of the same person over several occasions (or conditions). In Andersen's model, item difficulties are constant over occasions, but the ability that is involved depends on the occasion. Although Andersen's model is appropriate for data in which learning occurs, because ability is occasion specific, the model does not contain learning abilities.

The various item response models reviewed previously are important contributions because a single model is postulated for performance under multiple conditions or occasions. Furthermore, ability is a latent variable and is not directly equated with performance levels. However, none of these models contains parameters to assess person differences in changes across conditions. Thus, they are not appropriate for the measurement of learning abilities.

Initial Ability, Learning Ability, and Effective Ability

An MRMLC can be applied to data that contain two or more measurements of ability. The ability measurements may correspond to either multiple occasions or to multiple conditions present during a single occasion. Two distinct kinds of ability are measured with MRMLC, effective ability and learning ability. Effective ability is the latent potential of a person's performance on a particular occasion or under specified conditions of measurement. Effective ability on the first occasion, also referred to as initial ability, is the traditional ability measurement. Learning ability is the increment in effective ability between two successive measurements. At the second or later measurement, effective ability depends on initial ability and one or more learning abilities.

When items are presented under sequentially administered K conditions, the first test is the standard test condition, while the remaining tests follow $K - 1$ units of targeted instruction, structured cues, or practice. Underlying performance is item difficulty, b_i, and M abilities, θ_{jm} for each person j, so that θ_{j1} is the initial ability and θ_{j2} to θ_{jm} are learning abilities.

It is assumed that any increase in item performance for person j results from an increase in effective ability, which is due to a change in learning abilities rather than a change in item difficulty. Thus, item difficulties are constant over many conditions, so that a single item difficulty, b_i, applies to the item with any condition. Furthermore, items within the same condition are assumed to have equal discriminations, a_{km}.

Performance for any item that is administered under condition k is governed by the effective ability, θ_{jk}^*, which is given as follows:

$$\theta_{jk}^* = \sum_{m=1} a_{km}\theta_{jm}, \tag{1}$$

where a_{km} = discrimination for all items administered under condition k on dimension m. Because conditions are administered sequentially, learning abilities cannot be involved in item performance measurement prior to administering the condition k that is associated with dimension m. Thus a matrix of item discrimination parameters, $\mathbf{A}_{k \times m}$, is structured as follows:

$$\mathbf{A}_{k \times m} = \begin{bmatrix} a_{11} & 0 & 0 & \cdots & 0 \\ a_{21} & a_{22} & 0 & \cdots & 0 \\ \cdot & \cdot & \cdot & & \cdot \\ a_{K1} & a_{K2} & \cdot & & a_{km} \end{bmatrix} \tag{2}$$

Equations 1 and 2 define effective abilities as being governed by a set of equations representing the impact of initial ability and the learning abilities (Equation 3).

$$\theta_{j1}^* = a_{11}\theta_{j1}$$

$$\theta_{j2}^* = a_{21}\theta_{j1} + a_{22}\theta_{j2}$$

$$\vdots \qquad \vdots \tag{3}$$

$$\theta_{jk}^* = a_{K1}\theta_{j1} + a_{k2}\theta_{j2} \ldots + a_{km}\theta_{jm}$$

According to this general formulation, increasingly more abilities are involved in the effective ability under each successive condition k. Models of this form have often been proposed for longitudinal data (e.g., simplex models for correlations). However, the importance here is that a constrained structure of abilities is postulated as a measurement model. That is, effective abilities are postulated to be condition specific, even within the same measurement occasion. Thus, Equation 3 specifies a dynamic, rather than a static, concept of ability.

Equation 3 also specifies some constraints for a measurement model. For example, within condition k, the item discrimination parameters for each dimension m are equal for all items, i. Thus, although the model of effective ability is multidimensional for $k > 1$, θ_k^* is a weighted composite of abilities that is the same for all items within condition k. Therefore, within a condition, a single (composite) ability characterizes performance on each item.

Figure 12.1 presents a schematic representation of the relation among effective ability, initial ability, and learning ability, as well as items. However, the relation of item solving to ability is nonlinear and requires the specification of an item response model.

A MULTIDIMENSIONAL RASCH MODEL FOR LEARNING AND CHANGE

The Rasch Model

An important feature of MRMLC is that abilities are measured as latent variables in an item response theory (IRT) model (see Lord, 1980, for more detail). In the Rasch model, the most simple IRT model, the latent potential, ξ_{ij}, (that person j solves item i) is the difference between the person's ability, θ_j^*, and the item's difficulty, b_i, as follows:

$$\xi_{ij} = \theta_j^* - b_i. \tag{4}$$

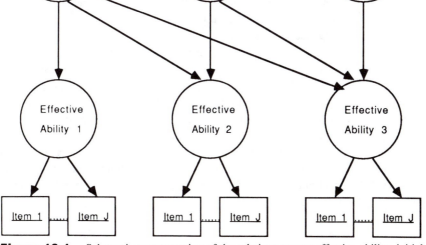

Figure 12.1   Schematic representation of the relations among effective ability, initial ability, and learning ability.

Thus, Equation 1 shows that latent response potential is greatest for a person of high ability encountering an easy item.

The Rasch model is a logistic model in which the latent response potential determines that the person solves a particular item as follows:

$$P\ (x_{ij}\ -\ 1|\theta_j^*,b_i)\ =\ \frac{\exp(\theta_j^*\ -\ b_i)}{1\ +\ \exp(\theta_j^*\ -\ b_i)}. \tag{5}$$

Ability is estimated from a person's responses to the test items, such that the differences between his or her item responses and the probability predicted by Equation 5 is as small as possible.

A major advantage of the Rasch model over classical test theory is that ability estimates are not biased by item difficulty. In classical test theory, the relative difference in ability between two persons or the same person on two occasions, depends on whether the test items are easy, moderate, or difficult. For example, two abilities that are measured by total score (or any linear transformation including z scores) may seem quite different on a set of moderately difficult items, but be virtually indistinguishable on very easy or very difficult items. In contrast, the difficulty of the items is controlled by the ability estimates provided by the Rasch model because item difficulty is a parameter in the model. Thus, the same differences between two abilities will be given in the Rasch model, whether the items are easy, moderate, or difficult. The independence of measurements from the measuring instrument is a very desirable property (see Rasch, 1961) and is crucial for measuring change.

MRMLC

Given the developments in Equations 1–3, the MRMLC may be formulated as an extension of the multidimensional Rasch model for binary data (Rasch, 1961) by introducing only one further constraint on the item parameters, namely that they are constant across occasions. The MRMLC has several advantages over the other binary data models (e.g., normal ogive model), including (a) the possibility of conditional maximum likelihood estimation for the item parameters, (b) specific objectivity of the parameters, (c) learning ability parameters that may be interpreted directly with respect to latent response potential, and (d) the fact that multivariate ability distribution need not be specified.

If we assume that the item difficulties, b_i, are constant across the K conditions and that effective ability is given as a combination of the initial ability and learning abilities, but that all nonzero item discriminations, a_{km}, are unity, then the matrix of item discriminations $\mathbf{A}_{k\ \times\ m}$ is

$$\mathbf{A}_{k\ \times\ m}\ =\ \begin{bmatrix} 1 & 0 & 0 & \cdots & 0 \\ 1 & 1 & 0 & \cdots & 0 \\ \cdot & \cdot & \cdot & & \cdot \\ 1 & 1 & 1 & \cdots & 1 \end{bmatrix}. \tag{6}$$

Furthermore, the effective abilities, θ_j^*, for a condition k may be given as

$$\theta_j^* = \mathbf{A}_{k \times m}\theta_j, \tag{7}$$

which shows that effective abilities have the following simple form:

$$
\begin{bmatrix} \theta_{j1}^* \\ \theta_{j2}^* \\ \theta_{j3}^* \\ \cdot \\ \theta_{jm}^* \end{bmatrix}
=
\begin{bmatrix}
1 & 0 & 0 & 0 & \cdots & 0 \\
1 & 1 & 0 & 0 & \cdots & 0 \\
1 & 1 & 1 & 0 & \cdots & 0 \\
& & \cdot & \cdot & \cdot & \\
1 & 1 & 1 & 1 & \cdots & 1
\end{bmatrix}
\begin{bmatrix} \theta_{j1} \\ \theta_{j2} \\ \theta_{j3} \\ \\ \theta_{jm} \end{bmatrix}. \tag{8}
$$

In Equation 8, a new learning ability is associated with each measurement occasion. Although $\mathbf{A}_{k \times m}$ could be easily constrained to fewer learning abilities, only the full model is described here.

The structure of $\mathbf{A}_{k \times m}$ shows that the effective abilities depend on an unweighted sum of initial ability and the $k - 1$ learning abilities. Although initial ability and learning ability may have unequal impact on performance, no item discrimination parameters other than unity are needed. Analogous to confirmatory factor analysis, unequal saturations of the variables (items) on the latent dimensions may be reflected in either the loadings (i.e., discriminations) or the ability variances. If the item discriminations are set to unity, then the differing impact will be reflected instead in the variances of the abilities.

Because $\mathbf{A}_{k \times m}$ shows that the summation for θ_{jk}^* includes only learning abilities up to condition k, we may write θ_{jk}^* as

$$\theta_{jk}^* = \sum_{m=1}^{k} \theta_{jm}. \tag{9}$$

The MRMLC, incorporating Equation 9 and assuming that item difficulties remain constant over conditions, can thus be given as

$$P(X_{i(k)j} = 1) = \frac{\exp(\sum_{m=1}^{k} \theta_{jm} - b_i)}{1 + \exp(\sum_{m=1}^{k} \theta_{jm} - b_i)}, \tag{10}$$

where θ_{j1} = initial ability at $k = 1$; $\theta_{j2}, \ldots, \theta_{jM}$ = learning abilities that correspond to $k > 1$; and b_i = item difficulty.

Note that the estimation of the item parameters in Equation 10 requires a counterbalanced design to preserve local independence. Thus, a design matrix that assigns the observation condition for an item to a group of persons must be incorporated into the estimates. Table 12.1 presents a Latin square design structure for three groups under these conditions.

A Monte Carlo study with two conditions (pretest and posttest) and three item sets (4 linking items and two 20-item test forms), which were counterbalanced

Table 12.1

DATA STRUCTURE FOR ITEMS ADMINISTERED UNDER THREE CONDITIONS

		Item assignment		
Group	Linking items	Block 1	Block 2	Block 3
1	1	1	2	3
2	1	3	1	2
3	1	2	3	1

Note: 1 = pretest, 2 = posttest 1, and 3 = posttest 2.

over two groups ($N = 1,000$ each), was undertaken for this chapter to demonstrate estimation of the item parameters. Good recovery of the item parameters ($r = .996$), initial ability ($r = .930$) and learning ability ($r = .901$) was found.

LEARNING ABILITY VERSUS CHANGE SCORES

In classical test theory (cf. Bereiter, 1963), the measurement of change is conceptualized as a difference score. Although later developments have refined the indices (e.g., Cronbach & Furby, 1970) by residualizing change scores with various indices of initial status, a difference score is still the essential concept.

The prototypic change score involves a pretest ability, z_{j1}^*, and posttest ability, z_{j2}^* for person j. These abilities are transformed into an initial ability and a change measurement, z_{j1} and z_{j2}, respectively, as follows:

$$\begin{bmatrix} z_{j1} \\ z_{j2} \end{bmatrix} = \begin{bmatrix} z_{j1}^* \\ z_{j2}^* - z_{j1}^* \end{bmatrix}, \tag{11}$$

and so

$$\begin{bmatrix} z_{j1} \\ z_{j2} \end{bmatrix} = \begin{bmatrix} 1 & 0 \\ -1 & 1 \end{bmatrix} \begin{bmatrix} z_{j1}^* \\ z_{j2}^* \end{bmatrix}. \tag{12}$$

It is interesting to compare the classical concept of change measurement to the multidimensional conceptualization of learning ability. In the multidimensional model, it is postulated that the underlying abilities, θ_j, produce the effective abilities, θ_j^*, as

$$\begin{bmatrix} \theta_{j1}^* \\ \theta_{j2}^* \end{bmatrix} = \begin{bmatrix} 1 & 0 \\ 1 & 1 \end{bmatrix} \begin{bmatrix} \theta_{j1} \\ \theta_{j2} \end{bmatrix}. \tag{13}$$

The classical concept of change scores in Equation 11 defined an index from the observed abilities rather than modeling observed abilities from underlying abilities that include change. However, because z_j^* obviously corresponds to effective abilities, θ_j^* and because

$$\begin{bmatrix} 1 & 0 \\ -1 & 1 \end{bmatrix}^{-1} = \begin{bmatrix} 1 & 0 \\ 1 & 1 \end{bmatrix}, \tag{14}$$

the classical change concept is inherently multidimensional. That is, the classical change concept implicitly involves the same relations of observed (effective) abilities to underlying abilities as the multidimensional model for learning and change that is proposed here, because Equation 12 can be written as

$$\begin{bmatrix} z_1^* \\ z_2^* \end{bmatrix} = \begin{bmatrix} 1 & 0 \\ 1 & 1 \end{bmatrix} \begin{bmatrix} z_1 \\ z_2 \end{bmatrix}. \tag{15}$$

Thus, it can be seen that the calculation of change scores from two observed abilities implicitly assumes that ability on the posttest, z_2^*, is multidimensional rather than unidimensional. Furthermore, the relative weights of initial ability and change in the posttest are identical to the unit-weighted relations that are postulated in Equation 11.

Although the multidimensional nature of posttest ability seems quite obvious in the preceding development, I will show that the reliability paradox in change measurement resulted from conceptualizing the posttest as unidimensional. If the emphasis had been on modeling the pretest and posttest from underlying dimensions (Equation 15) rather than on calculation (Equation 9), the multidimensionality would have been clear.

The Reliability of Change Scores

Evaluating the role of error in change scores has been a paradoxical issue in classical test theory. As the correlation of the pretest and posttest measures decreases, then the relative error in change scores also decreases (see Lord, 1963, for the classic formula for the reliability of change scores). However, as Bereiter (1963) pointed out, a low pretest–posttest correlation leads to difficulties in interpreting the meaning of "change," because it indicates that the tests do not measure the same dimension. This paradox results from not conceptualizing change as a separate dimension. If the pretest and the posttest are equivalent forms to measure the same dimension, then the pretest–posttest correlation is an index of reliability in classical test theory, and it must be high.

The MRMLC avoids this conceptual paradox because learning abilities are postulated as separate dimensions. Furthermore, because learning ability is defined in an item response model, evaluating the error in the learning ability estimates clearly does not involve pretest to posttest correlations. The variance for estimating learning ability depends on the information about the ability, which can be given for each person, j, by the MRMLC (Equation 10) probability $P(X_{i(k)j} = 1)$ [now written as $P(\theta_j)$], as

$$s^2_{\theta j2} = \sum_I^I P(\theta_j) (1 - P(\theta_j)) \Big/$$

$$\sum_I^{s_1-1} p(\theta_j) (1 - P(\theta_j)) (\sum_{s_1}^I p(\theta_j) (1 - P(\theta_j))), \qquad (16)$$

where items 1 to $s_1 - 1$ appear on the pretest and items s_1 to I appear on the posttest.

As in other item response models, Equation 16 implies that measurement error is minimized when item difficulties are close to the person's ability level. Because the model is multidimensional, minimizing measurement error for learning ability requires matching item difficulties to effective ability at both the pretest and posttest.

Change Scores at Different Levels of Initial Ability

Bereiter (1963) noted that a small change that occurs when initial ability is high may not have the same meaning as the same change that occurs when initial ability is more moderate. In the context of classical test theory, performance changes are linearly related to the estimated change score. Thus, the classical test theory model did not provide a means for formalizing Bereiter's observation. In item response theory, of course, the relation of ability to performance (expressed as response probabilities) is nonlinear, and, further, the exact change in probability between any two effective abilities depends on their relative location on the item response curve. In the MRMLC the expected changes in performance for a given level of learning ability will depend on both the level of initial ability and the item difficulties. Figure 12.2 presents an item characteristics curve, plotted against effective ability on the posttest. Two hypothetical persons with different initial ability levels, (θ_{11} and θ_{21}, respectively) but equal learning abilities (θ_{12} and θ_{22}) are shown. This figure shows that the increase in performance is far greater for Person 2 than for Person 1.

Figure 12.3 presents the expected change scores from the MRMLC for learning ability (Ability 2) at three levels of initial ability (Ability 1) on the Monte Carlo study subjects. Change scores were calculated as the difference between the expected true scores (see Lord, 1980, for the formula) at the pretest and the posttest. It can be seen that the change scores that are associated with learning ability depend on the initial ability level, because of the nonlinear relation of

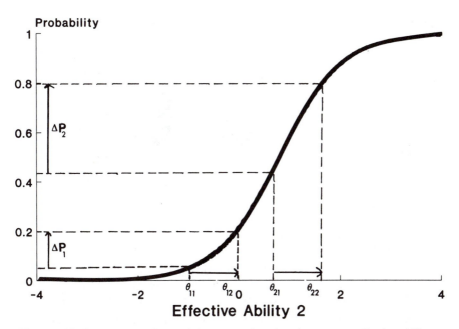

Figure 12.2   An item characteristics curve plotted against posttest effective ability.

effective ability to performance. In this example, high learning abilities (i.e., modifiabilities) were associated with more performance change for the lower initial abilities than for the higher initial abilities. The opposite pattern was found for low learning abilities. However, the exact relations of initial ability and learning ability to change scores will depend on the difficulty of the items.

The Negative Correlation of Change and Initial Ability

Another classical paradox is that the correlation of change scores with initial ability has a spurious negative bias because of the sharing of error variances. The error component of the first ability is also involved in the change score, but with a change of sign (Lord, 1963). Thus, a negative bias in the correlation of change with initial level is created.

Although the classical test theory derivation does not apply directly to the present model, a negative bias in the correlation between initial ability and learning ability was observed in a small Monte Carlo study. Although the generating correlation was .00, initial ability estimates and learning ability estimates had a negative correlation. This correlation was primarily due to the elimination of persons who had perfect scores on the posttest, which was likely if both the initial ability and learning ability were high. Thus, the correlation of the true initial

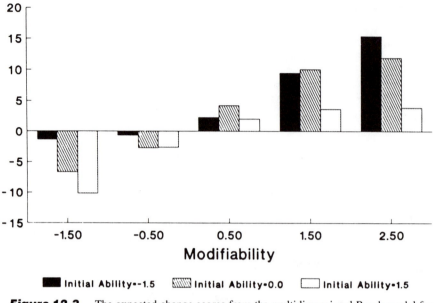

Figure 12.3   The expected change scores from the multidimensional Rasch model for learning and change (MRMLC) for learning ability at three levels of initial ability of the Monte Carlo study subjects.

ability with the true learning ability in the remaining sample was negative ($r = -.267$). However, the observed negative correlation between the estimates of initial ability and learning ability was even higher than this value ($r = -.403$), which indicates some negative bias in estimation.

Although beyond the scope of this chapter, item response theory provides methods that can reduce, if not eliminate, the negative bias. For example, adaptive testing can eliminate the problem of perfect scores, as well as optimize ability information at all levels. Thus, error variances for estimating initial abilities can be equalized across ability levels.

GROWTH CURVES

The growth and decline of ability across the life span have been a recurring research issue. In terms of the MRMLC model, growth curves for an individual or group could be derived from the effective abilities observed at the various occasions of measurement. However, the MRMLC ability growth curves will be different from ability growth curves obtained from observed performance levels, given by measures from classical test theory. Growth curves obtained from MRMLC abilities are more valid because MRMLC abilities are controlled for test properties.

Figure 12.3 shows that changes in observed performance levels are not linearly related to ability change. Both initial ability and item difficulty influenced the observed performance level change. These effects extend to growth curve shape. In general, growth in observed performance levels will be greatest for individuals (or groups) for whom item difficulty is most appropriate (i.e., an accuracy rate of .50). Observed performance levels will change less for individuals for whom the items are too easy or too difficult. Growth curves based on MRMLC abilities are not confounded with either item difficulty or initial ability, because both are included as parameters in the model. Although controlling for item difficulty is standard in IRT models, controlling for initial ability is a special advantage of MRMLC.

CONCLUSIONS

I have presented a latent trait model for the measurement of learning and change that is based on a multidimensional conceptualization of the learning process. A structure to relate performance to initial ability and learning ability has been specified, and with further constraints on the item parameters (i.e., unit weights), the MRMLC was presented. The Monte Carlo study indicated good recovery of both item and person parameters from the MRMLC model.

The measurement of learning ability with MRMLC has also been examined with respect to the classical issues in the measurement of change. It has been shown that whereas ability is regarded as unidimensional, the classical concept of change is inherently multidimensional in the manner postulated in MRMLC. However, the multidimensional latent trait formulation of learning ability has several advantages because (a) the paradox of the reliability of change disappears, (b) the different meaning of change at different initial ability levels is directly accommodated by the model, and (c) the spurious negative relation of initial level and change can be reduced by maximizing measurement precision at each level.

COMMENTS ON "IMPLICATIONS OF A MULTIDIMENSIONAL LATENT TRAIT MODEL FOR MEASURING CHANGE"

NORMAN CLIFF

Change is such an intuitively simple concept, yet it turns out to be one that is difficult to study statistically because of the ease with which artifacts can be introduced. The difficulties encountered by the simple difference score were identified early, Bereiter's (1963) study being an important source in this respect, along with Lord's (1963). The problem, therefore, is that of correlating a linear composite with its components.

There are a few early examples of trying to study changes attributable to learning within the context of an extensive aptitude battery that are more salient than Woodworth's (Woodrow, 1938). Allison's (1960) and Tenopyr's (1966) works come to mind. It is unfortunate that these dissertations did not become part of the wider literature, although both were rather widely circulated in Office of Naval Research (ONR) technical report form. These were more sophisticated attempts to relate the parameters of change across time to aptitude measures. Also deserving mention as a sophisticated model for studying mental growth is the work of Keats (e.g., 1983) on growth in mental age.

ITEM RESPONSE THEORY (IRT)

I am glad to see attempts like the one by Embretson to construct a specific model for changes across time. When dealing with test data, using an item response theory (IRT) model for this purpose has some advantages over trying to model the observed scores themselves, even though IRT models are subject to criticism.

Within the IRT context, Embretson's model is a well considered one. The IRT approach avoids the end effects that make it difficult to observe much change when an initial score is near the end of the scale where not much change can take place. IRT models are better able to circumvent this than observed-score models because they measure growth on the *latent* variable, which has potentially unlimited range. Modeling the latent variable virtually ensures that the score means as well as the covariances will be examined, rather than focusing on just one or the other. Using the IRT approach also enables the investigator to take advantage of the substantial number of results and programs that are available in this active research area.

Embretson's model used several properties that I find attractive (relative to other approaches that might have been taken within that framework). A scale is provided for the latent variable that is not subject to the indeterminacies that plague the more complex versions (Cliff, 1989a) and the latent scale is defined at the interval-scale level, rather than only ordinally.

As far as the model for the change in scores on the latent variable is concerned, one would call it a *path model*. At each stage in the process modeled, the current score on the latent variable is the score at the previous occasion plus an increment that results from the treatment or maturation that went on in the interval since the last measurement. The important feature here is that the score at $t - 1$ enters into performance at t in an unweighted fashion, (see Equations 4–6) rather than being discounted or magnified through the operation of a regression weight attached to the $t - 1$ score, as in some other path models. In this way, such a model is much more purely recursive than is the normal path model in which all the coefficients can vary. This feature leads to a much more parsimonious model with M parameters rather than $M(M + 1)/2$ (as in the more general version) and has the effect of predicting that the variance increases across the sequence of trials. This strikes me as realistic as well as parsimonious.

The methods for fitting the model show expertise insofar as I am competent to judge. Although the methods Embretson uses are among the ones that have come to be standard in these models over the last decade or so, employing them successfully in this context of modeling change represents a considerable achievement. An important and unusual feature is the employment of several subgroups of items in a design of presentation that is balanced across times. This avoids, or at least reduces, possible confounding of the effects of between occasions changes with practice effects, and deserves wider adoption.

DISCREPANCIES

Within this context, there are some features of the outcome of the simulation study that are disturbing. If one constructs data according to a model, using a certain parameter structure in the form of variances for the scores, correlations between scores, and the like, and then analyzes the data with a seemingly appropriate estimation procedure, one would expect to get back as results the parameter estimates that went in. In this case, there are some results that are somewhat disturbing. The analysis overestimates the ability variances considerably and gives small (but nontrivial) negative correlations with initial ability where they should be zero.

There are several possible sources for these discrepancies (which seem too large to be dismissed as chance). One is that they result from the necessity of discarding a substantial fraction of the cases because they correspond to zero or perfect scores. Embretson reports that this does not fully account for the discrepancies. Even if it did, this still creates a problem, because zero or perfect scores are fairly likely to occur with real data as well. (One hopes not to have to confine applications to tailored testing.) This finding indicates that the model will not return the ''true'' parameters of the model in any circumstance, and the discrepancy may be large if there are many zero or perfect scores. Another possible explanation is that there is an unrecognized indeterminacy in the equations, such as one frequently experiences in applications of covariance structure analysis. That is, the estimates of variances and correlations become confounded with each other. This possibility should be examined carefully.

Another possibility, and this I consider more likely, is that because initial ability can never be known, but only estimated, and since that estimate will be highly correlated with the initial observed score, it is not possible to remove the correlation between gain and error entirely with current methods. Because this *is* a path model, one is in some sense partialing out the earlier time scores. Because these are inevitably correlated with error, Bereiter's problem does not disappear. That is, there is no way to independently estimate the gain scores. Such a possibility merits further thought.

One aspect that would be worth including in the model is a model for the design structure of the order of presentation of the items. As it stands now, this appears only in the procedure. In most experimental design contexts, we not only counterbalance in this way but also estimate the effects of presentation position. This would be nice in the MRMLC also.

Knowing Embretson's other, more cognitive work in which item characteristics as well as person scores are explicitly modeled, I was a little disappointed not to find that feature here. Let me hasten to add that this expresses a disappointment, not a criticism, because it is quite understandable to take the steps reflected in the current work before the addition of the other complicating aspect. I hope to see, though, that consideration added in the future.

Having considered this approach within its own IRT framework, let me say a few words about the framework itself. The trouble with the Rasch model is that it is often contradicted by the data: The equal discrimination by items on the latent scale is typically not there if we look at it. Thus, the scale determinacy that the Rasch framework gives is, to some extent, artificial. Second, the Rasch model requires a lot of cases to estimate the parameters. Unless some adaptations can be made, the application of this model will be unavailable to the researcher trying to work with a couple hundred subjects. I believe the univariate Rasch model is satisfactory in that circumstance, but in this case, Embretson is trying to do a lot more.

A second worrisome aspect is the necessity of discarding cases with zero or perfect observed scores because their scale scores are then indeterminate. Depending on how many of each are discarded, I am sure this results in biased estimates of the model's parameters, to say nothing of the plight of the researcher who then has nothing to say about those cases that are discarded. The investigator in a treatment context will be particularly reluctant to discard first those cases who have the most opportunity to change (the zero scores) and then those who might display the most change (the perfect scores). This problem could be remedied by adopting methods such as those suggested in chapter 17 (Rubin) or by something like a Bayesian prior distribution on the scores (see Bock & Aitken, 1981). Without those developments, the person intending to apply this method will have to be sure to include enough very easy and very difficult items so as to minimize the number of lost cases.[1]

CONCLUSIONS

In summary, this IRT approach offers a promising avenue for evaluating change. It is more useful than others and reduces contamination by artifacts that result from using simple difference scores.

---

[1] The ordinal psychometric methods developed by Collins (Collins, chapter 9; Collins & Cliff, in press) and by me (Cliff, 1989a) do not have problems of this type.

REPLY TO CLIFF'S COMMENTS

SUSAN E. EMBRETSON

Cliff has thoughtfully raised several issues about the multidimensional Rasch model for learning change (MRMLC). The most important issues to respond to are (a) how the simulation study results bear on the feasibility of parameter estimation and (b) the practicality of applying MRMLC to typical research studies.

Results from the simulation study described in chapter 12 clearly indicate the estimability of MRMLC. The invertibility of the information matrix for the item parameters and for each subject's abilities clearly indicates that the model was identified. Estimation of the item parameters was extremely accurate ($r =$ .996), with the slope and intercept near 0 and 1, respectively. The estimated and generated abilities correlated .93 and .91, respectively, for the initial ability and learning ability. The level of the ability correlations depends on the relative error specified in the response patterns by the simulation parameters. So, more important, the distribution of the difference between the estimated and generated ability values, standardized for the estimated measurement error, approximated quite well the expected normal distribution for both abilities.

Some of the aforementioned results were not included in the draft of the chapter available for Cliff's review, and his concern shows this omission. A concern about data that was included in the draft was the larger standard deviations for the estimated abilities than for the generated abilities. This difference, however, is due to the random error that is assigned to the response probabilities in the simulation study to generate item response data. In classical test theory terms, the variance for estimated abilities is larger because it includes true variance plus error variance, whereas the generated abilities contain only true variance.

Two other concerns about the simulation results—the substantial number of cases with unestimable abilities (as a result of zero or perfect scores) and the too high negative correlations between ability estimates—arose from using non-optimal item parameters in generating the data. A subsequent simulation study (see Embretson, in press) resulted in only 3.4% of the cases with zero or perfect scores, and a much smaller negative correlation between estimation abilities ($r = -.201$). This negative correlation results at least partially from the poor estimation of extreme abilities with a fixed content test. Because the MRMLC is an IRT model, estimation of extreme abilities could be improved by adaptive testing, in which items with appropriate difficulties can be selected for each person.

One practical concern was the applicability of MRMLC to studies with only a couple hundred subjects. Estimation can be expected to be adequate for such small samples, just as for the ordinary Rasch model. Because the item difficulty parameters are held constant over occasions (and dimensions) in MRMLC, and item discriminations are fixed to zero or one, MRMLC contains no more item parameters than the ordinary Rasch model. Although small sample sizes are adequate for MRMLC, the multidimensionality does influence the number of items that must be administered, because measurement must be adequate for each dimension, rather than for just one dimension.

Another practical concern was the fit of the Rasch model to actual test data. This criticism is not as serious as it may seem, because most test developers behave implicitly as if the Rasch model were true. That is, they preselect items for high discriminations and compute abilities from unweighted total scores. Preselecting items increases the fit of the Rasch model, and using unweighted total scores for estimating abilities defines the Rasch model as the only appropriate IRT model.

Finally, Cliff was disappointed that a cognitive model was not incorporated in MRMLC. I am glad that he thought positively of this possibility, because I have already developed such a model and have applied it successfully to measuring spatial learning ability (Embretson, 1989).

CHAPTER 13

QUALITATIVE TRANSITIONS AMID QUANTITATIVE DEVELOPMENT: A CHALLENGE FOR MEASURING AND REPRESENTING CHANGE

KEITH F. WIDAMAN

Editors' Introduction

In human development, change is both quantitative and qualitative. From conception to death, not only do different length dimensions of the body change quantitatively, but the shape of the body changes qualitatively. To some extent, for some characteristics, qualitative change can be described in terms of relations among quantitative changes—but only if qualitative change is accurately specified. In other cases of qualitative change, there is emergence of new features that cannot be specified in terms of quantitative changes. In any case it is important to become aware of qualitative change and not confuse it with quantitative change or inappropriately try to describe and explain it as if it were quantitative change. To identify and explain qualitative change requires different research designs, different methods of measurement and different methods of analysis than are used for study of quantitative change. In chapter 13 Widaman clarifies these matters.

The present work was supported in part by Grants HD-21056 and HD-22953 from the National Institute of Child Health and Human Development and an intramural grant from the academic senate at the University of California at Riverside. I would like to thank John Horn and Linda Collins for their thorough and invaluable comments on previous drafts of this chapter. Their work improved the chapter immeasurably. Comments by Christopher Hertzog on the conference presentation on which this chapter is based and by Katherine Gibbs and Todd Little on a draft of this chapter are also gratefully acknowledged.

Widaman emphasizes that scientific theory should guide design, measurement, and analyses directed at identifying qualitative change. He uses his research on the development of arithmetic abilities to illustrate this point. The theory—the "paradigm" in Kuhn's terms—on which this research is based differs in several important ways from theory that has guided psychometric studies of quantitative change in arithmetic abilities. Widaman focuses on structural and functional processes specified in terms of parameters of models for reaction times in doing arithmetical tasks. With this chronometric paradigm, children can be characterized as progressing quantitatively in automatization of processes of counting at the same time as they progress qualitatively away from these processes toward processes of retrieving from a memory network. As in chapter 9, readers are alerted to the likelihood that unless they bear in mind that qualitative change is different from static differences, important development will not be seen.

Observing the changes in behavior that occur from childhood into adulthood gives rise to the conclusion that important qualitative transitions occur alongside marked quantitative changes. The psychological structures underlying many types of behavior undergo important changes in kind, as well as exhibiting changes in level. Although these broad statements may come as no surprise to researchers of developmental processes, the answers to questions concerning distinguishing qualitative from quantitative change are not clear. These questions arise in different forms: How are we to conceive of change? What changes? Why does change occur? How does change occur? How much change occurs? These are the questions that are confronted in this chapter.

Through examples from studies of the development of mental abilities, several conceptions of change are discussed. The domain of such abilities has been studied throughout this century, and several theories of mental abilities have been developed. These theories provide useful examples of the different meanings of change or the different foci involved when thinking about change. Using the ability domain to exemplify problems in the analysis of change is not limiting, however, because comparable problems regarding change occur in virtually all domains of human behavior.

SOME THEMES IN THE STUDY OF DEVELOPMENT

Qualitative Versus Quantitative Change

Qualitative change

One type of change that occurs with development is change in the organized form of behavior that the subject exhibits. Such an organized form of behavior may be identified as embodying a stage. The ontogenetic development of the organism is often conceived as the movement through a series of successively more adaptive and more mature stages. Organized forms of behavior obey certain laws at each particular stage. These laws reflect behaviors that are more adaptive and mature than behaviors exhibited at previous stages but not as mature as those at later stages. Changes in organization are qualitative in nature. Of course, a stage theory can apply to lessened as well as to improved adaptation, as in the loss of cognitive capabilities in later adulthood (Horn, 1988) or the development of alcoholic maladaption and maladjustment (Horn, Wanberg, & Foster, 1990).

A process of cumulation or agglomeration of skills or capabilities may underlie qualitative change. Until sufficient cumulation occurs, the attainment of a new skill or set of skills cannot support the movement from one stage to the next. Behavior at a given stage is mediated by all skills cumulated to that point; skills not yet attained limit the maturity of the forms of behavior exhibited. Attainment of the skills associated with a given stage may modify the execution of skills attained at previous stages, or may not modify previously attained skills, simply allowing the appearance of more complex and mature forms of behavior. This notion of the cumulation of skills is consistent with the stage theories proposed by Siegler (1981) and Fischer (1980).

Noncumulative evolution of the structure of behavior may also define qualitatively distinct stages. In this case, the structure or organization of thought entailed at a given stage undergoes a modification or transformation (without obvious cumulation of definable skills) to become the more mature structure that embodies the next stage. Again, development is characterized by the progressive elaboration of ever more mature structures. This may be the form of structural development in children's thinking postulated by Piaget (1955, 1962; Flavell, 1963). Piaget hypothesized that children's thinking proceeds through four major stages: sensorimotor, preoperational, concrete operational, and formal operational. Transition from one of these stages into the next seems (according to Piaget) to be characterized not by the accretion of new skills or mental operations onto those previously attained, but by a restructuring of the way in which problems of a certain sort are conceived and thereby solved. This restructuring results in a new mental organization that represents a new organic whole. Of course, the new mental organization enables the individual to exhibit more mature forms of behavioral or cognitive skills. But, the new mental organization is logically and epigenetically prior to the more mature behavioral skills exhibited by the person, rather than vice versa.

Regardless of whether qualitative development has a noncumulative or cumulative form, the period of transition from one stage to the next corresponds to an epoch during which reorganization or significant supplementation of mental structures occurs. Such a period of transition may be represented as a period of rapid growth, perhaps so rapid that it is not seen, in which case there is a jump from one stage to the next. Once the reorganization is completed, a period of relative stability ensues that appears as a plateau in performance. Because there might be quantitative growth in components of the structure reflecting a stage, such a plateau reflects stability in the structural sense only. A plateau in performance eventually gives way to a transition to the next stage, to a new organization of mental structures.

Quantitative change

In contrast to the dearth of studies of qualitative change is the multitude of studies of quantitative change. Indeed, in writings on the analysis of change, change is usually viewed only quantitatively. A quantitative index yields an indication of the relative amount or standing of a person on a particular variable, usually on a scale assumed to be at the interval level, and occasionally at the ratio level, of measurement. In developmental research, quantitative change has been studied through measures of physical stature or status (such as height and weight; Bayley, 1956 and Bock, chapter 8) as well as through measures of abilities and personality characteristics.

Quantitative indices often yield smooth trends relating performance to age. In order to place individuals at different ages on the same dimension, the typical quantitative index of performance is an abstraction that maintains similarity or identity at a surface level across all ages, such as the number of addition problems solved correctly within 2 min. However, it is difficult to establish comparability of measures taken at different times or ages. With the linear composite measures most often used in ability and personality measurement, metric factorial invariance is one requirement for establishing measurement comparability (Horn, McArdle, & Mason, 1983; Meredith, 1964a).

Structure Versus Function

In theory, qualitative and quantitative change can occur in structure, in function, or in both. The core meaning of structure concerns form. In Piagetian research, for example, two mental operations are identified as embodying the same general level of cognitive development because the mental transformations underlying or representing the solutions to two problems have the same form. Psychometrically, factorial invariance is indicative of the same linear form. If the same pattern of high and low loadings occurs across the several factors in each of two or more solutions, the factors can be said to have the same form over the different conditions sampled.

Here, I want to distinguish two forms of knowledge structure—two types of knowledge—that are important in the solution of intellective problems: declarative knowledge and procedural knowledge. Declarative knowledge consists of stored knowledge of facts in different domains. For example, knowing that "5" is the answer to the problem "2 + 3" and knowing that a "robin" is a member of the class "bird" are examples of declarative knowledge in arithmetic and semantic domains, respectively. Procedural knowledge, on the other hand, refers to stored knowledge about cognitive operations. In the arithmetic domain, procedural knowledge includes knowledge about procedural algorithms for computing the correct sum for a problem, procedural rules or heuristics for obtaining sums, and so forth. For example, a child can know a counting procedure for obtaining the sum of "2 + 3" without knowing that "5" is the sum. There is strong evidence that children learn and swiftly generalize certain rules for addition, rather than requiring practice with every combination that conforms to a rule (Baroody, 1983, 1984). One such rule is that adding zero to a number leaves the number unchanged, or "$x + 0 = x$."

Developmental changes in knowledge structures are usually reflected in improvements in both declarative and procedural knowledge, and these changes may be either qualitative or quantitative. Thus, declarative knowledge may develop quantitatively, gradually strengthened through practice, as procedural knowledge develops qualitatively, revealed in stage-to-stage transformations. The opposite might be true, too. The point is that whether declarative and/or procedural knowledge develops quantitatively, qualitatively, or in both ways, our research methods must be responsive to all of these possibilities.

I restrict my focus on function to two types of functional characteristics related to the accessing of knowledge structures: (a) the speed and facility with which declarative knowledge is retrieved and procedural knowledge is executed, and (b) the flexibility with which declarative and procedural knowledge are applied to nontypical applications. Across many types of chronometric tasks, reaction time on a given task is systematically reduced as a function of practice on that task. One way of characterizing this improvement in performance is that performance becomes automatized (e.g., Schneider, Dumais, & Shiffrin, 1984). Early in practice, performance is mediated by effortful, controlled processes; as practice ensues, performance becomes more skilled, enabling the release of effortful control as automatic processing mediates performance. The movement from controlled to automatic processing can be viewed as either a quantitative improvement in execution time or a qualitative shift from one form of processing to another. Regardless, developmental changes in intellective functions during childhood and adolescence can be viewed as the improvement and concomitant automatization of cognitive skills through practice.

In addition to the automatization of specific skills, flexibility in applying declarative and procedural knowledge to nontypical applications may be an important feature of intellective skills. Schneider et al. (1984) noted that dealing with novel applications usually requires the invocation of controlled, effortful processing. More important, individual differences in such flexibility in applying declarative and procedural knowledge may be a feature of the broad form of intelligence (i.e., fluid intelligence) discussed by Horn (1988).

The Organism's Response to Stimuli

The domain of human mental abilities has engendered several approaches to the investigation of abilities and the changes they undergo. The stimulus–organism–response, or S–O–R, formulation characterizes most approaches and therefore is useful in comparing and contrasting the several approaches. Each research approach to mental abilities presumes a stimulus, a problem of some sort. The organism is assumed to have structures that function to encode the problem and engage in mediating responses that, when completed, result in an overt response that represents a solution to the problem presented. In large measure, the core of research on the development and aging of human abilities is twofold in nature: (a) to determine the structural and functional organization(s) of the mediating responses by the organism, and (b) to investigate whether these structures and their functional characteristics undergo qualitative and/or quantitative change over time (i.e., age). The major research traditions in the study of mental abilities can be distinguished by comparing the relative emphasis each places on investigating the form of the mediating responses by the organism versus the quantitative levels of response, as well as the relative emphasis placed on investigating the structural versus functional characteristics of the abilities studied.

NUMERICAL FACILITY: WHAT IT IS AND HOW IT CHANGES

Theoretical musings and empirical findings related to the ability dimension of numerical facility are discussed in the following sections. My intent is to illustrate the influence of research approaches on the types of studies designed and the sorts of conclusions offered on the form of development in this domain. This brief review supports a general conclusion that a combination of theoretical, research, and analytical approaches is needed to represent accurately developmental change in any given domain.

Research Approaches

The psychometric approach
Numerical facility is an ability dimension identified in most hierarchical theories of intellectual abilities. It is an ability to produce, rapidly and accurately, answers to problems requiring simple numerical calculations such as addition, subtraction, and multiplication. In research by Thurstone and his associates (e.g., Thurstone, 1938; Thurstone & Thurstone, 1941), numerical facility was one of the seven Primary Mental Abilities defined in early studies and was one of the most clearly replicated across studies. The numerical facility primary ability is one of a set of dimensions identified as indicators of a broad form of intelligence (i.e., crystalized

intelligence) (Horn, 1988). Measured in the Primary Mental Abilities battery, changes in numerical facility with age have been reported in an array of cross-sectional (e.g., Horn, 1988) and longitudinal (e.g., Schaie, 1983; Nesselroade & Baltes, 1974) studies. In extant studies, consistent increases in numerical facility have been found during childhood and adolescence, with relative stability of mean levels of numerical facility during a large portion of the adult years.

Paper-and-pencil tests are the instruments used in most psychometric research on numerical facility. Typically, a test has rather homogeneous content (e.g., only addition problems or only subtraction problems), and a battery of such homogeneous tests is administered to a large sample of subjects. The intercorrelations among tests of addition, subtraction, multiplication, division, and beyond will usually have a quasisimplex form, indicating that people who score well on tests of higher levels of mathematics (e.g., algebra and division) also score well on tests of lower levels, whereas those who do poorly on higher level tests may score well on lower level tests. This pattern of correlations implies a step-functional relation among tests; persons at the higher steps have progressed up previous steps (Horn, 1978). But, within a battery of tests of other cognitive capabilities, these different measures of arithmetic abilities form the Numerical Facility factor. Given their loadings on a common factor, tests of addition, subtraction, multiplication, and division are assumed to have common elements. However, the identities of the common elements of numerical tasks—be they particular declarative or procedural knowledge structures or their functional characteristics—have not been studied in depth. The data collected in psychometric studies cannot support such study. Prophetically, Thurstone (1947) urged that factor analytic findings be followed up by laboratory studies designed to isolate the commonalities underlying tests that consistently define a given factor; however, his admonition has generally not been heeded.

Psychometric studies of developmental change have provided inspectional evidence of configural invariance for ability tests, but rigorous tests of metric invariance have only rarely been conducted (see chapter 7; Horn et al., 1983). Identity of factorial patterns implies identity of structure. If there is such identity, developmental change on each factor can be portrayed quantitatively by increases in scores on the factor; such increases can be interpreted as changes in functional characteristics. With regard to numerical facility, developmental change during childhood and adolescence might represent automatization of the unspecified cognitive processes that underlie performance on simple numerical tasks.

The order-of-processes approach

There is a sense in which the quasisimplex form indicating transition from addition to subtraction to multiplication to division represents a structure of knowledge, as just indicated. Addition can be said to be a process on which subtraction (another process) is built, and multiplication can be seen as a process built on understanding addition and as a prerequisite for understanding division. But, structural developmental theories often aim to go beyond, and analytically within, these gross processes to delineate sets of cognitive skills that underlie performance, the order in which these skills are acquired, and the changes in the organization of these skills as the child matures.

The design of much structural developmental research differs from the design of psychometric studies in three principal ways: (a) Subjects are administered a battery of heterogeneous tasks, each of which is designed to require a unique combination of skills; (b) on the basis of age differences in patterns of passing and failing items, analyses are directed at showing the order of acquisition of various unique cognitive skills; and (c) individual differences at a given age play little role in the analyses, because age differences are analyzed and play the major role in explanation. Given functional invariance across age, conclusions usually involve qualitative change in structure. As Collins (chapter 9) points out, methods for studying static traits are often used inappropriately to study the dynamic change that is the focus of such studies, whereas the aim of these studies is to identify the separate skills that emerge and the order (invariant, it is hoped) of emergence of these skills within individuals.

Applying this approach to numerical facility, Gelman (1982) described the skills underlying children's counting, which represents the way in which young children find the sum of things in two groups. The five skills that Gelman discussed were: (a) partitioning and tagging, breaking up items into those to be counted and those already counted and then tagging each item with a count as it is moved from the former to the latter partition; (b) the stable-order principle, by which tags (e.g., number words) are used in an invariant order; (c) the cardinal principle, according to which the last tag used denotes the number of items in the set; (d) the abstraction principle, which represents awareness that counting may be applied to any set of objects; and (e) the order-irrelevance principle, representing the idea that items may be counted in any order to arrive at the correct sum. Characterizing the level of a child's counting involves describing which of the five skills the child has attained, rather than noting how well or how fast the child can execute each skill.

The chronometric approach

Chronometric studies of numerical facility are based on reaction times to numerical problems and presuppose a conceptual model of the temporal flow of information processing. One processing model on which chronometric research on simple addition has been based is shown in Figure 13.1. The subject is presented with the addends, $a + b$, and a stated sum, c. The model assumes that presentation of a problem leads first to the encoding of the addends into an appropriate rep-

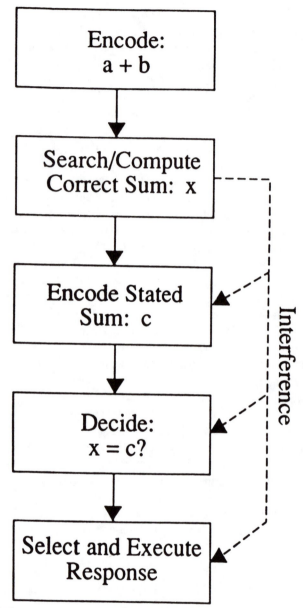

Figure 13.1   Flow diagram of cognitive processing on which chronometric research on simple addition has been based.

resentation in short-term memory. Then, the correct answer for the problem is either computed anew or retrieved from a long-term memory store, as discussed below. After arriving at the correct sum, the digits in the stated sum are encoded, allowing a comparison of the correct and stated sums. Depending on the correctness of the stated sum, a response of "yes," signifying correct, or "no," signifying incorrect, is selected and executed. Reaction times (RTs) to problems structured to emphasize more and less of the hypothesized processes provide a basis for estimating parameters of linear equations (e.g., regression models) specified to represent the processes. Evidence in support of, or threatening, different models of processing is adduced by tests of goodness of fit for models involving and not involving the critical model parameters. A more general componential model for mental addition, which is an elaboration on the model in Figure 13.1, was proposed by Widaman, Geary, Cormier, and Little (1989). In this model, all processes underlying solution of addition problems of any size—including the encoding of digits, the search for, or computing of, correct sums in each column, and the carrying to the next column—are represented. Given a satisfactory model of the flow of processing, regression modeling of RTs to addition problems represents, or is paramorphic to, the way in which individuals solve the problems.

Early chronometric research on digital, or counting, models of numerical facility was undertaken by Groen and Parkman (1972; Parkman & Groen, 1971). Groen and Parkman postulated that simple addition problems of the form "7 + 4 = 11" were solved using a mental counter. According to this theory, a person sets the mental counter at most one time and then increments the counter in a unit-by-unit fashion. The mental counter can be used in five different ways. For example, according to one model, the counter is set to the larger addend and then incremented a number of times equal to the smaller addend, or MIN. In this model, called the MIN model, the slope for the MIN variable is the predicted increase in solution time associated with each incrementing of the mental counter as the smaller addend is added onto the larger. In analyses of RT data from both children and adults, the MIN model, among the competing counting models, resulted in the highest amounts of variance explained, thereby attaining the best fit to the data. However, the MIN slope parameter was much larger for children than for adults. This suggests that adults use the same process as children use to solve simple addition problems, but they run through this process at a more highly automatized rate.

More recently, Ashcraft and Battaglia (1978) suggested that mental addition performance may reflect retrieval of the correct sum from a stored network of these facts. Following up this observation, my associates and I (Geary & Widaman, 1987; Geary, Widaman, & Little, 1986; Widaman et al., 1989; Widaman, Little, Geary, & Cormier, in press) found that a memory network retrieval model provided the best fit to RT data gathered from college students. The structural variable that had the highest level of fit, across four types of addition problems, was the product of the two addends (PRODUCT). A model including the PRODUCT of addends is consistent with a process of looking up answers in a table of addition facts in a memory network. This table is bounded by two entry nodes that contain values from 0 through 9, representing the addends in a simple addition problem. Answers to addition problems are assumed to be stored at the intersection of the nodal values corresponding to a problem; for example, the answer "5" is stored at the intersection of values of "3" on Node 1 and "2" on Node 2. In such a network, the PRODUCT corresponds to the area traversed from the origin, or (0, 0), intersection, to the intersection of the nodal values for a problem (see Widaman et al., 1989, for further details). In the studies by my associates and me, regression models including a PRODUCT variable had higher levels of fit to RT data than did models consistent with alternate counting and retrieval processes. Moreover, we (1990) found smooth developmental trends in automatization of this function, as discussed below.

Representing Change in Numerical Facility

Given these findings, a central question we ask is, Are changes in numerical facility qualitative or quantitative in nature? The answer we find is yes! Some changes in numerical facility appear to be qualitative in nature; others appear to be quantitative.

First, consider the developmental changes that conform to the pattern of qualitative change via cumulation of skills. The five basic operations underlying counting, discussed by Gelman (1982), must be present for a child to sum the number of objects in two groups. To proceed to addition, the child also must be able to (a) represent the numerosity of things in each of two groups with numerals, and then (b) combine the numerals to arrive at a sum. As more complex forms of addition are faced, the child must learn to carry to the next column. Also, a variety of rules and heuristics are being learned that enhance the speed of mental addition. Each of these changes reflects the acquisition of increasing numbers of skills that affect the level of maturity of numerical facility that the child may exhibit.

However, noncumulative qualitative changes appear to characterize other developmental transitions in numerical facility. In particular, the central stage during which the answer to an addition problem is obtained, the search/compute stage, appears to undergo a noncumulative evolution. Siegler and Shrager (1984) identified three early stages in children's strategy usage: (a) "counting fingers," in which the child holds up fingers corresponding to the number of units in each group and then explicitly counts all raised fingers; (b) "fingers," in which the child again raises fingers, but does not explicitly count them; and (c) "counting," in which there is some external referent (e.g., moving lips) indicating that the child is explicitly counting each unit. After these stages, the mental counting models (e.g., the MIN model of Groen & Parkman, 1972) and memory network retrieval models appear to characterize skilled performance on addition problems.

Relevant to the latter two stages, results from a study by Widaman et al. (in press) are presented in Table 13.1. These results indicate that there is an approximately 50/50 split between subjects using counting and retrieval strategies at the second grade level. At the sixth grade level and in college, approximately 80% of the students use retrieval, whereas 20% apparently still use counting to solve addition problems. Some persons may never reach the most mature stage, that of retrieval. Psychometric analyses, based on scores on numerical tests, can reveal metric stability of factor patterns from elementary school to college. However, such a demonstration of structural stability would mask the underlying qualitative changes in strategy usage uncovered using chronometric methods.

To see the quantitative changes in the functional characteristics of execution of cognitive processes, consider Figure 13.2. Here, the average slope parameter estimates for the PRODUCT structural variable are presented for each grade level sample across the two studies reported by Widaman et al. (in press). These data points are based on students identified as using memory network retrieval as the strategy for responding to addition problems. A simple nonlinear equation of the form $PRODUCT = 200 \, Grade^{-1.16}$ explains rather well the relation between PRODUCT parameter estimates and grade, $R^2 = .795$, $(p < .0006)$. Given the simple and smooth function fit to the data points, grade may provide a useful index of the amount of practice with addition problems that occurs as a function of school experiences, practice that leads to automatization of function.

CONCLUSIONS

The study of the development of human abilities would be a simpler enterprise if numerical facility were either unique or uncommon, that is, if the different types

Table 13.1

DISTRIBUTION OF PERSONS USING DIFFERENT PROCESSING STRATEGIES, BY GRADE LEVEL

| | | Processing strategy | | | |
| | | Digital | | Retrieval | |
Grade	N	n	%	n	%
Second	61	30	49	31	51
Fourth	65	20	31	45	69
Sixth	60	13	22	47	78
College	100	20	20	80	80

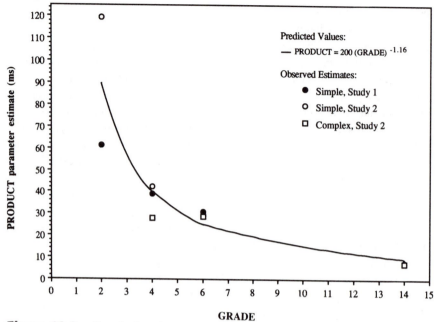

Figure 13.2   Quantitative changes with age in the functional characteristic of speed of retrieval of answers to addition problems.

of developmental change exhibited in the mental processes underlying the solution of arithmetic problems were found only in a small number of domains. But, it is likely that similar patterns of change occur in most domains of human thought and behavior. Kail (1984) has shown the sequential attainment of cognitive processes underlying memory, and investigations into such important abilities as verbal comprehension and spatial ability will probably require a similar portrayal. Moreover, behaviors in many other domains (e.g., aggression) appear also to undergo both qualitative and quantitative change.

The main message of this chapter is that both qualitative change and quantitative change occur in the development of mathematical capabilities and both are likely to characterize most human psychological development. Researchers must be alert to identify these two kinds of change, both when studying structure and when studying function. Different designs for research, methods of measurement, and methods of analysis are needed to distinguish and describe the two kinds of change. The three approaches described in this chapter are important, but other approaches are required. We must search out methods, at all levels of inquiry, that allow us to represent accurately the ways in which individuals develop skills and abilities in all domains of behavior.

A metaphor can be the most concise way of conveying the essence of a situation; the metaphor sought is one that represents research on behavioral development (in general) and human abilities (in particular). The metaphor is the familiar one of the five blind men asked to describe an elephant; each blind man, standing next to one particular part of the elephant—the trunk, a leg, and so on—described that part. The resulting descriptions of the elephant had little commensurability, a result that is both amusing and understandable. Such a metaphor for our current situation leads to at least two interesting conjectures: First, description of change in one feature of a set of abilities may have little relation to description of changes in other features of that set of abilities. More important, qualitative change in numerical abilities is a different part of the beast than that represented by quantitative change in these or other abilities. Second, in our focus on change, it is not clear that we are attempting to characterize changes in the human ability "elephant" at all. Rather, much research appears to involve huddling around the elephant's tail, carefully quantifying the elephant's output, then relating the levels of output to the chronological age and other characteristics of the elephant. Analyzing the fluid and crystallized features of the elephant's output can be intriguing, but it does not get at many major structural and functional characteristics of the elephant and the changes these characteristics undergo: We thereby fail to characterize the course of developmental change in the elephant, which is, after all, our ultimate goal.

COMMENTS ON "QUALITATIVE TRANSITIONS AMID QUANTITATIVE DEVELOPMENT: A CHALLENGE FOR MEASURING AND REPRESENTING CHANGE"

CHRISTOPHER HERTZOG

Widaman and his laboratory group represent the elephant of my measurement problem, and I am as handicapped as the general scientific field he characterized. Let me start by praising them for the nature of the careful work they are doing in this area. It is precisely this direction that is needed in ability research today, generically, and application of such techniques to developmental research on cognition is exciting. The problem of differentiating qualititative from quantitative developmental change in cognition has long been at the crux of theoretical and empirical work in developmental psychology (Lerner, 1986; Wohlwill, 1973). Widaman focuses on how one might use contemporary information-processing theory to assist in the identification of qualitative changes in basic arithmetic skills during childhood, but the theoretical approach and empirical techniques he employs can be used for different cognitive processes and across the human life span. For example, such approaches could be extended to examine late-life changes in intelligence (Hertzog, 1985; Hunt, 1983).

DEVELOPMENTAL APPROACH

The primary focus for a developmental approach to cognitive processes within an information-processing perspective, as with Widaman's work, is on differentiating between (a) changes in application of invariant cognitive processes at different developmental epochs and (b) qualitative shifts in the nature of the cognitive

218

structures and processes used to solve isomorphic classes of cognitive problems. Widaman argues that there are developmental shifts in numerical abilities as children first acquire basic cognitive structures (i.e., the concept of numerosity) and then develop mature skills (moving from the controlled process of counting toward automated retrieval of basic additive and multiplicative relations from memory). Two fundamental problems exist: First, failure to differentiate qualitative changes may lead to erroneous inferences about changes in molar performance levels on cognitive tasks (in this case, ability tests measuring addition). Second, how does one proceed to characterize the qualitative stage of development, and then measure quantitative change in skill acquisition? Certainly, the problems identified by Widaman generalize across different cognitive domains. For example, it appears that spatial relations skills, especially those involving ability to execute mental rotations, undergo major qualitative changes prior to ages 7–9 and are thereafter best characterized by quantitative changes in efficiency of process execution (Pellegrino & Kail, 1982). However, satisfactory answers to questions regarding the nature and extent of early developmental changes in spatial skills have not been found. Moreover, the possibility that qualitative differences in processing strategies may confound the developmental curves for mental rotation task performance, interpreted by Pellegrino and Kail (1982) as quantitative changes, has not seriously been entertained, let alone falsified.

Widaman's approach is to employ experimental variation in stimuli and conditions in reaction time (RT) tasks that assess quantitative skills as a means of identifying qualitative processing differences. He then uses componential models for RT to generate parameters estimating processing efficiency at different stages of solution generation. This sort of approach is exactly what is needed, especially in analyzing individual differences in adult cognitive development (Hertzog, 1985). An experimentally grounded psychometrics is required to move us away from static conceptions of abilities and toward more process-oriented theories and assessment techniques (e.g., Embretson, 1985).

REMAINING CHALLENGES

Nevertheless, Widaman's chapter is somewhat incomplete and unsatisfying. It can be regarded more as a general statement about what is needed in the field than as a compelling demonstration of the benefits of the componential approach. The challenge for all of us still remains—to address several issues regarding qualitative versus quantitative change. In this comment I shall identify many of the possible limitations of this approach. I do so not because I disagree with it, but because perhaps I am more daunted than Widaman by the problems posed, and perhaps also less sanguine about the limitations of componential approaches for dealing with qualitative differences in processing complex problems.

Theoretical Limitations

First, current cognitive theories now recognize that the serial processing models popular in componential theories of the 1970s are at best problematic, because many processes occur automatically, without awareness, and in parallel (e.g., Kihlstrom, 1987; McClelland, 1979). It is therefore important to recognize that the parameter estimates of componential models based on simple and parsimonious serial processing assumptions may not adequately characterize the actual process of problem solution. If so, whither the construct validity of the processing parameters estimated?

One can abandon the serial processing assumptions of most componential models and still learn much from a cognitive correlates framework, in which tasks thought to measure specific constellations of relevant cognitive processes are correlated with performance on molar tasks administered under different conditions (e.g., variation in item difficulty; see Horn, 1985; Hunt, 1983). Indeed, much of the work of Widaman and others can probably be justified under less restrictive assumptions than they themselves invoke. Nevertheless, the reader should not assume that the componential approach is above reproach as an instantiation of cognitive processing theory and its ability to model complex problem solution.

Second, the crucial issue for strategic processing is to recognize that we must differentiate between processing structures dictated by stage of cognitive (structural) development versus processing strategies dictated by metacognitive processes (i.e., strategy generation, selection, and identification). A child who has an inaccurate concept of numerosity makes many mistakes that will not characterize the behavior of a child who is counting. However, children just developing memory-based processing strategies will necessarily process problems differently, depending on the quality of the addition tables held in memory and the probability of successful retrieval of solutions from memory. There is a good chance that children are not one type of processor or the other, but that their responses on experimental trials are a mixture of multiple strategies, with the probability of which strategy they use depending in part on the problem's difficulty level. Such issues are usually not adequately addressed in componential theorizing, let alone empirical estimates of constituent processes. Note that criticism of quantitative comparisons of molar dependent variables such as ability tests leveled by Widaman also apply to his own componential parameter estimates if the processing assumptions of the componential model are inaccurate or oversimplified.

Third, in relation to the previous point, it is often the case that the crucial issue is the probability of a successful execution of a cognitive process, not the time taken for successful execution. Certainly this is the case in assessing qualitative level of cognitive development—one often uses patterns of errors to identify strategic processes. In more complex tasks, however, there is a high probability of failure to achieve correct output at various processing stages (e.g., imaged spatial transformations under high levels of working memory load). An adequate componential approach for most complex cognitive tasks (and real world problems) must simultaneously model error patterns and RTs, which is apparently not part of the approach used by Widaman for simple addition. Widaman's approach is probably appropriate for his problem, given that numerical facility is generally conceptualized as the ability to rapidly compute solutions to simple arithmetic problems and that the problem is chiefly one of limited generalizability to other cognitive domains. Even so, failure to account for errors could result in biased estimates of ability at the low end of the ability continuum.

Fourth, it is not always clear how one is to distinguish qualitative change from quantitative change, and it is possible to enter into a vicious tautological theoretical/empirical cycle here (Wohlwill, 1973). At a theoretical level, should the change from counting behavior to memory-based retrieval be considered a structural change, in the Piagetian sense? Or is it a qualitative transition only in the limited, mechanistic sense, of differential application of existing cognitive structures and processes? What are the criteria for differentiating the two? Does it matter?

Fifth, is it always the case that componential models are superior to the molar ability tests from classic psychometrics? Widaman may be overstating the case because he focuses exclusively on the issue of how item solutions are generated. Regarding predictive validity, it may eventually be shown that there is little specificity of prediction between different component process parameters for external criteria of real world behaviors and outcomes, as well as little incremental validity in prediction over and above traditional test scores. This is especially true if individual differences on tests are simply crude but effective ways of measuring the same processes identified by cognitive tasks (Keating, 1984).

Functionally, it is likely that overall test performance, and subjective assessments of it are the proximal causes of self-concept variables such as negative self-efficacy beliefs, achievement motivation in assessment contexts, and the like (Kanfer, 1987; Wood & Bandura, 1989), irrespective of the complex means by which right and wrong answers are generated. I do not contest the importance of understanding the cognitive processes for teaching, training, and evaluation—and indeed, I am more sympathetic to the approach taken by Widaman than I am of the position of Keating and other critics. However, we should not assume that every meaningful basic and applied research question requires usage of componential logic and methodology.

Sixth, Widaman does not discuss at length how quantitative change should be assessed after identification of qualitative differences. My own bias (Hertzog, 1985) is that it is quite reasonable to chart individual differences in change after assignment to qualitative processing subtypes, depending on whether that makes sense from a developmental perspective. That is, it makes no sense to chart quantitative improvements in children who do not have a well developed numerosity concept, but it does make sense to measure quantitative change in children as their efficiency in memory retrieval skills increases. This is where longitudinal covariance structures approaches of the type described by McArdle (1988; see also Hertzog & Schaie, 1988) may be ideal, for even when there is some shift in the strategic processing of difficult problems, one may still be able to identify the invariant process at the level of latent variables modeled as determinants of clusters of items varying in difficulty, under assumptions of partial metric invariance rather than complete metric invariance (see Cunningham, chapter 7).

Empirical Issues

How are strategic differences to be measured, once conceptualized? This is a difficult issue given that we are theorizing about the black box without being able to open it, relying largely on Pandora's leftovers. There are four basic techniques for identifying strategies: (a) inferences from patterns of reaction times and errors across conditions, (b) post-hoc self-reports, (c) changes in behavior under strategic processing instructions, and (d) think-aloud protocols. All have their problems, and the success of an investigation largely depends on whether specific predictions regarding reaction time (RT) and error patterns create an adequate opportunity for falsification of alternative strategic models and classification of subjects into particular strategic classes (see MacLeod, Hunt, & Mathews, 1978, for a success story). Classifications based solely on theoretically derived patterns of RTs are certainly not foolproof. For example, Ratcliff (1985) argued that qualitative interpretations of fast same RTs in perceptual discrimination tasks are unwarranted, given that his quantitative diffusion model for RT, which assumes different criteria for responding "same" and "different" by subjects, can account for the data. Widaman presents us with a typological classification of children into processing subgroups, but with essentially no information about his classification criteria. Caveat emptor!

Widaman's componential approach relies on modeling individual RTs as a function of experimental conditions in order to generate parameter estimates. It is not clear from the presentation how this is to be applied in the case of children at different qualitative processing stages. Presumably, one has a two-stage procedure in which children are classified into subtypes and then parameters are estimated within subtype groups. There are a number of issues here, including (a) attending to non-normal RT distributions; (b) whether parametric equations can be fitted to aggregated data, and the bias involved; and (c) the sampling distribution of individual parameter estimates when the aggregated regression equation is used to generate predicted scores.

In studies of different developmental groups, it is necessary to recognize that the dependent variable will be influenced by sources of variance other than the cognitive components of interest to the investigator. One of the chief strengths of the cognitive processing perspective is that it provides a basis for identifying hypothetical influences that are both construct-relevant and performance-specific. Hertzog (1989) recently showed that the perceptual and psychomotor speed components involved in marking computerized answer sheets have an increasingly high correlation with the Primary Mental Abilities (PMA) Verbal Meaning test in a cross-sectional sample of adults. These increases were specific to the PMA vocabulary test, not to two other tests of vocabulary. Moreover, this performance-specific component of variance appeared to contribute to greater cross-sectional age differences for the PMA test. The empirical challenge, then, is to identify multiple components of variance on dependent measures like RT and to isolate estimates of cognitive process from such influences in a fashion that recognized developmental changes in the sources of influences on the dependent measure. Currently, componential models presume that isolation is achieved through implementation of subtractive factors logic, as instantiated in the multiple regression equations for item RTs. Such assumptions may not actually be justified.

CONCLUSIONS

The foregoing sections are not intended to convey disagreement with Widaman's chapter and approach, but instead to convey respect for the complexity of the problems that confront us in this domain. Widaman was faced with the impossible task of presenting a complex theoretical and methodological perspective, including an example, to a general audience in a 30 min talk. My hope is than an expanded version of his chapter will address the issues that have been enumerated, which will benefit all of us. I have come behind Widaman and measured his output. I get the distinct and pungent sense of much more to come.

REPLY TO HERTZOG'S COMMENTS

KEITH F. WIDAMAN

Hertzog's reaction to my chapter is, in many respects, precisely the reaction I had hoped to elicit in thoughtful readers: He found the chapter provocative, yet not entirely satisfying, and therefore likely to entice readers to find out more about our work (as in Widaman et al., 1989). Good!

Hertzog raised several questions to which I shall respond (it is impossible to respond here to each of the issues he raised). Some of the problems outlined by Hertzog are ones with which we have yet to deal constructively; he provided a map of these regions of our research domain that should be investigated. Given limited space for a response, I shall make three general points rather than discuss in detail how we intend to explore these regions.

First, the problems Hertzog saw in our research on numerical facility are problems in almost all (if not all) studies of cognitive processes. The implications for representing patterns of data to deal better with many of these problems are not yet clear. The flaws in research to which Hertzog refers must be more clearly specified before they can be resolved; we need more acceptable ways of representing cognitive processes, and their developmental course, if we are to deal with the flaws once they have been clearly specified.

Second, the problems Hertzog notes are primarily problems with the chronometric approach, but equally serious problems obtain for the other approaches I discussed. What is lost when using these other approaches should be weighed against what is lost with the chronometric approach. In particular, the psychometric approach is biased toward misrepresenting developmental change as quantitative, even when the key aspects of change are qualitative. The chronometric approach yields evidence of both qualitative and quantitative change, although, granted, the information on quantitative change may not be commensurate with that derived from the psychometric approach.

This brings me to my third and most important point: the problems Hertzog discusses are not problems with the central argument of my chapter, namely, that although developmental change is often interpreted as either quantitative or qualitative, it is very likely both. Many researchers (e.g., in the Piagetian tradition) tend not to model important quantitative change, and many other researchers (e.g., in the tradition of Spearman) do not model qualitative change. The multimodel approach I presented is directed at identifying both qualitative and quantitative change, thus providing a more complete account of development, but very possibly also requiring that we consider forms of change we have not anticipated. A list of the problems inherent in one or another of the approaches I described is not a strong criticism against the multimodel approach, per se.

For the most part, I agree that the problems Hertzog identified should be solved and that the multimodel approach is, as he says, "exactly what is needed . . . to move us away from static conceptions . . . toward more process-oriented theories and assessment techniques." Let this be the main message of both my chapter and Hertzog's comments.

CHAPTER 14

BEHAVIOR GENETIC
STUDIES OF CHANGE

JOHN LOEHLIN

Editors' Introduction

Two major classes of influence, environmental and genetic, determine both stable individual differences and developmental changes in these differences. Loehlin describes models and methods that provide a basis for inference about these determinants in this chapter. The covariability across time and at each occasion of measurement can be partitioned into two components. One set, made up of biological relations—between parents and their children, siblings, twins, and so forth—is considered to represent genetic determinants. The other set, made up of components that are not estimated from information about biological relationships, is considered to represent environmental determinants plus error.

Loehlin illustrates this theory by taking a simple model and progressively adding to it to allow for ever more realistic ideas about what, in fact, can occur in development. The simple model is for data in which identical and fraternal twins are measured repeatedly along a single dimension across time. In this model, components of genetics and the environment account for the observed variability at each remeasure and are themselves determined by the persisting effects of the prior genetic and environmental influences, and by new such influences that come into effect over the time between the measure and remeasure. Keeping the basic features of this quasisimplex model intact, Loehlin expands it to deal with the possibility that for both one and more than one manifest variable there can be common-factor genetic and common-factor environmental influences operating to produce the individual differences of each remeasure.

These preliminaries set the stage for Loehlin to describe empirical data applications and further extensions of these ideas in studies in which measures of IQ, extraversion, emotional stability, and socialization were obtained in samples of adopted children and biological children in the same homes. The models for these data become intricate, but can be described in terms of persistence and lack of persistence in the phenotype as measured, and effects associated with genes, shared environment, correlations among specifics, and error. It may be useful for the reader to consider these models in the context of chapters 10 (Meredith) and 15 (Gollob and Reichardt).

As is widely known, behavior geneticists use data from informative groups—twins, adoptive families, the families of twins, and so forth—to partition variance. The basic division is into two parts: that due to the genes and that due to environment. Most currently used methods go a step further and break down the environmental part into that portion shared by families and that portion distinctive to the individual. With appropriate designs and using multiple informative groups, one can make further partitions—for example, of the genetic variance into simple additive effects and nonadditive genetic interactions. Or one can obtain variance components reflecting gene–environment interaction and correlation. However, in this chapter we shall stop at the three-way division: the effects of genes, the effects of shared family environment, and the effects of unshared environment.

Although the concept of partitioning variance is well known, it is perhaps less widely understood that trait covariance can be partitioned into components by the same methods as trait variance. This can be done for the covariance among a set of different traits, or for the covariance of a single trait measured on more than one occasion. The focus of this chapter is on the latter, the partitioning of cross-time covariance. Using standard behavior genetic techniques, one can divide such covariance into the various aforementioned genetic and environmental components. This can permit substantively interesting conclusions. For example, one might be able to infer for some trait of interest that the genetic influences on it tended to persist over time, whereas the environmental influences on it were transitory.

BEHAVIOR GENETIC MODELING OF COVARIANCE OVER TIME

Behavior geneticists are beginning to explore these possibilities. For example, Figure 14.1 presents a path diagram from Boomsma and Molenaar (1987). The underlying model is a quasi-simplex. That is, the value at each time point is a function of two factors—the value at the immediately preceding time point and a residual. These are shown in the diagram by the paths β and ζ, respectively. However, the model has two of these simplexes, one at the bottom for the genes

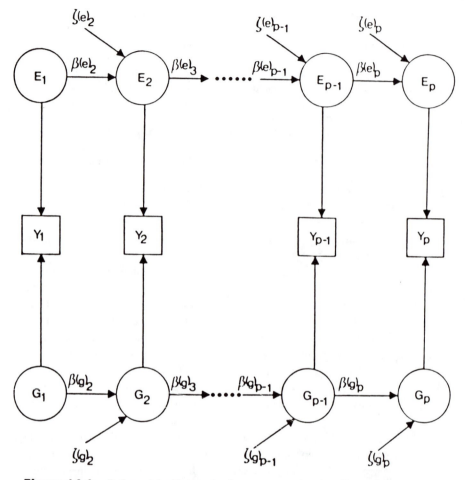

Figure 14.1   Path model with two simplexes representing the effects of genes (G) and
environment (E) on a behavior (Y) over time (subscripts 1–p). For dis-
cussions of paths β and ζ see text. From "The Genetic Analysis of
Repeated Measures" by D. I. Boomsma and P. C. M. Molenaar, 1987,
Behavior Genetics, 17, p. 113. Copyright 1987 by Plenum Publishing
Corporation. Reprinted by permission.

and one at the top for the environment, to be fit simultaneously. Using simulated
data for monozygotic and dizygotic twins measured on several occasions, Boomsma
and Molenaar showed that given the assumption of stable βs and ζs, one can
solve for the necessary four parameters from the cross-time variance–covariance
matrices of the observed variable **Y** in the two twin groups.

Figure 14.2 (from Eaves, Long, & Heath, 1986) shows a model with an
additional level of complication. In this case, two alternative hypotheses con-

cerning the covariance of a trait over time are represented on both the genetic and environmental sides of the diagram. One of these hypotheses is essentially the same simplex model as Boomsma and Molenaar's. The Gs and the γ paths on the right represent a simplex on the genetic side; the Es and the η paths on the left represent a simplex on the environmental side. Added to this simplex model is a factor analytic model represented by the G_c on the right, a genetic factor common to all four occasions, and the E_c on the left, a corresponding common environmental factor. The G_ss and the E_ss act as both residuals for the simplex model and specifics for the factor model. The paths down the center labeled p allow for the possibility of direct persistence over time of the phenotypic trait itself.

One can go a step further and expand the one-variable models of Figures 14.1 and 14.2 into a multivariable temporal model, by measuring more than one trait across time. Figure 14.3 shows an example from Boomsma, Martin, and Molenaar (1989). This particular model involves two variables measured on four occasions. The four occasions are a baseline measurement and three measurements at different times after ingesting a dose of alcohol. Thus, in this case, one is

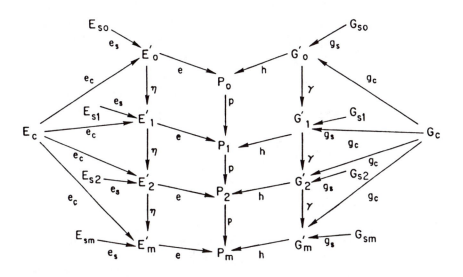

ENVIRONMENT   PHENOTYPE   GENOTYPE

Figure 14.2   Path model with both environmental and genetic simplexes (η, γ) and common factors (E_c, G_c) affecting a phenotype (P) over time (subscripts 0–m). For further details see text. From "A Theory of Developmental Change in Quantitative Phenotypes Applied to Cognitive Development" by L. J. Eaves, L. Long, and A. C. Heath, 1986, *Behavior Genetics*, *16*, 145. Copyright 1986 by Plenum Publishing Corporation. Reprinted by permission.

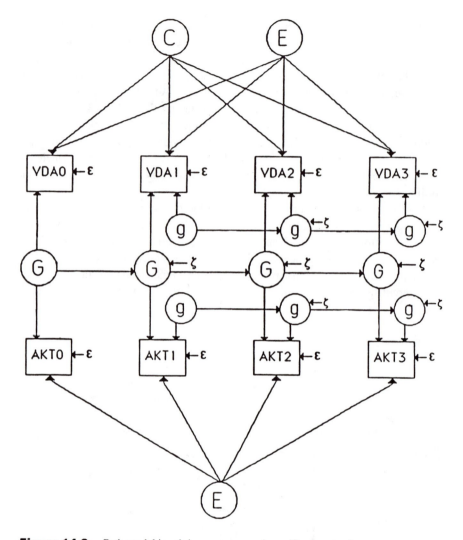

Figure 14.3 Path model involving common and specific aspects of two measures over
time. VDA = motor coordination task; AKT = arithmetic computation
task; Time 0 = before consuming alcohol; Times 1–3 = during recovery.
G = genes common to the two tasks; g = genes specific to a single
task; E = environmental factor specific to an individual; C = environmental factor common to twins; ϵ, ζ = residuals. From "Factor and
Simplex Models of Repeated Measures: Application to Two Psychomotor
Measures of Alcohol Sensitivity in Twins" by D. I. Boomsma, N. G.
Martin, and P. C. M. Molenaar, 1989, *Behavior Genetics, 19*, p. 91.
Copyright 1989 by Plenum Publishing Corporation. Reprinted by per-
mission.

dealing with short-term change rather than long-term development. The two traits are a measure of motor coordination (top squares) and a measure of arithmetic computation (bottom squares). In Figure 14.3, the genetic relations are assumed to be of the simplex type, as represented by the horizontal arrows in the center of the figure—G represents genes common to both tasks and g represents genes specific to each. In this example, the environmental effects, E and C, are hypothesized to be factors common over time but unique to each test. Arithmetic is shown as involving unshared environment only (bottom), and motor coordination as involving both shared and unshared environment (top). Residual time-specific genetic and environmental factors are also shown. One might at first find the notion of genetic factors unique to occasions an hour apart odd, but there is no fundamental difficulty here. Different physiological (or for that matter psychological) processes may come into play at different stages in the recovery from a dose of alcohol, and they may be affected by different genes.

TEMPORAL BEHAVIOR GENETIC MODELS IN THE TEXAS ADOPTION PROJECT

Several temporal behavior genetic models have been applied to data from the Texas Adoption Project. This research was carried out jointly with Joseph M. Horn and Lee Willerman at the University of Texas at Austin (e.g., Horn, Loehlin, & Willerman, 1979; Loehlin, Willerman, & Horn, 1987). In these applications we begin with the major handicap of only two-occasion measurement, the original adoption study and a 10-year follow-up. The potential for fitting elaborate over-time models is thus severely limited. Nevertheless, two examples will be described: one in which a model more or less in the spirit of those described earlier is fit to data on IQ, and one in which changes in group means on three personality rating composites are modeled.

But first, some background. The study began in the mid-1970s with 300 cooperating Texas families, each of whom had adopted a child from a particular church-related home for unwed mothers. At that time, all the available members of the adoptive family were given IQ and personality tests. This included the adopted child, the adoptive mother and father, other children who had been adopted into the family, and, in quite a number of cases, one or more children born to the adoptive parents, sometimes before and sometimes after the adoption in question. The adoptees ranged in age from 3 to 14 years of age when tested, with a median age of 8. Also available from the agency files were IQ test results and scores on the Minnesota Multiphasic Personality Inventory (MMPI) for many of the birth mothers who gave the children up for adoption (the tests were taken while the mothers were in residence at the home prior to the birth of their child). About 10 years after the initial testing, we followed up and retested the children in 181 families. The 258 twice-tested adopted children in these families and the 93 twice-tested biological children provide the data for the analyses to follow.

The measures that were available for most children at both ages were an individual IQ, based on the Stanford-Binet, Wechsler Intelligence Scale for Children (WISC), or Wechsler Adult Intelligence Scale (WAIS) (depending on age), and ratings of the child by a parent on 24 bipolar personality trait scales. On the basis of a factor analysis, the rating scales were combined into three major composites, labeled extraversion versus introversion, emotional stability versus maladjustment, and good versus poor socialization.

Figure 14.4 shows a highly schematic path model of the situation; measured variables are shown by rectangles. The parental generation, measured just once, is at the top. Symbolized are the IQs of an adoptive parent (P) and a birth mother (B) plus an index of the socioeconomic status (S) of the adoptive home, based on parents' education and father's occupational level. At the bottom are the IQ of an adopted child (AC) and the IQ of a child born to the adoptive parents (NC). The first occasion of measurement is shown at the left (subscript 1) and the second at the right (subscript 2). Each individual's IQ is assumed to be influenced by his or her genes (G), his or her family environment (E), and other factors represented by short, unlabeled residual arrows. These residual factors include environmental influences unique to the individual, errors of measurement, nonlinear genetic effects, gene–environment interactions, and so forth.

The paths between the top and bottom parts of the figure represent different forms of between-generations transmission. The path between birth parent's and child's genes is fixed at $\frac{1}{2}$, its value according to genetic theory. The path labeled x_1 is a parameter that allows for an effect of parent's IQ on the common family environment (CE) of the children; the path labeled f_1 allows for a similar effect of the socioeconomic circumstances of the family. The dashed lines allow for corresponding effects at Time 2.

The dotted horizontal lines from left to right across the figure represent various possibilities for persistence of effects from Time 1 to Time 2: Path y reflects the persistence of the genes; path z, the persistence of shared environment; and path n, the persistence of the developed trait itself. Also shown is a fourth possibility: The curved arrows at the bottom of the figure represent possible correlations between specifics of measurement on the two occasions, or other residual effects.

The model that was actually fit to the data was more complicated. Detailed discussion is unnecessary here, but some features omitted from Figure 14.4 should be mentioned. For example, the full model includes both mothers and fathers, and allows for correlations between their IQs and between their IQs and the socioeconomic status of the adoptive home. It allows for the presence of more than one child in a given category in an adoptive home (and hence for additional sets of birth parents). Also allowed for is selective placement—the tendency of

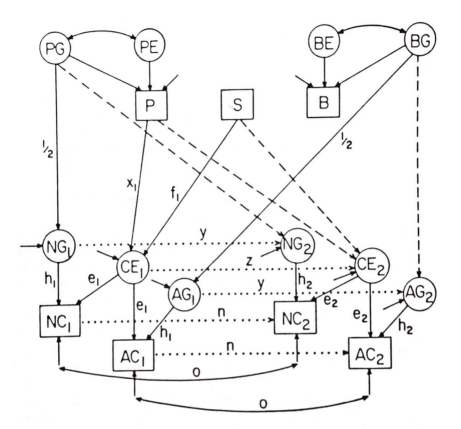

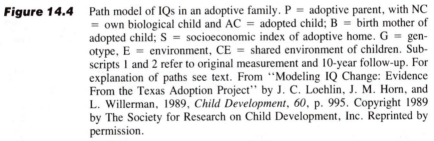

Figure 14.4   Path model of IQs in an adoptive family. P = adoptive parent, with NC = own biological child and AC = adopted child; B = birth mother of adopted child; S = socioeconomic index of adoptive home. G = genotype, E = environment, CE = shared environment of children. Subscripts 1 and 2 refer to original measurement and 10-year follow-up. For explanation of paths see text. From ''Modeling IQ Change: Evidence From the Texas Adoption Project'' by J. C. Loehlin, J. M. Horn, and L. Willerman, 1989, *Child Development, 60*, p. 995. Copyright 1989 by The Society for Research on Child Development, Inc. Reprinted by permission.

adoption agencies to try to match the child to the adoptive home. Finally, the model distinguishes between a latent variable representing an individual's true intelligence and that person's score on an IQ test, which is what is actually observed.

Variations of the full model were fitted to a set of 36 empirical correlations among the IQs of various categories of individuals in the study, and between IQs and socioeconomic status (SES). (For details, see Loehlin, Horn, & Willerman, 1989). A few of the main results may be described with reference to Figure 14.4.

We found that some form of horizontal, cross-time arrow was necessary in order to fit the data, and that phenotypic persistence (the path labeled n) was sufficient. Some form of cross-generational environmental transmission was necessary, but the data were adequately fit using either path x from parent's IQ or path f from socioeconomic status. The overall fit of the model was excellent, χ^2 = 18, with 26 *df*. The parameters of most interest are those labeled h and e, representing the effect of genes and of shared family environment on IQ: h_1 and e_1 represent these effects at Time 1, the first occasion of measurement; h_2 and e_2 represent further genetic and environmental effects on IQ that have been added by Time 2 to the effects persisting from Time 1. At Time 1, h_1 was .51 and e_1 was .25, both statistically significant. The additional contribution of the genes by Time 2 (h_2 of .45) was also statistically significant, but e_2 was not significantly different from zero; in fact, it came out slightly negative, at $-.11$. Apparently, the influences of shared family environment on children's IQs were real, though modest; they occurred relatively early in life and their effects persisted to some degree in the phenotype. By contrast, genetic effects on the development of intellectual skills appeared to occur throughout the period under study, with the genes making substantial new contributions to intellectual variation until late adolescence or early adulthood, when our second measurements were taken.

Recently Phillips and Fulker (1989) reported the fitting of somewhat similar behavior genetic models to longitudinal IQ data from families in the Colorado Adoption Project. These data are for an earlier age period (1–7 years) and the analyses are different from ours in a number of respects, so the comparison of results must be somewhat tentative. However, on the face of it, there appear to be some differences. For example, their analysis finds new genetic contributions to have almost ceased by age 7, whereas ours has them persisting at least into late adolescence. Clearly, some questions will require further exploration before the substantive issues can be considered settled.

The second example from the Texas Adoption Project differs from the first in several ways. It deals with personality rather than ability. It is multivariate rather than univariate, although only modestly so (i.e., three traits instead of one). It models age effects explicitly, rather than finessing them by using the age-normed measure, IQ. Finally, the analysis focuses on group means rather than on individual variation.

The personality dimensions are the three composites of parental ratings mentioned earlier: extraversion versus introversion, emotional stability versus instability, and good versus poor socialization. These were available only for the children in the study, not the parent generation.

One can think of the adopted and biological children as two groups growing up together in the same environment (the adoptive homes) but who have very different genetic parents. From other analyses (Loehlin, Willerman, & Horn, 1982) we know that the adoptive and biological mothers differed on at least two of the three personality dimensions under consideration. The birth mothers of the adopted children generally had elevated MMPI profiles, that is, they were less emotionally stable than the adoptive parents. They were also less well socialized, scoring considerably higher than the adoptive parents on the MMPI Psychopathic Deviate scale. Because the birth mothers had been given a shortened version of the MMPI lacking the Social Introversion scale, a direct comparison on the third dimension was not possible. No test scores were available for the genetic fathers of the adopted children, although it seems likely that the differences on emotional stability and socialization would hold for them as well.

To illustrate the model used for these data, Figure 14.5 presents a path diagram for a single trait, extraversion, measured on two occasions. The latent variable representing the true score on extraversion is related to the observed score at the bottom by a path corresponding to the square root of the reliability of the composite. This approach, which takes the measurement structure of the trait as given, means that any lack of fit of the model will reflect deficiencies in the structural rather than the measurement part of the model. This is appropriate, because it is in the structural part that our chief interest lies. The horizontal path a in Figure 14.5 represents the persistence of the trait from Time 1 to Time 2. The A1 and A1^2 at the top of the figure deal with the fact that the children in the study were measured at different ages. Inclusion of both age and age^2 terms allows for the possibility of nonlinear age effects. Finally, the triangle (after McArdle, 1986), represents a fixed constant of unity that handles the effects on means. The model is fit to moments (raw score products) rather than covariances, separately in the groups of adopted and biological children. The paths u and x are set to zero in one group and solved for in the other. Their values in the second group represent the difference in the mean level of extraversion between the two groups. As in the IQ example, the first path refers to the difference in means on the first occasion, the second to what is added by the time of the second occasion, over and above what persists along path a.

Figure 14.6 brings all three traits, extraversion, socialization, and stability, into the model. Age and age^2 have been omitted from this figure to keep it simpler (in the actual model paths went from age and age^2 to each of the six latent variables).

The model was fitted to moment matrices in the adoptive and biological children groups. The details are presented elsewhere (Loehlin, Horn, & Willerman, 1990). The model fits the data quite adequately, $\chi^2 = 33$, with 32 df. Both linear and nonlinear age effects were significant, and did not differ between the two groups. The cross-time paths a, b, and c ranged from about .4 to about .6, largest for extraversion, and again did not differ between the groups.

The paths u to z that represent mean differences and their changes tell an interesting story. At Time 1, as fairly young children, the adopted children were rated as a bit more extraverted and better behaved than the biological children of

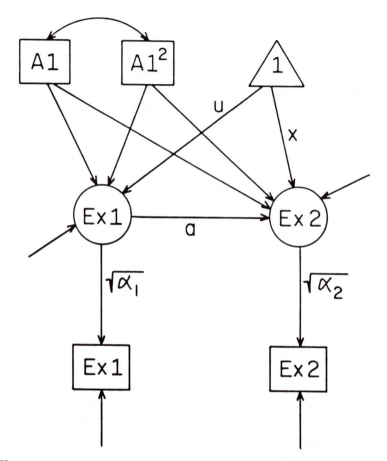

Figure 14.5   Path model for extraversion (Ex) measured at Times 1 and 2. A1 = age,; A1² = age²; α = reliability of extraversion measure. For explanation of paths see text. From "Heredity, Environment, and Personality Change: Evidence From the Texas Adoption Project" by J. C. Loehlin, J. M. Horn, and L. Willerman, 1990, *Journal of Personality, 58,* p. 234. Copyright 1990 by Duke University Press. Reprinted by permission.

the adoptive parents, although neither difference was statistically significant. There was essentially no difference in emotional stability. The changes, as reflected in the Time 2 paths, were significantly in the negative direction for the adopted children on both the socialization and the emotional stability dimensions. Another way of putting this is to say that as both groups of children grew older, the differences between them changed in the direction of the difference between their biological parents.

I don't want to give an exaggerated impression of the size of these changes in means—their estimated magnitude was about four tenths of a standard deviation

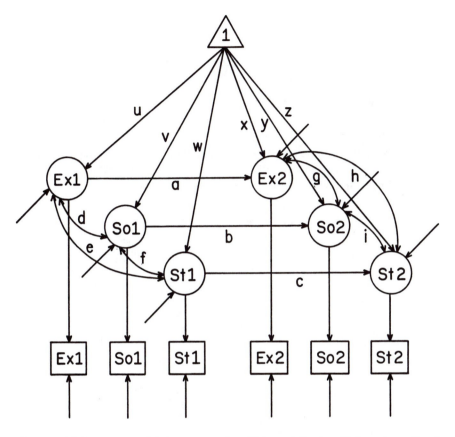

Figure 14.6   Path model for extraversion (Ex), socialization (So), and emotional stability (St) measured at Times 1 and 2. For explanation of paths see text. From "Heredity, Environment, and Personality Change: Evidence From the Texas Adoption Project" by J. C. Loehlin, J. M. Horn, and L. Willerman, 1990, *Journal of Personality*, *58*, p. 236. Copyright 1990 by Duke University Press. Reprinted by permission.

on the latent variables. Most adoptive parents still judged their adopted children to fall in the normal range of socialization and emotional stability.

One interesting additional point revealed by the path modeling was that the single greatest improvement in the fit of the model would result from the insertion of an additional path from extraversion at Time 1 to emotional stability at Time 2. One does not know, of course, whether extraverted behavior at Time 1 was a genuine precursor of emotional instability at a later age in this group of children, or whether the parents were rating the same behavior patterns at age 8 as extraverted and at age 18 as representing emotional immaturity. But in any event, the path model suggests hypotheses worth exploring in future research in this area.

CONCLUSIONS

To sum up the work in the behavior genetics of change, I want to make three points:

1. Simultaneously fitting models of two kinds of change—genetic and environmental—to data that reflect both is an exceptionally challenging enterprise.
2. Nevertheless, the results are potentially of great interest, and so behavior geneticists will almost certainly keep trying to do this.
3. They can use all the help they can get from others.

COMMENTS ON
"BEHAVIOR GENETIC STUDIES OF CHANGE"

LAURA A. BAKER

Developmental behavioral geneticists have an ambitious set of tasks indeed, and Loehlin presents some good examples of the questions being raised in this exciting new area. The primary objective is to understand how the complex interplay between dynamic genetic and environmental factors can produce individual differences in psychological development. To accomplish this zealous task requires the integration of at least three major areas of research: biometrics, psychometrics, and chronometrics (Cattell, 1966a; McArdle, 1986). In giving consideration to each of these areas in the context of Loehlin's chapter, several issues arise with respect to the biometrical and measurement aspects of his model of parent/offspring resemblance. I shall discuss some of these in detail here, and then provide a brief account of some alternative approaches to the study of change being made by others in this exciting area of investigation. Some possible directions for future research, based on presentations in this volume, are also noted.

MODEL SPECIFICATION IN PARENT/OFFSPRING DESIGNS

In considering the dynamic nature of latent genotypic variables, as discussed by Loehlin, there are a number of interesting implications for his model of parent/offspring resemblance that he does not discuss. The most important of these, and from which several problems may arise, concerns the specified value of ½ for the paths from biological-parent genotypes to adopted-child genotypes at each time of measurement. The fixing of these paths rests on the assumption that genetic effects important to the phenotype (in this case, IQ) in adulthood (i.e., the age at which the parents are tested) are perfectly correlated with genetic effects important to IQ at each of the ages when the children are measured (in Loehlin's example, childhood and late adolescence). This assumption may be plausible at the second time of testing, when the majority of the children were then well into their teenage years. In fact, the model makes an explicit assumption of cross-generational equivalence at Time 2, such that genetic influences in the children at Time 2 are isomorphic with those in the parents, and makes the additional constraint that heritabilities do not differ between adulthood and late adolescence (see Loehlin et al., 1989). The model does allow genetic factors at the first age of testing to differ from those at Time 2 and adulthood by including a separate parameter (h_1) for heritable influences in the children at Time 1. On the other hand, the fixed value of ½ on the path from biological parent to child's Time 1 genotype is less plausible, given that most of the adoptees were tested during early or late childhood.

It would be impossible, however, given the design of the study, to relax this constraint and place any value other than ½ on those paths. This is simply a limitation of all parent/offspring designs, with the rare exception of where the two generations are measured at different points in time when they have comparable ages. It is possible, on the other hand, to consider how the remaining parameters may have been affected by this potential misspecification.

For the sake of simplicity, consider only the situation in which genetic factors differ between Time 1 and adulthood, but cross-generational equivalence holds between Time 2 and adulthood. The actual value of the path from parental to child genotype is actually $\frac{1}{2}rG_1G_A$, where rG_1G_A represents the correlation between genetic factors important during adulthood and the children's age of measurement at Time 1. To the extent that rG_1G_A is less than unity, both the genetic and environmental parameters may be biased. In particular, the estimated h_1 is probably some function of the product between rG_1G_A and the true heritability at the first age of measurement in the children. This parameter (h_1) is therefore likely to be underestimated in Loehlin's analysis. Some of the "unreasonable" values obtained for the persistence paths (y, n) might also be due to the possible misspecification of the parent/offspring genetic transmission. Moreover, it has been shown elsewhere that when the necessary assumption of $rG_1G_A = 1.0$ is violated in designs involving twins and their parents, cultural transmission parameters are likely to be biased as well (Stallings, Baker, & Boomsma, 1989). In is unclear how the paths from parental IQ to child's environment (x) in Loehlin's model may be affected, but there is likely to be some bias as a result of the problems in specifying parent/offspring genotypic transmission.

This is not to say Loehlin's conclusion that "changes in genotypic expression continue at least into late adolescence" is necessarily wrong or misleading. It is simply unclear whether the changes in genetic effects between Time 1 and Time 2 are due to changes in the relative importance of genetic factors (h_1 vs. h_2), or due to a lack of genetic correlation between IQ at the two ages of testing. In essence, this emphasizes the inability of parent/offspring designs to disentangle questions about changes in heritability (i.e., relative portions of genetic variance) and changes in the composition of the genetic factors themselves (i.e., degree of genetic covariance among different time points). What is needed are additional data for contemporaneous relations such as biological siblings reared apart or identical and fraternal twins.

It should be noted that some investigators prefer to view this inseparability of heritability from genetic correlation as an asset to parent/offspring studies. As Plomin (1986) pointed out, any observed resemblance between biological parents and their offspring given up for adoption provides evidence that both heritabilities in the two generations and the genetic correlation between their respective ages of measurement must all be nonzero and substantial. This led Plomin to refer to an adoption study that includes only one time of measurement in both generations as an "instant longitudinal study."

MEASUREMENT LIMITATIONS

In addition to limitations of parent/offspring designs for separating different aspects of temporal changes in genetic and environmental effects, a number of measurement issues also arise. Using different measuring instruments in the parent and offspring generations is more a rule than an exception for most psychological characteristics, particularly when the offspring are measured at an early age. Even in Loehlin's data, different IQ measures were employed for biological parents and for adolescent offspring. This can result in a problem regarding the different ages of measurement; namely, the genetic transmission path is reduced from ½ to the extent that genetic factors important to the two measuring instruments are less than perfectly correlated. The use of varying measures at different times of assessment also presents a number of limitations in other designs, such as in the longitudinal study of twins. During childhood, most IQ and personality measures vary from one age to the next, even when they are purported to measure the same construct. This effectively prevents any comparison of observed means and variances across ages. Because many different models of development predict systematic changes in phenotypic variance (see Eaves et al., 1986), these inadequacies of our measuring instruments may lead to oversimplifications of potentially interesting (and perhaps more accurate) models.

Future longitudinal behavior genetic studies of cognitive development could yield considerably more informative results about genetic and environmental sources of change by employing a common measuring instrument at different ages. One example of such an instrument is the Woodcock-Johnson Cognitive Abilities Battery (Woodcock & Johnson, 1989), which has been standardized on a wide age range (24 months to 70 years) and allows comparisons of means and variances across ages. There is clearly a need for new developments of measures in other domains such as personality, so that meaningful age-to-age comparisons can be made in any longitudinal study.

ALTERNATIVE APPROACHES

Besides partitioning variance and covariance among observations at different ages of measurement, it is also possible to incorporate analyses of mean phenotypic changes. For example, Wilson (1977) presented a method for estimating genetic and environmental variance in developmental profiles based on longitudinal twin data. There the questions concern the degree to which individual spurts and lags in development are influenced by genetic or environmental variability across persons. There is still the concern with partitioning variance, but it is with respect to profiles over time, rather than individual time points.

Loehlin provides a very different approach for inspecting means using a structural modeling analysis of moment matrices. He makes no attempt to partition variance into genetic and environmental sources, but rather checks to see if temporal changes in personality variables arc in the direction predicted by the average genetic predisposition of the entire group of adoptees.

Other analyses of moment matrices allow the estimation of genetic and environmental variance for various parameters of individual growth curves, such as slopes and intercepts (McArdle, 1986; Sakai, Baker, Dawson, & Filion, 1988). Alternative growth models could also be employed in a similar type of analysis, such as the latent growth curve approach presented by Browne and Du Toit (chapter 4), in order to estimate genetic and environmental effects in rate of change and asymptote.

Survival analysis has also been used creatively by quantitative geneticists and biometricians to investigate genetic variation in age of onset of different mental disorders or diseases (Mack, 1988; Meyer, 1988). As Willet and Singer discuss in chapter 18, this kind of analysis may also be appropriate for the study of time-dependent characteristics other than rare or abnormal phenotypes. This might be useful to developmental behavioral geneticists for a wide variety of time-dependent phenotypes.

CHAPTER 15

INTERPRETING AND ESTIMATING INDIRECT EFFECTS ASSUMING TIME LAGS REALLY MATTER

HARRY F. GOLLOB AND CHARLES S. REICHARDT

Editors' Introduction

A principal aim of research on change is to infer cause. In chapter 15, Gollob and Reichardt describe three basic conditions that must obtain to provide a strong basis for inference about cause. They point out that because these conditions are met only in repeated measures longitudinal designs, cross-sectional designs provide a much weaker basis for causal inference. As a heuristic for examining the plausibility of assumptions needed to base causal inferences on cross-sectional data, Gollob and Reichardt develop a latent longitudinal model for cross-sectional data. The observations that are missing in cross-sectional data are imputed in latent longitudinal models by assumption and by use of latent variables. It is well to consider this model in the context of chapter 17 on combining cross-sectional and longitudinal data.

Often it is reasonable to suppose that causal influences operate not only directly, as when X causes Z, but also indirectly, as when X causes Y, which in turn causes Z. The analyses of Gollob and Reichardt demonstrate that researchers must be especially cautious and thoughtful in interpreting results from analyses aimed at isolating indirect effects. First, they show

We thank Robert M. McFatter and John L. Horn for helpful comments on earlier drafts of this chapter.

that when results from analyses based on simple cross-sectional models are used to distinguish direct and indirect causal effects, the estimates are likely to be biased, and the bias is likely to be more severe and complex than if only direct effects are estimated. Therefore it may be preferable to forego estimating indirect effects when only cross-sectional data are available. Second, Gollob and Reichardt show that even when the design is longitudinal, if the model uses fewer than $k + 2$ time points to estimate an indirect effect that contains a chain of k (or more) intervening variables, cross-sectional relations are necessarily present, and the obtained estimates of causal effects are likely to be biased.

Gollob and Reichardt's analyses lead to a sobering general principle: Although it is intuitively tempting to assume there is a single indirect effect operating over time, as from Time 1 to Time 2 to Time 3, in fact there is an infinity of indirect effects estimable under these conditions. Furthermore, the size of these indirect effects varies as a function of the amount of time between the intermediate time and the end-point times; that is, the positioning of Time 2 between Times 1 and 3. Gollob and Reichardt present concrete examples to show that, with end-points fixed, as the position of Time 2 varies from a few days to a few months after Time 1, the indirect effect would be estimated to be anything from near zero to large. The results thus demonstrate that there is no single indirect effect, but rather the size of an indirect effect is specific to a particular time interval. It is useful to consider these findings in the context of the issues raised by Cohen in chapter 2 on bias in longitudinal studies.

To move away from the difficulty of attempting to draw strong inferences about change from effects that are time specific, Gollob and Reichardt define *overall* direct and indirect effects, and explain how they can be estimated. They show that these overall effects not only provide a more dependable basis for inference than time-specific effects, but also correspond to the meanings intended in substantive theory.

Researchers who study cause and effect often ask two questions: What is the size of an effect due to a given cause? and How does an effect due to a given cause come about? In structural equation modeling, the first question can be addressed by estimating the size of the total effect for a given cause, and the second can be addressed by partitioning the estimate of the total effect into estimates of direct and indirect effects (Bollen, 1987; Fox, 1985; Heise, 1975; Loehlin, 1987). For example, a causal model that involves only the variables X, Y, and Z could partition the total effect of X on Z into an indirect effect that is mediated by Y and a direct effect that is not mediated by Y.

We (Gollob & Reichardt, 1985, 1987; Reichardt & Gollob, 1986) have shown that cross-sectional models (i.e., models containing relations only between variables at the same point in time) typically yield seriously biased estimates of total effects, and that latent longitudinal models can be used to avoid these biases. In this chapter we use our previous results to discuss biases and additional difficulties that arise when cross-sectional models are used to estimate direct and indirect effects. We also show that (a) conventional longitudinal estimates of direct and indirect effects typically vary as a function of when the mediating variable is measured, and (b) these conventional estimates usually are poor estimates of direct and indirect effects in the more general sense that usually is of interest to researchers.

USING CROSS-SECTIONAL DATA TO ESTIMATE TOTAL EFFECTS

It takes time for a cause to have an effect. For this reason, it usually is preferable to estimate effects by using longitudinal data rather than cross-sectional data (i.e., by using repeated measures data rather than data measured at only one point in time). Sometimes, however, only cross-sectional data are available. In such cases, it is common for researchers to estimate effects by fitting cross-sectional models. As explained later in this chapter, this use of cross-sectional data usually yields severely biased estimates. To help avoid these biases, we (Gollob & Reichardt, 1987) introduced the latent longitudinal model for estimating causal parameters when only cross-sectional data are available. Latent longitudinal models also are described below.

Using a Cross-Sectional Model

We (Gollob & Reichardt, 1987) have described three principles of causality. All three principles can be satisfied in longitudinal models. Cross-sectional models, however, satisfy none of the three principles. As a result, cross-sectional models usually produce poor estimates of effects.

The three principles of causality can be illustrated by comparing longitudinal and cross-sectional models of "X causes Y." Two such models are presented in Figure 15.1. The numerical subscripts on the variables denote points in time. For example, in Figure 15.1A, Y_1 and Y_2, respectively, denote the values of Y at Time 1 and Y at Time 2. To focus on causal issues, we assume throughout our discussion that population data are available and that variables are measured perfectly.

The first principle states that causes take time to exert their effects and, therefore, causal variables must occur before outcome variables. For example, the longitudinal model depicted in Figure 15.1A shows Y at Time 2 being caused in part by X at an earlier time, Time 1. In contrast, the cross-sectional model in Figure 15.1B shows Y at Time 2 being caused by X at the same time, rather than by X at an earlier time.

The second principle states that variables can have effects on themselves. Such autoregressive effects typically are not zero. For example, if a change were

A

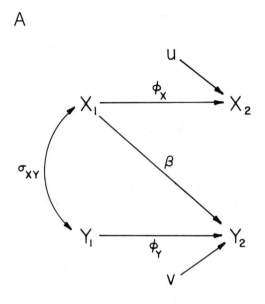

B

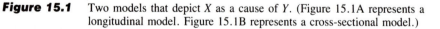

Figure 15.1   Two models that depict X as a cause of Y. (Figure 15.1A represents a longitudinal model. Figure 15.1B represents a cross-sectional model.)

made in X at Time 1, and other variables at Time 1 remained the same, X at Time 2 typically would be changed. The longitudinal model in Figure 15.1A allows for the possibility that the autoregressive effects of X and Y, Φ_X and Φ_Y, are nonzero. In contrast, the cross-sectional model omits autoregressive effects, implicitly assuming that they are zero.

The third principle states that the size of an effect typically varies with the length of the time lag. Thus, the size of an effect typically will vary depending on whether Time 1 and Time 2 are separated by a few seconds, a few days, or a few years. The longitudinal model in Figure 15.1A explicitly specifies both Time 1 and Time 2, so the length of the time interval is known. In contrast, the cross-sectional model specifies only Time 2, and therefore the time interval that is being studied is unspecified.

Because the cross-sectional model in Figure 15.1B violates the three causal principles, it is misspecified as a model of cause. As a result, fitting the cross-sectional model typically yields a seriously biased estimate of the true causal effect, β. Assuming the longitudinal model in Figure 15.1A is correct, the size of the bias in the cross-sectional estimate is a complex function of the values of the two autoregressive effects, the covariance of X and Y at Time 1, the variance of X at Time 1, and the variance of the disturbance term for X at Time 2. In addition, even if it were a good estimate of β, the cross-sectional estimate wouldn't be very useful and likely would be misinterpreted if the time interval weren't specified.

Using a Latent Longitudinal Model

The problems that arise when one uses a cross-sectional model can be avoided by using a latent longitudinal model. The first step in the latent longitudinal approach is to specify a longitudinal model that could be used to estimate causal parameters if longitudinal data were available. The approach is called *latent* longitudinal because the second step is to use explicitly stated assumptions in place of the longitudinal data that are missing. Although the requirement that assumptions be made explicit makes it more difficult to fit a latent longitudinal model than to fit a cross-sectional model, it also makes it possible to evaluate the degree of plausibility of the assumptions. Compared with fitting a cross-sectional model, fitting a latent longitudinal model enables one to fit more realistic (i.e., longitudinal) models of cause and thereby obtain less biased estimates of effects.

For example, given that data are available at only one point in time, Time 2, the latent longitudinal model depicted in Figure 15.2 can be used to estimate the effect that mother's IQ at Time 1 (MIQ_1) has on child's IQ at Time 2 (CIQ_2). The population comprises mother–child pairs in which the child is 45 months old at Time 2. To define a time lag that is theoretically interesting to study, we specify

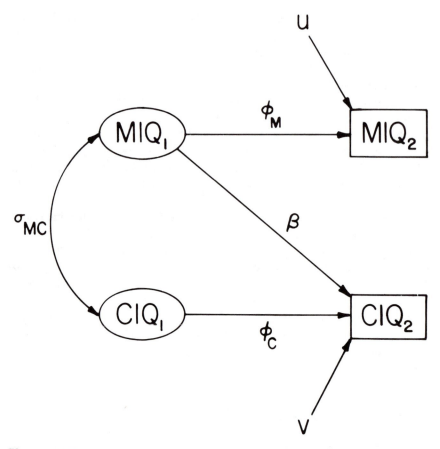

Figure 15.2   A latent longitudinal model that depicts mother's IQ (MIQ) and child's IQ (CIQ) at Time 1 (when the child is 27 months old) as causes of MIQ and CIQ at Time 2 (when the child is 45 months old).

Time 1 to be the time when the child is 27 months old. The model in Figure 15.2 has the same form as the model in Figure 15.1A, except that boxes are used to denote observations at Time 2 and ellipses are used to denote missing, or latent, observations at Time 1.

This model has eight unknown parameters, and the cross-sectional data at Time 2 provide three pieces of information (two variances and one covariance) that can be used in fitting the model. To estimate the eight model parameters, however, at least five constraints must be added to make up for having only cross-sectional data. For example, it would be possible to solve for the model parameters if, in addition to having the cross-sectional data, it were assumed that the test–retest correlations for mother's IQ and child's IQ were known and the variances and covariances at Time 1 and Time 2 were the same. Typically, a researcher would judge that such assumptions would be likely to hold only within a range. When such a range is specified, it is possible to estimate the model parameters within a range (Reichardt & Gollob, 1987). In this way, reasonable estimates of effects can be obtained even if only cross-sectional data are available. Similarly, Donaldson and Horn (in press; Horn & Donaldson, 1980; Horn & McArdle, 1980) have emphasized the value of making assumptions explicit when drawing causal inferences from the age, cohort, and time (ACT) model.

USING CROSS-SECTIONAL DATA TO ESTIMATE INDIRECT EFFECTS

Regardless of whether a cross-sectional or latent longitudinal model is used, the difficulties that arise in estimating causal effects using cross-sectional data are compounded when a total effect is partitioned into direct and indirect effects.

Using a Cross-Sectional Model

To see how difficulties are compounded when a cross-sectional model is used to estimate direct and indirect effects, consider the preceding IQ example with the additional assumption that the amount that a mother shapes her child's behavior using positive reinforcement (mother's positive control [MPC]) is a mediating variable. For example, according to the cross-sectional model in Figure 15.3, the total effect of mother's IQ at Time t (MIQ$_t$) on child's IQ at Time t (CIQ$_t$) is partitioned into a direct effect of β_3 units and an indirect effect of $\beta_1\beta_2$ units that operates via MPC at Time t (MPC$_t$). This indirect effect typically is interpreted as the combined result of the effect of MIQ on MPC and the effect of MPC, in

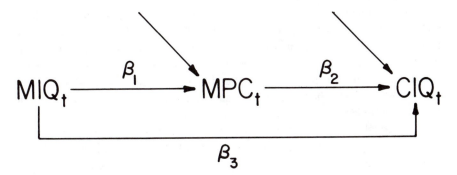

Figure 15.3   A cross-sectional model that shows relations among mother's IQ (MIQ), mother's positive control (MPC). and child's IQ (CIQ) at Time t. (The short, originless arrows denote disturbance terms.)

turn, on CIQ. In the social sciences, cross-sectional models such as this often are used to estimate direct and indirect effects.

Unfortunately, the estimate of the size of each individual effect in the cross-sectional model in Figure 15.3 (β_1, β_2, and β_3) is likely to be a biased estimate of the true effect, because the model violates the three principles of causality in the same fashion as does the model in Figure 15.1B. Moreover, because the cross-sectional estimates of the three effects in Figure 15.3 are not independent, the biases in the estimates of the direct and indirect effects are likely to be both more severe and more complex than those that result when only a total effect is estimated.

Using a Latent Longitudinal Model

As in the case when estimating total effects, if only cross-sectional data are available, it is preferable to use latent longitudinal models, rather than cross-sectional models, to estimate direct and indirect effects. But latent longitudinal models are even harder to fit when one is trying to partition direct and indirect effects than they are when one is trying to estimate only total effects.

To see what is required to fit a latent longitudinal model that includes an indirect effect of mother's IQ on child's IQ, suppose cross-sectional data are available only for Time 3 and that the longitudinal model in Figure 15.4 is correct. Times 1, 2, and 3 in this model are the times when the child is 27, 36, and 45 months old, respectively. Both the cross-sectional model in Figure 15.3 and the longitudinal model in Figure 15.4 include an indirect effect of mother's IQ on child's IQ via mother's positive control. In contrast to the cross-sectional model, however, the longitudinal model is consistent with the three aforementioned causal principles. Specifically, the longitudinal model specifies that causes occur before their effects, allows for autoregressive effects, and specifies the time intervals.

The longitudinal model depicted in Figure 15.4 contains 24 parameters, and the cross-sectional data at Time 3 provide six pieces of information (three variances and three covariances) that can be used in fitting the model. Therefore, assumptions that impose at least 18 constraints must be made to solve for the parameters in the model. For example, stationarity assumptions and knowledge of the test–retest coefficients would suffice, but background knowledge must be used to a much greater extent than when one is estimating total effects in a single-lag latent longitudinal model, as in Figure 15.2.

Although fitting a latent longitudinal model with cross-sectional data is preferable to fitting the cross-sectional model in Figure 15.3, it is usually better to fit a longitudinal model with longitudinal data. If the model in Figure 15.4 were fit by using longitudinal data for all three time points, the causal parameters could be estimated without making any additional assumptions. The advantage of having longitudinal data becomes even greater as the number of intervening vari-

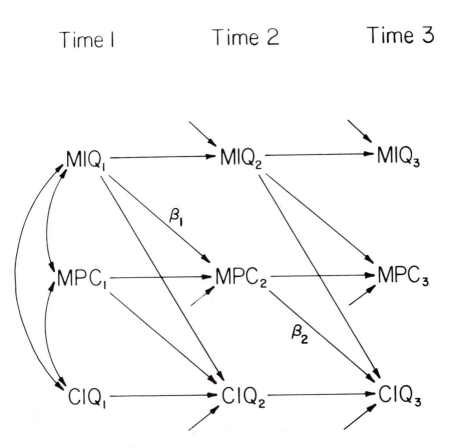

Figure 15.4   A three-wave model that depicts causal relations among mother's IQ (MIQ), mother's positive control (MPC), and child's IQ (CIQ) during two adjacent time lags that span Time 1 to Time 3.

ables in a causal chain increases. In general, to estimate an indirect effect that contains a chain of k intervening variables one must fit a model that has at least $k + 2$ time points. If longitudinal data are not available for at least $k + 2$ time points, it is necessary to use a latent longitudinal model and substitute for the missing data by using assumptions based on intuition, theory, and knowledge.

When a sound basis for making such assumptions is lacking, it often is preferable to forego estimating indirect effects when only cross-sectional data are available. Instead, it may be preferable to estimate only total effects by using a two-wave latent longitudinal model. For example, rather than fit a three-wave latent longitudinal model that corresponds to the structure in Figure 15.4, fit a two-wave model that specifies that CIQ_3 is caused directly by MIQ_1, MPC_1, CIQ_1, and a residual variable. Estimating the parameters in such a two-wave latent longitudinal model requires adding only half the number of constraints that would be required to estimate the parameters in the three-wave model.

USING INCOMPLETE LONGITUDINAL DATA TO ESTIMATE INDIRECT EFFECTS

Even when longitudinal data are available, researchers often use models with less than $k + 2$ time points to estimate indirect effects that involve a chain of k mediating variables. Such models necessarily include one or more cross-sectional relations (i.e., relations between variables at the same point in time) and therefore are likely to yield biased estimates of causal effects. These models also are ambiguous with respect to the time intervals that are being studied.

For example, Scarr (1985) had longitudinal data for mother–child pairs when the child was 27 and 45 months old. She used these data to fit a two-wave model that included the indirect effect of mother's IQ on child's IQ via mother's positive control. The model represented the indirect effect by using a path from MIQ_1 to MPC_1 (both at the time when the child was 27 months old) to CIQ (when the child was 45 months old). This part of the model is misspecified because the cross-sectional relation from MIQ_1 to MPC_1 does not allow time for mother's IQ to have an effect on mother's positive control.

Given longitudinal data for only Times 1 and 2, rather than fit a model that contains a cross-sectional relation, it would be preferable to use the latent longitudinal approach to estimate the indirect effect. For example, the latent longitudinal approach could be used to fit the model depicted in Figure 15.4. To use the latent longitudinal approach, however, the times must be specified for Times 1, 2, and 3. Time 3 is the time when a child is 45 months old, and data are available for this time point. Data also are available for the time when a child is 27 months old, but should one use these data for Time 1 or for Time 2? Consider both possibilities.

Suppose Time 1 is specified to be the time when a child is 27 months old. Then Time 2 must be chosen to fall in the interval between the time when the child is 27 months old and the time when the child is 45 months old, and assumptions must be made to compensate for the data that are missing at Time 2. Now suppose instead that Time 2 is specified to be the time when a child is 27 months old. Then Time 1 must be chosen to be a time when the child is younger than 27 months old, and assumptions must be made to compensate for the data that are missing at Time 1. The decision about which times to specify for Time 1 and Time 2 is an important one. The times that are chosen can influence the size of the effects, the number and plausibility of the assumptions that are used to constrain the model, and the substantive questions that can be answered by fitting the model.

Although the latent longitudinal approach provides a framework within which the indirect effect of MIQ_1 on CIQ_3 via MPC_2 can be estimated even though only two waves of data are available, this can be done only at the expense of making strong assumptions. It often may be better to reduce the number of assumptions by estimating only the total effect of each of the three variables at Time 1 (27 months) on CIQ at Time 3 (45 months). With data available for both of these times, the two-wave model is identified and can be fit without making the additional assumptions that would be required if an indirect effect were estimated.

THE CONVENTIONAL LONGITUDINAL ESTIMATE OF AN INDIRECT EFFECT IS TIME SPECIFIC

In this section we use both a substantive and an algebraic example to show that the conventional longitudinal estimate of the size of an indirect effect varies as a function of the time at which the mediating variable is measured. Such time-specific estimates do not provide a sound basis for partitioning total effects into direct and indirect effects in the sense that usually is of interest to researchers.

A Substantive Example

Suppose measures of MIQ, MPC, and CIQ are available for each mother–child pair at each of the three time points in Figure 15.4. Further suppose that Times 1, 2, and 3 are the times when the children are 27, 36, and 45 months old, respectively. Then, assuming this model is correct, the total effect of MIQ_1 on CIQ_3 is equal to the regression coefficient for MIQ_1 that would be obtained if CIQ_3 were regressed on the three variables at Time 1. This total effect is fixed regardless of how the total effect is partitioned into direct and indirect effects.

In causal modeling, the conventional estimate of the size of the indirect effect of MIQ_1 on CIQ_3 via MPC_2 is given by the product of β_1 and β_2. For example, if $\beta_1 = \beta_2 = 0.5$, the size of the indirect effect of MIQ_1 on CIQ_3 via MPC_2 would be $\beta_1\beta_2 = 0.25$. Typically, this result would be interpreted as though there were only one indirect effect of MIQ_1 on CIQ_3 via MPC, and the size of that one indirect effect were 0.25. Unfortunately, in most applications of causal modeling this interpretation is likely to be incorrect.

The problem arises because the size of the indirect effect usually varies as a function of the positioning of Time 2 between Times 1 and 3. To see this, suppose Time 1 and Time 3, respectively, are fixed at 27 and 45 months, but that Time 2 is chosen to be only 2 days after Time 1 rather than 9 months after Time 1 as originally assumed. In this case, β_1 would be small because any change in mother's IQ at Time 1 wouldn't have much time to affect mother's positive control at Time 2. Therefore, if the size of the indirect effect were to remain at 0.25, β_2

would have to become correspondingly larger. For example, if the time interval between Time 1 and Time 2 were so short that $\beta_1 = 0.01$, β_2 would have to equal 25. If the variables were standardized, this would mean that an increase of 1 standard deviation in MPC_2 would have to result in a 25 standard deviation increase in CIQ_3. But this is unlikely to occur. Is it reasonable to suppose that β_1 and β_2 would vary in such a way that their product would remain equal to the constant value of 0.25 regardless of where Time 2 was positioned? Probably not.

By generalizing the results of the preceding example, it can be shown that conventional longitudinal estimates of indirect effects, and therefore also estimates of direct effects, are *time specific*. When estimates of such effects are reported, it is important to emphasize their dependency on the time at which the intervening variable is measured. For example, rather than report that "the indirect effect of MIQ on CIQ via MPC is 0.25," one should report that "the time-specific indirect effect of MIQ at Time 1 on CIQ at Time 3 via MPC at Time 2 is 0.25."

An Algebraic Example

An algebraic example shows further how the conventional longitudinal estimates of direct and indirect effects are time specific. Suppose the variables X, Y, and Z all change continuously from Time 1 to Time 4. Suppose further that the values of these three variables are observed at four equally spaced points in time. Finally, suppose all of the true nonzero parameters that describe the causal system at Times 1, 2, 3, and 4 are depicted in Figure 15.5A. Then Figures 15.5B and 15.5C present two additional descriptions of the same causal system. Figure 15.5B describes the causal system at Times 1, 2, and 4, while Figure 15.5C describes the causal system at Times 1, 3, and 4.

Although they differ from each other and are incomplete relative to Figure 15.5A, both Figures 15.5B and 15.5C are correct because they are each implied by Figure 15.5A, which is assumed to be correct. Nevertheless, fitting the models in Figures 15.5B and 15.5C yields different estimates of the indirect effect of X_1 on Z_4 mediated by Y, depending on whether Y is assessed at Time 2 (Figure 15.5B) or at Time 3 (Figure 15.5C). Specifically, in Figure 15.5B the conventional estimate of the indirect effect of X_1 on Z_4 via Y is $\beta\gamma\delta + \beta\delta\omega$, whereas in Figure 15.5C it is $\beta\gamma\delta + \beta\delta\alpha$. These two estimates will be the same if and only if $\alpha = \omega$, in other words, if and only if the autoregressive effect of X is the same as the autoregressive effect of Z. Assuming this unlikely condition doesn't hold, the estimates of the indirect effects will be different. This again shows that conventional longitudinal estimates of indirect effects are time specific.

Because the causal system that underlies Figures 15.5A, 15.5B, and 15.5C is assumed to be a continuous one, the intervening variables could have been assessed at any one of an infinite number of alternative time points between Time

A

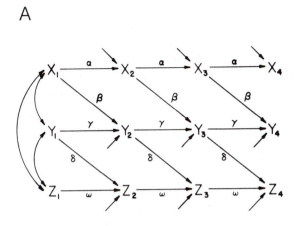

B

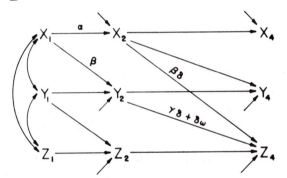

C

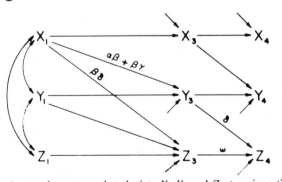

Figure 15.5   A causal structure that depicts X, Y, and Z at various times between Time 1 and Time 4. (Figure 15.5A represents data available for Times 1, 2, 3, and 4. Figure 15.5B represents data available for Times 1, 2, and 4. Figure 15.5C represents data available for Times 1, 3, and 4.)

1 and Time 4. In general, each of these other time points would yield a different estimate of the indirect effect of X_1 on Z_4 via Y. Each of these time-specific estimates would be equal to the indirect effect for the specific time at which Y was observed. Unfortunately, however, the time-specific estimates are not likely to provide good estimates of the direct and indirect effects that usually are of interest to researchers.

OVERALL DIRECT AND INDIRECT EFFECTS

In this section we define *overall* direct and indirect effects and also discuss ways to estimate such effects. We believe researchers usually think intuitively in terms of overall direct and indirect effects, yet typically estimate only time-specific direct and indirect effects.

Defining Overall Direct and Indirect Effects

For any variables, X and Z, the total effect of X at Time 1 (X_1) on Z at Time 2 (Z_2) is the change in Z that would have resulted at Time 2 if X had been one unit greater at Time 1, while the values of all other variables at Time 1 had remained the same. The total effect of X_1 on Z_2 presumably is mediated by a set of variables, only some of which can be explicitly specified in a model.

First, overall direct and indirect effects shall be defined for the case in which only variables X, Y, and Z are explicitly specified. In this case, the overall direct effect of X_1 on Z_2 is that part of the total effect of X_1 on Z_2 that would have occurred if Y had been constant throughout the entire interval from Time 1 to Time 2. The overall indirect effect of X_1 on Z_2 mediated by Y is that part of the total effect of X_1 on Z_2 that would not have occurred if Y had been constant throughout the entire interval from Time 1 to Time 2. The total effect of X_1 on Z_2 is equal to the overall direct effect plus the overall indirect effect that is mediated by Y.

A general definition of overall direct and indirect effects follows. Suppose a model explicitly specifies one or more mediator variables between X_1 and Z_2, and that neither X nor Z is treated as a mediator. Then, the overall direct effect of X_1 on Z_2 for this model is that part of the total effect that would have occurred even if *all* mediators specified by the model had been constant throughout the interval from Time 1 to Time 2. Now, let M denote a subset (or possibly all) of the mediators that the model specifies between X_1 and Z_2. Then, the overall indirect effect of X_1 on Z_2 via the mediators in M is that part of the total effect that would *not* have occurred if all the mediators in M had been constant throughout the interval from Time 1 to Time 2. If M contains all of the mediators specified by the model, the sum of the overall direct and the overall indirect effect will equal the total effect.

Our definitions of overall direct and indirect effects do not allow either X or Z to be a mediator variable. To see why, suppose Z had been treated as a mediator. Then, according to our definitions, the overall direct effect of X_1 on Z_2 would always be zero, and the overall indirect effect of X_1 on Z_2 via Z (or any set of mediators that included Z) would always equal the total effect. These conclusions follow because none of the total effect would have occurred had Z been constant throughout the interval from Time 1 to Time 2.

A similar difficulty arises if X is allowed to be a mediating variable. In addition, it seems natural to treat effects such as the time-specific indirect effect of X_1 on Z_3 via Z_2 and the time-specific indirect effect of X_1 on Z_3 via X_2 as parts of the overall direct effect of X_1 on Z_3, as is done by our definition.

Estimating Overall Direct and Indirect Effects

For purposes of estimation, it is useful to express overall direct and indirect effects in terms of various time-specific paths in a structural equation model of cause. To do so, we first define a "complete" causal model. A causal model is *complete* with respect to a set of variables during the interval from Time 1 to Time 2 if the variables are represented in the model at *every* time point at which any of the variables change between Time 1 and Time 2. In most applications of causal modeling, the variables change continuously within the interval from Time 1 to Time 2, but for present purposes, we assume that a discrete model can be used as an approximation. In a discrete model that is complete, it is assumed that changes in the variables occur only at the times that are explicitly specified in the model.

Suppose a given causal model is complete with respect to the variables X, Y, and Z during the interval from Time 1 to Time 2. Then the overall indirect effect of X_1 on Z_2 via Y is equal to the sum of all possible time-specific paths from X_1 to Z_2 via Y. Similarly, the overall direct effect of X_1 on Z_2 is equal to the sum of all possible time-specific paths from X_1 to Z_2 that do not involve Y. The total effect of X_1 on Z_2 is equal to the sum of all possible time-specific paths from X_1 to Z_2.

Figure 15.5A can be used to illustrate these ideas. We previously assumed that Figure 15.5A was an incomplete description of a continuous causal system, but we now assume that it is a complete description of a discrete causal system. In this figure, the total effect of X_1 on Z_4 is equal to the sum of the contributions of all the time-specific paths from X_1 to Z_4, but it also is equal to the regression coefficient obtained for X_1 when Z_4 is regressed on X_1, Y_1, and Z_1. Thus, the total effect can be calculated by using only observations at Time 1 and Time 4.

In contrast, calculation of the overall direct and indirect effects requires that X, Y, and Z be measured at every time point at which any of the variables change between Time 1 and Time 4. For example, because it is assumed to be complete with respect to the values of X, Y, and Z between Time 1 and Time 4, Figure 15.5A can be used to compute the overall direct and indirect effects. Specifically, because all paths from X_1 to Z_4 traverse Y, the overall direct effect is equal to zero. Both the overall indirect effect and the total effect are equal to $\alpha\beta\delta + \beta\gamma\delta + \beta\delta\omega$, which can also be written as $\beta\delta(\alpha + \gamma + \omega)$.

Because Figures 15.5B and 15.5C are incomplete with respect to the variables X, Y, and Z, they do not provide the correct overall direct and indirect effects that are implied by Figure 15.5A. Nevertheless, Figures 15.5B and 15.5C do provide correct total effects and correct time-specific direct and indirect effects. The time-specific direct and indirect effects given by Figure 15.5B are equal to $\beta\delta\alpha$ and $\beta\delta(\gamma + \omega)$, respectively. On the other hand, the time-specific direct and indirect effects given by Figure 15.5C are equal to $\beta\delta\omega$ and $\beta\delta(\alpha + \gamma)$, respectively. If all the causal parameters are positive, it can be seen that the time-specific estimates obtained from these two figures are underestimates of the overall indirect effect and are overestimates of the overall direct effect.

More generally, if all the causal parameters in a model are positive, a time-specific indirect effect is a lower bound for the size of the overall indirect effect. This follows because the overall indirect effect is equal to the sum of all possible time-specific indirect paths that traverse the relevant mediators, and this sum is at least as large as any one time-specific indirect path that also traverses the relevant mediators. By similar reasoning, if all the causal parameters are positive, a time-specific direct effect is an upper bound for the size of the overall direct effect.

If all the parameters in a causal system are positive, induction can be used to show that adding more time periods at which changes in the variables under study occur always reduces the bias in the estimates of the overall direct and indirect effects. If the causal system is continuous, the bias never can be eliminated, but it can be reduced.

If any of the causal parameters are negative, the situation is more complex. Specifically, both the direction and the size of the biases then depend on the particular model and effects being estimated. Nevertheless, under a wide range of conditions, adding additional waves of observations is likely to yield less biased estimates of the overall direct and indirect effects.

CONCLUSIONS

Models that contain cross-sectional relations are misspecified as models of cause, and usually yield severely biased estimates of total, direct, and indirect effects.

Better estimates typically can be obtained by fitting longitudinal models to longitudinal data. Nevertheless, if only cross-sectional data are available, the latent longitudinal approach provides a framework within which cross-sectional data can be used to estimate the size of effects.

The size of an indirect effect, as conventionally obtained by using longitudinal data to fit a longitudinal causal model, usually varies as a function of the time at which the mediating variable is observed. Although such time-specific indirect effects may sometimes be useful, they do not, in themselves, answer the more general question, How much of the effect of X_1 on Z_2 is mediated by Y over the interval from Time 1 to Time 2? Unfortunately, this is the question that researchers usually want to answer and seem to believe is being answered when they fit causal models to their data.

We recommend that the indirect effect of X at Time 1 (X_1) on Z at Time 2 (Z_2) mediated by Y over the interval from Time 1 to Time 2 be estimated by summing the contributions of all possible paths from X_1 to Z_2 via Y for all times at which Y is measured between Time 1 and Time 2. Other things being equal, the more time points between Time 1 and Time 2 at which X, Y, and Z are measured, the better the estimates of the size of the overall direct and indirect effects. We also recommend that researchers abandon the common practice of interpreting time-specific direct and indirect effects as though these were the same as the overall direct and indirect effects that they usually want to estimate.

COMMENTS ON "USING CAUSAL MODELS TO ESTIMATE INDIRECT EFFECTS"

ROBERT CUDECK

Gollob and Reichardt make four points. First, causal models must be longitudinal models. Second, autoregressive effects are expected as a matter of course in longitudinal studies. Third, functions of time (lag effects) must be included in the model, and the particular lags that are selected are of critical importance. Fourth, careful tinkering with data may help estimate models that are known to be more plausible than other models but that cannot be otherwise estimated. The third matter, that of deciding when to measure, presents one of the most difficult substantive problems associated with longitudinal designs and is one for which no satisfactory answer is available. When any of the first three matters are ignored, the authors contend, change models will be misspecified. Inferential problems are sure to arise if these misspecifications are ignored.

These points seem so clearly presented that there is little need to elaborate further about their relevance to longitudinal studies. Failing to account for these possible sources of error may render an otherwise serviceable model useless. The point that was not made, but which should also be stressed, is that the converse does not, and in fact cannot, hold: It is not true, for example, that changing from a cross-sectional model to a longitudinal model corrects the misspecification problem in any fundamental way. To believe otherwise is to expect much more from a model than a model is able to give.

To see this, consider Gollob and Reichardt's example in which a child's IQ at Time 2 is viewed as a function of maternal control and discipline at Time 1, but the child's IQ at Time 1 is not included. They argue that because the Time 1 measure of IQ is excluded, the regression coefficients associated with the other two variables are biased. Thus the parameter estimates in their example are .28

260

and .35 without the third variable, but when it is included, the estimates shrink to .09 and .14. Although the model without the third variable may be obviously wrong, it is incorrect to assume that including the third variable suddenly makes the model "true," whatever that may mean. For if maternal control and discipline is relevant for the child's IQ, how can the model possibly be correctly specified without paternal control and discipline? And if IQ has both an environmental effect as well as a genetic effect, how can the model be accurate if such variables as school experiences, or socioeconomic status (SES), or genetic influences are excluded? If important influences such as these are not represented in the model, how can the relative causal effects of variables that are in the model be accurately estimated?

Gollob and Reichardt argue that if the autoregressive effect of the dependent variable at an earlier time is excluded, then the model is incorrect and the computed causal effects are biased, a point that no doubt is often true. But this is another form of the omitted variable problem (e.g., Rao, 1971) that applies whenever any true cause is left out of a model. In any realistic model of behavior, it is virtually impossible to guarantee that all relevant variables are included, a condition that by no means is limited to longitudinal models applied to cross-sectional data. In fact, the problem can be stated as a general axiom, which most experienced researchers would not dispute.

A "correctly specified model" is, always has been, and always will be a fiction. A more realistic view of models is that they are simplifications of extremely complicated behavior. It is a mistake to assume that any model actually represents the underlying process absolutely correctly, even after certain obvious faults have been corrected. All that can be hoped is that a model captures some reasonable approximation to the truth, serving perhaps as a descriptive device or summarizing tool.

An approach that is more useful than trying to find the "true" model is to emphasize instead the performance of a model with new data. After all, if one model is supposedly more accurate than another, then it should be able to prove itself by accounting for new data more effectively than other contenders. The pertinent question is, Which of several models yields the best predictions of future data obtained from the same process that generated the original sample? This most often involves predicting responses for new subjects measured on the same variables at comparable time periods. Another possibility, which is important in change studies, is to consider observations and subjects as fixed, and predict to a new set of time points. Bock and Thissen (1980) have presented an impressive example of this kind of predictive validity using a model for heights from the Berkeley growth data (Tuddenham & Snyder, 1954). When fitting individual curves, they used the estimated total sample model and a height measurement from a single time point to predict, with great accuracy, the data at 17 other time periods. Another possibility of this kind would be to set aside every kth measurement, and then predict these omitted points from the fitted functions developed on all the others. In classic longitudinal studies, which often have only three or four time periods, it may not be feasible to evaluate the predictive validity of models to new occasions in this fashion, but it can be easily carried out in growth studies or in learning experiments.

The point of all of this, with respect to Gollob and Reichardt's presentation is: Suppose the model is wrong, not just in cosmetic, subtle features, but really badly misspecified. Suppose the available sample is haphazard. Suppose the variables have poor measurement properties, with distributions that do not resemble any known theoretical or empirical process. Suppose the available data are from a cross-sectional design instead of a longitudinal one. In short, suppose that compared with the true behavior or process, the models are a miserable scientific embarrassment. Even in this case, one can evaluate the relative performance of the models in an unambiguous, rigorous way by studying their predictive validity. Consider the importance of this issue from another direction. Think of trying to convince a doubting colleague that Figure 15.5A, which predicts new data well, is somehow less preferable than Figure 15.5B, which is supposed to be closer to the truth but performs more poorly with the same data.

A second aspect of Gollob and Reichardt's presentation is controversial. They note that the design of a study, and in particular the variables that are available, impose limitations on the kind of models that may be estimated, arguing specifically that a true longitudinal model cannot be fit to data that are simply cross-sectional. Their suggestion is to augment the sample statistics that are actually available with additional plausible values, perhaps obtained from another study, perhaps just made up. In other words, just add new numbers that represent a best guess at what the unavailable means, variances, or correlations might be. The authors sound a bit sheepish about this, but argue that making up data to estimate a reasonable model may be better than sticking with a model that is idiotic a priori.

Although this recommendation is unorthodox, it might possibly be justifiable in some cases. The suggestion to systematically modify aspects of the data is in the same spirit as the study of parameter sensitivity (e.g., Green, 1977), in which one slightly modifies parameter estimates to explore the response surface of a regression function. The suggestion is also related to trimming, Winsorizing, and weighting, which has been employed so successfully in robust statistics (Mosteller & Tukey, 1977). And after all, what are you going to believe: the data you actually collect, or the information you need to fit your favorite model?

Three important stipulations come to mind in contemplating this approach, however. First, small changes in a few elements of a sample covariance matrix can make a nice positive definite matrix singular. The minimum criterion for data tinkering is to ensure that the matrix used in the analysis is plausible. Olkin (1981), for example, has reviewed conditions that describe the permissible ranges of elements of a covariance matrix to ensure that things stay nonsingular.

Second, a small change to a few elements of the covariance matrix can also produce a large change to the estimated variance of a parameter as well as to the actual parameter estimate. It would seem important then to monitor estimated standard errors. If the effects of a range of values of a sample covariance are being studied, one might compute two one-sided confidence intervals for the parameters that correspond to the upper and lower limits of the range of values being considered, using the largest of the estimated standard errors as well. Parameters of some models have wide confidence intervals in the best of circumstances, such as the intraclass correlation of genetic models, for one notorious example. Dutifully report these bailing wire confidence intervals. If informed readers can live with an interval estimate for a correlation that may well cover the permissible parameter space, then so can I.

Third, do not take seriously any model developed by tinkering until its performance can be evaluated with honest, complete data of the appropriate kind, even if a study must be specially conducted to get them. Models must apply to real people measured on real variables. They cannot be made-up models that describe a nonexistent, imaginary population. This condition of requiring that the model be evaluated with real data is simply a variation on the theme of assessing its predictive validity, only applied to the case in which the model has been developed in an unusual manner.

If these three conditions could be met, especially the last, then tinkering with data as a means of developing a model otherwise inaccessible to one's design may be justified. On the other hand, tinkering with data without meeting these stipulations runs the risk of misleading colleagues or, worse still, misleading oneself, and it is essential to discourage creative model development of this kind. The way we discourage such poor scientific practice at Minnesota is to bury offenders up to their neck in the ground and run over them with a snowblower. This underscores the seriousness of the error and the extent of our displeasure with it to others who might contemplate the same behavior.

CHAPTER 16

WHERE HAVE ALL THE SUBJECTS GONE? LONGITUDINAL STUDIES OF DISEASE AND COGNITIVE FUNCTION

MERRILL F. ELIAS AND MICHAEL A. ROBBINS

Editors' Introduction

One of the major purposes of the "Best Methods for the Analysis of Change" conference was to uncover problems of data analysis that substantive researchers find to be important but for which there do not seem to be methods that can yield good solutions. The idea was to bring these problems to the attention of methodological experts and the scientific public in the hope that such exposure would help lead to better methods. Toward this end, Elias and Robbins present an issue that has probably bothered most who have been doing research for any length of time: small subject sample sizes. McArdle and Hamagami present a methodology for addressing this issue in chapter 17. Within chapter 17 is a comment by Rubin on chapters 16 and 17.

Collection of our data was supported by Research Grant AGO355 from the National Institute on Aging of the National Institutes of Health and Clinical Research Grant RR 229 from the Division of Research Facilities and Resources, U.S. Public Health Service. We acknowledge the collaboration of Penelope K. Elias; Thomas Pierce (University of Maine); Norman R. Schultz, Jr. (Clemson University); and Gunnar A. Anderson, Nancy Blakeman, and David H. P. Streeten (State University of New York Health Science Center, Syracuse).

The problem presented by Elias and Robbins is that most statistical procedures are based on the assumption that sample sizes are usually fairly large. The estimates of most statistical procedures and the inferences they can support are reasonable only asymptotically as the sample size increases. When many parameters must be estimated for variables of only moderate reliability and for relation that are not robust under even the most favorable of conditions, large sample sizes often are demanded. On the other hand, intensive, time-consuming, expensive observation may also be demanded, and the absolute number of subjects that can be sampled may be small. So what is a researcher to do?

Such conditions present a continuing problem in many areas of research, but especially in longitudinal research. In longitudinal research, many factors produce shrinking sample sizes, and only some of these factors are under the control of the researcher. Attrition inevitably occurs by death and illness (over which the researcher has no control) and by fatigue, loss of interest, fear, movement from the area, aversion to treatment, and other such factors over which the researcher has some, but usually not nearly enough, control. In the types of studies conducted by Elias and Robbins, decreasing sample sizes are unavoidable because of attrition and the need to categorize subjects in terms of medical diagnosis. Ironically, decreasing sample sizes also occur as a function of learning more about the phenomena of interest, improving observations, and improving measurements. As the researcher observes more carefully, measures more accurately, and learns more about the phenomena of interest, it becomes possible to divide samples of subjects more finely and thus produce smaller subsamples. This raises the question: Which subsamples are "too small" for the kinds of analyses one must do in order to advance understanding?

Although there are no solutions for some problems in life, there are ways to deal with even the worst conditions. That may be the reality we have to face in dealing with the problems Elias and Robbins raise. Therefore, researchers should carefully study these problems. In this frame of mind, the reader will want to look particularly at the procedures McArdle and Hamagami present in chapter 17. The comment by Rubin also provides a useful perspective.

The formal distinction between primary and secondary aging (Busse, 1969) facilitated the emergence of a new and important subdiscipline within adult developmental psychology: the health psychology of aging. Primary aging was conceptualized as inherited biological processes that are time related; secondary aging was seen as traumatic events and diseases that covary with chronological age and primary aging. Although the distinction has been challenged as conceptually incorrect and artificial, and even dangerous from a treatment standpoint (Evans, 1988), it focused attention on two important research goals: (a) characterization of the behavioral manifestations of healthy versus unhealthy aging and (b) understanding of the effects of specific diseases on changes in behavior over time.

Progress toward the first goal has been an inevitable by-product of longitudinal studies because health is a major methodological factor in longitudinal studies of behavior. Indeed, it is through longitudinal studies that we learned that mentally and physically healthy persons live longer, perform better (Hertzog, Schaie, & Gribbin, 1978; Siegler, 1975), and stay in studies longer than those who are diseased. We also learned that we must deal not only with attrition, but also with differential rates of attrition for healthy and unhealthy subjects.

In situations in which disease is a nuisance variable it may be possible to deal with it as a broadly defined construct or latent variable defined by aggregates of diseases (e.g., cardiovascular disease). However, an understanding of how disease effects changes in behavior over time necessitates examination of specific classes of disease (cf. Elias, Elias, & Elias, 1989). Rapid advances in diagnostic technology have resulted in the recognition of subtypes of disease (within classes) that were heretofore unknown. The study of disease subtypes is important to the understanding of how disease affects behavior when subtyping is done in terms of causal mechanisms. Yet, subtyping results in very small samples and reduction of sample size is further aggravated by attrition from longitudinal studies.

Longitudinal methodologists and clinical investigators often have different conceptions of small sample sizes. In the remaining sections of this chapter, some examples of small sample sizes are given and methodological issues related to small and shrinking samples are addressed.

AGGREGATE MODELS

One class of longitudinal studies makes use of existing longitudinal data sets to examine the role of disease in cognitive aging. For example, using medical records and data from their long-standing longitudinal study of intellectual functioning, Hertzog et al. (1978) demonstrated that a group of patients with a variety of vascular diseases (a disease aggregate) showed more accelerated cognitive change over time and higher levels of attrition than did healthy subjects. Their study is widely cited and serves as a good model for understanding the effects of healthy states versus unhealthy states on aging. These investigators encountered a sharp and inevitable reduction in sample size in each cell when they classified the aggregate vascular disease group into the 32 recognized categories of vascular disease. For example, there were as few as 10 or 12 hypertensive subjects per classification, depending on the diagnostic cutoff dates employed. Different cutoff dates were used because patients do not accommodate the longitudinal investigator by remaining in one diagnostic category over time; for example, they may move from hypertension without complications to hypertension with complications during the course of the longitudinal study. Thus there is attrition from specific diagnostic groups as well as attrition from the study. Obviously, one runs up against severe power and parameter restrictions with longitudinal samples this small. The problem does not lie with the investigator or the investigation, but rather with the absence of practical and easily applied methodologies for small-sample longitudinal studies.

CLASSES AND SUBTYPES OF DISEASE

One may maximize sample sizes by concentrating recruitment efforts with respect to a specific disease category. In a study sponsored by the National Institute on Aging, we have been doing just that for the past 16 years (e.g., Elias, Robbins, & Schultz, 1987; Elias, Schultz, Robbins, & Elias, 1989; Schultz, Elias, Robbins, Streeten, & Blakeman, 1989).

Modeled after Schaie (1965), our longitudinal design (Figure 16.1) allows comparisons of longitudinal cohorts (rows), effects of time lag (diagonal arrows) and interactions of blood pressure diagnosis with time of measurement (horizontal arrows). Age range is 18–87 years. The time between measurement periods (Time 1 vs. Time 2, etc.) is 5–6 years.

Figure 16.2 shows the number of subjects available in 1989 from rows 1–3. It is clear that attrition is significant from baseline (Time 1) to the second time of measurement (Time 2) and is greater for hypertensive subjects. However, the study is not over. Sample size will be enhanced by averaging the rows for the completed design and by testing much larger numbers of subjects at Time 1 (rows 3 and 4). Assuming the study can be funded until 1995, we project 147 hypertensive (mean arterial pressure greater than 105 mmHg) referrals for whom we have three measurement points (5–6 years apart) and 387 hypertensive referrals for whom

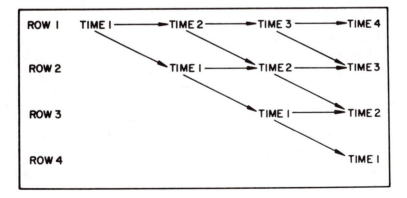

Figure 16.1   The longitudinal design. It allows comparisons of longitudinal cohorts (rows), effects of time lag (diagonal arrows), and time of measurement (horizontal arrows).

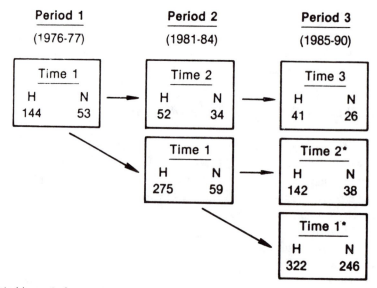

Period 1	Period 2	Period 3
(1976-77)	(1981-84)	(1985-90)

*Projected by end of current grant

Figure 16.2   Numbers of subjects tested and projected to be tested by the end of the current grant period.

we have two measurement points. Approximately 1,066 hypertensive subjects will be available for episodic analyses (Time 1 only) and for follow-up longitudinal studies, should they be pursued. Thus the longitudinal sample sizes are not unreasonably small. Yet hypertensive groups are aggregates of classes and subtypes of disease within classes.

The term *essential hypertension* is used very loosely. It is a broad class of hypertensive diseases distinct from very obvious forms of *secondary hypertension* (e.g., hypertension resulting from renal vascular lesions). All clinically elevated blood pressures are the end result of causal factors, some known and many unknown. Thus some forms of essential hypertension can be classified in terms of likely causal mechanism (or concomitant physiological phenomena). Sample sizes in each cell shrink, however, when one classifies them by physiological mechanisms (e.g., high, low, or normal renin hypertension; angiotensinogenic hypertension; and orthostatic hypertension), by pathophysiological correlates (e.g., isolated systolic hypertension), or by resultant effects (e.g., retinopathy).

Many categories are not mutually exclusive. Sample size is further reduced by hierarchical categorization. This is illustrated in Figure 16.3, which summarizes sample sizes at Time 1 (rows 1–3). The three major blood pressure classifications—normal, hypertensive, and high—are based on the criteria used by Wilkie and Eisdorfer (1971). Attrition will result in further reduction of sample sizes for

TOTAL HYPERTENSION CLINIC REFERRALS

(N = 741)

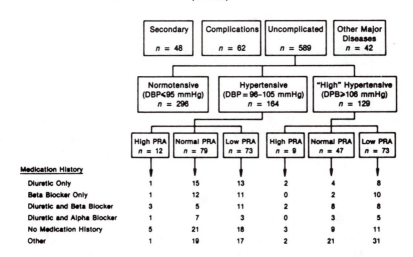

Figure 16.3 An illustration of the sharp reduction in sample size resulting from hierarchical arrangement of subjects into diagnostic categories and drug history groups.

longitudinal analyses. Moreover, diagnostic classifications can change from one longitudinal wave to another as the disease progresses. Thus there is attrition from specific diagnostic categories.

As neuropsychologists, we are interested in comparing the multiple domains of intellectual functioning affected by vascular disease and its complications. Thus in addition to the Wechsler Adult Intelligence Scale (WAIS) (Wechsler, 1955), our protocol includes an extensive neuropsychological test battery (Elias, Robbins, Schultz, Streeten, & Elias, 1987) and multiple measures of mood state. This places a limitation on the number of subjects who can be recruited at baseline (Time 1) and contributes to longitudinal attrition because more of each subject's time must be committed to repeated testing.

Faced with small samples and intimidated by traditional power considerations (Overall, 1987), there is often no alternative but to confine longitudinal analyses to aggregates of subgroups and relegate comparisons among subgroups to cross-sectional or episodic analyses. In other words, the design must be compromised for the sake of available longitudinal methods.

Let us assume (for purposes of exposition) that we have no methodological alternatives to designs employing disease aggregates. From a "models for aging" perspective there is something to be gained from studying aggregates of people with high blood pressure longitudinally; that is, hypertension provides a model for a subtle, cumulative pathophysiological process associated with chronic (but not catastrophic) disease. But does the aggregate model allow us to solve the problem of small samples? To answer this question we must turn to substantive data.

LONGITUDINAL STUDIES OF HYPERTENSION

Figure 16.4 summarizes data reported by Wilkie and Eisdorfer (1971) for three groups: normotensive subjects, borderline hypertensive subjects, and hypertensive subjects. In order to make Figure 16.4 similar to Figure 16.5, we redefined the groups as normotensive (N), moderate hypertensive (MH), and more severe hypertensive (HH). A group of subjects between the ages of 60 and 69 years was given the WAIS and then tested again 10 years later. The same procedure was followed for a group between the ages of 70 and 79 years of age at initial testing, but these data are not shown in Figure 16.4. WAIS score changes (in scaled score units) are shown on the ordinate. Change is shown as downward and upward trends from a zero point representing mean level of performance at initial testing (baseline). For the younger subjects, the N group showed no change ($n = 31$, $p > .05$), the MH group ($n = 10$) improved, and the HH group ($n = 10$) showed decline. The interpretation of decline for the HH group was straightforward: Pathophysiological processes associated with hypertension result in accelerated age-associated changes in performance. Improvement for the MH group was explained in terms of enhanced cerebral blood flow in subjects for whom cerebral

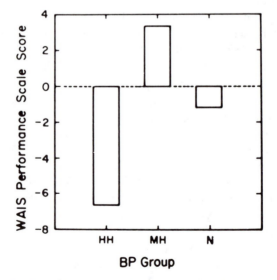

Figure 16.4   Wilkie and Eisdorfer (1971) longitudinal study of hypertension with 60- to 69-year-old subjects at baseline (Time 1).

blood flow may be compromised by atherosclerotic processes. Age at initial testing is clearly an important variable. When MH (borderline hypertensive) subjects were between 70 and 79 years old at baseline, decline rather than improvement was observed. Moreover, none of the HH (severe hypertensive) subjects survived to return to be tested (an extreme but not unexpected consequence of attrition in studies of disease).

Figure 16.5 shows Time 1 and Time 2 data from our study using the same kind of plot employed by Wilkie and Eisdorfer (1971); that is, change scores relative to WAIS scores (unweighted). Sample sizes were as follows: normotensive ($n = 38$); moderately hypertensive ($n = 34$); and hypertensive ($n = 28$). In Figure 16.5 we see significant ($p < .05$) but trivial change for N subjects, and no change for MH subjects (the equivalent of Wilkie and Eisdorfer's borderline group; diastolic blood pressure 95–105 mmHg). However, the HH group (diastolic blood pressure greater than 105 mmHg) shows significant ($p < .01$) though modest negative change.

Our HH group did not change as much as the equivalent group in the Wilkie and Eisdorfer (1971) study, but there are two important reasons. Our subjects were 44 years of age ($SD = 12.1$) at baseline, and they were measured every 5 years rather than every 10 years. The idea was to ultimately achieve more waves of testing, thus enhancing reliability of change measurement, and to test over a

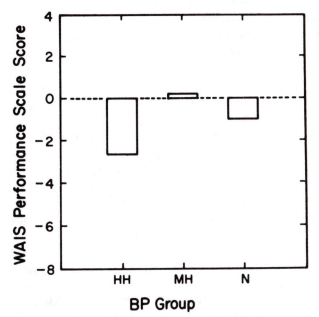

Figure 16.5   A summary of the authors' data presented in the same kind of plot as that used by Wilkie and Eisdorfer (Figure 16.4).

period we felt likely to yield change in hypertensive subjects but not normotensive subjects.

One may separate from the HH sample patients who remained free of complications ($n = 19$) and those who developed cardiovascular complications and other end organ changes produced by high blood pressure ($n = 19$). As expected, the group with complications performed more poorly than the group without complications. A further breakdown of hypertensive subjects with complications into subcategories of complication (e.g., cardiovascular and renal-vascular) resulted in some samples having only one subject. Even when we resort to analyses with the major aggregate groups (Figures 16.4 and 16.5), the problem of interpretation remains. For example, the question can be raised as to the extent that selective attrition of poorer performing hypertensives may have contributed to the improvement in performance for the 60- to 69-year-old MH subjects. Similarly, selective dropout by hypertensive subjects may have resulted in an underestimate of negative change for the more severely hypertensive patients of both studies. Furthermore, grouping subjects of different ages at a single baseline point is artificial and results in a loss of subjects who do not fit into reasonably homogeneous age categories; neither presentation of data (i.e., Figure 16.4 or 16.5) allows one to visualize data for the dropouts in relation to the persisters. Both presentations use mean change scores that, as is repeatedly stated throughout this book, may not accurately reflect individual patterns of change. Where more than two waves of data are presented, this problem becomes more acute.

Figures 16.6 and 16.7 (from a study by McArdle, Hamagami, Elias, & Robbins, in press) illustrate data from our longitudinal study. In order to maximize sample size, analyses were restricted to first- and second-occasion data, and borderline and hypertensive patients were combined into a single hypertensive group and compared with normotensive subjects. Slopes are shown for each subject for whom two data points were available. This is done by subtracting the score at Time 1 from the score at Time 2 and dividing by the difference in age between Time 1 and Time 2. In this analysis we were interested in Fluid factor scores. Rather than using scaled scores, as in Figure 16.5, we expressed raw scores as a percentage (100 is a perfect score). The + values represent subjects who dropped out and thus provided only first occasion data. Individual differences in growth curves are immediately apparent, as is the differential rate of attrition between hypertensive subjects and normotensive subjects. Unlike the normotensive group, dropouts in the hypertension group were the poorer performing subjects.

Of course a variety of growth curve analyses may be applied to level and slope as dependent variables (e.g., Rogosa, Brandt, & Zimowski, 1982). Here we were particularly interested in evaluating the effects of attrition on our data and in adjusting our change curves accordingly. Dr. J. J. McArdle and Mr. F. Hamagami (personal communication) were consulted with respect to this problem. Not only did they remind us about the importance of plotting data for each subject

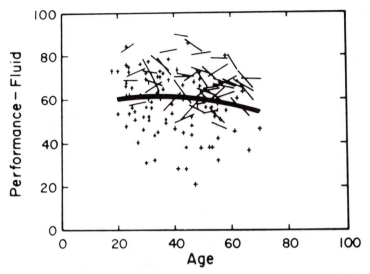

Figure 16.6 Longitudinal (lines) and cross-sectional (+) plots on an individual basis for hypertensives. From "Structural Modeling of Mixed Longitudinal and Cross-Sectional Data" by J. J. McArdle, F. Hamagami, M. F. Elias, and M. A. Robbins, in press, *Experimental Aging Research*. Copyright 1990 by Beech Hill Publishing Company. Reprinted by permission.

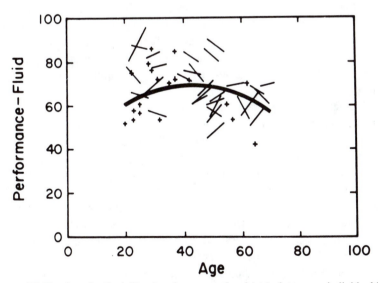

Figure 16.7 Longitudinal (lines) and cross-sectional (+) plots on an individual basis for normotensives. From "Structural Modeling of Mixed Longitudinal and Cross-Sectional Data" by J. J. McArdle, F. Hamagami, M. F. Elias, and M. A. Robbins, in press, *Experimental Aging Research*. Copyright 1990 by Beech Hill Publishing Company. Reprinted by permission..

(Figures 16.6 and 16.7), but they provided a solution (among possible solutions) to our problem that consisted of a multivariate structural equation model approach to mixed longitudinal and cross-sectional designs.

The McArdle et al. (in press) approach represents one of a number of possible solutions to attrition and a partial solution to sample size problems because it allows one to use all the data (i.e., cross-sectional data are not lost to the analysis). On the other hand, any structural equation modeling technique (even with restricted parameters) suffers from reduction in sample size. This is particularly true for multivariate applications. Thus we have not solved the problem of shrinking sample sizes.

Problems and solutions related to the use of small sample designs are, of course, closely related to those involving single subject designs. A small sample design is a single subject design with replications. Single subject designs have a relatively long history in psychology (Hayes, 1981), and the merits of the time series designs are worthy of consideration (Campbell & Stanley, 1963). Nesselroade and Jones (in press) turn adversity to advantage by helping us see the positive aspects of single subject designs. These authors remind us that investigators are always faced with difficult trade-offs involving numbers of subjects, numbers of dependent variables, and numbers of occasions of measurement. They note, "Studying the single subject with many measures on many occasions before trying to generalize across subjects is one way to deal with the various classification modes along which selection occurs" (Nesselroade & Jones, in press). How very applicable this argument is to our research. The short neuropsychological battery or single outcome measure allows for larger samples and thus facilitates generalizability to other persons, but decreases generalizability to the universe of relevant behaviors; that is, one can devise a very brief "neuropsychological battery" and learn a lot about little.

The advantage of single subject designs is eloquently stated by Nesselroade and Jones (in press): "One can exploit the rich information from the single case— patterns of intraindividual change and stability across multiple variables—and develop an understanding of how and how not to aggregate information across individuals if the aggregations are to represent something meaningful." Borrowing from Lamiell (1981) and Zevon and Tellegen (1982), Nessselroade and Jones argue convincingly that combining single subject designs with group designs "can put idiographic work in the service of developing a nomothetic science." The most refreshing aspect of the arguments made by Nesselroade and Jones is that we are directed to practical examples from actual research.

A neuropsychological approach to health psychology places heavy demands on the sampling of the universe of behavior associated with the diversity of brain function. The "twenty-minute battery" applied to subjects in broadly defined disease classes (e.g., cardiovascular disease or hypertension) results in statistical data of very little importance. An understanding of causal mechanisms precludes aggregates of diseases for the sake of enhanced sample size. Shrinking sample size is a well-recognized problem in longitudinal studies but, as we have emphasized in this chapter, it is further aggravated by methodological problems specific to the study of disease over substantial periods of time. For these reasons, we feel that idiographic methods must play an important role in the maturity of the health psychology of aging. Too often reductions in sample size are considered a design flaw rather than a trade-off. Given that they are inevitable, it seems inevitable that idiographic methods will receive increasing emphasis in the future.

CONCLUSIONS

In this chapter we have employed actual data to emphasize the inevitable reduction in sample size in each cell of the study that results when one studies longitudinally specific, well-defined diseases using a battery of tests that reflect the general and diverse nature of changes in brain function. We have illustrated two related problems: attrition and the individual patterns of change that defy description with conventional indices of central tendency. We made note of some relevant analyses and potential solutions.

CHAPTER 17

MODELING INCOMPLETE LONGITUDINAL AND CROSS-SECTIONAL DATA USING LATENT GROWTH STRUCTURAL MODELS

J.J. McARDLE AND FUMIAKI HAMAGAMI

Editors' Introduction

Old questions are often the best questions. McArdle and Hamagami address a question that has been at the core of discussion of research on adult development virtually from the very beginning: What inferences about change can correctly be drawn from cross-sectional study designs compared with longitudinal study designs? With the launching of pioneering empirical studies of human development in the 1940s and 1950s this question was analyzed in considerable detail—in writings that still stand among the most insightful in dealing with basic issues (Bell, 1953, 1954; Birren, 1959; Cattell, 1950; Jones, 1958). These writings made it clear that possibilities for incorrrect interpretations abound in both cross-sectional and longitudinal designs (as summarized by Horn & Donaldson, 1980), but that each, to some extent, corrects the other: Truth, it became clear, is most likely to be found in the confluence of results from well-designed and interrelated studies of both kinds. Out of this awareness the early writers developed the

We are indebted to John L. Horn for the free use of his ideas in this chapter. We also thank Mark Aber, Ed Anderson, Linda Collins, Pete Elias, John Nesselroade, Mike Robbins, Don Rubin, Ron Spiro, Carol Prescott, and John Willett for their thoughtful comments. This research has been supported by Grant AG07137 from the National Institute on Aging.

basic ideas of convergence analysis: the simultaneous use of cross-sectional and longitudinal data to provide a basis for drawing inferences about ontogenetic change, differences representing historical influences associated with time of birth, and effects produced by repeated measurements. In the particularly influential work of Schaie (1965, 1974), analyses of variance of different ways of arranging data were used to organize these ideas in a system of "age," "cohort," and "time" (ACT) effects. There followed a spate of articles pointing to illogical and incorrect interpretations spawned by the ACT analyses Schaie had proposed (Adam, 1978; Baltes, 1968; Botwinick & Arenberg, 1976; Cambell & Stanley, 1963; Donaldson & Horn, in press; Horn & Donaldson, 1976, 1977, 1980; Horn & McArdle, 1980; Mason, Winsborough, Mason, & Poole, 1973; Schaie & Hertzog, 1983). It became evident that in order to draw sound inferences, theory was needed to specify models that could be tested for adequacy in a crucible of comparisons with the realities of data.

Building on this foundation of prior work, McArdle and Hamagami first point to a grim truth: In practice it is almost impossible to design longitudinal research that closely approximates the conditions needed for strong inferences about ontogenetic change. They then show that grim though this truth may be, all is not lost: With reasonable substantive theory, a mixture of cross-sectional and longitudinal data and methods they have developed within multiple-group structural equation modeling, the different strengths and the lack of correspondence in weaknesses of cross-sectional and longitudinal gatherings of data can provide a sound basis for inference about change. Their results, although early and much in need of further study, suggest that these methods are robust under many conditions common in practice (see chapter 15, this volume).

Change is an important feature of everyday life. Our lives are often marked by events dealing with changes, especially death and birth, separation and reunion, firing and hiring, and failure and success. More often than not, the information we need to deal with these life changes is limited, and sometimes it is completely missing. It is a simple fact of life—we must understand and deal with changes on the basis of limited information.

It is not surprising that scientific studies of change also must deal with limited information. In most research in psychology, we almost always lose some important subjects, and we almost always think of better measurement techniques or better variables after an experiment is completed. The mathematical and statistical models we use to analyze our data should allow us to deal with these facts.

The purpose of this chapter is to explore uses of new methods for analysis of growth and change with limited observed data. The methods we examine come from the recent literature on structural equation modeling of growth curves. We show how most of these new methods are based on the earlier theories for linking cross-sectional and longitudinal data.

LONGITUDINAL DATA WITH LIMITED INFORMATION

The four plots of Figure 17.1 provide the context for our studies. These plots display different simulation samplings of data from a cohort sequential longitudinal study of age changes in intelligence (after Schaie, 1965). Plot A in Figure 17.1 contains scores for 100 individuals all measured twice over a 10-year period (1970 and 1980). Each single line represents 10 years and two scores for each person. Some individuals were measured at ages 20 and 30 while others were measured at ages 30–40, 40–50, and 50–60 years. Subjects were selected in a manner to ensure that the average time between measurements was approximately equal to the differences between the averages for different age groupings; for example, the age of the first group at the second measurement is approximately the age of second group at the first measurement (e.g., Botwinick & Siegler, 1980; Horn & McArdle, 1980; McArdle & Anderson, 1990).

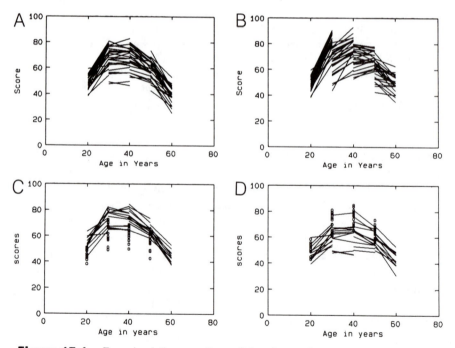

Figure 17.1   Four simulation samplings of data from cohort sequential longitudinal study. (Figure 17.1A represents random selection. Figure 17.1B represents random selection with retest effect. Figure 17.1C represents nonrandom selection based on level. Figure 17.1D represents nonrandom selection based on slope.)

In real psychological data the situation is often more complex than that indicated in plot A in Figure 17.1A. One complexity is illustrated in plot B. In this plot, data are displayed in the same way as in plot A, but a retest improvement (learning) effect has been built into the data. Here, for example, the Time 2 points of the Age 20 cohort do not match up well with the Time 1 points of the Age 30 cohorts because the Time 2 subjects have had the benefit of a first testing before the second testing, whereas the Time 1 subjects have not had this benefit. Retest is only one of many reasons why the longitudinal and cross-sectional gradients can be different (e.g., Baltes, Reese, & Nesselroade, 1988).

Plot C in Figure 17.1C adds another level of complexity. The small circles designate the available scores of people who dropped out of the study after the first testing; there is only one score for each person. Notice, too, those who dropped out had lower scores than their age cohorts at the first time of measurement. A correlation between low initial scores and dropout has been found in many psychological studies (e.g., Botwinick & Siegler, 1980). Dropout is also depicted in plot D, but in this case the people with the largest changes are the dropouts. The dropout mechanism appears to be more random throughout the plot, but, as indicated, dropout is not random. Later in this chapter we show that this dropout may have serious consequences.

One ideal in developmental research is to measure everyone over many appropriate intervals of time or during the entire period of development. Because this is impossible, the researcher must make the best of incomplete information such as that described in Figure 17.1. Even though information is lacking, the aim is to draw valid conclusions about development, changes over age, differences between birth cohorts, and combinations of these factors.

MODELS FOR CHANGE WITH LIMITED INFORMATION

Developmental researchers have been aware of the problems of dealing with limited data. Often they have stated the problems in the context of trying to figure out the kinds of inferences that can be accurately drawn from longitudinal data as compared with cross-sectional data (see Baltes et al., 1988; Campbell & Stanley, 1963; Cattell, 1950; Cook & Campbell, 1979; Harris, 1963; Wohlwill, 1973). Most important in the early formulations, although often neglected, is the work of Bell (1953, 1954) and Cattell (1950). Each put forth the basic idea of using both longitudinal data and cross-sectional data to recover, in the context of changing circumstances, information about developmental change. Bell (1954) stated one basic theme as follows:

> The method called "convergence" has been advocated as a means of meeting some research needs not satisfied by either a cross-sectional or longitudinal approach. This method consists of making limited remeasurements of

cross-sectional groups so that temporally overlapping measurements of older and younger subjects are provided. The remeasurements may be used as a way of determining whether trends which would otherwise be seen only between different age groups are corroborated within short time periods for each age group. The method may also provide a means of actually linking up individuals or sub-groups between adjacent segments of a developmental curve, each segment consisting of a limited longitudinal study on a different age group. (p. 281)

In order to link up the information from different curve segments Bell (1954) used a distance index to match different individuals between different curve segments. Although this was described by Bell as an ad hoc statistical technique, he showed how it recovered the full longitudinal curve information from different segments. Bell cautiously noted that the convergence method "will introduce considerable error into data collected, and that in some instances it might produce quite misleading results" (1954, p. 283). Nevertheless, Bell demonstrated the efficiency of the convergence approach by showing that a 10-year longitudinal curve could be approximated with only 3 years of data collection. Cattell (1950) also described how developmental curves might be estimated by remeasuring in cross-sectional samples.

Several researchers have described or used strategies similar to Bell's for the analysis of incomplete longitudinal data (Bryk & Raudenbush, 1987; Goldstein, 1987; Prahl-Andersen, Kowalski, & Heydendael, 1979). Prominent among these strategies are those encompassed by the techniques of linear structural equation modeling (e.g., LISREL; Jöreskog & Sörbom, 1988). Structural modeling has become well known and widely used in aging research (see Aldwin, Spiro, & Bosse, 1989; Loehlin, 1987; McArdle & Anderson, 1990). In many cases such analyses have been geared toward the causal analysis of time series (as in Horn & McArdle, 1980). This autoregressive approach has come under some criticism by Rogosa and colleagues (see Rogosa, Brandt, & Zimowski, 1982), who advocate older forms of growth curve analysis. Most recently, Meredith and colleagues (see McArdle, 1986; McArdle & Epstein, 1987; Meredith & Tisak, 1990) have demonstrated how a wide variety of growth curve concepts can be modeled using standard structural equation techniques. A structural equation modeling approach to incomplete growth curve analyses is relatively recent (e.g., Horn & McArdle, 1980; Jöreskog & Sörbom, 1988; McArdle & Anderson, 1990; McArdle, Anderson, & Aber, 1987; Meredith & Tisak, 1990).

An important concern in longitudinal data collection is the problem of subject self-selection, or nonrandom dropout (Baltes, Schaie, & Nardi, 1971; Botwinick & Siegler, 1980). Statistical models based on random and nonrandom data selection have been presented by Rubin and colleagues (Little & Rubin, 1987; Rubin, 1974, 1976, 1977). Allison (1987) showed how these techniques could be used within the context of LISREL models. Most recently, McArdle, Hamagami, Elias,

and Robbins (in press) applied these contemporary techniques to mixed longitudinal and cross-sectional growth data. Formulation of models of nonrandom subject
selection is now an active area of statistical research.

CURRENT PLAN

Our research builds on these recent developments. Our purpose in describing the
results of this research is primarily pedagogical. We aim to show how some new
technical results can be used. We shall first demonstrate how convergence models
can be used with incomplete longitudinal data. The special analyses required in
using convergence theory with actual data and models will be highlighted and the
conditions under which the models may fail as well as those under which they
can be seen to succeed are explored.

   In accordance with these objectives, we shall first lay out a very simplified
version of the basic problem with concrete examples of "what could be," using
statistical simulation. Our selection of examples is based on constructive repli-
cation of Bell's (1954) experimental study in previous work on aging (Horn &
McArdle, 1980; McArdle & Horn, 1990). We simulate one of these examples
and show how sampling from this simulated reality might occur in actual exper-
imentation. Different variations of our methods are applied to show the extent to
which this reality can and cannot be represented and recovered.

METHODS

Complete Longitudinal Growth Curves

To put the issues in concrete form before examining how fluid and complex they
can become (and do become in developmental research) we will work though a
substantive example. Suppose we measure change in visual cognitive capability
(Gv) over a period of adulthood extending from age 20 to age 60, as Horn and
his colleagues did (Horn & Cattell, 1967, 1985). The evidence of this research
indicated that in many people (whether sampled longitudinally or cross-sectionally)
Gv improves from age 20 to age 30, plateaus over the next 10 years, and then
declines. This situation is depicted in plot A in Figure 17.2, where to keep
conditions simple (but concordant with Horn's findings) we have assumed that
variable Y, representing individual differences in Gv, has been scaled to have a
mean over all measures and occasions of 50 and a standard deviation of 10.

   Plot A in Figure 17.2 shows data that might be obtained from a long-term
longitudinal study: 100 people have all been observed five times over a 40 year
period. In substantive research on growth and change this kind of data is rare. It
is nearly impossible to measure everyone over such a long period of time because

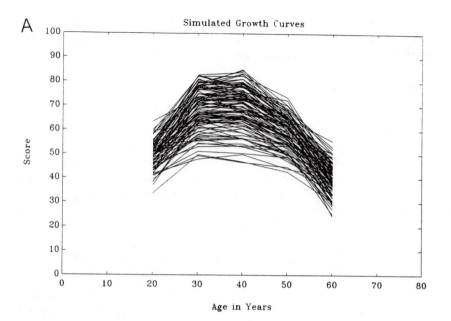

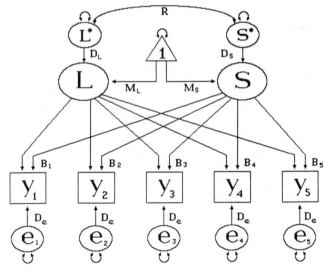

Figure 17.2   Latent growth model for longitudinal data. (Figure 17.2A represents simulated growth curves. Figure 17.2B represents longitudinal growth model.)

people move, people ask to drop out of the study, and people die. So, as much as we might hope to gather a complete data set similar to that depicted in plot A, we do not.

In reality, plot A is a plot of 100 growth curves randomly generated from a specific mathematical model that is described in the next section. The raw simulated data are formed into a matrix **Y** that has 100 rows and 5 columns—500 separate elements. The means and standard deviations of the five columns (simulated observed variables) of this matrix are listed in section A of Table 17.1; the variable intercorrelations are listed in section B. In order to fit these summary statistics with model expectations, we formed the moment matrix (of average cross-products) listed in section C. This symmetric matrix includes the average means in the first column as well as the average covariances in the remaining rows and columns. The unity constant in the first row and column of the matrix allows us to isolate the mean vector in further analysis.

Table 17.1

STATISTICS FOR LONGITUDINAL DATA OF 100 INDIVIDUALS MEASURED AT FIVE OCCASIONS OVER 40 YEARS

	Constant	Age 20	Age 30	Age 40	Age 50	Age 60
		A. Means and standard deviations				
M		49.57	68.94	68.93	59.37	39.99
SD		5.51	8.57	9.01	6.68	6.12
		B. Correlation matrices				
Age 20		1.000				
Age 30		.591	1.000			
Age 40		.612	.943	1.000		
Age 50		.750	.899	.893	1.000	
Age 60		.788	.253	.286	.486	1.000
		C. Scaled moment matrix				
Constant	1.000					
Age 20	.496	.249				
Age 30	.689	.345	.483			
Age 40	.689	.345	.482	.483		
Age 50	.594	.297	.414	.415	.357	
Age 60	.400	.201	.277	.277	.239	.164

D. Current Growth Model Simulation Values

$T = 5, N = 100,$
$ML = 50, DL = 5, V(L^*) = N(0, 1)$
$MS = 10, DS = 3, V(S^*) = N(0, 1)$
$ME = 0, DE = 2, V(E^*) = N(0, 1)$
$BLS = 0$
$B(20) = 0, B(30) = 2, B(40) = 2, B(50) = 1,$ and $B(60) = -1$

A Latent Growth Curve Model

The following are important details of the mathematical and statistical models postulated for this data. The path diagram of plot B in Figure 17.2 depicts a latent growth model for longitudinal data. The mathematical and statistical equations for this model are listed in Table 17.2. The data for the model are as follows: N = 100 individuals (n = 1, . . ., 100) measured on five occasions (t = 1, . . ., T) yielding the observed variables $Y(t, n)$: Each observed variable is represented as a square and each latent variable as a circle in plot B. The observed scores are specified to be a weighted sum of the following three individual latent (unobserved) variables:

1. $L(n)$—a level variable representing individual differences in level of performance. This can be formulated as an initial level or an average level. In either case, the L score is constant for each individual across the entire time series.
2. $S(n)$—a slope variable representing individual differences in the rate of change in performance over time. The positive or negative sign of this score gives the direction of change over time. Like the $L(n)$ score, this score remains the same for any individual across the time series. However, the contribution of this slope to the observed score $Y(t, n)$ changes because it is multiplied by the basis coefficient $B(t)$, as can be seen in the equation in section A of Table 17.2.
3. $E(n)$—an error or residual score represents an unobserved random score. This score has a mean of zero and zero correlations with all other variables over time. These scores may be interpreted as errors of measurement. Such errors are expected to change randomly over time for any individual.

The basis term, $B(t)$, in the equation in section A of Table 17.2 represents a concept that is new for many. This model is similar to the concept of an $f(t)$, representing a mathematical function. A function in mathematics is an equation of the form $Y(t\ n) = f(t)$, relating a variable Y to a variable t. For example, an $f(t)$ for $Y(t, a)$ might be a best fit for a straight-line function (equation) specifying that as age increases over time, visual capability increases linearly. This can be symbolized as follows:

$$Y(t, n) = f(t) \text{ or}$$

$$Y(t, n) = L(n) + S(n)A(t, n) + E(t, n).$$

Here $A(t, n)$ is an individual's age at time t, and $S(n)$ is an individual's slope of best fit (e.g., by least squares) for the straight-line relation. But for the data in plot A of Figure 17.2, one would be likely to think that such a straight-line

Table 17.2

MATHEMATICAL AND STATISTICAL FEATURES OF A LATENT GROWTH
CURVE MODEL (SEE FIGURE 17.2)

A. Mathematical population model

$$Y(t, n) = L(n) + B(t) S(n) + E(t, n),$$

where

$Y(t, n)$ = observed score at time t,
$L(n)$ = unobserved level score,
$S(n)$ = unobserved slope score,
$E(t, n)$ = unobserved error score,
$B(t)$ = basis coefficient for time t.

B. Statistical population model

$$L(n) = ML\ 1(n) + DS\ L^*(n),$$
$$S(n) = MS\ 1(n) + BLS\ L^*(n) + DS\ S^*(n),$$
$$E(t, n) = ME\ 1(n) + DE\ E^*(t, n),$$

where

X^* = any standardized random variable (unit variance, zero mean),
Mx = mean for component X,
Dx = residual deviation for component X,
Bxy = regression coefficient for Y on X, and
$1(n)$ = unit constant.

C. Expected values for growth model parameters

$$\mathcal{E}\{ My(t) \} = Ml + B(t) Ms + Bls\ Ml + Me,$$
$$\mathcal{E}\{ Vy(t) \} = Vl + B(t) Vs\ B(t)' + 2 B(t) Vl\ Bls' + Ve,$$
$$\mathcal{E}\{ Cy(t, t+i) \} = Vl + B(t) Vs\ B(t+i)' + B(t) Vl\ Bls' + B(t+i) Vl\ Bls',$$

where

$Vx = Dx\ Dx'$ = the variance of component X, and
$Cxy = Dx\ Rxy\ Dy'$ = the covariance of X and Y.

D. Statistical estimation based on maximum likelihood

$$LRT = -2N \ln LR = N\ [\ LR(d) + LR(t) + LR(m)\ ],\ \text{with}$$
$$LR(d) = \ln|\mathcal{E}\{Cy\}| - \ln|O\{Cy\}|,$$
$$LR(t) = tr\ [\ O\{Cy\}\ inv(E\{Cy\}\ )]\ - T,$$
$$LR(m) = [O\{My\} - \mathcal{E}\{My\}\ ]'\ inv(\ \mathcal{E}\{Cy\}\ )\ [O\{My\} - \mathcal{E}\{My\}\ ],$$

where

$O\{My\}$ = the observed means obtained from data,
$\mathcal{E}\{My\}$ = the expected means given by the model,
$O\{Cy\}$ = the observed covariances obtained from data,
$\mathcal{E}[Cy]$ = the expected covariances given by the model,
LRT = Likelihood ratio test statistics,
$LR(d)$ = the determinantal component of the LRT,
$LR(t)$ = the trace component of the LRT, and
$LR(m)$ = the mean component of the LRT.

function would not provide a good fit; for this reason, one might fit a quadratic function—that is, a function in which, in addition to the above, $A(t, n)$ is squared and multiplied by another "slope" value of say, $Q(t)$. Other such complex functions could be considered (and indeed are considered in chapters 4, 8, and 10).

The $B(t)$ of the equation in section A of Table 17.2 is similar to a function in this sense; it, too, represents a relation between age and Y, and this relation can be of many nonlinear forms. It differs from the usual function, however, in that it is specified in terms of linear departures from an origin. Specifying a straight line function in terms of $B(t)$ will illustrate this. For example, let $B(t)$ = [0, 1, 2, 3, 4] at ages 20, 30, 40, 50, and 60, respectively, for a representation of the equation in section A of Table 17.2 in which the mean level is 50 and the mean slope is 10. Thus, for all persons, the mean $L(t)$ is 100 and the mean $S(t)$ is 10. Omitting the error term to make the example particularly straightforward, the equation would be

$$Y_t = 100 + B(t) * 10.$$

$B(t) = 0$ at age 20 is an assumption of convenience that starts the curve of change at this age. Thus,

$$Y(20) = 100 + 0 * 10 = 100.$$

The curve thus begins at $Y = 100$, the group average. $B(t) = 1$ at age 30 indicates that from age 20 to age 30 there is one unit of change:

$$Y(30) = 100 + 1 * 10 = 110.$$

$B(t) = 2$ at age 40 indicates that from age 20 to age 40 there are two units of change.

$$Y(40) = 100 + 2 * 10 = 120.$$

In the same manner, $B(t) = 3$ and $B(t) = 4$ at ages 50 and 60, respectively, indicates that from age 20 to these other ages there are three and four units of change, and Y is 130 and 140, respectively.

Likewise, $B(t) = [0, 2, 2, 1, -1]$ indicates a nonmonotonic, nonlinear function similar in shape to the curves shown in plot A in Figure 17.2. In this case, $B(t) = 0$ at age 20 can be just the same as for the linear case, based on the same assumption of convenience, and $B(t) = 2$ at age 30 indicates that from age 20 to age 30 there are two units of change and that

$$Y(30) = 100 + 2 * 10 = 120.$$

$B(t) = 2$ at age 40 indicates that from age 20 to age 40 years there are again two units of change:

$$Y(40) = 100 + 2 * 10 = 120.$$

$B(t) = 1$ at age 50 indicates that from age 20 to age 50 years there is one unit of change and

$$Y(50) = 100 + 1 * 10 = 100.$$

$B(t) = -1$ at age 60 indicates that from age 20 to age 60 there is a drop of one unit: The average is 10 points below the average at age 20 years,

$$Y(60) = 100 + -1 * 10 = 90.$$

We thus see that $B(t)$ describes a nonlinear relation of change in terms of linear differences from a start point, rather in the way that spline regression is used to describe nonlinear relation. The $B(t) = [0, 2, 2, 1, -1]$ function represents the model from which random curves were generated to create the data of plot A in Figure 17.2. We will need to recover such a set of coefficients, therefore, to fit the data of Figures 17.1 and 17.2.

The average curves of these examples hide individual differences, as Tucker (1963) emphasized in the pioneering conference on the study of change (Harris, 1963). Given that $B(t)$ represents the same lawful relation for all people, there are likely to be individual differences not only in levels, $L(n)$, at each age (representing the likelihood that at any given age some individuals are above the mean, and others are below) but also in slopes, $S(n)$. Slopes represent the idea that the outcome scores of some individuals increase, whereas others decrease, and among those who increase or decrease, some do so more than others. These group- and individual-differences concepts are included by adding statistical assumptions about the means, deviations, and correlations given in Figure 17.2 and listed in Table 17.2. All latent components are assumed to be independent, but a correlation among the level and slope scores can be allowed (with coefficient R). The equation in section C of Table 17.2 lists the latent growth model expectations for the means, standard deviations, and correlations of any set of observed scores $Y(t, n)$.

Generating Incomplete Longitudinal Data

In order to generate the curves of plot A in Figure 17.2, we first defined a fixed set of population parameters (these are listed in section D of Table 17.1). Next we randomly generated standardized normal deviates for the three latent components $L^*(n)$, $S^*(n)$, and $E^*(n)$. We created the raw unobserved components using the equation in section B of Table 17.2 and created the raw observed scores $Y^*(t, n)$ using the equation in section A.

Plot A in Figure 17.2 can be directly related to the path model parameters of the latent growth curve model (the equation in Table 17.2, section B). The overall height of the curve is related to the mean level of 50, and the overall variance is related to the deviation level of 5. The individual differences in change over time are related to the mean slope of 10 and deviation slope of 3. The specific assignment of population values, in which the basis is $B(t) = [0, 2, 2, 1, -1]$ for the five ages, is crucial to the analysis. As pointed out in the previous section, this basis describes a curve that (a) starts at zero (age 20), (b) goes up two change units by the second occasion (age 30), (c) stays at that change unit for the third occasion (age 40), (d) goes down halfway by the fourth occasion (age 50), and (e) goes down two more change units, or one unit below the starting point, by the fifth occasion (age 60). The most striking feature of Figure 17.2 is the nonlinear basis, or shape, of the overall curves.

The initial plots of Figure 17.1 show the incomplete growth curves obtained by drawing samples from the complete data in plot A in Figure 17.2. The incomplete data of Figure 17.1 were obtained as subsets from the "complete" growth curve data by applying the following four selection mechanisms:

Sample A. Each individual in plot A in Figure 17.1 was randomly selected in one of four age groups (age 20, 30, 40, or 50), but only the first two data points were selected. The resulting randomly created data matrix **Y** includes only 100 rows and 2 columns— 200 elements—from the total data. These data are thus only 40% complete.

Sample B. Each individual in plot B in Figure 17.1 was randomly selected, as in plot A, but to each second data point was added a random retest score. To make this retest effect clear, this retest score was based on a retest mean of 10 with a retest deviation of 1. These data are also only 40% complete.

Sample C. Each individual in plot C in Figure 17.1 was randomly selected as in plot A, but then dropouts based on level scores were created. Dropouts were defined as all individuals at or below the median on their unobserved level scores, $L(n)$. This definition was designed to represent self-selection of a kind thought to be found by researchers in the field of cognition; that is, low-scoring persons tend to drop out whereas the high-scoring persons persist (see Baltes et al., 1971; Botwinick & Siegler, 1980).

Sample D. Each individual in plot D in Figure 17.1 was randomly selected as in plot A, but dropouts based on slope scores were created. Dropouts were defined as individuals at or above the median on slope scores $S(n)$. This selection was designed to represent a kind of self-selection found in studies of personality—persons who change a lot tend to drop out, whereas those who change little tend to persist (Horn, 1972).

Compared with the full set of data in plot A in Figure 17.2, the "obtained" data of Figure 17.1—the data available for analysis—are sparse. As indicated above, the data for plots A and B in Figure 17.1 are only 40% complete. The obtained data in plots C and D in Figure 17.1 are even more sparse. Here there are scores for only 48 persons tested twice. The number of data elements is only 96, about 20% of the original data. Moreover, there is nonrandom split of the already limited data in these sets. If the dropouts, tested only one time, are considered in these data, the obtained data are increased by 52 observed elements; the total number of elements is thus 148, which is only about 30% of the original information. Although these data sets are sparse by comparison with a complete data set that represents an ideal, they are typical of the best samplings obtained in repeated measures longitudinal research.

Modeling Incomplete Growth Curves

A structural equation model that can represent the data described in the previous section has been developed (McArdle & Anderson, 1989; McArdle et al., 1987; Meredith & Tisak, 1990). A new version of this model is described in the path diagrams of Figure 17.3.

In the left-hand column of Figure 17.3 is a latent growth model for each of four groups for which there are two variables. Two major assumptions are made in this model. First, we make the strong assumption that the identical path model, with the same numerical parameters, fits all groups, that is, is invariant over groups. Second, we assume latent (hidden) variables account for each data set: a different set of latent variables for each data set. For example, in the top diagram, for Group 1 (subjects measured at ages 20 and 30 years), the manifest variables (squares) are Y(1) and Y(2) and the latent variables (circles) represent unmeasured variables at ages 40, 50, and 60 years. In the next diagram down, for Group 2, the manifest variables are Y(2) and Y(3), and unmeasured variables at ages 20, 50, and 60 years are Y(1), Y(4), and Y(5). In the same manner, the path diagrams for Groups 3 and 4 represent different configurations of manifest and latent variables. The four diagrams represent four independent groups in each of which are hidden variables. These can be regarded as surrogates for the variables for which data are missing. Taking this view of the matter puts us in a position to test hypotheses about convergence across separate groups by using standard techniques for testing the invariance of factor loadings across groups (as discussed by Cunningham and Horn in chapter 7).

We also use the multiple-group growth model to examine, and account for, bias due to selective subject attrition. These analyses are indicated in the right-hand column of Figure 17.3, in which four additional path models are diagrammed.

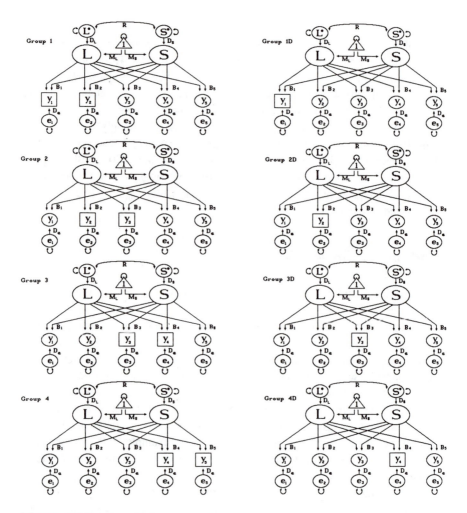

Figure 17.3   A multiple-group path model for latent growth with missing data and nonrandom attrition.

Each of these represents a case in which only one variable is measured. In isolation, these single time points of cross-sectional data would not provide enough information to uniquely estimate the model parameters $B(t)$. However, the information from the four groups can help indicate the model parameters for the longitudinal data. This model will not fit the data well if the first-occasion age functions differ, thereby providing direct evidence of nonrandom attrition. But even if this invariant model does not fit the data well, the invariant equation coefficients will represent the most informative estimate of the overall age function we seek (see Allison,

1987; Little & Rubin, 1987; Rubin, 1976). Analyses for an eight-group model (all the groups in Figure 17.3) provide informative tests of the major hypotheses outlined above.

We fit models to either one-group, four-group, or eight-group moment matrices using the LISREL computer program series (Jöreskog & Sörbom, 1988). As discussed in describing the equation in section C of Table 17.2, the moment matrices of these analyses are variance-covariance matrices augmented by a row and column of means. The equations in section C of Table 17.2 are the expected-value equations for standard maximum likelihood estimation. These model expectations can be matched up to a set of observed moments to form a likelihood function for estimation and testing (for more details, see Jöreskog & Sörbom, 1979; Little & Rubin, 1987; McArdle, 1988). Each model constraint will generate one degree of freedom (*DF*) for testing the fit of the constrained model against some less restricted alternative. Maximum likelihood estimation provides a basis for obtaining parameter standard errors and an overall likelihood ratio test (*LRT*) statistic for the evaluation of goodness of fit. Specific programming devices are needed to handle the staggered age of testing and the different numbers of observed variables. (A description of the LISREL program we used for input for this problem is provided in the appendix of this chapter.)

Results of the Latent Growth Model

A first set of analyses demonstrates the kinds of results obtained in fitting the full path model (Figure 17.2 and Table 17.2) to the full set of simulated data (Figure 17.1 and Table 17.1). Section A in Table 17.3 gives the numerical results of six models fitted to the moment matrix of section C in Table 17.1. Section B in Table 17.3 gives some statistical indices for the overall model goodness of fit.

Section A in Table 17.3 and Table 17.4 is organized so each column represents a specific model and each row represents a specific model parameter. The first column contains the population values for the simulation. The second column contains the parameters for fit of the latent growth model to the sample moment matrix with only the minimal model restrictions. In order to identify the parameters of this two-factor model we must impose the following constraints. Two loadings are fixed: (a) The constraint $B(1) = 0$ makes the slope factor, S, independent of the level factor, L; and (b) the constraint $B(5) = -1$ provides a needed scaling for the slope factor, S. Although these loadings are fixed at the correct population values, this is done only for comparative purposes; in theory, any two fixed values of $B(t)$ should work as well. For convenience in calculation, we also add a restriction that all error deviations equal a single value, $DE(t) = DE$, but this restriction is not generally required.

Table 17.3

NUMERICAL RESULTS FROM FITTING THE LATENT GROWTH MODEL TO
COMPLETE SIMULATED DATA ($N = 100$; FROM TABLE 17.1)

A. Maximum likelihood estimates (with standard errors in parentheses)

Model parameter	Population values	Latent growth	Fixed arrows	Linear growth	No slope baseline
Function means					
$1 \rightarrow L$[a]	50.0	49.5 (.6)	50.0 (==[b])	63.1 (??[c])	57.4 (.6)
$1 \rightarrow S$[d]	10.0	9.4 (.4)	10.0 (==)	11.5 (??)	.0 (==)
Function loadings[e]					
$S \rightarrow Y^t(20)$	0.0	0.0 (==)	0.0 (==)	0.0 (==)	.0 (==)
$S \rightarrow Y(30)$	2.0	2.1 (.1)	2.0 (==)	$-.25$ (==)	.0 (==)
$S \rightarrow Y(40)$	2.0	2.1 (.1)	2.0 (==)	$-.50$ (==)	.0 (==)
$S \rightarrow Y(50)$	1.0	1.1 (.1)	1.0 (==)	$-.75$ (==)	.0 (==)
$S \rightarrow Y(60)$	-1.0	-1.0 (==)	-1.0 (==)	-1.0 (==)	.0 (==)
Function deviations[g]					
$L^* \rightarrow L$	5.0	5.3 (.4)	5.3 (.4)	13.7 (??)	1.4 (2)
$S^* \rightarrow S$	3.0	2.9 (.2)	3.0 (.2)	.2 (??)	.0 (==)
$L^* \leftrightarrow S^*$	0.0	.12 (1)	.14 (.1)	-46.2 (??)	.0 (==)
$E(t) \rightarrow Y(t)$[g]	2.0	2.1 (.1)	2.1 (.1)	12.5 (??)	13.3 (.5)

B. Goodness of fit of model to simulation data

Fit index	Latent growth	Fixed arrows	Linear growth	No slope baseline
Likelihood ratio (LRT)[n]	10.6	13.1	1,186.3	1,246.2
Degrees of freedom (DF)[i]	11	16	14	17
Likelihood index[j] (LIP)	99%	99%	5%	0%

[a] Level.
[b] Indicates a parameter that is fixed.
[c] The standard error could not be calculated.
[d] Slope.
[e] All loadings from level component to scores $Y(t) = 1$.
[f] Year.
[g] All error deviations $E(t) \rightarrow Y(t)$ fixed to be equal.
[h] LISREL chi-square value.
[i] LISREL degrees of freedom $- 1$ (due to fixed unit).
[j] $(1.0 - \{[LRT(0) - LRT(1)]/LRT(0)\}) *100$, where $LRT(0) =$ baseline.

The numerical results of the second column in section A of Table 17.3 show
the parameters estimated for the latent growth model. All are very close to the
population values. For example, the population mean level is 50 and this parameter
is estimated as 49.5 with a standard error of .6 from this sample of 100. Also,
the latent basis coefficient $B(2)$ is 2.0 in the population, and it is estimated as 2.1
with a standard error of .1 from this sample. As indicated in section B of Table

Table 17.4

NUMERICAL RESULTS FROM FITTING THE LATENT GROWTH MODELS TO INCOMPLETE SETS OF SIMULATED DATA

A. Maximum likelihood estimates

Model parameter	40-Year study[a]	10-Year study[b]	10 + Retest study[c]	10 + Level study[d]	10 + Slope study[e]
Function means					
$1 \to L$	49.5 (.6)	48.5 (1.0)	49.6 (1.2)	49.8 (1.0)	50.1 (1.0)
$1 \to S$	9.4 (.4)	8.6 (1.4)	.2 (1.7)	7.3 (1.4)	5.3 (1.7)
Function loadings					
$S \to Y(20)$	0.0 (= =)	0.0 (= =)	0.0 (= =)	0.0 (= =)	0.0 (= =)
$S \to Y(30)$	2.1 (.1)	2.4 (.5)	119 (??)	2.6 (.7)	3.2 (1.1)
$S \to Y(40)$	2.1 (.1)	2.4 (.5)	143 (??)	2.5 (.7)	3.4 (1.2)
$S \to Y(50)$	1.1 (.1)	1.2 (.3)	97 (??)	1.3 (.5)	1.9 (.8)
$S \to Y(60)$	−1.0 (= =)	−1.0 (= =)	−1.0 (= =)	−1.0 (= =)	−1.0 (= =)
Function deviations					
$L^* \to L$	5.3 (.4)	5.3 (.5)	2.2 (2.3)	5.3 (.6)	5.1 (.6)
$S^* \to S$	2.9 (.2)	2.7 (.5)	.0 (.4)	2.5 (.7)	2.1 (.7)
$L^* \leftrightarrow S^*$	.12 (.1)	−.01 (.1)	.0 (.4)	−.03 (.2)	−.01 (.2)
$E(t) \to Y(t)$	2.0 (.1)	1.9 (.1)	5.7 (.6)	1.8 (.3)	1.5 (.3)

B. Goodness of fit of alternative models to simulation data

Model fit index	40-Year study	10-Year study	10 + Retest study	10 + Level study	10 + Slope study
Latent LRT (DF)	11 (11)	9 (11)	149 (11)	79 (19)	47 (19)
Fixed LRT (DF)	13 (16)	12 (16)	214 (16)	86 (24)	62 (24)
Linear LRT (DF)	1186 (14)	299 (14)	319 (14)	252 (22)	204 (22)
No slope LRT (DF)	1246 (17)	323 (17)	333 (17)	209 (25)	129 (25)
Latent LIP	99%	97%	96%	62%	64%

Note: In section A standard errors are in parentheses. Horizontal bar means the parameter is fixed. L = level, S = slope, Y = raw score, E = error. In section B degrees of freedom are in parentheses. *LRT* = likelihood ratio, *LIP* = likelihood index percentage.
[a]Plot A in Figure 17.2.
[b]Plot A in Figure 17.1.
[c]Plot B in Figure 17.1.
[d]Plot C in Figure 17.1.
[e]Plot D in Figure 17.1.

17.3, this model fits the data very well: $LRT = 10.6$ ($df = 11$). This overall good fit and the close estimates give us confidence that the simulation and the estimation program are working correctly.

The second column in section A of Table 17.3 represents the fixed arrows model. In this model we force the mean level (ML), mean slope (MS), and basis coefficients $[B(t)]$ to be fixed at the population model values. We allow free estimation of the stochastic model components: deviation level (DL), deviation slope (DS), deviation error (DE), and the correlation of the level and slope scores (RSL). This is a rigorous fitting of the population model. The model fits the data very well, with $LRT = 13.1$ ($DF = 16$). This result gives additional confidence that our simulation program is working correctly.

The next three columns in section A of Table 17.3 provides results for models that should be inconsistent with these data. The model in the fourth column is labeled "Linear growth" because it forces a linear basis on the growth model; that is, $B(t)$ = [.00, .25, .50, .75, 1.00] (multiplied by -1). The LRT of 1,186 ($DF = 14$) for this model indicates that many of the parameters could not be clearly identified and most standard errors are very large. This linear basis was fixed by a hypothesis often assumed in developmental analyses. Because there is curvilinearity in the relation between age and visual capability, as we simulated in the data, this model does not fit the data well and the parameter estimates are inconsistent.

The fifth column in section A of Table 17.3 is for a model in which no slope parameters are estimated; that is, $MS = 0$, $DS = 0$, and $B(t)$ is undefined. This model fits the data very poorly, with $LRT = 1,246$ ($df = 17$). Although this model does not fit these data, we use the results of this poor fit as a baseline [$LRT(0)$] against which to judge the goodness of fit of other models fitted to these data. The likelihood index percentage (LIP) in section B of Table 17.3 is the ratio of the goodness of fit of other models compared with this baseline. For example, under the assumptions of the linear growth model, $LIP = 100[LRT(0) - LRT(1)]/LRT(0) = (1,246 - 1,186)/1,246 = 4.8\%$, whereas under the assumptions of the fixed arrows model, $LIP = (1,246 - 13)/1,246 = 98.9\%$. The latent growth model accounts for 99% of the misfit between the available data and the no slope model, whereas the linear growth model accounts for only 5% of this between the data and the model.

Estimating Models Involving Only Two Time Points

The previous results help verify that the latent growth model fitting techniques can be used to recover the correct model parameters with a relatively small sample of subjects. However, the previous analyses used information from all five time points of measurement. In Table 17.4 we examine the results when the model is fitted to the four plots of Figure 17.1. In each case we have four age cohort groups measured at only one or two of the time points of the total data.

For ready comparisons, the first column in section A of Table 17.4 again provides the results of fitting the latent growth model described in section A of Table 17.3. These results come from the full 40-year study on 100 persons. But now the second column provides results obtained when only a 10-year study is done using four groups of 25 each (as in plot A in Figure 17.1). These results, overall, show a remarkable stability of parameter estimates and fit. Even with only the small proportion of the total data used to obtain these estimates, we would probably interpret the results in much the same way as when the total data set was used to give the results. The diminished sample, analyzed as proposed here, seems to have retained the overall picture of growth.

There are problems, however. The main problem shows up in the standard errors for the estimates. These are inflated relative to the standard errors obtained with the total data. It is quite reasonable that they should be inflated, considering that the dataset is 60% smaller, but this is not our only concern.

It is seen in section B in Table 17.4 that the *LRTs* are smaller and there is an overall loss of power in fitting the reduced data set relative to the total data set. Even so, with only two time points in a 10-year study, one would probably retain the hypothesis that the correct model fits ($LRT = 9; DF = 11$) and reject the hypothesis of linear growth model ($LRT = 299; DF = 14$). The large standard errors and lower *LRTs* alert us to a potential loss of information about growth from the loss of subjects and variables.

The model identified in the third column in section A of Table 17.4 is termed "10 + retest" because here we fit the single latent growth curve model to the data set of plot B in Figure 17.1, in which a retest effect was built in. The results show that the parameter estimates are biased (with $B(t) > 100$) and unstable ($seB(t) > 1,000$), and the model does not fit the data ($LRT = 149, DF = 11$). These results indicate a straightforward inconsistency between the model and the data. The model does not represent the retest effect. The data of plot B in Figure 17.1 can be better fitted, but a parameter to represent the retest effect is required. When we add a single component to represent this effect (i.e., with *MR* and *DR*), an excellent fit is obtained ($LRT = 10, DF = 9$), and the parameters are closely estimated and well behaved (for details on retest models, see McArdle & Anderson, 1990). The main point is that a model must come close to representing the reality of the data if good fit in convergence analysis is to be achieved.

Estimating Models With Nonrandom Dropouts

The model in the fourth column of section A in Table 17.4 is labeled "10 + level." This was fitted in two pieces. In the first piece, the fit was based on the 48 subjects having the highest level scores. The results show the effects of selection: The mean level is higher ($ML = 54.7$), the deviation level is lower ($DL = 3.2$), and we have generated a correlation between level and slope ($RLS = -.36$). The latent growth model fits these data very well ($LRT = 11.2, DF = 11$), but the fixed arrow model does not ($LRT = 45.1, DF = 16$). The difference between the two fits ($dLRT = 34.9, dDF = 5$) is noteworthy.

In the second piece of analysis we include both the 52 "dropouts" and the 48 "persisters." (Programming for this model is presented in the appendix to this chapter.) Thus, in these analyses all the available information in the reduced data set is used to get parameter estimates. The results in this case indicate that the estimated mean level (49.8) and deviation level (5.3) are much closer to the true population values of 50 and 5, respectively.

It is important to consider the goodness of fit of this model relative to that for the model evaluated in the first column of these analyses. In the second analysis the LRT is 79.4 ($DF = 19$); this is a relatively poor fit. For a direct comparison of this eight-group model with the previous four-group model, the difference in fit is dLRT $= 68.2$ ($DF = 8$); this is significant. Following the logic used by Rubin (1976) and Allison (1987), one can now conclude that (a) dropout is a nonrandom process, and (b) the parameter estimates from the second piece of analysis are best guesses about the true population values. Experienced modelers may find this conclusion at odds with usual model fitting strategies—here the model "doesn't fit" but we accept the values as being "best." But here the simulation results show the parameter estimates of the "corrected" model are indeed corrected.

We also notice a few potentially disturbing outcomes in these results. First, the eight-group model seems to correct the level parameters, but it doesn't do as well with the slope parameters. In the persister model the slope values are close to the true population values ($MS = 10.3$, $DS = 3.2$), but the addition of the dropouts decreases these estimates ($MS = 7.3$, $DS = 2.5$) and thus makes them less accurate. Second, the standard errors of the basis coefficients $B(t)$ are large. This may lead to mistakes in interpretation of the overall shape of the function. The parameters MS, DS, and $B(t)$ in this model are not, in a practical sense, strong enough to overcome the importance of the level correction. Nevertheless, these parameters are centrally important to developmental interpretations of the model. Thus, although the correction for nonrandom attrition seems to have worked in general, there are indications that the results must be interpreted carefully, probably in the context of having results for analyses on different subsets of the available data.

The final column in section A of Table 17.4 shows the results of fitting a model under conditions of slope selection (plot D in Figure 17.1). Again we did the analyses in two parts. When we fit a model for the 48 persisters only, we find anticipated results—a decreased mean slope (4.9) and a decreased deviation slope (2.0). We also see much larger parameters and standard errors for the basis coefficients: $B(40) = 3.1$, $SEB(40) = 1.4$. These values may lead to misinterpretations of the shape of the curve.

When the dropouts are included and invariance is required across all eight groups, the resulting model does not fit the data as well as when the four-group model is fit ($LRT = 46.7$, $DF = 19$), and the difference between the two fits is significant ($dLRT = 36.4$, $dDF = 8$). Again following the model comparison strategy outlined earlier, one can correctly conclude that dropout is a nonrandom process. In this case the corrected estimates are not very different from the uncorrected estimates.

Using the knowledge of the correct population model, we can see, first, that the estimates for corrected model yield only a slightly better fit to the population model ($dLRT = 15.7$, $dDF = 5$) than the estimates for the uncorrected model ($dLRT = 32.9$, $dDF = 5$), and, second, that even in the corrected model the parameter estimates for the slope are severely underestimated and the basis coefficients are overestimated. Thus, these model parameters are "not corrected" in the presence of this kind of slope selection. Perhaps this should not be surprising. In these analyses we do not have any information about slope for the dropouts. Surely, some such information is needed to make an accurate correction in a model.

CONCLUSIONS

The basic ideas of accelerated longitudinal study by convergence analysis were initially most fully developed by Bell (1953, 1954) and in broad overview by Cattell (1950). These ideas were most vigorously applied in analyses of variance by Schaie (1965, 1974). The use of moment matrices and multiple staggered groups are also central methodological features of convergence models. These basic ideas were developed by Horn and McArdle (1980) in an autoregressive context, and more generally by Meredith and Tisak (1990), McArdle et al. (1987), and McArdle and Anderson (1990). Further details on these kinds of growth models have been offered by McArdle (1986, 1988, 1989) and McArdle and Epstein (1987). The attrition models are based most fundamentally on the presentations of Rubin (1976), Little and Rubin (1987), and Allison (1987).

Our results demonstrate the utility of structural equation modeling techniques for convergence analysis with incomplete data in the study of change. The data in Table 17.3 shows that one can recover models based in latent growth curves, and reject plausible models that are inappropriate. Even with a sample as small as 100, there may be enough statistical power to obtain accurate parameter estimates and make meaningful model comparisons. Our second set of results (the 10-year and 10 + retest models in Table 17.4) show that by using a convergence model one can obtain reasonable estimates of parameters when data are randomly missing. Even when the samples were very small ($N = 25$ at $T = 2$), parameter estimates were close to the correct values; with adequate statistical power, a hypothesis for a reasonable model for the data was not rejected. The results from our third set of analyses (the 10 + level and 10 + slope models in Table 17.4), focusing on nonrandom dropout, were mixed and complex. We found we could recover reasonable estimates of the parameters for good models when self-selection occurred on score levels, but we could not recover some of the important features of correct models when self-selection occurred on score slopes. We conclude that some forms of subject self-selection are "correctable" using the simple specifications of our examples; however, to correct for other forms of self-selection one would need more direct information about the selection than would become available with the sampling designs we considered.

The results help to indicate the complexities involved in recovering missing longitudinal information. It is clear that judgments about change and growth that are based on incomplete, degraded data will differ from what they would be if data were complete. In fact, they will be wrong. But they may not be so wrong that they are useless. Our analyses essentially show that information missing at random poses little threat to the validity of the model interpretation, even when more than half the data are missing. In contrast, we found that when data were missing in a nonrandom fashion, serious threats to valid interpretation of modeling results could occur.

Our results show that the effects of nonrandom sampling can be demonstrated and that distinct developmental models are separable as long as there are strong enough "signal" of the correct model and there are enough data (compare Rogosa & Willett, 1985b). These issues obviously need more detailed study, and new alternatives to standard analysis need to be developed. Our results lead us to reconsider the use of designed experiments that optimize measurement in the areas of maximal change. Indeed, the kinds of analyses described in this study may actually be most useful in guiding the design of future longitudinal studies of change (see Johnston, 1980), rather than in use in the aftermath of data already collected.

One remarkable feature of the plots of the incomplete data of this study is that the basic shape of the relation is still apparent even in the most severely degraded data sets of plots B–D in Figure 17.1. If the naked eye can see it, then perhaps it is not surprising that we get nearly correct answers with our elegant analyses, and perhaps it is surprising when we don't. The visual clarity that we experience is based in part on the fact that we have the prototype of the curve in mind—the complete set of curves of plot A in Figure 17.2. Another way of saying this is that we have a good hunch (hypothesis) about the nature of the relations among our variables. Given prior knowledge, we have a reasonable chance of getting the correct result. This may be the most important factor to understand in seeking to understand change with limited information. One must have a strong frame of reference against which other ideas can be compared and contrasted. Deeper appreciation of the need to develop such frames of reference will lead to better sampling designs, better substantive theory, and better decisions about individual change.

APPENDIX

A LISREL-7 PROGRAM FOR LATENT GROWTH CURVE MODEL ON NONRANDOMLY INCOMPLETE DATA BASED ON SLOPE SELECTION

A LISREL-7 program listing is included here. For ease of programming and presentation we use RAM notation instead of standard LISREL notation (see McArdle & Boher, 1990; McArdle & McDonald, 1984). The first group model of the Appendix shows how we can fit this model into the RAM form of three matrices: a matrix of one-headed arrows (A = Beta), a matrix of two-headed arrows or slings (S = Phi), and a matrix to filter out the manifest variables (F = Lambda Y). The unit constant is simply considered another observed variable in this notation, and all path diagram rules apply to moments around zero (as in Horn & McArdle, 1980; McArdle & Epstein, 1987).

Other features of our LISREL programming are unique to this specific problem. The programming of the staggered pattern of two time points can be seen across the first four groups. To correctly place these variables we force the A(Beta) and S(Phi) matrices to be totally invariant but we alter the fixed F(Lambda Y) matrix for each group. The inclusion of attrition groups requires a model with different numbers of observed variables in each group. In the programming of Groups 5–8 we add an extra variable to the input data matrix but we then remove this variable from the estimation problem by fitting these statistics with zero residuals (using the Theta Epsilon matrix).

We also found the LISREL-7 program to be sensitive to starting values for these problems. In order to counteract these problems, we tried several alternative input options. First, we tried to rescale the input moment matrix so it was closer to a diagonal matrix. The moment matrix of plot D of Figure 17.2 was formed simply by dividing each score by 100 and recalculating the moment matrix.

Second, we placed the model constants into a scaling that was as close to being correct as possible; that is, we started the $ML = .50$ and the $MS = .10$. Third, we made the error variance relatively large (i.e., $DE = 5.0$). These specific additions to the program helped us obtain solutions that were otherwise untractable using the current version of LISREL.

Although the current versions of LISREL can produce correct calculations, they are difficult to use at best. This seems to be especially true when working with small sample sizes and moment matrices. One colleague even suggested, "LISREL is a good program for calculating values to the third decimal place as long as you are willing to input the first two" (E. Turkheimer, May 1989). We expect future versions of structural modeling programs to have special features for dealing with these kinds of problems.

A LISREL-7 PROGRAM FOR LATENT GROWTH CURVE MODEL

Group 1: Ages 20 and 30

```
Simulated Growth Curve Model: Eight-Group Model
DA  NI = 6 NG = 8 NO = 12 MA = MM
ME file = groups.mom
SD  file = groups.mom
LA  file = groups.mom
KM file = groups.mom
SE
     6,1,2 /
MODEL NY = 3 NE = 15 BE = FU,FI PS = SY,FI LY = FU,FI TE = FI,DI
LE
    Const Score20 Score30 Score40 Score50 Score60
    DS1 DS2 DS3 DS4 DS5
    Level Slope L* S*
MA   LY
1 0 0 0 0 0  0 0  0 0 0 0 0  0 0
0 1 0 0 0 0  0 0  0 0 0 0 0  0 0
0 0 1 0 0 0  0 0  0 0 0 0 0  0 0
MA BE
0 0 0 0 0 0  0 0  0 0 0 0  0 0 0
0 0 0 0 0 0 .1 0  0 0 0 1  0 0 0
0 0 0 0 0 0  0 .1 0 0 0 1  2 0 0
0 0 0 0 0 0  0 0 .1 0 0 1  2 0 0
0 0 0 0 0 0  0 0 0 .1 0 1  1 0 0
0 0 0 0 0 0  0 0 0 0 .1 1 -1 0 0
0 0 0 0 0 0  0 0  0 0 0 0  0 0 0
```

```
0 0 0 0 0 0  0 0  0 0  0 0 0  0 0
0 0 0 0 0 0  0 0  0 0  0 0 0  0 0
0 0 0 0 0 0  0 0  0 0  0 0 0  0 0
0 0 0 0 0 0  0 0  0 0  0 0 0  0 0
1 0 0 0 0 0  0 0  0 0  0 0 0  .3 0
1 0 0 0 0 0  0 0  0 0  0 0 0  0 .2
0 0 0 0 0 0  0 0  0 0  0 0 0  0 0
0 0 0 0 0 0  0 0  0 0  0 0 0  0 0
MA PS
0
0 0
0 0 0
0 0 0 0
0 0 0 0 0
0 0 0 0 0 0
0 0 0 0 0 0  1
0 0 0 0 0 0  0 1
0 0 0 0 0 0  0 0  1
0 0 0 0 0 0  0 0  0 1
0 0 0 0 0 0  0 0  0 0  1
0 0 0 0 0 0  0 0  0 0  0 1
0 0 0 0 0 0  0 0  0 0  0 0 1
0 0 0 0 0 0  0 0  0 0  0 0 0  1
0 0 0 0 0 0  0 0  0 0  0 0 0  .1 1
FR BE 2 7 BE 3 8 BE 4 9 BE 5 10 BE 6 11
FR BE 3 13 BE 4 13 BE 5 13
FR BE 12 14 BE 13 15
FR BE 12 1 BE 13 1
FR PS 14 15
OU NS RS SE TV PT PC FD add = off SS WP
```

Group 2: Ages 30 and 40
```
DA NI = 6 NO = 12 MA = MM
ME file = groups.mom
SD file = groups.mom
LA file = groups.mom
KM fu file = groups.mom
SE
   6,2,3 /
MODEL NY = 3 NE = 15 BE = in PS = in LY = FU,FI TE = fi,DI
LE
   Const Score20 Score30 Score40 Score50 Score60
```

```
    DS1 DS2 DS3 DS4 DS5
    Level Slope L* S*

MA   LY
1 0 0 0 0 0  0 0  0 0  0 0 0  0 0
0 0 0 1 0 0  0 0  0 0  0 0 0  0 0
0 0 0 0 1 0  0 0  0 0  0 0 0  0 0

OU NS SE PC TV pt ND = 3 add = off so to it = 100
```

Group 3: Ages 40 and 50
```
DA NI = 6 NO = 12 MA = MM
ME file = groups.mom
SD file = groups.mom
LA file = groups.mom
KM fu file = groups.mom
SE
    6,3,4 /
MODEL NY = 3 NE = 15 BE = in PS = in LY = FU,FI TE = fi,DI
LE
    Const Score20 Score30 Score40 Score50 Score60
    DS1 DS2 DS3 DS4 DS5
    Level Slope L* S*

MA LY
1 0 0 0 0 0  0 0  0 0  0 0 0  0 0
0 0 0 1 0 0  0 0  0 0  0 0 0  0 0
0 0 0 0 1 0  0 0  0 0  0 0 0  0 0

OU NS SE PC TV pt ND = 3 add = off so to it = 100
```

Group 4: Ages 50 and 60
```
DA NI = 6 NO = 12 MA = MM
ME file = groups.mom
SD file = groups.mom
LA file = groups.mom
KM fu file = groups.mom
SE
    6,4,5 /
MODEL NY = 3 NE = 15 BE = in PS = in LY = FU,FI TE = fi,DI
LE
    Const Score20 Score30 Score40 Score50 Score60
    DS1 DS2 DS3 DS4 DS5
    Level Slope L* S*
```

```
MA LY
1 0 0 0 0 0  0 0  0 0  0 0 0  0 0
0 0 0 0 1 0  0 0  0 0  0 0 0  0 0
0 0 0 0 0 1  0 0  0 0  0 0 0  0 0
OU NS SE PC TV pt ND = 3 add = off so to it = 100
```

Group 5: Age 20 only
```
DA NI = 7 NO = 13 MA = MM
ME file = groups.mom
SD file = groups.mom
LA file = groups.mom
KM fu file = groups.mom
SE
   6,1,7 /
MODEL NY = 3 NE = 15 BE = in PS = in LY = FU,FI TE = fi,DI
LE
  Const Score20 Score30 Score40 Score50 Score60
  DS1 DS2 DS3 DS4 DS5
  Level Slope L* S*
MA   LY
1 0 0 0 0 0  0 0  0 0  0 0 0  0 0
0 1 0 0 0 0  0 0  0 0  0 0 0  0 0
0 0 1 0 0 0  0 0  0 0  0 0 0  0 0
va 1.08341 te 3 3
OU NS SE PC TV pt ND = 3 add = off so to it = 100
```

Group 6: Age 30 only
```
DA NI = 7 NO = 13 MA = MM
ME file = groups.mom
SD file = groups.mom
LA file = groups.mom
KM fu file = groups.mom
SE
   6,2,7 /
MODEL NY = 3 NE = 15 BE = in PS = in LY = FU,FI TE = fi,DI
LE
  Const Score20 Score30 Score40 Score50 Score60
  DS1 DS2 DS3 DS4 DS5
  Level Slope L* S*
MA   LY
1 0 0 0 0 0  0 0  0 0  0 0 0  0 0
0 0 1 0 0 0  0 0  0 0  0 0 0  0 0
```

```
0 0 0 1 0 0  0 0  0 0  0 0 0 0  0 0
va 1.08341 te 3 3
OU NS SE PC TV pt ND = 3 add = off so to it = 100
```

Group 7: Age 40 only
```
DA NI = 7 NO = 13 MA = MM
ME file = groups.mom
SD file = groups.mom
LA file = groups.mom
KM fu file = groups.mom
SE
    6,3,7 /
MODEL NY = 3 NE = 15 BE = in PS = in LY = FU,FI TE = fi,DI
LE
    Const Score20 Score30 Score40 Score50 Score60
    DS1 DS2 DS3 DS4 DS5
    Level Slope L* S*
MA LY
1 0 0 0 0 0  0 0  0 0  0 0 0 0  0 0
0 0 0 1 0 0  0 0  0 0  0 0 0 0  0 0
0 0 0 0 1 0  0 0  0 0  0 0 0 0  0 0
va 1.08341 te 3 3
OU NS SE PC TV pt ND = 3 add = off so to it = 100
```

Group 8: Age 50 only
```
DA NI = 7 NO = 13 MA = MM
ME file = groups.mom
SD file = groups.mom
LA file = groups.mom
KM fu file = groups.mom
SE
    6,4,7 /
MODEL NY = 3 NE = 15 BE = in PS = in LY = FU,FI TE = fi,DI
LE
    Const Score20 Score30 Score40 Score50 Score60
    DS1 DS2 DS3 DS4 DS5
    Level Slope L* S*
MA   LY
1 0 0 0 0 0  0 0  0 0  0 0 0 0  0 0
0 0 0 0 1 0  0 0  0 0  0 0 0 0  0 0
0 0 0 0 0 1  0 0  0 0  0 0 0 0  0 0
va 1.08341 te 3 3
OU NS SE PC TV pt ND = 3 add = off so to it = 100
```

COMMENTS ON "WHERE HAVE ALL THE SUBJECTS GONE?" AND "MODELING INCOMPLETE LONGITUDINAL AND CROSS-SECTIONAL DATA USING LATENT GROWTH STRUCTURAL MODELS"

DONALD B. RUBIN

Chapters 16 and 17 (which I refer to collectively by an acronym of the authors' names, ERMH) have several features that make them consistent with modern themes in the field of statistics, and consequently I'm quite positive about the material. First, they involve the serious consideration of an actual (as opposed to simulated) data set that addresses questions of scientific interest. Second, they use appealing visual displays of data to help convey insight. And third, conclusions are not overstated; in particular, structural equations models (SEMs) are used to describe relationships and not to make causal inferences. My comments concern (a) three general themes in their data analyses, (b) the power of cogent visual displays of information, (c) two important modern statistical tools for handling missing data, and (d) four ultramodern statistical tools to facilitate the analysis of complicated models and help display results visually.

GENERAL ISSUES IN THE ERMH ANALYSES

Longitudinal data sets typically suffer from attrition and other forms of missing data. As a result, sample sizes in important subgroups become too small to analyze in traditional ways. Some "borrowing of strength" across subgroups is needed to address the scientific questions of interest. There are two distinct ways of doing this. First, the number of parameters can be reduced by setting some to zero, as when fitting an additive analysis of variance (setting interactions to zero), or, equivalently in a formal sense, by setting some parameters equal to others, as when setting some longitudinal and cross-sectional parameters equal to each other. This is the approach ERMH take in their SEMs. Another approach, currently very popular within the field of statistics itself, is called the Bayesian (or empirical-Bayesian or hyperparameter) approach, whereby some parameters are given distributions governed by a smaller set of parameters. The parameters with distributions, the random parameters, can be treated formally as missing data. Such models allow the data analyst to avoid setting some parameters equal to zero by instead giving them a distribution with mean and variance to be estimated. Relatively early accessible references include Efron and Morris (1977) and Rubin (1980). Social scientists with data sets like those of ERMH may wish to acquaint themselves with these techniques because they have proved successful in a variety of applications with sparse data.

My second general comment on the work of ERMH concerns the inclusion of both respondents and dropouts in data analyses. Doing so is an extremely important component of analyses that adjust for biases due to systematic differences between respondents and dropouts. Regardless of whether statistical tests reject the hypothesis that there is no bias, it is crucial to adjust for observed differences between respondents and dropouts, as ERMH do. A statistical analysis should almost never end with a rejection of a null hypothesis but rather with the formulation of a model that fits the data. This can often be accomplished in simple problems by calculating effect-size estimates with associated standard errors, but in more complicated problems, such as those of ERMH, visual summaries of models that fit the data are usually very helpful.

This leads to a third general point. Complicated analyses are often necessary in complicated problems, but unless their conclusions can be presented in transparent summaries that can be supported directly by the raw data, they should not be trusted. Too often, the results of complicated analyses are summarized without making clear how the conclusions are consistent with the raw data. The role of fancy analysis is to discover structure in the raw data, but once the structure is discovered (or formulated), the fancy analysis should be either supplemented with simple, direct summaries or displayed in meaningful ways that allow the conclusions to be understood and compared with the raw data.

THE POWER OF VISUAL DISPLAYS

The power of a visual display of a complicated analysis is illustrated by reconstructed images of the brain, such as those presented by Albert at the "Best Methods for the Analysis of Change" conference. Such images are actually the result of very complicated analyses, which often can be viewed as analyzing missing data problems. With positron emission tomography, observations are not made inside the brain but rather in detector pairs placed in a ring around the brain, where an observation in a detector pair implies a positron emission somewhere in the tube joining the two detectors. The missing datum is the exact location in the tube from which the emission emanated. The expectation-maximization (EM) algorithm, discussed in the next section, can be used to reconstruct the brain image by explicitly considering the problem as one of missing data (Vardi, Shepp, & Kaufman, 1985).

The visual reconstruction actually summarizes approximately 10,000 parameters giving intensities in a 100×100 grid of pixels in the brain, but it is wonderfully evocative of the underlying science in a way the list of the 10,000 parameters is not. When the raw data in the form of the relative counts in the detector pairs are compared with the implied counts from the reconstruction, the correspondence between the visual summary and the raw data can be directly evaluated.

TWO MODERN TOOLS FOR THE ANALYSIS OF DATA WITH MISSING VALUES

EM Algorithm

Two modern statistical tools play a major role in the analysis of data with missing values: factored likelihoods (Rubin, 1974) and the EM algorithm (Dempster, Laird, & Rubin, 1977). Both have been extensively discussed by Little and Rubin (1987) as well as a variety of other places, and consequently the presentation here is cursory.

Attrition in longitudinal studies often creates a missing-data pattern that is nearly monotone: Some people provide data at all time periods, some miss only the last, and others miss all but the first period. In such cases with common models, the analysis can proceed sequentially using a series of regressions, first predicting the least observed group of variables from all other variables using the subjects who provided responses on all variables, second predicting the second least observed group of variables from the more observed variables using all subjects who provided data on this second group of variables, and so on. After all of these analyses are complete, the answers from the various regressions can be combined to provide one summary analysis.

When using complicated models that constrain parameters in different time periods to be related, the factored-likelihood approach is not really appropriate, nor is it directly applicable when the pattern of missing data is not monotone. In such cases, the EM algorithm can often be applied (Dempster, Laird, & Rubin,

1977). EM is iterative, and each iteration has two steps, the E step, which calculates the expectation of the missing data (actually, the expectation of the incompletely observed sufficient statistics) given current estimates of parameters, and the M step, which applies standard complete-data maximum likelihood estimation, assuming the complete-data statistics estimated at the E step were actually observed. Each iteration increases the likelihood, and in most problems EM converges to the maximum likelihood estimate of the parameter for the missing data problem.

The key idea of EM is that it uses standard complete-data tools (for maximum likelihood estimation and obtaining conditional expectations) iteratively to solve the problem, thereby capitalizing on the widespread availability of modern computing. For some problems, EM cannot be easily applied, typically because of analytic difficulties in carrying out the E step, and in other problems the large-sample assumptions underlying maximum likelihood estimation itself may not be justifiable. Other methods are then needed.

Ultramodern Statistical Tools Based on Simulation Techniques

Obtaining inferences by taking random draws of missing values or of parameters themselves is a rapidly growing topic in statistics today. Four techniques are briefly introduced here; more extensive discussion, although still brief, is offered by Rubin (1991).

Multiple imputation (Rubin, 1987a) replaces each missing value by a set of $M > 1$ plausible values chosen to represent the uncertainty, given the observed data, about which values to impute. A multiply-imputed data set implies M completed data sets, each created by filling in one of the M sets of imputations. Each such completed data set is analyzed by complete-data methods, and these analyses are easily combined to yield valid inferences under the model used to create the imputations.

Data augmentation (Tanner & Wong, 1987) can be viewed as a small sample version of EM with multiple imputation used for both the E step and the M step. That is, at the E step, the missing values are multiply-imputed to create a distribution for the missing values given the current estimate for the distribution of the parameters, and at the M step the parameters are multiply-imputed to create a distribution for the parameters given the current estimate of the distribution of the missing data obtained at the E step. The sequence of iterations converges to the correct joint distribution of missing values and parameters.

Stochastic relaxation is similar to data augmentation with $M = 1$ and k independent replications. Also, stochastic relaxation can partition the missing data and parameters into p sets of random variables, $\phi_1, \ldots, \phi_p$. At each iteration, stochastic relaxation cycles through the p parts drawing a value of ϕ_i given values for all the other parts ϕ_j, $j \neq i$. It too converges to the correct joint posterior distribution of the missing data and the parameters. It is especially appropriate in problems with complicated clique (or neighborhood) structures on the random variables, as naturally arise in Markov random field models with Gibbsian prior distributions for image reconstruction (Geman & Geman, 1984). Because of its extensive application to these models in recent years, the method is now more commonly known in statistics as the Gibbs sampler (Gelfand & Smith, 1990). The iterative procedure can also be useful for multiply-imputing data, as shown by Rubin and Schafer (1991).

Another important tool in such problems is the sampling, importance re-sampling (SIR) algorithm (Rubin, 1987b), which is a noniterative method for helping to draw values from intractable distributions. The key idea is to take many draws, say N, from an approximation to the desired distribution, and then to redraw a few ($M < N$) with probability proportional to the N importance ratios, calculated as the ratio of the density of the drawn value under the correct distribution to its density under the drawing distribution. SIR has been used to create multiple imputations of industry and occupation codes in U.S. Census Bureau public-use files (Rubin & Schenker, 1987) and seems to have many applications in problems that are otherwise difficult to handle.

BACK TO THE ERMH DATA

One of the advantages of drawing inferences via the simulation techniques just outlined is that drawn values are closer to the data than are the usual summaries (e.g., parameter estimates, standard errors, and p values). To illustrate in the context of the ERMH study, the dropouts could have their missing data multiply imputed with $M = 2$ to create two possible lines emanating from each $+$ in Figures 16.6 and 16.7. An even more extensive use of simulation could also visually display the drawn values of the parameters themselves. I strongly encourage the continued use of modern statistical ideas and the consideration of some even newer methods based on simulation techniques to analyze such data.

CHAPTER 18

HOW LONG DID IT TAKE? USING SURVIVAL ANALYSIS IN EDUCATIONAL AND PSYCHOLOGICAL RESEARCH

JOHN B. WILLETT AND JUDITH D. SINGER

Editors' Introduction

Advances in one area of science often do not pass into other areas as readily as it seems they should. Part of the reason for this is that each area of science speaks in its own language. A method developed in one field is described in the argot of that discipline and from the point of view of that discipline, which makes it difficult for outsiders to understand the method and see its relevance for work in their own field.

Chapter 18 adroitly helps to effect the smooth transfer of an important method from the biological sciences, where the method has proved to be of considerable value, to the behavioral sciences, where the method is likely to have many worthy applications. The method to which we refer is survival analysis. Willett and Singer present this method in language that social scientists readily can understand and with examples that clearly show its relevance for dealing with research questions of importance to these scientists.

Earlier versions of this chapter were presented at the Workshop on Long-Term Follow-Up Strategies, National Institutes of Child Health and Human Development, Bethesda, Maryland, June 1989, and the biennial meeting of the Society for Research in Child Development, Kansas City, Missouri, April 1989. The order of the authors has been determined by randomization.

Survival analysis can be important in the study of change because basic questions of change often are, albeit implicitly, questions of duration and survival. For example, research questions framed as questions of "success"—success in school, in work, or in aging—can be seen to be, implicitly, questions of how many and how long (for some people never get to a specified end point). For example, How many completed the program? How many are still doing X (e.g., working or attending school) after y months, z years, and so on? How long do people continue to live before Alzheimer's disease sets in? How long do adolescents delay before taking up regular use of alcohol if they have (vs. have not) taken part in an alcohol use prevention program? How long does it take before students in a remedial program read at, or above, their grade level? Do convicts who pass from prison through a halfway house to the community spend more time arrest free than comparable convicts who do not get the halfway house experiences? Questions such as these can be effectively studied with the methods Willett and Singer describe in chapter 18.

In addition to posing questions about individual growth (in which time is a predictor), researchers can also frame their research questions so that time is treated as an outcome (Willett & Singer, 1989). Instead of asking how rapidly children change over time, researchers can inquire how much time must pass before a specific type of change or a specific event occurs. Such questions are about duration and differences in duration from child to child.

In this chapter, we identify problems that arise when duration data are collected and analyzed, and present a conceptual introduction to new methods that resolve these problems. We begin by identifying types of research questions that appropriately frame time as the outcome. We then describe innovative statistical methods for answering such questions, discuss their advantages, and comment on estimation strategies that use existing, and widely available, statistical software.

QUESTIONS THAT TREAT TIME AS THE OUTCOME

Many research arenas involve the study of time as an outcome. Some examples include (a) mothers' response times (How long does it take a mother to respond to her baby's cry? Do first-time mothers respond more quickly than second-time mothers?), (b) children's attention spans (How long are children's attention spans? Do boys have shorter attention spans than girls?), and (c) time to master a task (How long does it take to acquire a skill? Is the length of time shorter for children who attended an innovative training program?). Other examples include questions about recidivism, attrition, time to qualification, career length, and mortality.

Furthermore, many research questions that have traditionally treated time as a predictor can profitably be reformulated with time as the outcome. Rather than asking "Does children's moral behavior develop systematically over time?"

we can ask "How much time must pass before children reach a given moral stage?" Powerful new statistical methods can be brought to bear when research questions are reframed in terms of the amount of time needed to achieve a criterion. A different and useful perspective can then be achieved through alternative data analyses.

For each aforementioned research domain, two types of questions can be posed. The first concerns the average length of time that must pass before a specific event of interest occurs. The second concerns the association between duration and predictors. Research is concerned with more than what happens on the average; it seeks to determine which background characteristics can predict variation around the average. Why do some mothers breastfeed for years, whereas others breastfeed for a few months? Why do some friendships last a lifetime, whereas others fizzle out quickly? These relational questions focus on variation in duration as a function of predictors: Does duration differ by group membership, treatment, environment, or background?

HOW ARE QUESTIONS ABOUT DURATION ANSWERED?

Researchers studying duration typically collect data on a sample of children for a preselected period of time (usually as long as the researcher can afford it). The outcome variable is then the amount of time that passes before the event of interest—mother's response, task mastery, graduation, or job quitting—occurs. At issue is how the data are to be analyzed.

One might think that an appropriate analytic approach is to estimate the mean length of time until the event of interest occurs. Then, subsequent analyses could focus on factors associated with interindividual variation in duration and perhaps could be conducted using duration (or, alternatively, log duration) as the outcome in regression analyses or analyses of variance. But if this is attempted, an analytic dilemma is encountered. What value of duration should be ascribed to those who do not experience the event of interest before data collection ends? These people provide us with "censored" durations—we know only that the event did not happen to them within the period of observation. With limited resources, data collection invariably ends before every individual has experienced the event in question.

One tempting, but unsatisfactory, solution is to eliminate the censored observations from the analyses entirely and study only the people who were not censored. This strategy necessarily distorts (negatively biases) the complete distribution of the waiting times. If some people waited longer than the entire period of data collection, then the average length of time to event is certainly longer than that found among the uncensored people. Data on the censored cases tell us much, especially about the possibility that the average duration is likely to be longer than the length of data collection. Accurate analysis of duration data must attend to the censored cases, even though their durations are unknown.

SURVIVAL ANALYSIS

Survival analysis is the preferred analytic alternative, a technique that incorporates both censored and uncensored cases in a single analysis (Cox, 1972; Kalbfleisch & Prentice, 1980).[1] In survival analyses, we do not examine duration directly. Instead, we make use of two mathematical transformations of duration that remain meaningful in the face of censoring: the *survivor function* and the *hazard function*. Although not examining duration directly may make it appear that survival analysis avoids the very outcome of interest—time—this inference is incorrect. Because the survivor and hazard functions are transformations of duration, findings can be retransformed after data analysis and interpreted in the original metric of duration.

We shall illustrate survival analysis with a simulated example based on data collected in the National Day Care Home Study (NDCHS; Singer, Fosburg, Goodson, & Smith, 1978).[2] Although our example describes how long children stayed in family day care, we could just as easily be analyzing data describing how long friendships last, how long before juvenile delinquents commit another crime, or how long it takes to master a task.

The Survivor Function

Survival analysis begins with the survivor function, in this case, a display of the probability of remaining in (''surviving'') day care plotted against time. Providing the sample of children has been representatively drawn, this plot describes the likelihood that a randomly selected child will remain in day care longer than a specific period of time—6 months, 1 year, 2 years, and so on. At the beginning of a study, when all children have entered day care, 100% are surviving, and the survival probability is 1.00. Over time, children leave day care and the survivor function drops steadily toward zero, although, because some children are usually censored, the sample survivor function rarely reaches zero. Formal mathematical definitions of the survivor function have been given by Allison (1984) and Kalbfleisch and Prentice (1980).

---

[1]In a separate but parallel development, economists and sociologists refer to survival analysis as ''event-history analysis'' (Allison, 1984; Blossfeld, Hamerle, & Mayer, 1989; Tuma & Hannan, 1984).

[2]The original NDCHS raw data were no longer available to us. Therefore, we used computer simulation to reconstruct individual level duration and covariate information on the basis of available published summary statistics (including estimated survivor and hazard functions).

Figure 18.1 shows the empirical survivor function for all of the children in our sample. About 82% of the children survived (remained in day care) more than 1 year, about 72% survived more than 2 years, and about 50% survived more than 3.1 years. This last number is the estimated *median lifetime*, an intuitively meaningful summary statistic indicating how long before half the sample leave day care. The estimated median lifetime answers the descriptive question, How many years, on average, does a family day-care arrangement last? The statistic takes both censored and uncensored cases into account.

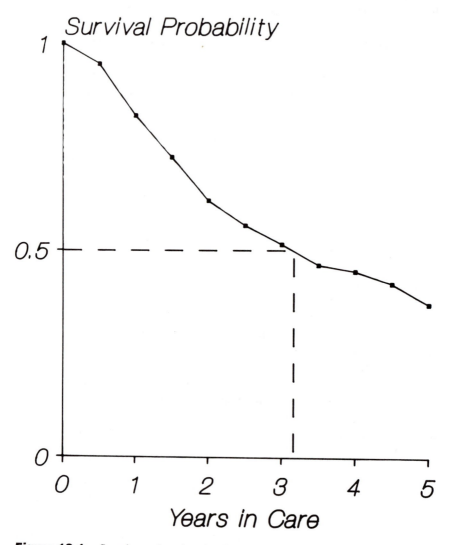

Figure 18.1   Sample survivor function for the children in the day-care study.

Rigorous treatments of survival analysis distinguish between duration measured *continuously* and duration measured *discretely*. (See Kalbfleisch & Prentice, 1980, for a thorough discussion of this issue.) In the former case, the sample durations can take on any nonnegative value. Such continuity, however, is not a condition that is easily realized in the practice of research. More often than not, duration is known only at specific points in time because the events under investigation only occur, or can only be measured, at particular times. For instance, in the present example, the length of time that children spent in family day care was known only to the nearest 6 months. For this reason, the present empirical survivor and hazard functions are not displayed as continuous functions but as chains of short line segments (see Miller, 1981).

The Hazard Function

If a large fraction of continuing children suddenly leave day care in a particular time period, the survivor function drops sharply, as happens in our example in the latter halves of Years 1 and 2. Sudden changes in the slope of the survivor function indicate periods of time when children are at a higher risk of leaving day care. This suggests that an accurate way to identify particularly risky time periods is to examine the slope of the survivor function for dramatic fluctuations. A refinement is to examine the hazard function, a sensitive barometer that detects changes in the slope of the survivor function. When duration has been measured discretely (as in this analysis), hazard can be defined as the conditional probability that a child will leave day care in a specific time period given that he or she has remained in care until that time.[3]

Like the survivor function, the hazard function can also be plotted out as a profile to describe the risk of a child's leaving day care at each time period given that the child has remained in day care up to that point. The magnitude of the hazard indicates the risk associated with each time period. Figure 18.2 presents the sample hazard profile corresponding to the survivor function in Figure 18.1. Comparing hazard at different time periods helps identify particularly risky time periods. In Figure 18.2, for instance, notice that the risk of leaving day care is elevated during the second year and then gradually declines through the fourth year, only to rise again when children begin to reach elementary school age.[4]

---

[3]Explicit definitions of the hazard function distinguish between duration measured *discretely* and duration measured *continuously*. In the former case, hazard is a conditional probability, and in the latter case it is a rate (Kalbfleisch & Prentice, 1980). Because the duration data in this analysis are measured discretely, we have framed our discussion in terms of conditional probability.

[4]Statistical methods are available for constructing confidence intervals around both survivor and hazard functions and for testing differences in these functions among groups (see Kalbfleisch & Prentice, 1980).

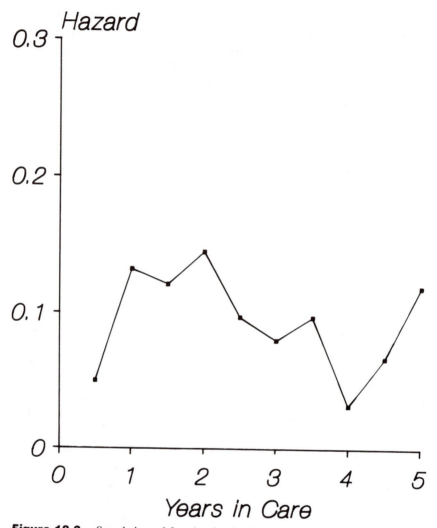

Figure 18.2   Sample hazard function for the children in the day-care study.

Identifying Predictors of Duration

Having described the sample as a whole, the next step in a survival analysis is to investigate predictors of interindividual variation in duration. A good exploratory strategy for investigating such relations is to compare sample survivor plots and hazard plots computed separately for children who share specific values of the predictors. This strategy is illustrated in Figure 18.3, which shows sample survivor functions and hazard functions for two groups of children: those in the care of a

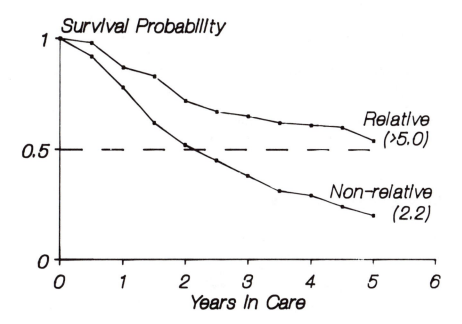

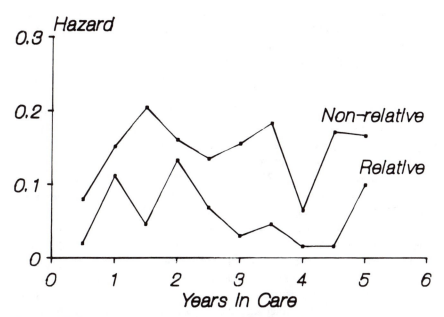

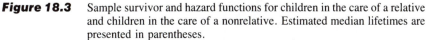

Figure 18.3 Sample survivor and hazard functions for children in the care of a relative and children in the care of a nonrelative. Estimated median lifetimes are presented in parentheses.

relative and those in the care of a nonrelative. The two pairs of profiles are distinct and clearly separated and indicate that children placed in the care of a relative are more likely to stay in day care.

The sample median lifetimes given in Figure 18.3 are one summary of the overall effect of type of care. For children in the care of a relative, median lifetime is more than 5 years; for children in the care of a nonrelative, it is 2.2 years. We conclude that, in this sample, care provided by a relative lasts at least 2.8 years longer, on average, than care provided by a nonrelative.

Building Statistical Models of Hazard

Plots of sample survivor and hazard functions depict relations between duration and each of the predictors. But for the same reasons that linear regression models are fitted to represent relations between an outcome and multiple predictors, we seek methods for summarizing the relations between duration and several predictors.

One good approach is to model the relation between the entire hazard profile and the predictors. To understand the concept behind such *hazard models*, examine the hazard profiles presented in Figure 18.3 and think of the type of care as a dummy predictor (RELCARE) which can take on the value 0 or 1. In this conceptualization, ignoring for the moment minor differences in the shape of the profiles, the effect of RELCARE is to displace the two hazard profiles vertically, relative to each other. When RELCARE takes on the value of 1 (relative care), the entire hazard function is lower compared with its location when RELCARE takes on the value of 0 (nonrelative care). A statistical model that captures this vertical displacement represents the logit transformation of the hazard profile (to account for the bounded nature of discrete hazard) as a function of predictors in much the same way as any outcome is expressed as a function of predictors in an ordinary multiple regression model. A population discrete-duration hazard model with RELCARE as a predictor is as follows: $\text{logit } h(t) = \beta_0(t) + \beta_1 \text{RELCARE}$. $\beta_0(t)$ is the baseline (logit) hazard profile or *intercept*, which indicates the value of (logit) hazard when RELCARE takes on the value of 0. We write this intercept as $\beta_0(t)$, a function of time, because the hazard profile is a function of time, the risk of a child leaving day care rising and falling with the passing years. The slope parameter β_1 summarizes the effect of RELCARE on the baseline profile, indicating the vertical shift in (logit) hazard attributable to a one-unit difference in RELCARE (in our case, the vertical shift is negative because children in the care of a relative have a lower risk of leaving day care than children in the care of a nonrelative). We can estimate β_1 and use the estimate (in comparison to its standard error) to decide whether RELCARE is statistically associated with hazard (and duration).

SOME ADVANTAGES OF SURVIVAL ANALYSIS
WITH HAZARD MODELS

Hazard modeling has several advantages for the developmental researcher. In many ways the methodology is similar to, and has the same advantages as, multiple regression analysis. First, because many predictors can be included in one model, several effects can be examined simultaneously or the influence of one predictor can be investigated while others are controlled. Second, both continuous and categorical variables can be treated as predictors. Third, both main effects and interaction effects can be incorporated in the same model. Hazard models are as flexible as linear regression models; interactions between predictors can be examined by adding cross-product terms to main effects models. Fourth, fitted models can be used to display findings (and the median lifetime statistic can be used to summarize them).

Figure 18.4 shows fitted hazard and survivor functions from a discrete-time hazard model with three predictors: the child's ethnicity, the child's age at entry into day care, and a two-way interaction between these main effects. Notice that (a) children entering day care at a younger age tend to stay longer (the main effect of entry age), (b) Black children tend to stay longer than White children (the main effect of ethnicity), and (c) White children entering day care at an older age leave unusually quickly (the two-way interaction of entry age and ethnicity). Other methods of displaying the results of survival analyses have been provided by Murnane, Singer, and Willett (1988, 1989) and Singer and Willett (1988).

Hazard modeling also has two additional advantages unique unto itself. First, variables whose values change or fluctuate with time can also be used as predictors. The cost of day care, for example, will change over time and yet may maintain a constant per dollar effect on duration. Such time-varying covariates can be included directly as predictors in the hazard model rather than having to build a prior growth model to summarize the temporal trend. This feature is especially important for developmental research because incorporating time-varying covariates into hazard models permits relations between different developmental attributes to be investigated.

A second unique advantage is that we can test whether the *effect* of a predictor varies with time. When we begin building hazard models, we usually assume that a predictor has the same effect in Year 1, Year 2, Year 3, and so on. In the discrete-time model this is equivalent to assuming a constant vertical separation between the two (logit) hazard profiles on every occasion that duration is known. This is called the *proportional hazards assumption*. But if a predictor has a different effect at different times, then the proportional hazards assumption is violated and we must include an interaction between the predictor and time in our model to capture this additional effect.

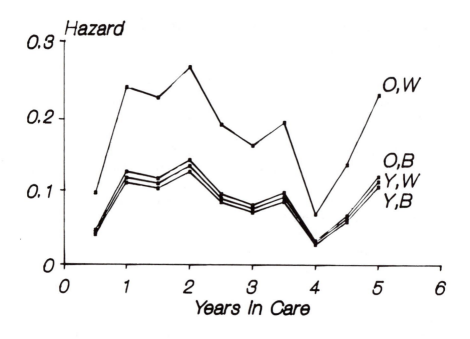

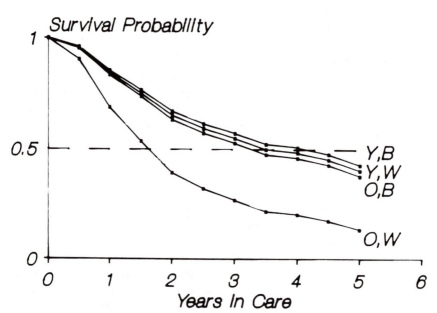

Figure 18.4   Fitted hazard and survivor functions obtained from a hazard model in which there were three effects: (a) the age of the child on entry into day care (Y = younger than 6 months, O = older than 6 months); (b) the ethnicity of the child (W = White, B = Black); and (c) the two-way interaction between the child's age and ethnicity.

STATISTICAL METHODS FOR FITTING HAZARD MODELS

The most common strategy for estimating the parameters of continuous-time hazard models is the method of partial likelihood (Cox, 1972). Although the estimation is based on complex statistical theory, these models are being used more often by empirical researchers because popular statistical packages such as SAS and BMDP now include procedures for their estimation (see Allison, 1984; Blossfeld, Hamerle, & Mayer, 1989). Without giving mathematical details, suffice it to say that the model parameters, their standard errors, and an overall chi-square goodness-of-fit statistic can be estimated for each model and inferences made to evaluate the relation between the predictors and duration. Good data analytic practice in continuous-time survival analysis is discussed by Willett and Singer (1988).

When duration has been measured discretely, as in this chapter, hazard is a conditional probability—the probability that an event will occur in a specific time period, given that it has not yet occurred. Discrete-time hazard modeling does not require dedicated software. Instead, model parameters can be estimated using standard log-linear modeling or logistic regression techniques. The use of logistic regression analysis to fit discrete-time hazard models requires the data analyst to restructure the data set before analysis (see Allison, 1982; Efron, 1988). In the rest of this chapter, we present a brief overview of discrete-time estimation strategy and we provide, in the appendix, SAS code for performing the required data manipulation, fitting discrete-time hazard models using logistic regression, and constructing fitted hazard and survivor profiles for interpretation and display.

Practically speaking, the procedure is simple. The original data set contains a single "line" of information for each person being investigated, with the following entries: (a) duration (measured discretely), (b) a dichotomous variable indicating whether the person's lifetime is censored, and (c) values of the selected predictors. Before the discrete-time analysis, this "person-oriented" data set is converted into a "person-period" data set in which each discrete time period for every person becomes a separate line containing termination, censoring information, and predictor information. For a child who stayed in day care through three time periods and left day care during the fourth time period (after two years, duration was measured discretely at 6-month intervals), the person-period data set has four discrete lines, one for each of the four time periods. Each of these new lines contains values of

> ◪ a new dichotomous dependent variable derived from the original duration information and censoring information, and designed to record whether the child is still in day care in each discrete time period. For a child who left day care during the fourth time period, the values of the new dependent variable would be 0, 0, 0, and 1. For a child who

was censored in the fourth time period, the new outcome would take
on values of 0, 0, 0, and 0.

- ☑ all the predictors. For time-invariant covariates, these values are identical to the initially measured value. For a child in the care of a relative for 2 years, RELCARE would have values 1, 1, 1, and 1. Time-
  varying covariates are given an appropriate and (potentially) different
  value in each time period. If the number of children present in the
  day-care home was to be treated as a time-varying covariate in the
  analyses, its values might be 11, 13, 7, and 7, as the size of the day-
  care group fluctuated with the passing months.

- ☑ a set of dummy variables denoting the time period to which each line
  in the new person-period data set corresponds. For instance, in the 5-
  year day-care example (with 6-month data collection), 10 dummy
  variables are required to represent all time periods. For each child, the
  first dummy takes on a value of 1 for the first 6 months (all other
  dummies are set to 0), the second dummy takes on a value of 1 for
  the second six months, and so on. When the discrete-time hazard
  model is fitted by logistic regression analysis, the estimated coefficients associated with the dummy predictors describe the shape of the
  baseline hazard function.[5] Interactions between the time period dummies and other predictors permit the effect of a given predictor to vary
  with time.

Using logistic regression analysis and the person-period data set, the new
dichotomous outcome is regressed on the time period dummies and the predictors.
Parameter estimates, standard errors, and goodness-of-fit statistics from these
analyses are exactly those required for the testing of the hazard models we have
described (Allison, 1982). Fitted probabilities from the obtained logistic regression
models provide estimates of the hazard probability in each discrete time period
so that both fitted hazard and survivor plots can be reconstructed (see this chapter's
appendix). Allison (1982) has provided further details of this procedure as well
as a worked example.

CLOSING THE CIRCLE

To recap, we began with a question about duration. To circumvent negative biases
associated with right censoring, the sample survivor function was constructed. To

---

[5] Of course, when the discrete-time hazard model is fitted, one of these "time dummies"
(usually the first) must be omitted from the logistic regression analyses to prevent multicollinearity.
After this selected time dummy has been dropped from the model, parameter estimates associated
with the remaining time dummies describe deviation of the baseline hazard from an initial value
provided by the fitted intercept in the logistic regression model.

increase sensitivity, the survivor function was expressed as a hazard function, and hazard was modeled as a function of predictors. On the basis of fitted models, predicted survivor and hazard functions were obtained at substantively interesting values of the predictors. Then, our analytic results were transformed back into the metric of interest—duration—using the median lifetime statistic. Thus, although a somewhat circuitous path was trodden, our data have been modeled appropriately and we are able to make statements about time as an outcome.

APPENDIX

SAS (Version 5) Code for
Estimating the Discrete-Time Hazard Models in This Chapter

* CREATING THE PERSON-PERIOD DATA SET *;

```
DATA FIRST;
  INFILE EXAMPLE;
  INPUT ID RELATIVE YOUNG MINORITY DURATION CENSOR;
  YOUNGMIN = YOUNG*MINORITY;

  ARRAY YRNO[10] YEAR01-YEAR10;
  DO YEAR = 1 TO DURATION;
    DO INDEX = 1 TO 10;
      IF YEAR = DURATION AND CENSOR = 0 THEN LEAVE = 1;
        ELSE LEAVE = 0;
      IF YEAR = INDEX THEN YRNO[INDEX] = 1;
        ELSE YRNO[INDEX] = 0;
    END;
    OUTPUT;
  END;

PROC FORMAT;
  VALUE GFMT  1="OLD WHITE"  2="YNG WHITE" 3="OLD MIN" 4="YNG MIN";
  VALUE TFMT  1="0.5 YRS" 2="1.0 YRS" 3="1.5 YRS" 4="2.0 YRS" 5="2.5 YRS"
              6="3.0 YRS" 7="3.5 YRS" 8="4.0 YRS" 9="4.5 YRS" 10="5.0 YRS";
  VALUE RFMT  1="NON-REL" 2="RELATIVE";
```

* MAIN EFFECTS OF YOUNG & MINORITY AS WELL AS THEIR INTERACTION *;

PROC LOGIST DATA=FIRST NOSIMPLE OUT=EST1;
    TITLE1 "MAIN EFFECTS OF YOUNG, MINORITY & THEIR INTERACTION";
    MODEL LEAVE = YEAR02-YEAR10 YOUNG MINORITY YOUNGMIN;

* COMPUTING FITTED HAZARD AND SURVIVAL FUNCTIONS *;

DATA EST1;
    SET EST1;
    IF _N_ = 1;

    YEAR01=0;
    GROUP1=0;
    GROUP2=YOUNG;
    GROUP3=MINORITY;
    GROUP4=YOUNG+MINORITY+YOUNGMIN;

    ARRAY GRP   [4] GROUP1-GROUP4;
    ARRAY YRNO [10] YEAR01-YEAR10;
    DO GROUP = 1 TO 4;
       DO TIME = 1 TO 10;
          X = INTERCEP + YRNO[TIME] + GRP[GROUP];
          HAZARD = 1/(1 + (EXP(-X)));
          IF TIME = 1 THEN SURVIVAL = (1 - HAZARD);
             ELSE SURVIVAL = (1 - HAZARD)*SURVIVAL;
          OUTPUT;
          END;
       END;
    KEEP GROUP TIME HAZARD SURVIVAL;

* DISPLAYING FITTED HAZARD AND SURVIVAL FUNCTIONS *;

PROC TABULATE FORMAT=10.4 DATA=EST1;
    CLASS GROUP TIME;
    VAR HAZARD SURVIVAL;
    FORMAT GROUP GFMT. TIME TFMT.;
    TABLE TIME, (HAZARD SURVIVAL)*GROUP/RTS=10;

PROC PLOT DATA=EST1;
    PLOT (SURVIVAL HAZARD)*TIME=GROUP;
    FORMAT TIME TFMT.;

* MAIN EFFECT OF RELATIVE, NO INTERACTION WITH TIME *;

```
PROC LOGIST DATA = FIRST NOSIMPLE OUT = EST2;
  TITLE1 "MAIN EFFECT OF RELATIVE CARE";
  MODEL LEAVE = YEAR02-YEAR10 RELATIVE;

DATA EST2;
  SET EST2;
  IF _N_ = 1;

  YEAR01  = 0;
  REL1    = 0;

  ARRAY YRNO [10] YEAR01-YEAR10;
  ARRAY REL   [ 2]  REL1 RELATIVE;
  DO RELCARE = 1 TO 2;
    DO TIME = 1 TO 10;
      X = INTERCEP + YRNO[TIME] + REL[RELCARE];
      HAZARD = 1/(1 + (EXP(-X)));
      IF TIME = 1 THEN SURVIVAL = (1 - HAZARD);
        ELSE SURVIVAL = (1 - HAZARD)*SURVIVAL;
      OUTPUT;
    END;
  END;
  KEEP RELCARE TIME HAZARD SURVIVAL;

PROC TABULATE FORMAT = 10.4 DATA = EST2;
  CLASS RELCARE TIME;
  VAR HAZARD SURVIVAL;
  FORMAT RELCARE RFMT. TIME TFMT.;
  TABLE TIME, (HAZARD SURVIVAL)*RELCARE/RTS = 10;

PROC PLOT DATA = EST2;
  PLOT (SURVIVAL HAZARD)*TIME = RELCARE;
  FORMAT TIME TFMT.;
```

* MAIN EFFECT OF RELATIVE AND AN INTERACTION WITH TIME *;

```
DATA SECOND;
  SET FIRST;

  ARRAY YRNO    [10] YEAR01-YEAR10;
  ARRAY RYEAR   [10] RYEAR01-RYEAR10;
  DO YEAR=1 TO 10;
    RYEAR[YEAR] = RELATIVE*YRNO[YEAR];
  END;

PROC LOGIST DATA=SECOND NOSIMPLE OUT=EST3;
  TITLE1 "MAIN EFFECTS OF RELCARE AND INTERACTIONS BET RELATIVE AND YEAR";
  MODEL LEAVE = YEAR02-YEAR10 RELATIVE RYEAR02-RYEAR10;

DATA EST3;
  SET EST3;
  IF _N_ = 1;

  YEAR01  = 0;
  RYEAR01 = 0;
  REL1    = 0;

  ARRAY YRNO    [10] YEAR01-YEAR10;
  ARRAY REL     [ 2] REL1 RELATIVE;
  ARRAY RELYR   [10] RYEAR01-RYEAR10;
  DO RELCARE = 1 TO 2;
    DO TIME = 1 TO 10;
      X   = INTERCEP + YRNO[TIME] + REL[RELCARE] + (RELCARE-1)*RELYR[TIME];
      HAZARD = 1/(1 + (EXP(-X)));
      IF TIME = 1 THEN SURVIVAL = (1 - HAZARD);
        ELSE SURVIVAL = (1 - HAZARD)*SURVIVAL;
      OUTPUT;
    END;
  END;
  KEEP RELCARE TIME HAZARD SURVIVAL;

PROC TABULATE FORMAT=10.4 DATA=EST3;
  CLASS RELCARE TIME;
  VAR HAZARD SURVIVAL;
  FORMAT RELCARE RFMT. TIME TFMT.;
  TABLE TIME, (HAZARD SURVIVAL)*RELCARE/RTS=10;

PROC PLOT DATA=EST3;
  PLOT (SURVIVAL HAZARD)*TIME=RELCARE;
  FORMAT TIME TFMT.;
```

References

Abelson, R. W., & Tukey, J. (1963). Efficient utilization of nonnumerical information in quantitative analysis: General theory and the case of simple order. *Annals of Mathematical Statistics, 34*, 1347–1369.

Adam, J. (1978). Sequential strategies and the separation of age, cohort, and time-of-measurement contributions to developmental data. *Psychological Bulletin, 85*, 1309–1316.

Agresti, A. (1984). *Analysis of ordinal categorical data.* New York: Wiley.

Ahmavaara, Y. (1954). The mathematical theory of factorial invariance under selection. *Psychometrika, 19*, 27–38.

Aitken, A. C. (1934). Note on selection from a multivariate normal population. *Proceedings of the Edinburgh Mathematical Society, 4*, 106–110.

Akaike, H. (1973). Information theory and an extension of the maximum likelihood principle. In B. N. Petrov & F. Csaki (Eds.), *Second international symposium on information theory.* Budapest: Akademiai Kiado.

Aldwin, C. M., Spiro, A., III, & Bosse, R. (1989). Longitudinal findings from the normative aging study: 1. Does mental health change with age? *Psychology and Aging, 4*(3), 295–306.

Allison, P. D. (1982). Discrete-time methods for the analysis of event histories. In S. Leinhardt (Ed.), *Sociological methodology* (pp. 61–98). San Francisco: Jossey-Bass.

Allison, P. D. (1984). *Event history analysis: Regression for longitudinal event data* (No. 07-046 in the Sage University paper series on quantitative applications in the social sciences). Beverly Hills, CA: Sage Publications.

Allison, P. D. (1987). Estimation of linear models with incomplete data. In C. C. Clogg (Ed.), *Sociological methodology* (pp. 71–103). San Francisco: Jossey-Bass.

Allison, R. B. (1960). *Learning parameters and human abilities.* Unpublished doctoral dissertation, Princeton, NJ.

Allport, G. W. (1937). *Personality.* New York: Holt.

Anderson, E. B. (1985). Estimating latent correlations between repeated testings. *Psychometrika, 50*, 3–16.

Anderson, T. W. (1978). Repeated measurements on autoregressive processes, *Journal of the American Statistical Association, 73*, 371–378.

Anderson, T. W. (1984). *An introduction to multivariate statistical analysis* (2nd ed.). New York: Wiley.

Aoki, M. (1987). *State space modeling of time series*. New York: Springer-Verlag.

Arminger, G., & Sobel, M. E. (1987). *Pseudo maximum likelihood estimation of mean and covariance structures with measurements from different data sources*. Unpublished manuscript.

Ashcraft, M. H., & Battaglia, J. (1978). Cognitive arithmetic: Evidence for retrieval and decision processes in mental addition. *Journal of Experimental Psychology: Human Learning and Memory*, 4, 527–538.

Baltes, P. B., Reese, H. W., & Nesselroade, J. R. (1977). *Life-span developmental psychology: Introduction to research methods*. Monterey, CA: Brooks/Cole.

Baltes, P. B., Reese, H. W., & Nesselroade, J. R. (1988). *Introduction to research methods: Life-span developmental psychology*. Hillsdale, NJ: Lawrence Erlbaum.

Baltes, P. B., Schaie, W., & Nardi, A. H. (1971). Age and experimental mortality in a seven-year longitudinal study of cognitive behavior. *Developmental Psychology*, 5, 18–26.

Baroody, A. (1983). The development of procedural knowledge: An alternative explanation for chronometric trends for mental arithmetic. *Developmental Review*, 3, 225–230.

Baroody, A. (1984). A reexamination of mental arithmetic models and data: A reply to Ashcraft. *Developmental Review*, 4, 148–156.

Bartholomew, D. J. (1987). *Latent variable models and factor analysis*. New York: Oxford University Press.

Bayley, N. (1956). Individual patterns of development. *Child Development*, 27, 45–74.

Bayley, N., & Pinneau, S. (1952). Tables for predicting adult height from skeletal age. *Journal of Pediatrics*, 40, 432.

Bell, R. Q. (1953). Convergence: An accelerated longitudinal approach. *Child Development*, 24, 145–152.

Bell, R. Q. (1954). An experimental test of the accelerated longitudinal approach. *Child Development*, 25, 281–286.

Bereiter, C. (1963). Some persisting dilemmas in the measurement of change. In C. W. Harris (Ed.), *Problems in measuring change*. Madison, WI: University of Wisconsin Press.

Bloomfield, P. (1976). *Fourier analysis of time series: An introduction*. New York: Wiley.

Blossfeld, H.P., Hamerle, A., & Mayer, K.U. (1989). *Event history analysis: Statistical theory and application in the social sciences*. Hillsdale, NJ: Lawrence Erlbaum.

Bock, R. D. (1976). Basic issues in the measurement of change. In D. N. M. de Gruijter & L. J. T. van der Kamp (Eds.), *Advances in psychological and educational measurement*. New York: Wiley.

Bock, R. D. (1983). The discrete Bayesian. In H. Wainer & S. Messick (Eds.), *Principals of modern psychological measurement: A festschrift for Frederick M. Lord* (pp. 103–115). Hillsdale, NJ: Lawrence Erlbaum.

Bock, R. D. (1986). Unusual growth patterns in the Fels data. In A. Demirjian & M. B. Duboc (Eds.), *Human growth: A multidisciplinary review* (pp. 69–84). London: Taylor and Francis.

Bock, R. D. (1989a). Measurement of human variation: A two-stage model. In R. D. Bock (Ed.), *Multilevel analysis of educational data* (pp. 319–342). San Diego: Academic Press.

Bock, R. D. (Ed.). (1989b). *Multilevel analysis of educational data*. San Diego: Academic Press.

Bock, R. D. (1990). *Marginal maximum likelihood estimation for the two-stage random regressions model with second stage covariates*. Unpublished manuscript.

Bock, R. D., & Aitkin, M. (1981). Marginal maximum likelihood estimation of item parameters: Application of an EM algorithm. *Psychometrika*, 46, 443–459.

Bock, R. D., & Thissen, D. (1976). Fitting multi-component models for growth in stature. *Proceedings of the 9th International Biometrics Conference, 1*, 431–442.

Bock, R. D., & Thissen, D. (1980). Statistical problems of fitting individual growth curves. In F. E. Johnston, A. F. Roche, & C. Susanne (Eds.), *Human physical growth and maturation: Methodologies and factors* (pp. 265–290). New York: Plenum.

Bock, R. D., & Thissen, D. (1983). *TRIFIT: A program for fitting and displaying triple-logistic growth curves.* Mooresville, IN: Scientific Software, Inc.

Bock, R. D., Wainer, H., Petersen, A., Thissen, D., Murray, J., & Roche, A. (1973). A parameterization for individual human growth curves. *Human Biology, 45*, 63–80.

Bollen, K. A. (1987). Total, direct, and indirect effects in structural equation models. In C. Clogg (Ed.), *Sociological methodology* (pp. 37–69). San Francisco: Jossey Bass.

Boomsma, A. (1983). *On the robustness of LISREL maximum likelihood estimation against small sample size and non-normality.* Unpublished doctoral dissertation, Department of Statistics and Measurement, University of Groningen, Groningen, Holland.

Boomsma, D. I., Martin, N. G., & Molenaar, P. C. M. (1989). Factor and simplex models of repeated measures: Application to two psychomotor measures of alcohol sensitivity in twins. *Behavior Genetics, 19*, 79–96.

Boomsma, D. I., & Molenaar, P. C. M. (1987). The genetic analysis of repeated measures. I. Simplex models. *Behavior Genetics, 17*, 111–123.

Botwinick, J., & Siegler, I. (1980). Intellectual ability among the elderly: Simultaneous cross-sectional and longitudinal comparisons. *Developmental Psychology, 16*, 49–53.

Box, G. E. P., & Tiao, G. C. (1977). A canonical analysis of multiple time series. *Biometrika, 64*, 355–365.

Box, G. E. P., & Taio, G. (1981). Modeling multiple time series with applications. *Journal of the American Statistical Association, 76*, 802–810.

Bracewell, R. N. (1986). *The Hartley transform.* London, UK: Oxford University Press.

Bracewell, R. N. (1989). *The Fourier transform.* London, UK: Oxford University Press.

Brillinger, D. R. (1973). The analysis of time series collected in an experimental design. In P. A. Krishnaiah (Ed.), *Multivariate analysis III* (pp. 241–256). New York: Academic Press.

Browne, M. W. (1984). Asymptotically distribution free methods for the analysis of covariance structures. *British Journal of Mathematical and Statistical Psychology, 37*, 62–83.

Browne, M. W. (1989, June). *Asymptotic robustness of normal theory methods for the analysis of latent curves.* Paper presented at the Summer Research Conference: Statistical Analysis of Measurement Error Models and Applications. Humboldt State University, Humboldt, CA.

Browne, M. W., & Cudeck, R. (1989). Single sample cross-validation indices for covariance structures. *Multivariate Behavioral Research, 24*, 445–455.

Browne, M. W., & Du Toit, S. H. C. (1987). *Automated fitting of nonstandard models* (Report WS-39). Pretoria: Human Sciences Research Council.

Brunswick, E. (1956). *Perception and the representative designs of experiments.* Berkeley, CA: University of California Press.

Bryk, A. S., & Raudenbush, S. W. (1987). Application of hierarchical linear models to assessing change. *Psychological Bulletin, 101*, 147–158.

Burt, C. (1937). *The backward child.* New York: Appleton-Century.

Busse, E. W. (1969). Theories of aging. In E. W. Busse & E. Pfeiffer (Eds.), *Behavior and adaptation in later life* (pp. 11–32). Boston: Little Brown.

Campbell, D. T., & Fiske, D. W. (1959). Convergent and discriminant validation by the multitrait-multimethod matrix. *Psychological Bulletin, 56*, 81–105.

Campbell, D. T., & Stanley, J. C. (1963). Experimental and quasi-experimental designs for research on teaching. In N. L. Gage (Ed.), *Handbook of research teaching*. Chicago: Rand McNally.

Campbell, D. T., & Stanley, J. C. (1967). *Experimental and quasi-experimental designs for research*. Chicago: Rand McNally.

Carroll, J. D. (1968). Generalization of canonical correlation to three or more sets of variables. *Proceedings of the American Psychological Association*, 227–228.

Cartwright, P. H. (1984). A note on using state-dependent models with a time dependent variance. *Journal of Business and Economic Statistics*, 2(4), 410–413.

Cattell, R. B. (1950). *Personality: A systematic theoretical and factual study*. New York: McGraw Hill.

Cattell, R. B. (1952a). *Factor analysis*. New York: Harper.

Cattell, R. B. (1952b). The three basic factor analytic research designs—their interrelationships and derivatives. *Psychological Bulletin*, 49, 499–520.

Cattell, R. B. (1964). Validity and reliability: A proposed more basic set of concepts. *Journal of Educational Psychology*, 55, 1–22.

Cattell, R. B. (1966a). Patterns of change: Measurement in relation to state dimension, trait change, lability, and process concepts. In R. B. Cattell (Ed.), *Handbook of multivariate experimental psychology*. Chicago: Rand McNally.

Cattell, R. B. (1966b). The data box: Its ordering of total resources in terms of possible relational systems. In R. B. Cattell (Ed.), *Handbook of multivariate experimental psychology*. Chicago: Rand McNally.

Cattell, R. B. (1988). The data box: Its ordering of total resources in terms of possible relational systems. In J. R. Nesselroade & R. B. Cattell (Eds.), *Handbook of multivariate experimental psychology*. New York: Plenum.

Cliff, N. (1977). A theory of consistency of ordering generalizable to tailored testing. *Psychometrika*, 42, 375–401.

Cliff, N. (1979). Test theory without true scores? *Psychometrika*, 44, 373–393.

Cliff, N. (1989a). Ordinal consistency and ordinal true scores. *Psychometrika*, 54, 75–91.

Cliff, N. (1989b). "*Multiple regression*" with ordinal variables: A new approach. Unpublished manuscript.

Cliff, N., & Charlin, V. C. (in press). Covariances of Kendall's tau. *Multivariate Behavioral Research*.

Cliff, N., & Donoghue, J. R. (1990). *Ordinal test fidelity estimated by an item sampling model*. Unpublished manuscript.

Cliff, N., McCormick, D. J., Zatkin, J. L., Cudeck, R. A., & Collins, L. M. (1986). BINCLUS: Nonhierarchical clustering of binary data. *Multivariate Behavioral Research*, 21, 201–227.

Collins, L. M. (in press). The measurement of dynamic latent variables in longitudinal aging research: Quantifying adult development. *Experimental Aging Research*.

Collins, L. M., & Cliff, N. (1985). Axiomatic foundations of a three-set Guttman simplex model with applicability to longitudinal data. *Psychometrika*, 50, 147–158.

Collins, L. M., & Cliff, N. (1990). Using the longitudinal Guttman simplex as a basis for measuring growth. *Psychological Bulletin*, 108, 128–134.

Collins, L. M., Cliff, N., & Dent, C. W. (1988). The longitudinal Guttman simplex: A new methodology for measurement of dynamic constructs in longitudinal panel studies. *Applied Psychological Measurement*, 12, 217–230.

Collins, L. M., & Dent, C. W. (1986). *LGSINDEX user's guide. Technical Report 86–100*. Los Angeles: Health Behavior Research Institute.

Collins, L. M., Wugalter, S. E., & Chung, N. K. (1991). *Latent class models for stage-sequential dynamic latent variables*. Manuscript submitted for publication.

Conover, W. J. (1980). *Practical nonparametric statistics* (2nd ed.). New York: Wiley.

Cook, T., & Campbell, D. (1979). *Quasi-experimentation: Design and analysis issues for field settings.* Boston: Houghton Mifflin Company.

Coombs, C. H. (1964). *A theory of data.* Ann Arbor: Mathesis Press.

Corballis, M. C., & Traub, R. E. (1970). Longitudinal factor analysis. *Psychometrika, 35*(1), 79–98.

Cox, D. R. (1972). Regression models and life tables. *Journal of the Royal Statistical Society, Series B, 34,* 187–202.

Cronbach, L. J., & Furby, L. (1970). How should we measure "change"—or should we? *Psychological Bulletin, 74,* 68–80.

Cronbach, L. J., Gleser, G. C., Nande, H., & Rajaratnum, N. (1972). *The dependability of behavioral measurements: Theory of generalizability for scores and profiles.* New York: Wiley.

Cudeck, R. (1989). Analysis of correlation matrices using covariance structure models. *Psychological Bulletin, 105,* 317–327.

Cunningham, W. R., & Birren, J. E. (1980). Age changes in the factor structure of intellectual abilities in adulthood and old age. *Educational and Psychological Measurement, 40,* 271–290.

Dearborne, D. F. (1921). Intelligence and its measurement: A symposium. *Journal of Educational Psychology, 12,* 123–147 & 195–216.

Dempster, A. P., Laird, N. M., & Rubin, D. B. (1977). Maximum likelihood from incomplete data via the EM algorithm (with discussion). *Journal of the Royal Statistical Society, Series B, 39,* 1–38.

Dempster, A. P., Rubin, D. B., & Tsutakawa, R. K. (1981). Estimation in covariance component models. *Journal of the American Statistical Association, 76,* 341–353.

Donaldson, G., & Horn, J. L. (in press). Age, cohort, and time developmental muddles: Easy in practice, hard in theory. *Experimental Aging Research.*

Donoghue, J. R., & Cliff, N. (in press). An investigation of ordinal true score test theory. *Applied Psychological Measurement.*

Du Toit, S. H. C. (1979). *The analysis of growth curves.* Unpublished doctoral dissertation, Department of Statistics, University of South Africa, Pretoria.

Eaves, L. J., Long, L., & Heath, A. C. (1986). A theory of developmental change in quantitative phenotypes applied to cognitive development. *Behavior Genetics, 16,* 143–162.

Efron, B. (1988). Logistic regression, survival analysis, and the Kaplan–Meier curve. *Journal of the American Statistical Association, 83,* 414–425.

Efron, B., & Morris, C. (1977). Stein's paradox in statistics. *Scientific American, 236,* 119–127.

Elias, M. F., Elias, P. K., & Elias, J. W. (1989). Biological and health influences on behavior. In J. E. Birren & K. W. Schaie (Eds.), *Handbook on the psychology of aging* (pp. 79–102). San Diego: Academic Press.

Elias, M. F., Robbins, M. A., & Schultz, N. R., Jr. (1987). Influence of essential hypertension on intellectual performance: Causation or speculation. In J. W. Elias & P. H. Marshall (Eds.), *Cardiovascular disease and behavior* (pp. 67–101). Washington, DC: Hemisphere.

Elias, M. F., Robbins, M. A., Schultz, N. R., Jr., Streeten, D. H. P., & Elias, P. K. (1987). Clinical significance of cognitive performance by hypertensive patients. *Hypertension, 9,* 192–197.

Elias, M. F., Schultz, N. R., Jr., Robbins, M. A., & Elias, P. K. (1989). A longitudinal study of neuropsychological performance by hypertensives and normotensives: A third measurement point. *Journal of Gerontology, 41,* 503–505.

El Lozy, M. (1978). A critical analysis of the double and triple logistic growth curves. *Annals of Human Biology, 5*, 389–394.

Embretson, S. E. (1985). *Test design: Developments in psychology and psychometrics.* New York: Academic Press.

Embretson, S. E. (1987). Improving the measurement of spatial ability by a dynamic testing procedure. *Intelligence, 11*, 333–358.

Embretson, S. E. (in press). A multidimensional item response model for learning processes. *Psychometrika.*

Emmerich, W. (1968). Personality development and concepts of structure. *Child Development, 39*, 671–690.

Engle, R. F., & Watson, M. (1979). *A time domain approach to dynamic factor and MIMIC models.* San Diego: University of California Press.

Engle, R. F., & Watson, M. (1981). A one factor multivariate time series model of metropolitan wage rates. *Journal of the American Statistical Association, 76*(376), 774–781.

Evans, J. G. (1988). Aging and disease. In D. Evered & J. Whelan (Eds.), *Research and the aging population* (pp. 38–57). New York: Wiley.

Ferguson, G. A. (1965). *Nonparametric trend analysis.* Montreal: McGill University Press.

Fischer, G. H. (1976). Some probabilistic models for measuring change. In D. N. M. de Gruijter & L. J. T. van der Kamp (Eds.), *Advances in psychological and educational measurement.* New York: Wiley.

Fischer, K. W. (1980). A theory of cognitive development: The control and construction of hierarchies of skill. *Psychological Review, 87*, 477–531.

Fischer, K. W., & Pipp, S. L. (1985). Processes of cognitive development: Optimal level and skill acquisition. In R. J. Sternberg (Ed.), *Mechanisms of cognitive development* (pp. 45–80). San Francisco: W. H. Freeman.

Fiske, D. W., & Rice, L. (1955). Intraindividual response variability. *Psychological Bulletin, 52*, 217–250.

Flavell, J. H. (1963). *The developmental psychology of Jean Piaget.* Princeton, NJ: Van Nostrand.

Fligler, M. A., & Policello, G. E. (1981). Robust rank procedures for the Behrens-Fisher problem. *Biometrika, 69*, 221–226.

Fox, J. (1985). Effects analysis in structural equation models II: Calculation of specific indirect effects. *Sociological Methods and Research, 14*, 81–95.

Friedman, M. (1937). The use of ranks to avoid the assumption of normality implicit in the analysis of variance. *Journal of the American Statistical Association, 32*, 675–701.

Gasser, T., Kohler, W., Muller, H. G., Kneip, A., Largo, R., & Molinari, L. (1984). Velocity and acceleration of height growth using kernel estimation. *Annals of Human Biology, 11*, 397–411.

Geary, D. C., & Widaman, K. F. (1987). Individual differences in cognitive arithmetic. *Journal of Experimental Psychology: General, 116*, 154–171.

Geary, D. C., Widaman, K. F., & Little, T. D. (1986). Cognitive addition and multiplication: Evidence for a single memory network. *Memory and Cognition, 14*, 478–487.

Gelfand, A. E., & Smith, A. F. M. (1990). Sampling-based approaches to calculating marginal densities. *Journal of the American Statistical Association, 85*, 398–409.

Gelman, R. (1982). Basic numerical abilities. In R. J. Sternberg (Ed.), *Advances in the psychology of human intelligence: Vol. 1* (pp. 181–205). Hillsdale, NJ: Lawrence Erlbaum.

Geman, S., & Geman, D. (1984). Stochastic relaxation, Gibbs distributions and the Bayesian restoration of images. *IEEE Transactions on Pattern, Analysis and Machine Intelligence, 6*, 721–741.

Geweke, J. F. (1975). *Employment turnover and wage dynamics in U.S. manufacturing: Appendix B: Estimation and hypothesis testing in the frequency domain factor analysis model*. Doctoral thesis, University of Minnesota, Minneapolis, MN.

Geweke, J. F. (1977). The dynamic factor analysis of economic time-series models. In D. Aigner, & A. Goldberger (Eds.), *Latent variables in socio-economic models* (pp. 365–383). Amsterdam: North-Holland.

Geweke, J. F., & Singleton, K. J. (1977). *A general approach to latent variable models for time series*. New York: University of Wisconsin.

Geweke, J. F., & Singleton, K. J. (1981). Maximum likelihood "confirmatory" factor analysis of economic time series. *International Economic Review, 22*, 37–54.

Glass, J., Bengtson, V. L., & Dunham, C. C. (1986). Attitude similarity in three-generation families: Socialization, status inheritance, or reciprocal influence? *American Sociological Review, 51*, 685–698.

Goldstein, H. (1987). *Multilevel models in educational and social research*. London: Oxford University Press.

Goldstein, H. (1989). Models for multilevel response variables with applications to growth curves. In R. D. Bock (Ed.), *Multilevel analysis of educational data* (pp. 107–125). San Diego: Academic Press.

Goldstein, H. & McDonald, R. P. (1988). A general model for the analysis of multilevel data. *Psychometrika, 53*, 455–467.

Gollob, H. F., & Reichardt, C. S. (1985). Building time lags into causal models of cross-sectional data. In *Proceedings of the Social Statistics Section of the American Statistical Association: 1985* (pp. 165–170). Alexandria, VA: American Statistical Association.

Gollob, H. F., & Reichardt, C. S. (1987). Taking account of time lags in causal models. *Child Development, 58*, 80–92.

Graham, J. W., Collins, L. M., Wugalter, S. E., Chung, N. K., & Hansen, W. B. (1991). Modeling transitions in latent stage-sequential processes: A substance use prevention example. *Journal of Consulting and Clinical Psychology, 59*, 48–57.

Granger, C. W. J. (1969). Investigating causal relations by econometric models and cross spectral methods. *Econometrica, 37*, 424–438.

Granger, C. W. J., & Newbold, P. (1977). *Forecasting economic time series*. New York: Academic Press.

Green, B. F. (1977). Parameter sensitivity in multivariate methods. *Multivariate Behavioral Research, 12*, 263–288.

Groen, G. J., & Parkman, J. M. (1972). A chronometric analysis of simple addition. *Psychological Review, 79*, 329–343.

Grossman, M., & Koops, W. J. (1988). Multiphasic analysis of growth curves in chickens. *Poultry Science, 67*, 33–42.

Gulliksen, H. (1950). *Theory of mental tests*. New York: Wiley.

Guttman, L. (1944). A basis for scaling qualitative data. *American Sociological Review, 9*, 139–150.

Guttman, L. (1950). The basis for scalogram analysis. In S. A. Stouffer, L. Guttman, E. A. Suchman, P. Lazarsfeld, S. A. Star, & O. A. Clausen (Eds.), *Measurement and production* (pp. 60–90). Princeton, NJ: Princeton University Press.

Hagenaars, J. L., & Luijkx, R. (1990). *LCAG users' manual*. Tilburg University, The Netherlands, Department of Sociology. Working paper series #17.

Hannan, E. J. (1974). Time series analysis. *IEEE Transactions on Automatic Control, 19*, 707–715.

Hannan, E. J. (1976). The identification and parameterization of ARMAX and state space forms. *Econometrica, 39*, 751–765.

Harlow, L. L. (1985). *Behavior of some elliptical estimators with nonnormal data in a covariance structures framework: A Monte Carlo study.* Unpublished doctoral dissertation, Department of Psychology, University of California, Los Angeles.

Harris, C. W. (Ed.). (1963). *Problems in measuring change.* Madison: University of Wisconsin Press.

Harvey, A. C. (1981). *Time series models.* New York: Wiley.

Hawkes, R. J. (1971). The multivariate analysis of ordinal measures. *American Journal of Sociology, 76,* 908–926.

Hayes, S. C. (1981). Single case experimental design and empirical clinical practice. *Journal of Consulting and Clinical Psychology, 49,* 193–211.

Heckman, J. (1976), The common structure of statistical models of truncation, sample selection, and limited dependent variables and a simple estimator for such models. *Annals of Economic and Social Measurement, 5,* 475–492.

Hedeker, D. R. (1989). *Random regression models with correlated errors: Investigating drug plasma levels and clinical response.* Unpublished dissertation, Department of Behavioral Sciences, University of Chicago.

Hedeker, D. R., & Bock, R. D. (1990). *Random regression models with correlated errors.* Manuscript submitted for publication.

Heise, D. R. (1969). Separating reliability and stability in test-retest correlation. *American Sociological Review, 34,* 93–101.

Heise, D. R. (1975). *Causal analysis.* New York: Wiley.

Henderson, A. S., Byrne, D. G., & Duncan-Jones, P. (1981). *Neurosis and the social environment.* Sydney, Australia: Academic Press.

Hertzog, C. (1985). An individual differences perspective: Implications for cognitive research in gerontology. *Research on Aging, 7,* 7–45.

Hertzog, C. (1989). The influence of cognitive slowing on age differences in intelligence. *Developmental Psychology, 25,* 636–651.

Hertzog, C., & Nesselroade, J. R. (1987). Beyond autoregressive models: some implications of the trait–state distinction for the structural modeling of developmental change. *Child Development, 58,* 93–109.

Hertzog, C., & Schaie, K. W. (1988). Stability and change in adult intelligence: 2. Simultaneous analysis of longitudinal means and covariance structures. *Psychology and Aging, 3,* 122–130.

Hertzog, C., Schaie, K. W., & Gribbin, K. (1978). Cardiovascular disease and changes in intellectual function from middle to old age. *Journal of Gerontology, 33,* 872–883.

Hettmansperger, T.P. (1984). *Statistical inference based on ranks.* New York: Wiley.

Holland, P. W. (1986). Statistics and causal inference. *Journal of the American Statistical Association, 81,* 945–970.

Holtzman, W. H. (1963). Statistical models for the study of change in the single case. In C. W. Harris (Ed.), *Problems in measuring change.* Madison, WI: University of Wisconsin Press.

Horn, J. L. (1967). On subjectivity in factor analysis. *Educational and Psychological Measurement, 27,* 811–820.

Horn, J. L. (1972). State, trait, and change dimensions of intelligence. *British Journal of Educational Psychology, 42,* 159–185.

Horn, J. L. (1978). Human ability systems. In P. B. Baltes (Ed.), *Life-span development and behavior: Vol. 1* (pp. 211–256). New York: Academic.

Horn, J. L. (1985). Remodeling old models of intelligence. In B. Wolman (Ed.), *Handbook of intelligence.* New York: Wiley.

Horn, J. L. (1988). Thinking about human abilities. In J. R. Nesselroade & R. B. Cattell (Eds.), *Handbook of multivariate experimental psychology* (2nd ed.) (pp. 645–685). New York: Plenum.

Horn, J. L., & Cattell, R. B. (1967). Age differences in fluid and crystalized intelligence. *Acta Psychologica, 26*, 107–129.

Horn, J. L., & Donaldson, G. (1980). Cognitive development in adulthood. In O. G. Brim & J. Kagan (Eds.), *Constancy and change in human development* (pp. 445–529). Cambridge: Harvard University Press.

Horn, J. M., Loehlin, J. C., & Willerman, L. (1979) Intellectual resemblance among adoptive and biological relatives: The Texas Adoption Project. *Behavior Genetics, 9*, 177–207.

Horn, J. L., & McArdle, J. J. (1980). Perspectives on mathematical/statistical model building (MASMOB) in research on aging. In L. W. Poon (Ed.), *Aging in the 1980's: Psychological issues* (pp. 503–541). Washington, DC: American Psychological Association.

Horn, J. L., & McArdle, J. J. (in press). A practical and theoretical guide to measurement invariance. *Experimental Aging Research*.

Horn, J. L., McArdle, J., & Mason, R. (1983). When is invariance not invariant: A practical scientist's look at the ethereal concept of factor invariance. *Southern Psychologist, 1*, 179–188.

Horn, J. L., Wanberg, K. W., & Foster, F. M. (1990) *Guide to the Alcohol Use Inventory (AUI)*. Minnetonka, MN: National Computer Systems.

Horst, P. (1961a). Generalized canonical correlations and their applications to experimental data. *Journal of Clinical Psychology, Monograph Supplement, 14*, 331–347.

Horst, P. (1961b). Relations among m sets of measures. *Psychometrika, 26*, 129–149.

Hotelling, H. (1935). The most predictable criterion. *Journal of Educational Psychology, 26*, 139–142.

Hotelling, H. (1936). Relations between two sets of variates. *Biometrika, 28*, 321–377.

Humphreys, L. G. (1962). The organization of human abilities. *American Psychologist, 17*, 475–483.

Hunt, E. (1983). On the nature of intelligence. *Science, 219*, 141–146.

Johnston, F. E. (1980). Research design and sample selection in studies of growth and development. In F. E. Johnston, F. E. Roche, & C. Susanne (Eds.), *Human physical growth and maturation: Methodologies and factors* (pp. 5–19). New York: Plenum.

Jones, C. J., & Nesselroade, J. R. (in press). Multivariate, replicated, single-subject designs and P-technique factor analysis: A selective review of intraindividual change studies. *Experimental Aging Research*.

Jones, K. J. (1982). *A comparison of state transition and vector ARMA modeling procedures*. Cincinnati, OH: American Statistical Association.

Jones, K. J. (1983). An empirically derived vector ARMA model for monetary and financial variables. In O. D. Anderson (Ed.), *Time series analysis: Theory and practice, 7* (pp.289–292). Amsterdam: North-Holland.

Jöreskog, K. G. (1971). Simultaneous factor analysis in several populations. *Psychometrika, 36*, 409–426.

Jöreskog, K. G. (1979). Statistical estimation of structural models in longitudinal- developmental investigations. In J. Nesselroade & P. Baltes (Eds.), *Longitudinal research in human development: Design and analysis*. New York: Academic Press.

Jöreskog, K. G. (1982). The LISREL approach to causal model-building in the social sciences. In K. Jöreskog & H. Wold (Eds.), *Systems under indirect observation: Part 1*. New York, North-Holland.

Jöreskog, K. G., & Sörbom, D. (1979). *Advances in factor analysis and structural equations models.* Cambridge, MA: ABT Books.

Jöreskog, K. G., & Sörbom, D. (1986). *LISREL VI user's guide.* Chicago: International Educational Services.

Jöreskog, K. G,. & Sörbom, D. (1988). *LISREL VII: A guide to the program and applications.* Chicago: SPSS Inc.

Judd, C. M., & Kenny, D. A. (1981). *Estimating the effects of social interventions.* New York: Cambridge University Press.

Kail, R. V., Jr. (1984). *The development of memory in children* (2nd ed.). San Francisco: W. H. Freeman.

Kalbfleisch, J. D., & Prentice, R. L. (1980). *The statistical analysis of failure time data.* New York: Wiley.

Kalman, R. E. (1960). A new approach to linear filtering and prediction problems. *Journal of Basic Engineering, 82,* 35–45.

Kanfer, R. (1987). Task-specific motivation: An integrative approach to issues of measurement, mechanisms, processes, and determinants. *Journal of Social and Clinical Psychology, 5,* 237–264.

Kanfer, R., & Ackerman, P. L. (1989). Motivation and cognitive abilities: an integrative/ aptitude-treatment interaction approach to skill acquisition. *Journal of Applied Psychology, 74,* 657–690.

Keating, D. P. (1984). The emperor's new clothes: The "new look" in intelligence research. In R. J. Sternberg (Ed.), *Advances in the psychology of human intelligence* (Vol. 2, pp. 1–45). New York: Academic Press.

Kendall, M. G. (1938). A new measure of rank correlation. *Biometrika, 30,* 81–93.

Kendall, M. G. (1970). *Rank correlation methods.* London: Charles Griffin.

Kettenring, J. R. (1971). Canonical analysis of several sets of variables. *Biometrika, 58,* 433–451.

Kihlstrom, J. F. (1987). The cognitive unconscious. *Science, 237,* 1445–1452.

Koopmans, L. H. (1974). *The spectral analysis of time series.* New York: Academic Press.

Koreisha, S. G., & Pukkila, T. M. (1987). Identification of nonzero elements in the polynomial matrices of mixed VARMA processes. *Journal of the Royal Statistical Society, Series B, 49,* 112–126.

Krantz, D. H., Luce, R. D., Suppes, S., & Tversky, A. (1971). *Foundations of measurement.* New York: Academic Press.

Labovitz, S. (1967). Some observations on measurement and statistics. *Social Forces, 46,* 151–160.

Laird, N. M., & Ware, J. H. (1982). Random effects models for longitudinal data. *Biometrics, 38,* 963–974.

Lamiell, J. T. (1981). Toward an idiothetic psychology of personality. *American Psychologist, 36,* 276–289.

Lanczos, C. (1966). *Discourse on fourier series.* New York: Hafner Publishing Co.

Largo, R. H., Gasser, T., Prader, A., Stultzle, W., & Huber, P. J. (1978). Analysis of the adolescent growth spurt using smoothing splines. *Annals of Human Biology, 5,* 421–434.

Lawley, D. N. (1943). A note on Karl Pearson's selection formulae. *Proceedings of the Royal Society of Edinburgh* (Section A), *62,* 28–30.

Lebo, M. A., & Nesselroade, J. R. (1978). Intraindividual differences dimensions of mood change during pregnancy identified in five P-technique factor analyses. *Journal of Research in Personality, 12,* 205–224.

Lerner, R. M. (1986). *Concepts and theories of human development* (2nd ed.). New York: Random House.

Lidz, C. (1987). *Dynamic testing*. Beverly Hills, CA: Guilford Press.

Litterman, R. B. (1980). *A Bayesian procedure for forecasting with vector autoregressions*. Cambridge, MA: Massachusetts Institute of Technology.

Little, R. J. A. (1985). A note about models for selectivity bias. *Econometrica, 53*, 1469–1474.

Little, R. J. A., & Rubin, D. B. (1987). *Statistical analysis with missing data*. New York: Wiley.

Little, R. J. A., & Rubin, D. B. (1989). The analysis of social science data with missing values. *Sociological Methods and Research, 18*, 292–326.

Liu, L., & Hudak, G. (1983). *Unified econometric model building using simultaneous transfer function equations*. (Available from Scientific Computing Associates, Box 625, DeKalb, IL, 60115)

Loehlin, J. C. (1987). *Latent variable models: An introduction to factor, path, and structural analysis*. Hillsdale, NJ: Lawrence Erlbaum.

Loehlin, J. C., Horn, J. M., & Willerman, L. (1989). Modeling IQ change: Evidence from the Texas Adoption Project. *Child Development, 60*, 993–1004.

Loehlin, J. C., Horn, J. M., & Willerman, L. (1990). Heredity, environment, and personality change: Evidence from the Texas Adoption Project. *Journal of Personality, 58*, 221–243.

Loehlin, J. C., Willerman, L., & Horn, J. M. (1982). Personality resemblances between unwed mothers and their adopted-away offspring. *Journal of Personality and Social Psychology, 42*, 1089–1099.

Loehlin, J. C., Willerman, L., & Horn, J. L. (1987). Personality resemblance in adoptive families: A 10-year follow-up. *Journal of Personality and Social Psychology, 53*, 961–969.

Loevinger, J. A. (1947). A systematic approach to the construction and evaluation of tests of ability. *Psychological Monographs, 61*, (Whole No. 285).

Loevinger, J. A. (1948). A technique of homogeneous test evaluation compared with aspects of "scale analysis." *Psychological Bulletin, 45*, 507–529.

Longford, N. T. (1987). A fast scoring algorithm for maximum likelihood estimation in unbalanced mixed models with nested effects. *Biometrika, 74*, 817–827.

Longford, N. T. (1989). Fisher scoring algorithm for variance component analysis of data with multilevel structure. In R. D. Bock (Ed.), *Multilevel analysis of educational data*. New York: Academic Press.

Lord, F. M. (1963). Elementary models for measuring change. In C. W. Harris (Ed.), *Problems in measuring change*. Madison: University of Wisconsin Press.

Lord, F. W. (1980). *Applications of item response theory to practical testing problems*. Hillsdale, NJ: Lawrence Erlbaum.

Lord, F. W., & Novick, M. R. (1968). *Statistical theories of mental test scores*. Reading, MA: Addison-Wesley.

Luborsky, L., & Mintz, J. (1972). The contribution of P-technique to personality, psychotherapy, and psychosomatic research. In R. M. Dreger (Ed.), *Multivariate personality research: Contributions to the understanding of personality in honor of Raymond B. Cattell*. Baton Rouge, LA: Calitor's Publishing Division.

Mack, W. (1988). *Frailty models for the study of familial aggregation of disease*. Unpublished dissertation, University of Southern California.

MacLeod, C. , Hunt, E. B., & Mathews, N. N. (1978). Individual differences in the verification of sentence-picture relationships. *Journal of Verbal Learning and Verbal Behavior, 17*, 493–507.

Mann, H. B., & Whitney, D. R. (1947). On a test of whether one of two variables is stochastically larger than the other. *Annals of Mathematical Statistics, 18*, 50–60.

McArdle, J. J. (1982). *Structural equation modeling of an individual system.* Report to the National Institute on Alcohol Abuse and Alcoholism (NIAAA AA-05743).

McArdle, J. J. (1986). Latent variable growth within behavior genetic models. *Behavior Genetics, 16,* 163–200.

McArdle, J. J. (1988). Dynamic but structural equation modeling of repeated measures data. In J. R. Nesselroade & R. B. Cattell (Eds.), *Handbook of multivariate experimental psychology* (2nd ed.). New York: Plenum.

McArdle, J. J. (in press). Structural modeling experiments using multiple growth functions. In P. Ackerman, R. Kanfer & R. Cudeck (Eds.), *Learning and individual differences: Abilities, motivation, and methodology.*

McArdle, J. J., & Anderson, E. (1989). Latent growth models for research on aging. In J. E. Birren & K. W. Schaie (Eds.), *The handbook of the psychology of aging, Volume III* (pp. 21–44).

McArdle, J. J., Anderson, E., & Aber, M. S. (1987). *Convergence hypotheses modeled and tested with linear structural equations* (pp. 347–352). Proceedings of the 1987 Public Health Conference on Records and Statistics. National Center for Health Statistics, Hyattsville, MD.

McArdle, J. J., & Epstein, D. (1987). Latent growth curves within developmental structural equation models. *Child Development, 58,* 110–133.

McArdle, J. J., Hamagami, F., Elias, M. F., & Robbins, M. A. (in press). Structural modeling of mixed longitudinal and cross-sectional data. *Experimental Aging Research.*

McArdle, J. J., & Horn, J. L. (1989). *A mega-analysis of aging and the WAIS.* Manuscript submitted for publication.

McArdle, J. J., & Horn, J. L. (in press). An effective representation of linear structural equation models. *Multivariate Behavioral Research.*

McArdle, J. J., & McDonald, R. P. (1984). Some algebraic properties of the Reticular Action Model for moment structures. *British Journal of Mathematical and Statistical Psychology, 37,* 234–251.

McCleary, R., & Hay, R. A., Jr. (1980). *Applied time series analysis for the social sciences.* Newbury Park, CA: Sage.

McClelland, J. L. (1979). On the time relations of mental processes: An examination of systems of processes in cascade. *Psychological Review, 86,* 287–330.

McDonald, R. P. (1968). A unified treatment of the weighting problem. *Psychometrika, 33,* 351–381.

McDonald, R. P. (1983). Exploratory and confirmatory nonlinear factor analysis. In H. Wainer & S. Messick (Eds.), *Principals of modern psychological measurement: A Festschrift for Frederick M. Lord* (pp. 103–115). Hillsdale, NJ: Lawrence Erlbaum.

McDonald, R. P. (1989). An index of goodness of fit based on noncentrality. *Journal of Classification, 6,* 97–103.

McGaw, B., & Joreskog, K. G. (1971). Factorial invariance of ability measures in groups differing in intelligence and socioeconomic status. *British Journal of Mathematical and Statistical Psychology, 24,* 154–168.

Mehra, R. K. (1974). Identification in control and econometrics similarities and differences. *Annals of Economic & Social Measurement, 3,* 21–47.

Meredith, W. (1964a). Notes on factorial invariance. *Psychometrika, 29,* 177–185.

Meredith, W. (1964b). Rotation to achieve factorial invariance. *Psychometrika, 29,* 187–206.

Meredith, W. (1965). A method for studying differences between groups. *Psychometrika, 30,* 15–29.

Meredith, W., & Tisak, J. (1982). Canonical analysis of longitudinal repeated measures data with stationary weights. *Psychometrika, 47*, 47–67.

Meredith, W., & Tisak, J. (1984, July). *"Tuckerizing" curves.* Paper presented at the annual meeting of the Psychometric Society, Santa Barbara, CA.

Meredith, W., & Tisak, J. (in press). Latent curve analysis. *Psychometrika, 55*, 107– 122.

Meyer, J. (1988). Estimating genetic parameters of age of onset distributions: A survival analysis approach. *Behavior Genetics, 18*, 724–725.

Miller, R. G., Jr. (1981). *Survival analysis.* New York: Wiley.

Millsap, R. E., & Meredith, W. (1988). Component analysis in cross-sectional and longitudinal data. *Psychometrika, 53*, 123–134.

Mislevy, R. J. (1987). Recent developments in item response theory with implications for teacher certification. In E. Z. Rothkopf (Ed.), *Review of research in education, Vol. 14.* Washington, DC: American Educational Research Association.

Mokken, R. J. (1971). *A theory and procedure of scale analysis.* Hawthorne, NY: Mouton & Co.

Molenaar, P. C. (1985). A dynamic factor model for the analysis of multivariate time series. *Psychometrika, 50*, 181–202.

Mosteller, F., & Tukey, J. W. (1977). *Data analysis and regression.* Reading, MA: Addison-Wesley.

Mulaik, S. A. (1972). *Foundations of factor analysis.* New York: McGraw-Hill.

Murnane, R. J., Singer, J. D., & Willett, J. B. (1988). The career paths of teachers: Implications for teacher supply and methodological lessons for research. *Educational Researcher, 17(6)*, 22–30.

Murnane, R. J., Singer, J. D., & Willett, J. B. (1989). The influences of salaries and ''opportunity costs'' on teachers' career choices: Evidence from North Carolina. *Harvard Educational Review, 59*, 325–346.

Muthén, B. (1983). Latent variable structural equation modeling with categorical data. *Journal of Econometrics, 22*, 43–65.

Muthén, B. (1987). *LISCOMP. Analysis of linear structural equations with a comprehensive measurement model. Theoretical integration and user's guide.* Mooresville, IN: Scientific Software.

Muthén, B. (1989). Latent variable modeling in heterogenous populations [presidential address to the Psychometric Society, July, 1989]. *Psychometrika, 54*, 557–585.

Muthén, B., & Kaplan, D. (1985). A comparison of some methodologies for the factor analysis of non-normal Likert variables. *British Journal of Mathematical and Statistical Psychology, 38*, 171–189.

Nesselroade, J. R. (1972). Note on the ''longitudinal factor analysis'' model. *Psychometrika, 37(2)*, 187–192.

Nesselroade, J. R. (1983). Temporal selection and factor invariance in the study of development and change. In P. B. Baltes & O. G. Brim, Jr. (Eds.), *Life-span development and behavior* (Vol. 5). New York: Academic Press.

Nesselroade, J. R. (1988). Sampling and generalizability: Adult development and aging research issues examined within the general methodological framework of selection. In K. W. Schaie, R. T. Campbell, W. M. Meredith, & S. C. Rawlings (Eds.), *Methodological issues in aging research.* New York: Springer.

Nesselroade, J. R. (1990). The warp and the woof of the developmental fabric. In R. Downs, L. Liben, & D. S. Palermo (Eds.), *Visions of development, the environment, and aesthetics: The legacy of Joachim F. Wohlwill.* Hillsdale, NJ: Lawrence Erlbaum.

Nesselroade, J. R., & Baltes, P. B. (1974). Adolescent personality development and historical change: 1970–1972. *Monographs of the Society for Research in Child Development, 39*, (1, Serial No. 154).

Nesselroade, J. R., & Featherman, D. L. (in press). Intraindividual variability in older adults' depression scores: Some implications for developmental theory and longitudinal research. In D. Magnusson, L. Bergman, G. Rudinger, & B. Torestad (Eds.), *Stability and change: Methods and models for data treatment.* London: Cambridge University Press.

Nesselroade, J. R., & Ford, D. H. (1985). P-technique comes of age: Multivariate, replicated, single subject designs for research on older adults. *Research on Aging, 46–80.*

Nesselroade, J. R., & Ford, D. H. (1987). Methodological considerations in modeling living systems. In M. E. Ford & D. H. Ford (Eds.), *Humans as self-constructing living systems: Putting the framework to work.* Hillsdale, NJ: Erlbaum.

Nesselroade, J. R., & Jones, C. J. (in press). Multi-modal selection effects in the study of adult development: A perspective on multivariate, replicated, single–subject, repeated measures designs. *Experimental Aging Research.*

Olkin, I. (1981). Range restrictions for product-moment correlation matrices. *Psychometrika, 46,* 469–472.

O'Reilly, D. F. X., Hui, B. S., Jones, K. J., & Sheehan, K. (1981). *Macroeconomic forecasting with multivariate ARMA.* Lexington, MA: Data Resources, Inc.

Overall, J. E. (1987). Estimating sample size for longitudinal studies of age-related cognitive decline. *Journal of Gerontology, 42,* 137–141.

Parkman, J. M., & Groen, G. J. (1971). Temporal aspects of simple addition and comparison. *Journal of Experimental Psychology, 89,* 335–342.

Pearson, K. L. (1903). On the influence of natural selection on the variability and correlation of organs. *Philosophical Transactions of the Royal Society, Series A, 200,* 1–66.

Pellegrino, J. W., & Kail, R. V. (1982). Process analyses of spatial aptitude. In R. J. Sternberg (Ed.), *Advances in the psychology of human intelligence* (Vol. 1). Hillsdale, NJ: Lawrence Erlbaum.

Pena, D., & Box, G. E. P. (1987). Identifying a simplifying structure in time series. *Journal of the American Statistical Association, 82,* 836–843.

Phillips, K., & Fulker, D. W. (1989). Quantitative genetic analysis of longitudinal trends in adoption designs with application to IQ in the Colorado Adoption Project. *Behavior Genetics, 19,* 621–658.

Piaget, J. (1955). *The language and thought of the child.* New York: Meridian.

Piaget, J. (1962). *Play, dreams and imitation in childhood.* New York: W. W. Norton.

Pierce, D. A. (1977). *R-2 Measures for time series* (pp. 297–301). Alexandria, VA: American Statistical Association.

Pierce, D. A., & Haugh, L. D. (1977). Causality in temporal systems: Characterizations and a survey. *Journal of Econometrics, 5,* 265–293.

Plomin, R. (1986). Multivariate analysis and developmental behavioral genetics: Developmental change as well as continuity. *Behavior Genetics, 16,* 25–44.

Prahl-Andersen, B., Kowalski, C. J., & Heydendael, P. H. J. M. (1979). *A mixed-longitudinal interdisciplinary study of growth and development.* New York: Academic Press.

Preese, M. A., & Baines, M. J. (1978). A new family of mathematical models describing the human growth curve. *Annals of Human Biology, 5,* 1–24.

Priestly, J. B. (1981). *Spectral analysis and time series.* London: Academic Press.

Priestly, M. B., Rao, T. S., & Tong, H. (1973). Identification of the structure of multivariable stochastic systems. In P. A. Krishnaiah (Ed.), *Multivariate analysis III* (pp. 351–368). New York: Academic Press.

Priestly, M. B., Rao, T. S., & Tong, H. (1974). Applications of principal component analysis and factor analysis in the identification of multivariable systems. *IEEE Transactions on Automatic Control*, *19*, 730–734.

Randles, R. H., & Wolfe, D. A. (1979). *Introduction to the theory of nonparametric statistics*. New York: Wiley.

Rao, C. R. (1958). Some statistical methods for comparison of growth curves. *Biometrics*, *14*, 1–17.

Rao, P. (1971). Some notes on misspecification in multiple regression. *American Statistician*, *25*, 37–39.

Rasch, G. (1961). On the meaning of measurement in psychology. In J. Neyman (Ed.), *Proceedings of the Fourth Berkeley Symposium on Mathematical Statistics and Probability* (Vol. 5). Berkeley: University of California Press.

Ratcliff, R. (1985). Theoretical interpretations of the speed and accuracy of positive and negative responses. *Psychological Review*, *92*, 212–225.

Raudenbush, S., & Bryk, A. (1988). Methodological advances in studying effects of schools and classrooms on student learning. *Review of Research in Education, 1988*.

Reichardt, C. S. (1988). *Estimating effects*. Denver: University of Denver, Department of Psychology. Unpublished report.

Reichardt, C. S., & Gollob, H. F. (1986). Satisfying the constraints of causal modeling. In W. M. K. Trochim (Ed.), *Advances in quasi-experimental design. New directions in program evaluation*, *31*, 91–107. San Francisco: Jossey-Bass.

Reichardt, C. S., & Gollob, H. F. (1987). Taking uncertainty into account when estimating effects. In M. M. Mark & R. L. Shotland (Eds.), *Multiple methods for program evaluation*. (New Directions for Program Evaluation, No. 35, pp. 7–22). San Francisco: Jossey-Bass.

Resnick, L.B., & Neches, R. (1984). Factors affecting individual differences in learning. In R.J. Sternberg (Ed.), *Advances in the psychology of human intelligence* (Vol. 2). Hillsdale, NJ: Lawrence Erlbaum.

Reynolds, T. J., & Suttrick, K. H. (1986). Assessing the correspondence of a vector to a symmetric matrix. *Psychometrika*, *51*, 101–112.

Richards, F. J. (1959). A flexible growth function for empirical use. *Journal of Experimental Biology*, *10*, 290–300.

Richards, L. N., Bengtson, V. L., & Miller, R. B. (1989). The 'generation in the middle:' Perceptions of adults' intergenerational relationships. In K. Kreppner & R. M. Lerner (Eds.), *Family systems and life-span development* (pp. 341–366). Hillsdale, NJ: Lawrence Erlbaum.

Roberts, R. E. L., & Bengtson, V. L. (1990). Is intergenerational solidarity a unidimensional construct?: A second test of a formal model. *Journal of Gerontology: Social Sciences*, *45*, S12–S20.

Robertson, T. B. (1908). On the normal rate of growth of an individual, and its biochemical significance. *Archives of Entwicklungs Mechanik den Organismen*, *25*, 581–614.

Robinson, E. A. (1959). *An introduction to infinitely many variates*. New York: Hafner Publishing Co.

Robinson, E. A. (1967). *Multichannel time series with digital computer programs-revised edition* (rev. ed.). San Francisco: Holden-Day.

Roche, A. F., Wainer, H., & Thissen, D. (1975) Predicting adult stature for individuals. *Monographs in pediatrics*. Basel: Karger.

Rogosa, D. R. (1987). Causal models do not support scientific conclusions: A comment in support of Freedman. *Journal of Educational Statistics*, *12*, 185–195.

Rogosa, D. R., Brandt, D., & Zimowski, M. (1982). A growth curve approach to the measurement of change. *Psychological Bulletin*, *92*, 726–748.

Rogosa, D. R., & Willett, J. B. (1985a). Satisfying a simplex structure is simpler than it should be. *Journal of Educational Statistics, 10*, 99–107.

Rogosa, D. R., & Willett, J. B. (1985b). Understanding correlates of change by modeling individual differences in growth. *Psychometrika, 50*, 203–228.

Rosenbaum, P. R. (1984). From association to causation in observational studies: The role of strongly ignorable treatment assignment. *Journal of the American Statistical Association, 79*, 41–48.

Rosenbaum, P. R., & Rubin, D. B. (1983). The central role of the propensity score in observational studies for causal effects. *Biometrika, 70*, 41–55.

Rubin, D. B. (1974a). Estimating causal effects of treatments in randomized and nonrandomized studies. *Journal of Educational Psychology, 66*, 688–701.

Rubin, D. B. (1974b). Characterizing the estimation of parameters in incomplete data problems. *Journal of the American Statistical Association, 69*, 467–474.

Rubin, D. B. (1976). Inference and missing data. *Biometrika, 63*, 581–92.

Rubin, D. B. (1977). Assignment of treatment groups on the basis of a covariate. *Journal of Educational Statistics, 2*, 1–26.

Rubin, D. B., (1980). Using empirical Bayes techniques in the law school validity studies. *The Journal of the American Statistical Association, 75*, 801–827.

Rubin, D. B. (1987a). *Multiple imputation for nonresponse in surveys*. New York: John Wiley.

Rubin, D. B. (1987b). A noniterative sampling importance resampling alternative to the data augmentation algorithm for creating a few imputations when fractions of missing information are modest: The SIR algorithm. Discussion of ''The calculation of posterior distributions by data augmentation'' by Tanner and Wong. *Journal of the American Statistical Association, 82*, 543–546.

Rubin, D. B. (1991). EM and beyond. *Psychometrika*.

Rubin, D. B., & Schafer, J. S., (1991). Efficiently creating multiple imputations for incomplete multivariate normal data. In *Proceedings of the 1990 American Statistical Association*. Alexandria, VA: American Statistical Association.

Rubin, D. B., & Schenker, N. (1987). Interval estimation from multiply-imputed data: A case study using agriculture industry codes. *Journal of Official Statistics, 3*, 109–136.

Runkle, D. E. (1987). Vector autoregressions and reality (with comments). *Journal of Business & Economic Statistics, 5*(4), 437–454.

Sacher, A. M., Young, A. C., & Meredith, W. M. (1960). Factor analysis of the electro cardiogram. *Circulation Research, 8*, 519–526.

Sakai, L. M., Baker, L. A., Dawson, M. E., & Filion, D. L. (1988). Effects of inheritance on sustained attention in 9- to 16-year-old twins. *Behavior Genetics, 18*, 730.

SAS Institute. (1980). *Procedure state space*. Cary, NC: SAS Institute.

Satorra, A., & Bentler, P. M. (1986). *Robustness properties of ML statistics in covariance structure analysis*. Unpublished manuscript.

Scarr, S. (1985). Constructing psychology: Making facts and fables for our times. *American Psychologist, 40*, 499–512.

Schaie, K. W. (1965). A general model for the study of developmental problems. *Psychological Bulletin, 64*, 92–107.

Schaie, K. W. (1974). Translations in gerontology—from lab to life: intellectual functioning. *American Psychologist, 29*, 802–807.

Schaie, K. W. (1983). The Seattle longitudinal study: A 21-year exploration of psychometric intelligence in adulthood. In K. W. Schaie (Ed.), *Longitudinal studies of adult psychological development* (pp. 64–135). New York: Guilford.

Scher, A. M., Young, A. C., & Meredith, W. M. (1960). Factor analysis of the electrocardiogram. *Circulation Research, 8*, 519–526.

Schmidt, W. H., & Wisenbaker, J. M. (1986). *Hierarchical data analysis: an approach based on structural equations.* (CEPSE, No. 4., Research Series). East Lansing, MI: Michigan State University, Department of Counseling, Educational Psychology, and Special Education.

Schneider, W., Dumais, S. T., & Shiffrin, R. M. (1984). Automatic and control processing and attention. In R. Parasuraman & D. R. Davies (Eds.), *Varieties of attention* (pp. 1–27). New York: Academic Press.

Schoenberg, R. J. (1987). *LINCS: Linear covariance structure analysis.* Kensington, ND: RJS Software.

Schultz, N. R., Jr., Elias, M. F., Robbins, M. A., Streeten, D. H. P., & Blakeman, N. A. (1989). Longitudinal study of performance of hypertensive and normotensive subjects on the Wechsler Adult Intelligence Scale. *Psychology and Aging, 4,* 496–499.

Shapiro, A. (1985). Asymptotic equivalence of minimum discrepancy estimators to G. L. S. estimators. *South African Statistical Journal, 19,* 73–81.

Short, R., Horn, J. L., & McArdle, J. (1984). Mathematical-statistical model building in analysis of developmental data. In R. N. Emde & R. J. Harmon (Eds.), *Continuities and discontinuities in development* (pp. 371–401). New York: Plenum.

Siegel, S. (1956). *Nonparametric statistics for the behavioral sciences.* New York: McGraw-Hill.

Siegel, S., & Castellan, J. (1988). *Nonparametric statistics for the behavioral sciences* (2nd ed.). New York: McGraw-Hill.

Siegler, I. C. (1975). The terminal drop hypothesis: Fact or artifact? *Experimental Aging Research, 1,* 169–185.

Siegler, R. S. (1981). Developmental sequences within and between concepts. *Monographs of the Society for Research in Child Development, 46* (2, Serial No. 189).

Siegler, R. S., & Shrager, J. (1984). Strategy choices in addition and subtraction: How do children know what to do? In C. Sohpian (Ed.), *Origins of cognitive skill* (pp.229–293). Hillsdale, NJ: Erlbaum.

Sims, C. A. (1977). *Exogenicity and causal ordering in macroeconomic models.* Minneapolis, MN: Federal Reserve Bank of Minneapolis.

Sims, C. A. (1980). Macroeconomics and reality. *Econometrica, 48,* 1–4.

Singer, J. D., Fosburg, S., Goodson, B. D., & Smith, J.M. (1978). *National day care home study research report. Final report of the National Day Care Home Study* (DHHS Pub. No. 80-30283). Rockville, MD: U.S. Department of Health and Human Services.

Singer, J. D., & Willett, J. B. (1988). Detecting involuntary layoffs in teacher survival data: The year of leaving dangerously. *Educational Evaluation and Policy Analysis, 10,* 212–224.

Singleton, K. J. (1980). A latent time series model of the cyclical behavior of interest rates. *International Economic Review, 21*(3), 559–575.

Slutzky, E. (1927). The summation of random causes as the source of cyclic processes. *Econometrica, 5,* 105–146.

Smith, R. B. (1972). Neighborhood context and college plans: an ordinal path analysis. *Social Forces, 51,* 199–217.

Somers, R. H. (1974). Analysis of partial rank correlation measures based on the product-moment model: Part One. *Social Forces, 53,* 229–246.

Somers, R. H. (1976). A caution regarding partial rank correlation based on the product-moment model. *Social Forces, 54,* 694–700.

Sörbom, D. (1974). A general method for studying differences in factor means and factor structures between groups. *British Journal of Mathematical & Statistical Psychology, 27,* 229–239.

Sörbom, D. (1982). Structural equations models with structured means. In K. Jöreskog & H. Wold (Eds.), *Systems under indirect observation: Part 1*. New York: North-Holland.

Stallings, M., Baker, L. A., & Boomsma, D. (1989). Estimating cultural transmission from extended twin designs. *Behavior Genetics, 19*, 777.

Steiger, J. H., & Lind, J. C. (1980, June). *Statistically based tests for the number of common factors*. Paper presented at the annual meeting of the Psychometric Society, Iowa City, IA.

Steiger, J. H., Shapiro, A., & Browne, M. W. (1985). On the asymptotic distribution of sequential chi-square statistics. *Psychometrika, 50*, 253–264.

Sternberg, R. J. (1985). *Beyond IQ: A triarchic theory of intelligence*. Cambridge, England: Cambridge, University Press.

Stouffer, S. A., Guttman, L., Suchman, E. A., Lazarsfeld, P., Star, S. A., & Clausen, J. A. (Eds.). (1950). *Measurement and prediction*. Princeton, NJ: Princeton University Press.

Strenio, J. F., Weisberg, H. I., & Bryk, A. S. (1983). Empirical Bayes estimation of individual growth curve parameters and their relationship to covariates. *Biometrics, 39*, 71–86.

Tanner, J. M. (1986). Growth as a mirror of the condition of society: Secular trends and class distinction. In A. Demirjian & M. B. Duboc (Eds.), *Human growth: A multidisciplinary review* (pp. 3–34). London: Taylor and Francis.

Tanner, J. M., Whitehouse, R. H., Marshall, W. A., Healy, M. J. R., & Goldstein, H. (1975). *Assessment of skeletal maturity and prediction of adult height*. London: Academic Press.

Tanner, M., & Wong, W. (1987). The calculation of posterior distributions by data augmentation. *Journal of the American Statistical Association, 82*, 528–558.

Thurstone, L. L. (1938). Primary mental abilities. *Psychometric Monographs*, No. 1.

Thurstone, L. L. (1947). *Multiple factor analysis*. Chicago: University of Chicago Press.

Thurstone, L. L., & Thurstone, T. G. (1941). Factorial studies of intelligence. *Psychometric Monographs*, No. 2.

Tisak, J., & Meredith, W. (1989). Exploratory longitudinal factor analysis in multiple populations. *Psychometrika, 54*, 261–282.

Tsay, R. S. (1989). Parsimonious parameterization of vector autoregressive moving average models. *Journal of Business and Economic Statistics, 7*, 327–341.

Tucker, L. R. (1958). Determination of parameters of a functional relation by factor analysis. *Psychometrika, 23*, 19–23.

Tucker, L. R. (1966). Learning theory and multivariate experiment: Illustration by determination of parameters of generalized learning curves. In R. B. Cattell (Ed.), *Handbook of multivariate experimental psychology*. Chicago: Rand McNally.

Tuddenham, R. D., & Snyder, M. M. (1954). Physical growth of California boys and girls from birth to eighteen years. *University of California Publications in Child Development, 1*, 183–364.

Tukey, J. W. (1978). Can we predict where "time series" should go next? In D. R. Brillinger & G. C. Tiao (Eds.), *Directions in time series* (pp. 1–31). Ames, IA: Iowa State University.

Tuma, N. B., & Hannan, M. T. (1984). *Social dynamics: Models and methods*. New York: Academic Press.

van de Pol, F., & Langeheine, R. (1989). Mover-stayer models, mixed Markov models and the EM algorithm; with an application to labour market data from the Netherland Socio-Economic Panel. In R. Coppi & S. Bolasco (Eds.), *Multiway data analysis* (pp. 485–495). Amsterdam: North Holland.

van de Pol, F., & deLeeuw, J. (1986). A latent Markov model to correct for measurement error. *Sociological Methods and Research, 15,* 118–141.

Vardi, Y., Shepp, L. A., & Kaufman, L. (1985). A statistical model for positron emission tomography. *Journal of the American Statistical Association, 80,* 8–37.

Watson, M., & Engle, R. F. (1983). Alternative algorithms for the estimation of dynamic factor, MIMIC, and varying coefficient regression models. *Journal of Econometrics, 23,* 385–400.

Watson, M. W., & Kraft, D. F. (1984). Testing the interpretation of indices in a macroeconomic index model. *Journal of Monetary Economics, 13,* 165–181.

Wechsler, D. (1955). *Manual for the Wechsler adult intelligence scale.* New York: Psychological Corporation.

West, B. J. (1985). *An essay on the importance of being nonlinear.* Berlin: Springer-Verlag.

Wheaton, B., Muthén, B., Alwin, D., & Summers, G. (1977). Assessing reliability and stability in panel models. In D. R. Heise (Ed.), *Sociological methodology* (pp. 84–136). San Francisco: Jossey-Bass.

White, N., & Cunningham, W. R. (1987). The age comparative construct validity of speeded cognitive factors. *Multivariate Behavioral Research, 22,* 249–265.

Widaman, K. F., Geary, D. C., Cormier, P., & Little, T. D. (1989). A componential model for mental addition. *Journal of Experimental Psychology: Learning, Memory, and Cognition, 15,* 898–919.

Widaman, K. F., Little, T. D., Geary, D. C., & Cormier, P. (in press). Individual differences in the development of skill in mental addition: Internal and external validation of chronometric models. *Learning and Individual Differences.*

Wiener, N. (1948). *Cybernetics.* New York: Wiley.

Wiener, N. (1949). *Extrapolation, interpolation, and smoothing of time series with engineering applications.* New York: Wiley.

Wilcox, R. (1987). *New developments in statistical methods.* Hillside, NJ: Lawrence Erlbaum.

Wilcoxon, F. (1945). Individual comparisons by ranking methods. *Biometrics,* 80–83.

Wiley, D. E., & Wiley, J. A. (1970). The estimation of measurement error in panel data. *American Sociological Review, 35,* 112–117.

Wilfgong, H. D. (1980). *ASVAB technical supplement for the counselor's guide.* Fort Sheridan, IL: Directorate of Testing, United States Military Processing Command.

Wilkie, F., & Eisdorfer, C. (1971). Intelligence and blood pressure in the aged. *Science, 172,* 959–962.

Willett, J. B., & Singer, J. D. (1988, April). *Doing data analysis with proportional hazards models: Model building, interpretation and diagnosis.* Paper presented at the annual meeting of the American Educational Research Association, New Orleans.

Willett, J.B., & Singer, J.D. (1989). Two types of question about time: Methodological issues in the analysis of teacher career path data. *International Journal of Educational Research, 13,* 421–437.

Wilson, R. (1977). Analysis of longitudinal twin data: Basic model and applications to physical growth measures. *Acta Geneticae Medicae et Gemellologiae: Twin Research, 28,* 93–105.

Wissler, C. (1901). The correlation of mental and physical traits. *Psychological Monographs, 3*(6, Whole No. 16).

Wohlwill, J. F. (1973). *The study of behavioral development.* New York: Academic Press.

Wold, H. (1954). *A study in the analysis of stationary time series* (2nd ed.). Stockholm: Almquist & Wiksell.

Wolfram, S. (1988). *Mathematica.* Reading, MA: Addison-Wesley.

Wood, R. E., & Bandura, A. (1989). Impact of conceptions of ability on self-regulatory mechanisms and complex decision making. *Journal of Personality and Social Psychology, 56,* 407–415.

Woodcock, R. W., & Johnson, M. B. (1989). *Woodcock-Johnson psycho-educational battery* (rev. ed.). Allen, TX: DLM Teaching Resources.

Woodrow, H. (1938). The relationship between abilities and improvement with practice. *Journal of Educational Psychology, 29,* 215–230.

Working, H. (1960). Note on the correlation of first differences of averages in a random chain. *Econometrica, 28,* 916–918.

Yen, W. (1986). The choice of scale for educational measurement: An IRT perspective. *Journal of Educational Measurement, 23,* 299–325.

Yule, U. (1926). Why do we sometimes get nonsense correlations between time series? A study in the sampling and nature of time series. *Journal of the Royal Statistical Society, 89,* 1–65.

Zevon, M. A., & Tellegen, A. (1982). The structure of mood change: An idiographic/nomothetic analysis. *Journal of Personality and Social Psychology, 43,* 111–122.

INDEX